Understanding Deafness and the Rehabilitation Process

Related Titles of Interest

Principles and Applications in Auditory Evoked Potentials
John T. Jacobson (Editor)
ISBN: 0–205–14846–8

Speech-Language Pathology and Related Professions in the Schools
Robert J. Lowe (Editor)
ISBN: 0–205–13499–8

Speech, Language, and Hearing Disorders: A Guide for the Teacher, Second Edition
Herbert J. Oyer, Barbara J. Hall, and William H. Haas
ISBN: 0–205–14908–1

Toward a Psychology of Deafness: Theoretical and Empirical Perspectives
Peter V. Paul, Dorothy W. Jackson
ISBN: 0–205–14112–9

Understanding Digitally Programmable Hearing Aids
Robert E. Sandlin (Editor)
ISBN: 0–205–14845–X

Orientation to Deafness
Nanci A. Scheetz
ISBN: 0–205–13438–6

Speech-Language Pathology Services in the Schools, Second Edition
Joyce S. Taylor
ISBN 0–205–13262–6

Understanding Deafness and the Rehabilitation Process

HV
2380
.U53
1994
West

Edited by
Richard C. Nowell
Laura E. Marshak
Indiana University of Pennsylvania

Allyn and Bacon
Boston • London • Toronto • Sydney • Tokyo • Singapore

Series Editor: Mylan Jaixen
Editorial Assistant: Susan Hutchinson
Cover Administrator: Linda Knowles
Manufacturing Buyer: Megan Cochran
Editorial-Production Service: Walsh Associates
Cover Designer: Suzanne Harbison

Copyright © 1994 by Allyn and Bacon
A Division of Paramount Publishing
160 Gould Street
Needham Heights, Massachusetts 02194

Library of Congress Cataloging-in-Publication Data

Understanding deafness and the rehabilitation process / edited by
   Richard C. Nowell, Laura E. Marshak.
      p.   cm.
   Includes bibliographical references and index.
   ISBN 0–205–15628–2
    1. Deaf.   2. Deaf—Rehabilitation.   I. Nowell, Richard C.
II. Marshak, Laura E.
HV2380.U53   1994
362.4'28'0973—dc20
                                       93–50768
                                        CIP

Printed in the United States of America

10   9   8   7   6   5   4   3   2   1   99 98 97 96 95 94

Contents

Preface

The purpose of this book is to help you better understand deafness, deaf people, and the many challenges that deaf people face in preparing themselves for and finding jobs. The last of these is our primary focus. Many books currently exist in which various topics related to deafness, including education, cognitive development, language development, and, more recently, cultural development and the psycholinguistics of American Sign Language are examined in depth. These topics are referred to briefly in this book, as a general orientation before we move on to our primary focus—the means by which deaf people make the transition from school to work, resolve personal and family situations, receive appropriate guidance, find and obtain access to appropriate jobs, and receive appropriate support to succeed in those jobs.

Some people who are deaf are quite successful in finding employment without significant intervention from educators or rehabilitation specialists. However, many deaf people need specialized interventions because of the great barriers that deafness often erects for deaf individuals as they try to cope with family, develop English skills, implement aspects of vocational plans, and develop communication skills needed to interact with hearing people.

This book begins with a brief overview of hearing loss and the development of deaf people, with suggestions for hearing professionals working with them (Chapter 1). Then there is an in-depth look at the effects of deafness on language and communication (Chapter 2), cognition (Chapter 3), and affective development (Chapter 4). Next we examine the critical aspect of helping deaf individuals make the transition from school to work (Chapter 5). One must, of course, know the skills of a prospective worker, and we look at the important area of assessment in general (Chapter 6), and how the outcomes of assessment are applied in vocational guidance for the deaf worker (Chapter 7). The deaf worker's personal adjustment is critical to vocational success, and therapeutic interventions are discussed, in terms of individual and group counseling with cognitive behavior therapy (Chapter 8), and family intervention with a systems approach (Chapter 9). Chapter 10 contains an overview of the legal framework which impinges on the deaf worker. Chapter 11 addresses the technological and personal support services available to assist deaf workers. Finally, once the system is in place to train and support deaf workers, jobs must be found, and the process of job placement is discussed in Chapter 12.

We hope this book provides—for the student preparing to enter the field of rehabilitation, for the professional faced with assisting a deaf client, and for deaf people themselves—a framework within which appropriate services will be provided to assist deaf adults in finding jobs that are suitable for their skills and are personally rewarding. We are in the age of the Americans with Disabilities Act, a law which is intended to provide equal access to all of the benefits of living in this country for individuals with disabilities. Deaf people are truly "differently abled" and not disabled, and we hope this book helps professionals acquire skills to facilitate the vocational development of those deaf individuals in need of assistance.

One of the most difficult aspects of writing a book such as this one, especially when a group of authors is involved, is the use of terminology which is accurate, consistent, and unoffensive to as many people as possible. We have made an attempt, but some inconsistencies may have slipped through. For example, we have tried to use the terms "deaf people" and "hard-of-hearing" people instead of "the deaf", or "hearing-impaired" people. When this book was begun, the acceptable acronym for a device used by deaf people to communicate by phone was "TDD", but over the last two years, we have seen a growing preference for the formerly used term "TTY", and so we have changed this term. If the reader does not always agree with our terminology, we hope he or she will agree with our goals to provide better opportunities for deaf people in our society.

RCN
LEM

Acknowledgments

An undertaking like this book requires the support, both direct and indirect, of many individuals. We would like to express our appreciation for the hard work of all of our contributors, and for the support of the editorial staff of Allyn and Bacon, especially Ray Short, Mylan Jaixen, and Susan Hutchinson. Kathy Whittier, our copyeditor, did a wonderful job in the final production stages of the book. We would like to thank Bruce Godsave, SUNY Geneseo, and Sue Philip, Northeastern University, for their comments on the first draft of the book. We appreciate the sharing of experiences by deaf individuals in the Pittsburgh and Indiana, Pennsylvania, area. We received great encouragement and support from our colleagues in the Department of Special Education and Clinical Services of Indiana University of Pennsylvania, and we wish to thank them—especially our departmental secretary, Vickie Johnson, and our chairperson, Clarice Reber. Finally, no undertaking like this is possible without the personal and emotional support from our families, and we wish especially to thank our spouses, Susan Polk Nowell and Edward Kramer.

Contributing Authors

RICHARD C. NOWELL is an associate professor in Education of Persons with Hearing Loss at Indiana University of Pennsylvania. He holds an M.A. from New York University in Audiocommunicative Disabilities and an Ed.D. from the University of Rochester in Educational Psychology. Dr. Nowell also spent three years at the Pennsylvania State University as a post-doctoral student in Education of the Hearing Impaired and Audiology. He holds certification as a Teacher of the Deaf from the Council on Education of the Deaf, as an audiologist from the American Speech/Language/Hearing Association, and as an interpreter from the Registry of Interpreters for the Deaf. He has worked as an interpreter, an interpreter-trainer, a teacher, a teacher-trainer, an educational audiologist, a parent-counselor, a research associate, and an administrator. Dr. Nowell is the editor of *A Handbook on the Education of Multiply Handicapped, Hearing Impaired Children* and author of many articles on the providing of services to deaf children and adults. Previously Chairperson of the Special Interest Group: Research on the Education of Deaf Persons of the American Educational Research Association, Dr. Nowell is currently President of the Division for Children with Communication Disorders of the Council for Exceptional Children.

LAURA E. MARSHAK is an associate professor in Rehabilitation at Indiana University of Pennsylvania and a licensed psychologist whose practice includes persons with disabilities and family members facing vocational and adjustment problems. She received her doctorate in Rehabilitation Counseling from the University of Pittsburgh. Dr. Marshak is co-author of *Counseling Persons with Physical Disabilities: Theoretical and Clinical Perspectives,* and co-editor of *Group Psychotherapy: Intervention with Special Populations.* In addition, she has published several chapters and articles which focus on improving the coping abilities and self-sufficiency of persons with disabilities. Dr. Marshak teaches skill-oriented courses, such as vocational assessment, facilitating adjustment of persons with disabilities, and counseling.

C. TANE AKAMATSU works as a psychoeducational consultant for the Toronto (Ontario) Board of Education, serving deaf and hard-of-hearing students from preschool through high school. She received her Ph.D. in psychology from the University of Rochester, and has been employed at the National Technical Institute for the Deaf and Michigan State University.

THOMAS E. ALLEN received his Ph.D. from the University of Minnesota. He is Director of the Center for Assessment and Demographic Studies, Gallaudet University. He has developed achievement test norms with students with hearing loss and is the principal author of the book, *Deaf Studies and the School to Work Transition.*

FRANK G. BOWE, Ph.D., is Professor, Department of Counseling, Research, Special Education, and Rehabilitation, at Hofstra University. Dr. Bowe received the Distinguished Service Award from the President of the United States in 1992 in recognition of more than 15 years of national advocacy on disability. Among his books are *Equal Rights for Americans with Disabilities* (Watts, 1992) and *Approaching Equality* (TJ Publishers, 1991).

HELEN CRAIG has been Director of Research, Western Pennsylvania School for the Deaf, and co-editor of the Reference Issue of the *American Annals of the Deaf* since 1970. She has published over 70 professional articles, chapters, and booklets on cognitive development, pragmatic language, behavioral strategies, parent-infant programming, and hearing loss.

JAMES J. DECARO holds a B.S. and M.S. in civil engineering from the State University of New York at Buffalo and a Ph.D. in instructional technology from Syracuse University. Since 1985, he has served as Dean of the National Technical Institute for the Deaf, a college of the Rochester Institute of Technology. His current scholarly interest is in strategic planning in higher education.

ROSEMARY P. GARRITY is the administrative director at the Western Pennsylvania School for the Deaf and Center on Deafness. She is a graduate of Mercyhurst College and received her Master's from the University of Pittsburgh. Mrs. Garrity has been responsible for developing a wide range of services for deaf students and adults and has made several presentations statewide and nationally.

MICHAEL HARVEY, Ph.D. A.B.P.P., is a clinical psychologist in private practice in the Boston, Massachusetts area. He is an adjunct faculty member at Gallaudet University and Boston University. He has authored many publications, including a book entitled *Psychotherapy with Deaf and Hard of Hearing Persons: A Systemic Model.* He has lectured extensively across the country.

T. ALAN HURWITZ, a deaf son of deaf parents, is a professor and Associate Vice President for Outreach and External Affairs, and Associate Dean and Director of the Division of Educational Support Service Programs at the National Technical Institute for the Deaf/Rochester Institute of Technology. He holds a B.S. (Washington University) and M.S. (St. Louis University) in Electrical Engineering and an Ed.D. in Curriculum and Teaching (University of Rochester). Dr. Hurwitz is past president of the National Association of the Deaf and co-chaired the National Task Force on Educational Interpreting.

PAUL A. LOERA received Bachelor's and Master's degrees in Rehabilitation Psychology from the University of Arizona. He completed his Doctorate in Rehabilitation Psychology from the University of Pittsburgh. He is Director of Mental Health for the Western Pennsylvania School for the Deaf and Center on Deafness, and Associate Director for the Center on Deafness in Pittsburgh. He also has a private practice in psychology.

NANCY M. LONG received her Ph.D. in clinical psychology from Northern Illinois University. With more than 15 years in vocational rehabilitation with deaf people, Dr. Long has authored 30 publications and conducted 150 workshops on this topic. She is currently Associate Professor and Director of Research at the Research and Training Center on Traditionally Underserved Persons who are Deaf.

DAVID S. MARTIN is Professor and Dean of the School of Education and Human Services at Gallaudet University. He has been a teacher, school administrator, curriculum developer, and teacher educator. His writing and research includes publications in the field of education of deaf persons, cognitive education, and social studies education.

PATRICIA A. MUDGETT-DECARO holds a B.A. in Biology from Earlham College, and M.Ed. in Counseling from the State University of New York at Brockport, and is completing a dissertation in pursuit of a Ph.D. in curriculum at the University of Rochester. Her research and scholarly interest relate to the ways in which various perspectives on deafness are incorporated into everyday structures and conversations.

DOUGLAS D. NOBLE holds an M.A. in philosophy and a Ph.D. in education from the University of Rochester. He is author of the book *The Classroom Arsenal: Military Research, Information, Technology, and Public Education*. His scholarly interests are the political economy of educational technology and corporate influence on schooling.

STEVEN R. SLIGAR holds a B.A. in Sociology from West Georgia College and an M.A. in Education with a specialization in Vocational Evaluation from Auburn University. He is currently director of the Georgia Sensory Rehabilitation Center. A past president of the American Deafness and Rehabilitation Association, he received the national Eugene Petersen Award for services to traditionally underserved persons who are deaf.

MICHAEL STINSON is a research associate and associate professor at the National Technical Institute for the Deaf. He also teaches a course on the psychological, social, and cultural aspects of deafness in the NTID/University of Rochester Program in Preparing Teachers of the Deaf. He is the author of more than 35 research publications, including 5 recently completed chapters for books or monographs.

HOWARD E. "ROCKY" STONE has a B.A. from the University of Southern California and completed one year in the master's program at the School of Advanced International Studies, John Hopkins University. Recipient of an honorary doctorate from Gallaudet University, he is the founder and executive director emeritus of Self Help for Hard of Hearing People, Inc. (SHHH).

► 1

An Orientation for Professionals Working with Deaf Clients

RICHARD C. NOWELL
Indiana University of Pennsylvania

LAURA E. MARSHAK
Indiana University of Pennsylvania

This book examines critical issues related to the effective rehabilitation of persons who are deaf. As a foundation for subsequent chapters, this introductory chapter provides a brief orientation for the professional or professional-in-training about hearing loss and typical patterns in the development of deaf individuals. It also suggests some critical principles for the professional to follow when working with deaf clients.

Any addressing of such complex issues requires generalization. However, the reader should be aware that the "typical" patterns discussed here may not hold true for all deaf people. Members of the deaf community are individuals, and that individualism is a critical aspect underlying how we believe deaf clients should be viewed in the successful rehabilitation process. Furthermore, we are primarily focusing on those individuals who can be classified as "deaf" as opposed to those who are more likely to be classified as "hard-of-hearing."[1] (These terms are explained later in this chapter.) The needs of the latter group, although sometimes similar, are often quite different.

---

[1]We avoid using the term "hearing-impaired," a term which often is used as a generic term for "deaf and hard-of-hearing," but also is used as a euphemism for "deaf."

THE AUDITORY SYSTEM AND HEARING LOSS

The basic areas of the auditory system include the outer, middle, and inner ears, the VIII cranial nerve, the brainstem, and the cortex of the brain. If the auditory system is damaged, the site of lesion, or where the damage takes place, is a critical factor in how the individual's processing of sound is affected. The site of lesion is also an important variable, along with the degree of the loss, the age of onset of the loss, and the presence or absence of other disabilities, affecting how the individual with a hearing loss functions.

The outer ear is composed of the fleshy auricle, or pinna (what we often refer to as "the ear"), and the outer ear canal. It is separated from the middle ear by the eardrum or tympanic membrane. The middle ear contains three small bones, or ossicles, which bridge the space between the eardrum and the inner ear. Together the outer and middle ears comprise the conductive aspect of the auditory system. Sound vibrations are conducted into the outer ear canal, strike the eardrum, and are carried by the ossicles to the inner ear.

Damage to the conductive system tends to be less severe than sensorineural damage and often may by corrected by medical intervention. Furthermore, although hearing sensitivity may be decreased by such damage, there is usually not a severe effect on the ability of the individual to discriminate speech sounds, as long as appropriate amplification is provided. Although "deaf" people may have conductive losses in addition, their hearing loss typically is sensorineural.

The sensorineural part of the auditory system is primarily the inner ear, or cochlea, and the VIII cranial nerve. Damage to this part of the auditory system not only causes a loss in sensitivity to sound but also often results in a decrease in the individual's ability to understand speech, even with amplification. Although sensorineural damage may be mild or moderate, it can also be profound, that is, of such an extreme that an individual can hear little or no sound. Furthermore, in general, sensorineural losses cannot be corrected by medical intervention.

Damage can also occur at the brainstem level or in the cortex itself. Brainstem damage may lead to what is often referred to as central auditory processing problems. Damage to the cortex may cause processing difficulties and higher order cognitive problems related to the use of auditory information. Although it is certainly possible for deaf individuals to have damage in these areas as well, as stated before, in general, this text focuses on individuals who have damage which we assume lies within the cochlea.

Etiologies and Additional Disabilities

Sensorineural hearing loss can have various sources and can be acquired during prenatal development, at birth, or later in the individual's life. About forty percent of the etiologies of children served in educational programs for deaf children are unknown, although it is likely that many of these are related to recessive genetic sources (Brown, 1986). Known sources include dominant as well as recessive genetic traits, but fewer than ten percent of deaf children are born to one or two deaf parents (Northern & Downs, 1984). Other primary sources of hearing loss include diseases, such as rubella or German measles, which attack the developing fetus during gestation; perinatal complications associated with prematurity; Rh incompatibility; and diseases often associated with the birth process, such as cytomegalovirus and herpes. Hearing loss may also be caused by certain childhood diseases; infections in the neurological system, including meningitis and encephalitis; ototoxic drugs, including those used in treating life-threatening illnesses; and, rarely, trauma.

One of our primary concerns regarding etiology is the manner in which the individual may be affected in other areas. Although various estimates vary widely, about thirty percent of deaf individuals may have secondary disabilities (Wolff & Harkins, 1986). These disabilities may affect sensory, physical, affective, or cognitive functioning. For example, rubella acquired by the fetus during pregnancy, in addition to hearing loss, may cause visual problems, auditory processing difficulties, attention-deficit and related disorders, and/or mental retardation (Northern & Downs, 1984). Obviously, if other disabilities are present, educational and vocational outcomes can be affected.

Degree of Hearing Loss

Hearing loss may be measured in a variety of ways. Two of the most common ways are the puretone audiogram and Speech Reception Thresholds. In the former, thresholds of hearing (the softest intensity level at which the client can hear the tone half the time) are determined at distinct octave intervals across the primary range of hearing. In the latter, threshold levels are determined by asking the client to repeat bisyllabic words presented with equal stress on both syllables. Each ear is tested separately in both tests.

Although it is more accurate to use detailed measures of the above tests, one specific number (puretone average loss) often is used to indicate the degree of an individual's hearing loss (e.g., "she has a 75 decibel [dB] loss"). This figure is usually the average loss on a relative dB scale at the frequencies of 500, 1000, and 2000 Hz (Hertz or cycles per second) in the better ear. In most test results this figure corresponds closely with the Speech Reception Threshold.

Descriptive terms—mild, moderate, severe, and profound—are also frequently used to describe a hearing loss. Because most hearing losses are not flat, i.e., there are not similar thresholds at all measured frequencies, these terms are once again usually applied to the average loss. In real world functioning, a person with a mild loss is just able to perceive the sound of soft conversational speech. A person with a moderate loss may be barely aware of average conversational speech. One with a severe loss may just be able to hear loud conversational speech. A profound loss usually means the individual would not hear the sound of conversational speech at all.

Other Parameters of Hearing

The primary question regarding hearing ability to be asked about a person with a hearing loss is how well that person is able to *understand* speech. If an individual with a hearing loss is able to receive language aurally, that is, by hearing it, either with or without amplification, that individual is functionally "hard-of-hearing." On the other hand, if that person is unable to understand speech aurally, even with amplification, that person is usually referred to as "deaf" (Scheetz, 1993).

In addition to the degree of a hearing loss and ability to discriminate speech, a critical aspect concerning how an individual will function is the age of the onset of the loss. Individuals who are born deaf will tend to have much more difficulty in mastering the language of the majority culture, especially in its oral/aural form (that is, speaking and understanding spoken English) than individuals who lose their hearing after they have had an opportunity to develop language skills during the first several years of life (see Chapter 2). In fact, many of the latter who are "post-lingually" deaf refer to themselves as "hard-of-hearing," indicating significant aspects about how they function as well as their own cultural identification.

Technological Interventions

Technology has, of course, done a lot to remediate the functioning of those with hearing loss. Modern hearing aids have provided an opportunity for many people with less than a profound loss to communicate very well with hearing people. Hearing aids also often help even one with a profound hearing loss to receive a lot of speech information, even though the individual may not be able to receive and produce speech fluently. Some deaf individuals are able with a combination of speechreading and amplification to communicate orally quite well. Again, this is much more often the case with a post-lingually deaf person.

In recent years the development of cochlear implants has provided the possibility of improved hearing for even those with profound hearing losses. How much cochlear implants will contribute to the development of prelingually, profoundly deaf children remains to be seen (Berger & Millin, 1989).

Hearing aids and other technological devices (see Chapter 11) may assist deaf individuals in their daily lives, but they do not change deaf people into hearing people. That is, a deaf person who communicates well with hearing people in many situations is still a deaf person, and even those with the best oral/aural communication skills will have difficulty in many, if not most, situations with hearing people. Prelingual deafness also results in most individuals' developing less than fluent English skills (see Chapter 2).

EDUCATION AND THE COMMUNICATION CONTROVERSY

Deaf people grow up in a hearing world within a system dominated by hearing people, including the educational system. In the nineteenth century, deaf people themselves were a dominant force in educational programs for deaf children in the United States, but that was to change (Moores, 1987). Increasing emphasis upon the teaching of speech to deaf children was to result in a marked decrease in the number of deaf teachers. This change of emphasis by the turn of the century reflected another phase in the ongoing communication controversy.

The controversy about communication methodology, that is, what method of communication to use in school programs for deaf children, had existed since the first recorded positions on educational approaches in Europe around the beginning of the seventeenth century. The two basic opposing positions in the ongoing controversy are often referred to as "oral" and "manual." In the early days of education of deaf children, proponents of oralism held the position that, in order to function in a hearing world, deaf children must learn to speak and understand speech (through residual hearing and speechreading). The "manualists" opposing this position generally held that sign language was the only way deaf people could communicate and that speech was irrelevant for them (Scouten, 1984).

The founding of the first permanent school for deaf children in the United States in 1817 by Thomas Gallaudet included the implementation of the latter method, based upon the French "silent method," and the first teacher at the school was a French deaf man, Laurent Clerc. Although Gallaudet's son, Edward Miner Gallaudet, was to embrace the position that both speech and sign language were appropriate for deaf children (Moores, 1987), the oral-only forces, following international trends, were to dominate the field by the end of the nineteenth century. All schools were basically oral in the U.S. during the first six decades of the current century (Scouten, 1984).

In the 1970s, educational programs began to swing back to a philosophy of "Total Communication," a position that holds that any and all communication methods (including speech and sign language) should be used where appropriate with deaf children (Scouten, 1984). The great majority of schools for deaf children in this country now follow this philosophy, which generally means that teachers both sign and speak during classroom instruction, and that the school encourages students to both speak and sign.

Currently a new controversy has arisen regarding whether to use some form of Manually Coded English, that is, sign language in English word order and with English grammatical inflections, or American Sign Language (ASL), the language which is used by most prelingually deaf adults in the U.S. and Canada. ASL has a word order usually different from English and a grammar unique to a visual/manual language. Proponents of teaching ASL to young deaf children often suggest that English then be taught as a second language (see Chapter 2).

With the swing to oral-only education at the end of the nineteenth century, deaf teachers became a rarity (Moores, 1987). Now that Total Communication is the predominant philosophy of educational programs, we are now seeing an increase in deaf teachers and in general the influence of the deaf subculture on the raising of deaf children. Although some of the outspoken deaf advocates strongly support the use of ASL with young deaf children, there is no consensus as to the type of sign language to be used.

There are, of course, many other important aspects of educating deaf children in addition to the communication mode used. In this age of the mainstreaming of individuals with disabilities, there is an ongoing controversy as to the advisability of mainstreaming deaf children, especially those who rely upon manual communication. Although mainstream advocates claim that deaf children in special schools are "isolated" from society, those deaf children in a regular school with hearing children with whom they have little or no communication may be much more isolated.

In some cases, hearing parents wish their deaf children to be in regular schools with their hearing peers, whether or not the educators involved believe that is the best placement for the children. In other cases, parents may want their children to go to a special school for deaf children, even when their local schools provide services for deaf children and strongly push for placement of deaf children in their programs, drawing upon laws requiring "least restrictive environment" (see Chapter 10). A directive from the U.S. Department of Education in late 1992 (U.S. Department of Education, 1992) states that special schools for deaf children may be considered the "least restrictive environment." This controversy is not likely to be resolved in the near future.

Evaluations of educational programs for deaf children have been less than complimentary in their assessment of society's efforts to give deaf children the same opportunities as hearing children. Although in 1965 the Babbidge Report, the end product of the work of a presidential commission on education of deaf children, was very influential in changing the field, a more recent presidential commission's report (Bowe, 1988) still indicates that we have far to go before we can be satisfied about the opportunities we are providing for these children. Some specific outcomes of educational efforts for deaf children are discussed in terms of language in Chapter 2 and in terms of cognitive ability in Chapter 3.

COMMON PATTERNS OF DEVELOPMENT

Although there are many varied patterns of development of deaf individuals, the most common patterns follow. Most deaf children are born to hearing parents, most of whom know little or nothing about deafness. These children are identified as deaf on the average at eighteen months (SKI*HI Institute, 1992). They often receive hearing aids and some limited early intervention services, usually focused on providing parents with methods of stimulating early language and communication development (Scheetz, 1993). Although the emphasis in the past has been on oral communication, we now see more and more of these services including sign language training for parents and their deaf children. Additionally, many programs are now focusing on the extensive need for emotional support of these hearing families.

When deaf children reach preschool age, they usually have some type of educational program available for them, especially if they live in an urban area (although members of minority groups are less often found in these programs [Moores, 1987]).

Upon reaching school age, deaf children most often enter special school programs, either residential (live-in) or day (daily commuting) programs, although we see a large percentage of deaf students now being served in self-contained classrooms or resource rooms in the regular public schools (Paul & Quigley, 1990).

Often deaf students do not graduate from high school until they are 20 or 21. Their average reading level at that time is about grade 4.5 (King & Quigley, 1987). Their overall academic skills are on the average behind those of their hearing peers, and their entry into post-secondary programs is less common than with hearing students (Paul & Quigley, 1990). When they do attend post-secondary schools, most often it is at one of the national programs (Gallaudet University or the National Technical Institute for the Deaf), one of the federally sponsored regional college and technical schools for deaf students, or, more rarely, a college or university which has a program of special support services for deaf students (Moores, 1987). Some will attend colleges and universities with limited services for deaf students.

We are now seeing the appearance of transition programs to help deaf students make the move from high school to post-secondary training or work (see Chapter 5). With recent legislation requiring more accessibility to training (see Chapter 10), we are also seeing more opportunity for vocational training for deaf adults. It remains to be seen how effective recent trends will be in preparing deaf individuals for the world of work on a national level, although the outcomes in some programs are very encouraging.

DEAF ADULTS IN SOCIETY

Most pre-vocationally deaf people, that is, those who lose their hearing before entering the work force or specific training for jobs (defined by Quigley & Kretschmer, 1982, as age 19), will identify to some degree with the deaf subculture (Furth, 1973). In fact, many individuals who grow up with a hearing loss, but according to our former functional definition are "hard-of-hearing," still choose to identify with the deaf subculture. Within this subculture they will socialize extensively with other deaf people, usually marry other deaf people, and belong to various organizations operated by and for deaf adults.

Most deaf people do not consider their hearing loss as a "handicap." They see it, rather, as a characteristic that sets them apart from the mainstream society in many ways. Although they may struggle, just as hearing people do, to succeed in a hearing world, they see their deafness and their membership in the deaf subculture as something about which to be proud—deafness is not something to be overcome (Paul & Jackson, 1993).

Currently we see that, although some deaf adults are fluent in written and signed English, in general their communication often relies upon some degree of ASL or a combination of ASL and signed English (see Chapter 2). Although there are many deaf adults who are quite skilled speechreaders and who have intelligible speech, the majority of prelingually, profoundly deaf individuals will rely upon some type of sign language to facilitate any extensive communication situations (Hipskind, 1989).

MINORITY GROUP STATUS

To work effectively with deaf adults in the rehabilitation process, one must understand the social consequences of deafness. Many of the problems experienced by persons who are deaf have nothing to do with the direct effects of hearing loss. Rather, they are related to the effects of differing from the social norm and reactions of the larger society to such differences. Wright (1983) discusses how societies tend to idolize normal standards and the implications of this for those who differ from the norm:

> Idolizing normal standards . . . means that the normal standards of behavior are rigidly defined and held forth as the single criterion for the desirable or even allowable. Those who fall below those standards are devaluated. Their needs are underserved, their well-being neglected.

As a result of the significant ways in which deaf persons deviate from rigid societal standards about what constitutes an "adequate" person, they often find themselves in the position of other disadvantaged minority groups.

> . . . they are subject to the same problems that other minority groups face: *the demand that the minority people come up to the expectations of the majority, and the majority's utter disregard for the real needs of the minority group* (italics added); and in addition the preconceived opinions, the prejudices, the power structure, the self-perpetuation, the superiority complex (paternalism), and the authority held by the members of the majority over the minority segment. (Jacobs, 1974, p. 61)

Differentness becomes equated with deviance and inadequacy. Idolization of normal standards prompts many to believe that the solution for persons who differ is to become as much like the social norm as possible.

In part, as a response to the majority culture's reaction to deaf individuals, a deaf culture has developed which holds great value for its members. This subculture is characterized by its own language patterns, its members' acceptance of being socially and culturally deaf, behavioral norms, endogamous marital patterns, the historical awareness of its members, and networks of voluntary organizations (Paul & Jackson, 1993). Although some people who are audiologically deaf do not choose to belong to this subculture, they are likely to be seen by the hearing world as members.

For vocational rehabilitation efforts to be successful, one must be aware that many problems experienced by deaf persons are a result of their status as a minority group rather than their own deficiencies. This orientation is crucial because it provides a way to think about how to open up options for clients rather than accept the status quo. For all too long, the status quo meant that workers who are deaf were primarily guided toward a limited range of blue collar jobs such as printing press operators and shoemakers. In addition, problems which hindered their abilities (i.e., significant academic deficiencies or lack of work adjustment skills) were often accepted as necessarily concomitant with deafness.

In reality, many of these problems have resulted from a lack of flexibility in meeting the needs of individuals who differ from the norm. With regard to deafness, this is best illustrated by the controversy regarding manual versus oral communication. As long as persons who are deaf are expected to meet rigid societal standards (i.e., the one right way to converse is through the spoken word), solutions to communication problems are not readily identified and the functional effects of the disability are exacerbated. We recognize the existence of a significant conflict for many, because (on an individual basis) deaf persons who speak better and understand speech better "succeed" more readily in the majority culture.

The relationship that is formed between the professional and the individual with deafness is the cornerstone of the vocational-rehabilitation process. It is important that these relationships do not unintentionally mirror the mistakes made by society at large in the perception and treatment of persons who are deaf. The following principles are useful in this regard.

1. *The professional needs to check the accuracy of perceptions of clients.* Professionals must be able to perceive deaf individuals objectively in order to collaborate effectively to improve their vocational situation. Human perception is far from accurate and tends to be particularly distorted in terms of individuals who differ from the norm. Persons with deafness clearly differ from the norm and are consequently subject to several phenomena which result in distorted perceptions. These distorted perceptions often culminate in what has been termed as a "fundamental negative bias" (Wright, 1988). This term applies to the fact that discernment of a disability "steers perception, thought and feeling along negative lines to such a degree that positives remain hidden" (Wright, 1988, p. 3).

Deafness has such a powerful impact on how others view the deaf individual that it often calls forth the perceptual phenomenon of *spread*: ". . . the power of single characteristics to evoke inferences about a person" (Wright, 1983, p. 32). With spread, the discernment of a single disability often leads us to perceive other impairments (regardless of whether they actually exist). For example, perception of impaired hearing evokes inferences of impaired intelligence . . . which evokes inferences of impaired emotional functioning . . . which evokes inferences of impaired vocational potential, ad infinitum. This is not to say that multiple problems do not cluster for some persons with disabilities, but rather that, we run the danger of making *automatic* inferences on the basis of a single disability.

Another threat to accurate perception is the tendency to overlook the environment when interpreting the behavior of persons who differ from the norm. Behavior can best be understood as a function of the interaction between a person and his or her environment (Lewin, 1935). However, when an individual differs from the norm, we tend to focus solely on the individual and disregard the environmental influence on behavior (Wright, 1983). This type of perceptual error has contributed to many professionals' stereotypes of clients who are deaf. For example, while speaking about her experiences as a psychologist working with deaf individuals, a colleague recently described them as "paranoid and difficult." Whereas lack of trust may have been a prominent feature in many of her interactions with clients, she had overlooked the environmental sources of this paranoid approach. Members of minority groups are often inherently distrustful of members of the majority. What one considers paranoia can also be considered caution based on experience.

2. *Professionals need to form collaborative relationships with clients.* Vocational rehabilitation must be based on a relationship in which the client and the professional form an equal partnership to address rehabilitation issues. The professional can effectively view his or her role as a "resource collaborator" (Tyler, Pargament, & Gatz, 1983). Egan (1990) described this type of professional-client relationship in the following manner:

> . . . either helper or client can approach the other to originate the helping process. Both have equal status in defining the terms of the relationship, in originating actions within it, and in evaluating both outcomes and the relationship itself. (p. 79)

All too often within rehabilitation, the concept of an equal partnership becomes lost in practice—especially in circumstances where the obstacles to rehabilitation are the greatest. As the challenges mount, professionals can lose sight of the importance of fostering and maintaining the requisite genuinely collaborative relationship. At times it is regarded as a luxury because of the amount of time it takes to truly integrate a client into a partnership.

Relationships between hearing professionals and deaf clients are particularly prone to this problem because of communication problems. However, problems can also occur between deaf professionals and clients. Lack of equal status in the helping relationship can jeopardize the best laid rehabilitation plans. Clients who are not engaged as equal status participants in the rehabilitation process are inclined naturally to resist. Sometimes this resistance is mistakenly regarded as evidence of a lack of social skills, motivational problems, or idiosyncracies of deaf culture, when it is actually a manifestation of resentment over being controlled by another.

3. *Helping must empower clients.* The nature of helping is such that it can either lead to improved self-sufficiency or it can increase the recipient's feelings of powerlessness (Stensrud & Stensrud, 1981). An awareness of the need to empower clients is necessary in order to avoid paternalistic methods. Empowerment means that persons with disabilities need to have choices and control in the rehabilitation process. Condeluci (1991) writes, "people who have been devalued must have opportunities

and experiences to make choices and be in charge (p. 125)." Within this context the professional's role is to facilitate clients' decision making rather than make choices for them (Condeluci, 1991).

Empowerment is a concept that can be applied on an individual and/or a group basis. On an individual basis, empowerment builds self-esteem. Condeluci writes of the relationship between empowerment and self-esteem, ". . . the quickest way to self-esteem is to focus on capacities. Give people control and support them in their efforts (p. 122)." An obvious way to implement the principle of empowerment on a group basis is to learn about and respect deaf culture.

4. *Helping must attend to environmental factors which contribute to the vocational problems experienced by persons with deafness.* As discussed earlier, the most significant problems experienced by those with deafness do not lie solely within the structures which govern hearing. Rather, they are to a great extent environmentally based. Within this context, societal attitudes, common practices, and regulations comprise part of the deaf individual's environment. Whereas the vocational rehabilitation process needs to focus on changing the individual (through training, education, counseling, etc.), it is important that equal attention be paid to changing the environment. In practical terms, this means fostering more realistic attitudes about the capabilities of persons who are deaf and promoting the use of necessary accommodations, such as interpreters, job restructuring, and assistive devices.

As the reader progresses through the following chapters, we hope these principles are kept in mind, and that persons with deafness are regarded as competent members of a subculture rather than deficient members of a hearing culture. The following chapters contain information that will help the reader to gain a comprehensive understanding of the many ways that deafness often impacts individuals. In this process many common misconceptions about deafness will be addressed. In addition, many of the following chapters describe ways in which the needs of deaf persons can be met in a flexible manner in order to empower them to implement realistic and satisfying vocational plans successfully.

REFERENCES

Berger, K.W., & Millin, J.P. (1989). Amplification/assistive devices for the hearing impaired. In R.L. Schow & M.A. Nerbonne (Eds.), *Introduction to aural rehabilitation* (pp. 31–80). Austin, TX: Pro-Ed.

Bowe, F. (Ed.) (1988). *Toward equality: Education of the deaf.* Washington, DC: U.S. Government Printing Office.

Brown, S.C. (1986). Etiological trends, characteristics, and distributions. In A.N. Schildroth & M.A. Karchmer (Eds.), *Deaf children in America* (pp. 33–54). San Diego, CA: College-Hill Press.

Condeluci, A. (1991). *Interdependence: The root to community.* Orlando, FL: Paul M. Deutsch Press.

Egan, G. (1990). *The skilled helper.* Pacific Grove, CA: Brooks/Cole.

Furth, H.G. (1973). *Deafness and learning: A psychosocial approach.* Belmont, CA: Wadsworth.

Hipskind, N.M. (1989). Visual stimuli in communication. In R.L. Schow & M.A. Nerbonne (Eds.), *Introduction to aural rehabilitation* (pp. 125–180). Austin, TX: Pro-Ed.

Jacobs, L.M. (1974). *A deaf adult speaks out.* Washington, DC: Gallaudet College Press.

King, C., & Quigley, S.P. (1987). *Reading and deafness.* San Diego, CA: College-Hill.

Lewin, K. (1935). A dynamic theory of personality. New York: McGraw-Hill.

Moores, D.F. (1987). *Educating the deaf: Psychology, principles, and practices* (3rd edition). Boston: Houghton-Mifflin.

Northern, J., & Downs, M. (1984). *Hearing in children* (3rd ed.). Baltimore: Williams & Wilkins.

Paul, P.V., & Jackson, D.W. (1993). *Psychology of deafness: Theoretical and empirical perspectives.* Boston: Allyn and Bacon.

Paul, P.V., & Quigley, S.P. (1990). *Education and deafness.* New York: Longman.

Quigley, S.P., & Kretschmer, R.E. (1982). *The education of deaf children: Issues, theory, and practice.* Austin, TX: Pro-Ed.

Scheetz, N.A. (1993). *Orientation to deafness.* Boston: Allyn and Bacon.

Scouten, E.L. (1984). *Turning points in the education of deaf people.* Danville, IL: Interstate.

SKI*HI Institute. (1992). Final Report, Early intervention research project, Logan, Utah.

Stensrud, R., & Stensrud, K. (1981). Counseling may be hazardous to your health: How we teach people to feel powerless. *Personnel and Guidance Journal, 59,* 300–304.

Tyler, F.B., Pargament, K.I., & Gatz, M. (1983). The resource-collaborator role: A model for interactions involving psychologists. *American Psychologist, 38,* 388–398.

U.S. Department of Education. (1992, October 30). Notice of policy guidance. *Federal Register,* pp. 49274 ff.

Wright, B.A. (1983). *Physical disability: A psychosocial approach.* New York: Harper & Row.

Wolff, A.B., & Harkins, J.E. (1986). Multihandicapped students. In A.N.Schildroth & M.A. Karchmer (Eds.), *Deaf children in America* (pp. 55–81). San Diego, CA: College-Hill Press.

Wright, B.A. (1988). Attitudes and the fundamental negative bias: Conditions and corrections. In H.E. Yuker (Ed.), *Attitudes toward persons with disabilities.* New York: Springer Publishing Co.

▶ 2

Language and Communication Development

C. TANE AKAMATSU
Toronto Board of Education

In this chapter, the development of language and communication will be discussed from a cognitive developmental point of view. It begins with working definitions, theoretical foundations, some of the historical reasons why the field is as complex as it is, and why the clientele is so varied in its communication skills. From there, the milestones in normal language development are reviewed in terms of form, content, and use. Included in this discussion are both hearing children of hearing parents and deaf children of deaf parents. Following this is a review of the most common development of deaf youth who have hearing parents. The chapter concludes with some typical communicative, linguistic, and functional outcomes, and implications for the rehabilitation practitioner.

DEFINITIONS AND THEORETICAL FOUNDATIONS

This chapter begins with a few words about the relationships among communication, cognition, language, and culture. At the risk of over-simplification but for the sake of clarity, communication itself can be described as consisting of five parts: message, sender, receiver, channel, and feedback. Communication begins with a need to send a message of some kind. This message can be information, a greeting, a summons, or whatever. This message is generated by the sender, and goes from the sender to the receiver. Messages must be sent via a channel, such as speech, sign, writing, code (e.g., Morse code), radio, television, etc. For the receiver to receive the message, it is clearly necessary that the message be intelligible and accessible. It is not necessary for the message to be verbal (i.e., linguistic); international signs such as those seen in airports and on international highways are examples of nonverbal messages. Finally, the receiver must confirm whether or not a message has been received. This confirmation is called feedback, and can take the form of an answer to a query, a simple acknowledgment, a behavioral response to a command, or similar responses.

The use of language is one form of communication. Language is best described in terms of its form, content, and use (Bloom & Lahey, 1988). In form, language is a system of communication that is symbolic (uses arbitrary symbols that everyone agrees upon), rule-governed, and generative (new messages can be put together—generated—from a finite number of "parts"). The symbols of a language can be either spoken or signed. Some languages also have written forms, although a language does not have to have a written form to be considered a language. For example, English is a spoken language that also has a written form, whereas American Sign Language (ASL) is a signed language that does not have a widely accepted standardized written form, although some ways of transcribing signs in written form have been developed (e.g., Stokoe, Casterline, & Croneberg, 1965). The form of a language is defined as its grammar and syntax—how words are put together to form sentences, and how sentences that express minute differences in meaning are made.

Language content is defined in terms of the meaning or semantics expressed. This includes both word meanings and the semantic relationships among the people, objects, and actions in the sentences. For example, in the sentence "Mary reads a book," Mary is the agent of read, and book the object of Mary's reading. Thus, if a young child said, "Mary book" to convey the meaning of this sentence, we would say that she had expressed the agent and object of the sentence.

Language use refers to the function of an utterance. That is, an utterance can be used to inform, question, command, or otherwise manipulate the behavior of the listener. The primary, pragmatic function of language is communication, and more importantly and specifically, language can be used to represent and manipulate understanding of the world among the people who use that particular language.

As mentioned earlier, languages can be either signed or spoken. English is an example of a spoken language and is used by the majority of hearing people in the United States and English-speaking Canada. ASL is an example of a signed language, and is used by the majority of deaf people in the same areas. These two languages, English and ASL, will be the focus of the discussion in this chapter.[1]

As the reader will have noted from the previous chapter, deaf people make up a very heterogeneous population. The heterogeneity of the population means that the demographic and environmental factors alone create many, many possibilities for both normal and less-than-optimal social interaction. As such, language development in deaf individuals can take many different routes, each with its own outcome. The next section is a discussion of the various influences that bear on language development, and an attempt to tie together apparently conflicting research findings in a unified theory of language development. It is important to remember that developing a usable adult language is extremely difficult for most deaf individuals, and many adult deaf clients will not have an adult's command of a language. This can create difficulties in communication, but is not an insurmountable obstacle.

Such an approach imparts a sense of the possible and does not perseverate on deficits. The adult deaf client may have plenty of information about his or her failures, but very little information about alternative possibilities. Adopting a positive vantage point will encourage the rehabilitation specialist to look at the possibilities inherent in a client's interests and talents, rather than to focus exclusively on "repairing" what the client *cannot* do.

Language and Culture

Different groups of people use different languages. The conventions for behavior, including the use of language, differ from group to group, and are part of each group's culture. Just as we think of American culture as different from, say, Japanese culture, or French culture, so is hearing culture different from that of deaf culture.

There are many sources for what is called deaf culture, but perhaps American Sign Language is the strongest influence through which deaf people have created their own culture that bears distinct differences from hearing culture (Padden & Humphries, 1988; see also Chapter 4). Although deaf culture is so strongly influenced by ASL (as well as by attendance at residential schools for deaf students, suffering the consequences of discriminatory practices at home, in school, and on the job, and by experiencing the world primarily through vision), one should remember that not all deaf people participate in deaf culture because not all deaf people sign or go to residential schools. This culture is a highly variable one, transmitted largely from peer to peer, rather than from parent to child. The reason for this is simple: Most deaf people are born into hearing families, and only as a result of contact with deaf adults and children born into deaf families do they learn the knowledge, practices, and beliefs that underlie deaf culture.

Sometimes this contact comes upon entry into a residential school for deaf children, which can happen at any age. Some individuals, however, spend their entire school careers in schools for hearing children with special services or classes for deaf students. These individuals may not be influenced by the deaf community until after they graduate and associate with deaf adults on a social basis. Consequently, the age at which they begin to socialize as deaf people varies considerably.

Some individuals, in spite of contact with the deaf community, choose not to socialize within that community. This may be a reflection of their own self-image ("I'm not a deaf person; I just don't hear well,") or their own perception of their potential ("I can fit in—or function as a hearing person—if I only try hard enough."). People who lose their hearing in adulthood, in particular, should not be thought of as deaf people, but as hearing people who can no longer hear, because culturally, they are indeed hearing. These people often may associate with deaf people to practice signing, or to lobby as a group for workplace reforms, since discriminatory practices affect deaf people regardless of the age at which the deafness occurred. Many of these people belong to organizations such as Self-Help for the Hard-of-Hearing (SHHH) or the Association of Late-Deafened Adults (ALDA).

Language and Cognition

Although the next chapter discusses cognitive development of deaf people in greater detail, it is important to understand the relationship between language and cognition. Language and cognition are intimately tied. Language can be used to manipulate cognition (for teaching/learning; for memory; for creating new knowledge). After his curiosity was piqued by observations of deaf people, Vygotsky began a series of theoretical discussions about cognitive development which have only recently had an impact in the field of deafness. Vygotsky (1986) suggested that, although all humans have the capacity for higher mental functions (e.g., deliberate memory, organization, learning), these higher mental functions come about only as a result of having been "taught" or *mediated*. Mediation is defined as the process by which the more knowledgeable (teacher, parent, older peer) models the function to be acquired for the less knowledgeable. This mediation occurs most efficiently through the use of language. Indeed, Vygotsky maintains that the single most differentiating characteristic of humans is the ability of verbal (i.e., linguistic) mediation.

Verbal mediation is a powerful tool for cognitive development. Much teaching and learning, both formal and informal, occurs because of verbal mediation, and mediation is the one are that is usually most affected by deafness. Although the effects are obviously remediable, intervention in the area is extremely difficult. The deaf child of hearing parents is not able to take advantage of the verbal mediation in spoken English that the parents are able to provide. The parents are usually not equipped to provide equivalent mediation in either spoken or signed English, nor in ASL. So although the parents make valiant efforts to communicate with the child (including learning how to sign), these efforts fall short in their ability to provide the complex verbal mediation needed by the child.

The deaf child of deaf parents is somewhat more fortunate. This child is able to use the verbal mediation the parents provide in ASL. Thus linguistic and cognitive development proceeds normally and naturally as for hearing children of hearing parents. However, once the child enters school, the teachers may not be fluent in either signed English or ASL. Indeed, research shows that most teachers are unable to provide complete, consistent models of either ASL or signed English (Marmor & Petitto, 1978; Stewart, Akamatsu, & Bonkowski, 1948). Thus, the quality of verbal mediation provided to this deaf child is reduced.

Research also documents that deaf children of deaf parents do better in school (Corson, 1973; Meadow, 1968; Stuckless & Birch, 1966). The explanation usually provided is that these children "have language." While it cannot be denied that these children will probably have been exposed to a more complete language than deaf children of hearing parents, it is also true that deaf children of deaf parents have had their understanding of the world mediated, and are thus better equipped than deaf children of hearing parents to engage in structuring information, remembering, and manipulating thought in complex ways. The resulting achievements—academic, social, and emotional—should not be surprising.

SYNOPSIS OF "NORMAL" LANGUAGE DEVELOPMENT

In this section, language development in children who acquire their first language under normal circumstances will be reviewed. This discussion includes deaf children acquiring their first signed language from a communicatively rich environment. One must recognize, however, that the proportion of deaf children who are so fortunate is extremely low, less than 10% of the deaf population (Schein & Delk, 1974).

Prelinguistic Communication

Humans are fundamentally social beings. All children begin with a need to communicate. This need expresses itself initially in the cries of the infant, and by the end of the first year, in specific intentional gestures and/or vocalizations (Bates, 1976; Bates, Camaioni, & Volterra, 1975; Scoville, 1983). Adults interact with infants with the expectation that, although babies may not understand adult's utterances at the moment, they will develop an understanding through extensive interaction. Even in the absence of complete language input, babies will invent and create bits and pieces of language, as in the case of pidgin and creole speakers (Bickerton, 1977), or deaf children with no access to signed language (Goldin-Meadow, 1982).

Prelinguistic development of language is related to cognitive development. The increasing amount of interpersonal experiences, particularly those involving language, leads to the development of cognitive, semantic, and social schemas, which enable the further development of both language and cognition (Bruner, 1975; Sugarman, 1978; Vygotsky, 1986).

Vocabulary and semantic relations

Young children's' vocabularies grow rapidly, with several words being acquired daily between the ages of 2½ to 4½ (Smith, 1926). Signing children are no different. Emergence of the first word/sign occurs on average between the ages of 10–14 months (Klima & Bellugi, 1979; Siple & Akamatsu, 1986), and vocabulary growth proceeds rapidly thereafter. The content of these early vocabularies seem universal, despite differences of culture and upbringing, largely consisting of names of people, animals, and objects in the child's environment, and actions of eating, sleeping, and playing (Gleason, 1985).

Vygotsky (1986) suggests that the continued growth and refinement in word meaning depends heavily on the extended use of language to talk about words, such that words themselves become (psychological) objects that children can manipulate to develop even more complex understandings of the words they use. Under normal circumstances, this occurs naturally. Very young children are observed to misuse words, sometimes overgeneralizing meanings (using "dog" to refer to all four-legged furry animals), at other times undergeneralizing (using "dog" to refer only to the family dog, and some other word for other dogs). The practice of categorizing, based on the adults' practices, applies not only to objects, but to words as well. It is clear to see that without the extensive linguistic mediation available in the normal language environment, the development of a child's vocabulary will be delayed, and at times, bizarre.

Vocabulary and semantic development is the one area of language development that continues throughout an individual's lifetime, although at a much slower pace in adulthood. Indeed, Hammermeister (1971) found that deaf adults' English abilities continued to develop as their vocabularies expanded to meet the needs of the workplace and independent living.

Morphology and Syntactic Development

Upon the acquisition of some 50–75 words by the second half of the second year, a new stage in productive language development begins. The child begins to string two words together, and the beginnings of syntax emerge. At this time, researchers and clinicians measure language development in terms of mean length of utterance (MLU). This is a measure of the average number of morphemes per utterance (Brown, 1973). It is believed that children with the same MLU are at the same stage of language development, regardless of age. MLU has been used as an indicator of signed and spoken language development.

When children's utterances are only two words long, it is difficult to determine whether they actually have a knowledge of the target language's syntax, but given a combination of children's utterances and context clues, some educated guesses can be made about their intended meaning (Bowerman, 1975; Bates, 1976).

With the three-word stage, two significant developments occur (Brown, 1973). First, grammatical morphemes can be embedded in a phrase to express a specific grammatical relationship among the words. For example, <u>no work</u> inserted into <u>Mommy work</u> produces <u>Mommy no work</u>. The second is that phrases can be conjoined: <u>Baby hug</u> and <u>hug teddy</u> become <u>Baby hug teddy</u>. These two grammatical processes indicate that chunks of language are being manipulated, rather than individual words or morphemes.

Further syntactic development includes the use of functional and inflectional morphology, the little words and word endings that indicate grammatical and semantic relationships among words in sentences. In his classic study of the acquisition of 14 grammatical morphemes in English, Brown (1973) discovered that these morphemes were acquired in roughly the same order by the three children he studied, a finding that has since been replicated in whole or in part in English-based sign systems (Bornstein, Saulnier, & Hamilton, 1980, 1983; Crandall, 1978; Gilman & Raffin, 1975).

By the age of five years, children have acquired all of the simple syntax and much of the complex syntax of their native language. Language development under normal circumstances proceeds quickly, and indeed almost effortlessly, but is predicated on fully accessible linguistic communication and mediation of the environment by adults and more advanced peers.

INFLUENCES ON DEAF CHILDREN'S LANGUAGE DEVELOPMENT

Sensory Channels

It is clear that beyond a certain hearing threshold level, around 90 dB HL, vision takes over as the primary modality for communication (Conrad, 1979; Ling, 1976; McAnally, Rose, & Quigley, 1987). This single fact means that the process of acquiring spoken language becomes a task both extremely difficult and somewhat unnatural for the child. In this case, deafness is more than a lack of auditory input. It also usually means a lack of visual input of the right kind, specifically, a lack of socially mediated, comprehensible, linguistic communication. In this situations, the typical deaf child is put at a grave disadvantage in learning language.

Attitudes of Parents and Other Important People

A secondary influence on the language development of deaf children is attitudes of parents, teachers, and others who work with them. If the prevailing message is one of the child's inadequacy because of hearing impairment, the child will not develop a sense of self-efficacy, or have any expectation that the future holds anything other than failure. If, on the other hand, there is a sense that the child can and will accomplish life's tasks, including learning language, there is much hope for the future of the child (Schlesinger, 1988).

Language is acquired through meaningful interaction between caregivers and children. Sometimes, however, the creation of meaningful interaction is short-circuited by disadvantaging conditions such as organically based language disorders, mental retardation, or in the present case, deafness. Because deafness is usually unexpected and often unsuspected, caregivers usually find themselves in the untenable position of talking to a sporadically responsive child. That is, the child appears to respond normally at times, and not at all at other times. The confirmation of deafness serves as an impetus for caregivers to change the nature of communication with the child. In some cases, the caregivers attempt to learn to sign. In other cases, the quantity and quality of the interaction simply decline.

For example, hearing mothers often speak less to their deaf children than to hearing children, use atypical rhythmic and intonational patterns, give more commands and fewer verbal praises to their children, and are generally more dominant in their interaction patterns (Cheskin, 1982; Gross, 1970; Weddell-Monig & Lumley, 1980). In contrast, Greenberg and his colleagues (Carmichael & Greenberg, 1980; Greenberg, Kusche, Gustafson, & Calderon, 1984) found that interaction between deaf mothers and their deaf children is much more like hearing mothers and their hearing children. That is, interaction is conducive to complex, sustained, mature, and reciprocal interaction, where the child is an equal partner in the communicative interaction.

EDUCATIONAL CONSIDERATIONS

Signing Systems

From the late 1960s through the 1970s was a turbulent time in the deaf community. ASL was recognized as a full-fledged language, and much research into the linguistics and psycholinguistics of ASL was being conducted (Klima & Bellugi, 1979; Siple, 1978; Stokoe, 1960; Stokoe & Volterra, 1985; Wilbur, 1987). The concept of "total communication" (see Chapter 1) was advocated as one way to improve the dismal achievement of deaf children. Legislation such as Public Law 94–142 (Education for All Handicapped Children Act, 1975) required schools and programs to modify delivery of education to deaf children. The civil rights movement was underway, and deaf people began to recognize their own power to control their destiny. Deaf culture was recognized as independent from hearing culture.

All of these factors combined to force a rapid and unplanned change in programs for deaf children. Primarily, this change centered around how teachers and parents were to communicate with their young charges. The ultimate goal of English language development remained. The schools were not ready to accept ASL as a language, either as a language in which to teach or as a language to be taught, yet were willing to allow "signing" in the classrooms in order to increase the quality of communication between teacher and student. In general, parents, teachers, and administrators still expected deaf students to conform to the norms of the hearing culture.

During this same timeframe, a number of English-based signing systems were developed and refined for use in the educational sphere. Basically, these systems use signs from ASL, sometimes modified by the practice of initializing or using the manual alphabet letter that corresponds to the first letter of a target English word, with a corpus of signs invented specifically for the purpose of representing English grammatical structure. Among the more common of these systems are Seeing Essential English (Anthony, 1966), Signing Exact English (Gustason, Pfetzing, & Zawalkow, 1975), and Signed English (Bornstein, Saulnier, & Hamilton, 1983). Collectively, these are known as English-based signing systems, or manually coded English (MCE). There is considerable doubt about whether these systems constitute a real language. Those who argue that they do not contend that although MCE is based on English, which is a natural language, MCE itself is not naturally acquired as a first language by anyone (Baker & Cokely, 1980; Luetke-Stahlman, 1986). It is a system contrived out of necessity, to be used for a specific purpose, i.e., making English visible on the hands for real-time communication (English is already visible in written form). However, there are those who suggest it might at least function as a natural first language if complete input is available to deaf children (e.g., Stewart, Akamatsu, Hunter, Krugh, & Ng, 1989).

The main difficulty that educators and deaf people have had with MCE is that such a variety of systems were developed within a very short timespan, and virtually no research on its use was conducted before wide-scale implementation took place. This wide-scale use was often mandated without proper training in the use of MCE or in any follow-up monitoring of its use. Consequently, teachers were forced to learn it in isolation (violating a major principle of language acquisition) and without meaningful feedback (violating a second principle). The result was an incomplete knowledge and production of MCE, sometimes mixed with whatever co-existing ASL there was. It is this pidgin to which most preschool and school-age deaf children were exposed in the name of English.

The Complexity of the Task

Any thorough discussion of the language of deaf individuals must take into account at least three varieties of language (ASL, English, and Pidgin Sign), three modes of expression (signed, spoken, and written), and two sense modalities (vision and audition) (Bochner & Albertini, 1988). This complicated picture is the natural result of the cultural, educational, and physical characteristics that interact with deafness.

There are deaf adults who, because of the lack of sufficient comprehensible, linguistic mediation during childhood, have not acquired either ASL or English to a point where they can apply their language skills well in the workplace. They may be unable to read English well enough to fill out an application form. They may not be able to either speak or write English well enough to ask questions of someone who is unfamiliar with deaf people or sign language. They may be able to use Pidgin Sign well enough to use an interpreter, but may not know ASL well enough to benefit as much as someone who does know ASL. As such, one may consider many deaf adults, particularly those who participate in rehabilitation programs, as still in the process of learning language, but now as adults instead of as children.

Methods of Language Instruction in the Schools

For the rehabilitation specialist to understand the source of the variety of communication styles evident among deaf people, it is important to understand the variety of communication systems in educational practices to which deaf people have been exposed. As was described above, MCE or some pidgin derivative thereof was adopted for use with deaf children on a widespread scale during the 1970s, as part of the "total communication" revolution. MCE was intended to be signed while simultaneously speaking English, a practice that is known as *simultaneous communication*.

Early studies of the efficacy of this communication system suggested that teachers were unable to rise to the task of signing and speaking in this fashion while maintaining coherence and a complete representation of English on the hands (Marmor & Petitto, 1979; Reich & Bick, 1977). These studies were conducted on teachers who had not been given specific training in how to communicate using MCE and/or simultaneous communication, nor for that matter in ASL. Even to this day, teacher training programs do not typically have more than one or two courses in signing, and very few have courses specifically in an MCE system or in ASL (Maxwell, 1985; Akamatsu & Stewart, 1987). Few school districts specifically endorse a communication policy that specifies either an MCE system and/or ASL for use in the classroom, nor do they often back up such a policy with in-services and monitoring assistance to the teachers to encourage complete, comprehensible linguistic input to deaf students (Stewart et al., 1989).

The fact remains that the language of education is English. Over the years, educators have tried many approaches to teaching this language, with differing amounts of success. With younger children, natural approaches are usually tried. In its broadest sense, the natural approach consists of adults using language in meaningful communication as occurs naturally in the environment. In practice, this means either that adults speak only English to the child, or attempt a combination of spoken and signed English. The difficulty for the child arises either because in the first instance, spoken English is not fully accessible to the child, or in the second case, because the resulting "language" looks more like a pidgin (Maxwell, Bernstein, & Matthews, 1986; Stewart et al., 1988). In either event, although communication may be taking place, there is no complete language model for the child to acquire.

It is important for teachers and counselors to realize the implication of the exclusive use of English, and the specific banning of ASL, in the classroom. The unequivocal message—hidden, yet profound—is that the language of power is English, and the culture of power is that of hearing people. While this may be true in the "outside" world, the message to the children is that they are deaf and cannot have access to this power. Deaf children have but to look around to see that the powerful people in their lives are hearing—parents, teachers, counselors, and administrators. Without full access to this language, deaf children are doomed to a position of impotence.

Theoretically, ASL could be used in the schools as the first complete language of deaf children. However, because only recently have a handful of schools endorsed its use, not much research has been conducted for us to make judgments about its efficacy.

Given the difficulties inherent in trying to acquire a language that one cannot hear, from teachers and parents who cannot sign it, using materials and methods that do not always work, and being tested with materials that are standardized on hearing, English-speaking populations, it is not surprising that academic achievement of deaf students is low, relative to the hearing population. The average deaf high school graduate reads at about the grade 4 level (Moores, 1987), and writes sentences that are grammatically imperfect and often very ambiguous (Charrow, 1981; Moores, 1987).

These descriptions of the English language achievements of the average deaf person, while commonly found in textbooks about deafness, do not do justice to a description of how a deaf adult might be expected to function in society. First, it is clearly unreasonable to assume that simply because someone has only achieved a grade 6 reading level that the person thinks and acts like a sixth grader. Indeed, a 20-year-old deaf adult is of legal age and can be expected to carry the typical responsibilities of a 20-year-old, such as renting an apartment, buying groceries, doing laundry, driving a car, handling a checking account, and so forth. By the age of 30, it is not surprising to see the deaf adult married, perhaps with a child or two, perhaps purchasing a home.

It is also not unusual to find deaf adults who cannot read or write English, and who have led such protected lives that they are truly incapable of living independently. On the other end of the scale, there are high school graduates who go on to college and university, who excel academically, and who ultimately become leaders in their chosen profession. Thus, it is important to remember that "average" achievement is just that—average—not typical, and certainly not stereotypical.

OUTCOMES

Consideration of communication characteristics is important in working with deaf adults. The population is extremely heterogeneous in this respect. Demographic factors alone explain much of the variety in communication skills that deaf adults display. As mentioned in Chapter 1, among the demographic factors one must consider are: age of onset, degree and type of hearing impairment, communication in the home, type of school program attended, and ethnic status.

Signing

It is important to note that most of the younger clientele are the oldest group of students with the opportunity to have had signing used throughout their education. As such, the information to be reported here contains valuable first approximation information for the clients rehabilitation specialists will serve.

Most deaf clients who apply for rehabilitation services use some form of signing and attended educational programs in which signing was used. However, many do not sign at home. In general, one can expect that potential clients from residential schools, day schools, and full-time special education programs are more likely to sign than potential clients who were educated in the mainstream (Jordan & Karchmer, 1986). Since the ability to communicate in the aural/oral modality is one of the factors in the decision to integrate youngsters in mainstream classes, one can expect that deaf clients who prefer signing do not have functionally intelligible speech (see next section).

It is interesting to note that a greater percentage of ethnic minorities[2] come from educational programs that include sign than their White counterparts (Jordan & Karchmer, 1986). Some of these clients may also come from homes where English is not the primary language, and where the "handicap" of deafness poses serious consequences for the integrity of the family. This suggests a mismatch in home and school communication modes that may have seriously hampered the development of communication. In general, more research is needed to better understand the interaction of deafness and ethnicity and communication skills. Perhaps the majority culture may be more accepting of deaf ethnic minorities signing, and not as concerned that they develop standard English skills.

What distinguishes signers from non-signers? Degree of hearing loss is one factor. The more severe the hearing loss, the more likely potential clients are to sign. As a group, ethnic minority potential clients are more likely to sign than their White peers. Finally, age at onset of the hearing loss is predictive of signing; prelingually deaf individuals are far more likely to sign than are those who are postlingually deafened.

Among deaf adults, Stewart (1983) found that, although most deaf adults preferred ASL as a language, they also recognized the utility of English for work purposes and advocated the bilingual use of ASL and English for deaf children in educational programs. Many are highly motivated to improve their English skills but may not have a clear sense of what functional literacy and interactive skills entail. Indeed, many deaf adults are unaware that ASL and English are two separate languages, and may labor under the false belief that they have "bad language" when they are actually quite skilled in ASL but lacking in functional English skills. Rehabilitation programs that offer bilingual instruction in ASL and English may be most beneficial for these individuals.

Spoken English

English is first and foremost a spoken language. It is the dominant language in the United States. The ability to speak is so highly valued in hearing culture that individuals without intelligible speech are often undervalued in their other abilities to contribute to society. Measures of "speech" as traditionally used in the schools with hearing-impaired people are measures of articulation and speaking ability in the English language. Tests of articulation of individual phonemes are only for the phonemes of English. Furthermore, intelligibility as a whole is aided by the use of connected discourse, which, for an English speaker, means connected English. It is with this in mind that the reader should consider this section.

The speech of deaf people has been described at length by investigators such as Nickerson (1975) and Ling (1976). Despite the many advances in technology, the speech intelligibility of deaf individuals has not improved significantly (Ling, 1976; Jensema, Karchmer, & Trybus, 1978).

As can be expected, speech intelligibility is strongly related to hearing. Wolk and Schildroth (1986) found that 86 percent of the students with a "less-than-severe" hearing loss were rated as having intelligible speech, whereas 75 percent of the students with profound hearing losses were rated as unintelligible. Most signers (93 percent) were unintelligible, regardless of their hearing loss. Of those students who use both speech and sign, about 60 percent were rated as unintelligible. These data suggest that those who are intelligible will tend to use speech as their preferred mode of communication, but the majority of deaf people have a great deal of difficulty with speech and will seek alternative modes of communication.

Wolk and Schildroth (1986) found that ethnic background seems to influence ratings of intelligibility. In their study, ethnic minority students were consistently and more often rated as less intelligible than their white peers. These data did not address the possibility that ethnic minority students came from non-English speaking homes, and that part of the difficulty they had with intelligibility might be that they actually had foreign-language accents.

Possession of additional handicapping conditions also influences intelligibility (Wolk & Schildroth, 1986). Students with handicaps in addition to deafness are less likely to be judged intelligible.

It is important, on the one hand, for clients to have an accurate assessment of their speech so they can determine how they wish to interact with hearing people. On the other hand, it is important for the rehabilitation specialist and others with whom the deaf client works to respect the deaf person's choice of a modality *other* than speech.

Literacy: Reading Outcomes

Contrary to what might be expected, teaching deaf children to read and write is not at all like teaching any other children, in the sense that hearing children typically learn to read the language that they speak natively and fluently. Unlike the hearing child who enters school with a fully developed spoken language, the deaf child often has to learn to read and write a language with which they are unfamiliar. As is the case with speech, the dominant language of literacy in the United States is English. With an increasing Hispanic population, particularly in the southwest, it is likely that literacy in Spanish will become a desirable and even necessary goal, as well.

Although the *process* of becoming literate seems to be the same for deaf and hearing children (Andrews, 1986; Ewoldt, 1981, 1985; Stanovich, 1980), the *outcomes* of literacy instruction have favored hearing children. In addition, among deaf students, certain patterns are observed. On standardized tests of reading, White deaf students in general outperform ethnic minority deaf students, and deaf students with no cognitive or behavioral handicapping conditions performed better than those with such handicaps. To a lesser extent, females tended to score higher than males. Although regional differences do occur, there is a general trend for those deaf students educated in local school districts to outperform those in special schools (Allen, 1986). Finally, other factors related to achievement in reading comprehension are degree of hearing loss (less-than-profoundly deaf students tended to score better than pro-foundly deaf) and age of onset of deafness (those who become deaf at or after age 3 tend to score higher than those who become deaf prior to age 3).

With regard to functional literacy, however, we can expect deaf adults to be able to read material on topics with which they are familiar with little difficulty, but to have more difficulty with unfamiliar topics (Gormley, 1981, 1982; McGill-Franzen & Gormley, 1980). Subtleties of grammar and vocabulary may continue to elude the client (Moores, 1970), so the rehabilitation specialist will have to be careful to check on deaf adults' comprehension of written material to ensure that no misunderstandings arise. Such "checking" must be done in such a way that the client does not feel mistrusted or patronized. It is more beneficial, for example, to review the content *with* clients without quizzing them, or to ask what clients would do based on the information they just read. What may appear to be reluctance on the part of the client to "learn independently" may simply be frustration at not being able to understand a given pamphlet or manual. At the same time, with increased experience and successes with new material, the deaf client can be expected to become increasingly independent in the use of written material.

Literacy: Writing Outcomes

There are no standardized tests of writing that are used with deaf children for the purposes of educational placement. The inescapable fact is that writing is performed in English, and measured against a standard for English. Much of the literature until fairly recently has focused on the difficulties that deaf children experience in learning to write English, compared with their normally hearing peers. For example, Myklebust (1964) found that on average deaf children's sentences were shorter and simpler in structure than those of hearing children. Further, they tended to overuse a limited number vocabulary words rather than varying word choice. Grammatically, deaf individuals have difficulty with features such as verb tense and agreement, and function words such as articles, prepositions, and coordinating and subordinating conjunctions (Greenberg & Withers, 1965).

These findings, though somewhat dated, point to results of an inefficient pedagogy for teaching both the English language and writing. By the time they graduate from high school, deaf students may harbor a mistaken belief that writing grammatical sentences is tantamount to being literate. Many have never written for audiences other than their teachers and may not realize that different situations call for different writing styles. For example, a project report to one's superior requires a more formal style than does a note to a peer about when the next meeting is.

Several researchers have suggested that a constructive way of viewing the written English of deaf people is to take the perspective that English is their second language (Charrow, 1981; Maxwell, 1989). As such, we might expect that the kinds of errors that appear in their writing might be similar to errors that other speakers of English as a second language might make. Indeed, this does seem to be the case.

The following samples of deaf people's writing give the flavor of what one might expect. This first sample, an excerpt from a synopsis of the King Midas story, was written by a grade 8 student:

> King Midas who loved gold and wished to touch turn gold.
>   One day, Midas sat down and counted the pile of gold coins. Then he saw the strange in the room. There was the god which he asked him if he was a rich man. Midas said that may be true. He wished to touch would turn to gold. (Charrow, 1981, p. 180)

This next sample was written by an adolescent:

> Hi, I'm very happy now and also vacation. I have to swim my pool with my friends everyday.
>   Last week, I practice to play my golf long time. I like it very much. I played a fresbee with my friends. I dreamed about Gold finger who throw my black hat that is as sharp as a blade. And also an ant drive in a flying saucer that called U.F.O. (from Charrow, 1981, pp. 179–180.)

Another sample from a college student (also from Charrow, 1981):

> This morning the kids had a small strike showing their complaints of what they have not learned anything from the English department . . . and sure enough the English teachers are under very pressure and in this situation I know it is out of question that you have a 1 to 10 basis or a mass meeting with English teachers and then you will still find no way to convince them. (p. 181)

More recent researchers have explored writing in the context of the process for learning to write (Graves, 1984). In this paradigm, the focus of instruction is on developing authors of meaningful text used to convey information to a real audience. As such, the writing process is more like the meaningful communicative interactions so necessary for language development. Investigations of deaf students learning to write under this model at high school (Nower, 1985) and college levels (Staton, 1985) all show that they focus their efforts on meaning-making when given the freedom to do so. Therefore, it does not suffice to simply say that deaf people have difficulty writing. The most important message here is that deaf people intend meaning when they write and are struggling with what is probably their second language. As such, it is important that meaning be assumed when reading a deaf person's writing, and that the rehabilitation process include instruction in writing based on principles of natural language learning. This includes writing for specific purposes, with specific audiences in mind, and writing as a process of meaning-making, rather than as a product to be judged on correctness of grammar.

On the job, it is helpful to think of deaf people's writing as much like the writing of a foreign speaker of English. We assume that hearing foreign speakers can perform their jobs competently, even though their English is not perfect. Given the English learning situation of deaf people, a similar assumption about their on-the-job competence is warranted. Supervisors and co-workers must be helped to understand that although deaf adults' writing can seem peculiar and garbled, there is a communicative intent behind the writing. People must be willing to see beyond the mistakes to the meaning that the deaf adult intends. Features of grammar and spelling are relatively less important for short notes than formal reports. If a text contains relatively few grammatical and spelling errors, secretaries might be obliged to simply correct these, without passing judgment on the deaf person's intelligence or skill. Where the writing is truly ambiguous, simple questions ("Did you mean X or Y?") often clear up the matter very quickly.

For most of us, writing is used when speech is impractical, or as a supplement to speech. For many deaf people, writing replaces speech. Although some deaf people have speech intelligible enough for others to understand, they may have a great deal of difficulty understanding speech. When intelligible deaf people request that communication be written, it is best to comply rather than to continually frustrate them because it seems that they "ought" to be able to understand speech. Although writing can be time-consuming compared to speaking, it is generally a good practice because it reduces the chance for misunderstanding and ensuing frustration.

Synthesis

In the discussions of sign, speech, and literacy, several threads of findings seem consistent across all communication modalities. First, deaf clients who have been in integrated settings in school tend to do better with speech and literacy than those who have not been. Second, White students are more likely to have been integrated than ethnic minorities. Third, signers are less likely to have been integrated, and more likely to be members of ethnic minorities.

These findings point to a consistent and unspoken set of values in the research that is conducted and how it is reported. They suggest that the more like White, hearing people deaf people are, the "better" it is for them, and the more opportunity for integration they will have had. Conversely, profoundly, prelingually deaf people born to hearing families as well as deaf ethnic minorities, are more likely to stay in a segregated special education setting, and more likely to become members of the deaf community upon leaving school. Persons with hearing loss born to deaf families should be the most advantages, given the rich opportunity for social interaction and complete and complex language input, yet those who are profoundly, prelingually deaf are more likely to encounter unproductive communication and language differences between their home environment and the outside world.

CONCLUSIONS AND IMPLICATIONS
FOR PRACTICE

From the literature reviewed in this chapter, three major conclusions can be drawn:

Deaf people are potentially capable of functioning fully in a hearing environment despite their language differences, provided certain accommodations are made. In some cases, the accommodation may be as simple as providing an interpreter that can interpret between English and the deaf individual's preferred language or communication system. Providing certain technological devices such as hearing aids or telecommunication devices for the deaf (TDDs) for those who choose to use them, and the proper training in the use of these devices is helpful (see Chapter 11).

Grade equivalent reading level on achievement tests does not indicate functional literacy or general level of intellectual function. Standardized tests measure an individual's ability to perform on standardized tests, and tests similar to those found in school. On-the-job performance is often a matter of exercise of judgment and ability to apply what one knows to a variety of novel situations. Although high levels of English literacy definitely open up avenues for advancement, one would be remiss to suggest that low levels of literacy indicate that an individual is incapable of adequate, if not superior, job performance, depending on the job.

Further, deaf adults have a great deal of life experience that can make up for certain deficits in performance on standardized tests. This situation may be compared to that of new immigrants and refugees from non-English speaking countries. These people may have been highly trained professionals before they were forced to leave their homeland. Yet, their inability to speak or read and write English often forces them into jobs that underutilize their skills.

Aspects of deaf culture must be understood and respected when communicating with deaf people. Signing is only one aspect of deaf culture. Professionals should associate with deaf adults in their community to learn their culture. A better understanding of the cultural differences both within deaf culture and between deaf and hearing cultures will help them anticipate and prevent cultural clashes and improve communication (See Chapter 13).

Hearing people do not have a monopoly on knowledge about deaf people. Competent deaf adults from the community must be used as resources and models for communicating with and understanding other deaf youth and adults. In showing one's respect for the deaf community, one will gain deaf people's respect, and become a more facile mediator of the two cultures.

SUMMARY

Language, communication, and culture are intimately related. A description of language and communication development in deaf individuals must take into account two cultures (deaf and hearing), two languages (ASL and English), two sense modalities (vision and audition), and three modes of expression and reception (signing/ reading sign, speaking/listening, and reading/writing). Research into normal language development reveals that when complete, comprehensive input is available, language is acquired rapidly and effortlessly within the first years of life. When language input is limited, as is usually the case with deaf children, language development is much more difficult, and extends over a much longer period of time.

Despite the difficulties inherent with deafness, deaf youth do have the potential to become fully functioning, contributing citizens in our communities. Their success depends in large part on the attitudes of their parents, teachers, and counselors, assumptions about their eventual success, and the kinds of language and social mediation they receive during childhood. It is important to remember that most deaf adults are gainfully employed, often as a result of post-secondary education and training, and in spite of communication difficulties that deafness presents. They become increasingly sophisticated in the workplace, sometimes taking on leadership roles. For some, rehabilitation is a continuation of the habilitation process begun early in childhood. For others, it is a second chance for a productive life.

ENDNOTES

1. There are, of course, deaf people in this country who do not come from English-speaking homes. For these people, the language learning situation becomes more complex, but the general principles described in this chapter still apply.

2. For this discussion, "ethnic minorities" encompass non-Hispanic Black, Black and White Hispanic, Asian-American, and Native-American students. "White" refers to non-Hispanic Caucasian students.

REFERENCES

Akamatsu, C.T., & Stewart, D. (1987). *A survey of sign language instruction in training programs for teachers of the hearing impaired.* Research in Evaluation and Teacher Training Program Evaluation Series No. 22. East Lansing, MI: Michigan State University, College of Education.

Allen, T. (1986). A study of the achievement patterns of hearing-impaired students: 1974–1983. In A. Schildroth & M. Karchmer (Eds.), *Deaf children in America* (pp. 161–206). San Diego: College Hill Press.

Andrews, J. (1986). How do deaf children learn about prereading? *American Annals of the Deaf, 131,* 210–217.

Anthony, D. (1966). *Seeing essential English.* Unpublished master's thesis, Eastern Michigan University, Ypsilanti, MI.

Baker, C., & Cokely, D. (1980). *American Sign Language: A teacher's resource on grammar and culture.* Silver Spring, MD: TJ Publishers.

Bates, E. (1976). *Language and context: The acquisition of pragmatics.* New York: Academic Press.

Bates, E., Camaioni, L., & Volterra, V. (1975). The acquisition of performatives prior to speech. *Merrill-Palmer Quarterly, 21,* 205–226.

Bickerton, D. (1977). Pidginization and creolization: Language acquisition and language universals. In A. Valdman (Ed.), *Pidgin and creole linguistics* (pp. 49–69). Bloomington: Indiana University Press.

Bloom, L., & Lahey, M. (1988). *Language development and language disorders.* New York: Wiley.

Bochner, J., & Albertini, J. (1988). Language varieties in the deaf population and their acquisition by children and adults. In M. Strong (Ed.), *Language learning and deafness* (pp. 3–48). Cambridge: Cambridge University Press.

Bornstein, H., Saulnier, K., & Hamilton, L. (1980). Signed English: A first evaluation. *American Annals of the Deaf, 125* (3), 468–481.

Bornstein, H., Saulnier, K., & Hamilton, L. (1983). *A comprehensive Signed English dictionary.* Washington, DC: Gallaudet College Press.

Bowerman, M. (1975). Cross linguistic similarities at two stages of syntactic development. In E.H. Lenneberg & E. Lenneberg (Eds.), *Foundations of language development: A multidisciplinary approach* (Vol. 1, pp. 267–282). New York: Academic Press.

Brown, R. (1973). *A first language: The early stages.* Cambridge, MA: Harvard University.

Bruner, J. (1975). The ontogenesis of speech acts. *Journal of Child Language, 2,* 1–19.

Carmichael, H., & Greenberg, M. (1980). A comparison of functional communication in deaf vs. hearing mother-child dyads: Descriptive analysis and intervention implications. Paper presented at the Annual International Interdisciplinary Conference on Piagetian Theory and the Helping Professions, Los Angeles.

Charrow, V. (1981). The written English of deaf adolescents. In M. Whiteman (Ed.), *Writing: The nature, development, and teaching of written communication* (Vol. 1: Variation in Writing: Functional and linguistic-cultural differences, pp. 179–188). Hillsdale, NJ: Erlbaum.

Cheskin, A. (1982). The use of language by hearing mothers of deaf children. *Journal of Communication Disorders, 15,* 145–153.

Conrad, R. (1979). *The deaf school child.* London: Harper and Row.

Corson, H. (1973). *Comparing deaf children of oral parents and deaf parents using manual communication with deaf children of hearing parents on academic, social, and communication functioning.* Unpublished doctoral dissertation, University of Cincinnati, Cincinnati, OH.

Crandall, K. (1978). Inflectional morphemes in the manual English of young hearing impaired children and their mothers. *Journal of Speech and Hearing Research, 21,* 373–386.

Ewoldt, C. (1981). A psycholinguistic description of selected deaf children reading in sign language. *Reading Research Quarterly, 13* (1), 58–89.

Ewoldt, C. (1985). A descriptive study of the developing literacy of young hearing-impaired children. *Volta Review, 87,* 109–126.

Gilman, L., & Raffin, M. (1975). Acquisition of common morphemes by hearing-impaired children exposed to the Seeing Essential English sign system. Paper presented at the Annual Meeting of the American Speech and Hearing Association, Washington, DC.

Gleason, J. (1985). *The development of language.* Columbus, OH: Charles E. Merrill.

Goldin-Meadow, S. (1982). The resilience of recursion: A study developed without a conventional language model. In E. Wanner and L. Gleitman (Eds.), *Language acquisition: The state of the art* (pp. 51–77). Cambridge: Cambridge University Press.

Gormley, K. (1981). On the influence of familiarity on deaf students' text recall. *American Annals of the Deaf, 126,* 1024–1030.

Gormley, K. (1982). The importance of familiarity on hearing impaired readers' comprehension of text. *The Volta Review, 84,* 71–80.

Graves, D. (1984). *Writing: Teachers and children at work.* Portsmouth, NH: Heinemann Educational Books.

Greenberg, B., & Withers, S. (1965). *Better English usage: A guide for the deaf.* Indianapolis, IN: Bobbs-Merrill.

Greenberg, M. (1980). Mode use in deaf children: The effects of communication method and communication competence. *Applied Psycholinguistics,1,* 65–79.

Greenberg, M., Kusche, C., Gustafson, F., & Calderon, R. (1984). The paths project: A model for the prevention of psychosocial difficulties in deaf children. In G.B. Anderson & D. Watson (Eds.), *The habilitation and rehabilitation of deaf adolescents.* Washington, DC: The National Academy of Gallaudet College.

Gross, R. (1970). Language used by mothers of deaf children and mothers of hearing children. *American Annals of the Deaf, 115,* 93–96.

Gustason, G., Pfetzing, D., & Zawalkow, E. (1975). *Signing Exact English* (rev. ed.). Rossmoor, CA: Modern Signs Press.

Hammermeister, F. (1971). Reading achievement in deaf adults. *American Annals of the Deaf, 116,* 25–28.

Heider, F., & Heider, G. (1940). A comparison of sentence structure of deaf and hearing children. *Psychological Monographs, 52,* 42–103.

Jensema, C., Karchmer, M., & Trybus, R. (1978). *The rated speech intelligibility of hearing-impaired children: Basic relationships and a detailed analysis* (Series R, No. 6). Washington, DC: Gallaudet College, Office of Demographic Studies.

Jordan, I., & Karchmer, M. (1986). Patterns of sign use among hearing-impaired students. In A. Schildroth & M. Karchmer (Eds.), *Deaf children in America* (pp. 125–138). San Diego, CA: College-Hill Press.

Klima, E., & Bellugi, U. (1979). *The signs of language.* Cambridge, MA: Harvard University Press.

Ling, D. (1976). *Speech and the hearing-impaired child: Theory and practice.* Washington, DC: A.G. Bell Association for the Deaf.

Luetke-Stahlman, B. (1986). Building a language base in hearing-impaired students. *American Annals of the Deaf, 131,* 220–228.

Marmor, G., & Petitto, L. (1979). Simultaneous communication in the classroom: How well is English grammar represented? *Sign Language Studies, 23,* 99–136.

Maxwell, M. (1985). Sign language instruction and teacher preparation. *Sign Language Studies, 47,* 173–180.

Maxwell, M. (1989). Discourse structure in visual narratives of the deaf. Paper presented at the National Reading Conference, Austin, TX.

Maxwell, M., Bernstein, M., & Matthews, K. (1986). Bimodal language production. Paper presented at the Theoretical Issues in Sign Language Research Conference, Rochester, NY.

McAnally, P., Rose, S., & Quigley, S. (1987). *Language learning practices with deaf children.* Boston: College Hill.

McGill-Franzen, A., & Gormley, A. (1980). The influence of context of deaf readers' understanding of passive sentences. *American Annals of the Deaf, 125,* 937–942.

Meadow, K. (1968). Early manual communication in relation to the deaf child's intellectual, social, and communicative functioning. *American Annals of the Deaf, 113,* 29–41.

Moores, D. (1970). Investigation of psycholinguistic abilities of deaf adolescents. *Exceptional Children, 36,* 645–654.

Moores, D. (1987). *Educating the deaf: Psychology, principles, and practices* (3rd edition). Boston: Houghton Mifflin.

Myklebust, H. (1964). *The psychology of deafness.* New York: Grune and Stratton.

Nickerson, R. (1975). Characteristics of the speech of deaf persons. *Volta Review, 77,* 342–362.

Nower, B. (1985). Scratching the itch: High school students and their topic choices for writing. *Volta Review, 87,* 171–185.

Padden, C., & Humphries, T. (1988). *Deaf in America.* Cambridge: Harvard University Press.

Rawlings, B., & King, S. (1986). Postsecondary educational opportunities for deaf students. In A. Schildroth & M. Karchmer (eds.), *Deaf children in America* (pp. 231–257). San Diego, CA: College-Hill Press.

Reich, P., & Bick, M. (1977). How visible is visible English? *Sign Language Studies, 14,* 59–72.

Schein, J., & Delk, M. (1974). *The deaf population of the United States.* Silver Spring, MD: National Association of the Deaf.

Schlesinger, H. (1988). Questions and answers in the development of deaf children. In M. Strong (Ed.), *Language learning and deafness* (pp. 261–291). Cambridge: Cambridge University Press.

Scoville, R. (1983). Development of the intention to communicate: The eye of the beholder. In L. Feagans, C. Garvey, & R. Golinkoff (Eds.), *The origins and growth of communication.* Norwood, NJ: Ablex.

Siple, P. (Ed.) (1978). *Understanding language through sign language research.* New York: Academic Press.

Siple, P.A., & Akamatsu, C.T. (1986). Language acquisition in a set of fraternal twins of deaf parents. Paper presented at Theoretical Issues in Sign Language Research, Rochester, NY, June 13–16.

Smith, M. (1926). *An investigation of the development of the sentence and the extent of vocabulary in young children* (Studies in Child Welfare, Vol. 3, No. 5). Iowa City: University of Iowa.

Stanovich, K. (1980). Toward an interactive-compensatory model of individual differences in the development of reading fluency. *Reading Research Quarterly, 16,* 32–71.

Staton, J. (1985). Using dialogue journals for developing thinking, reading, and writing with hearing-impaired students. *The Volta Review, 87,* 127–154.

Stewart, D. (1983). The use of signs by deaf children: The opinions of a deaf community. *American Annals of the Deaf, 128,* 878–883.

Stewart, D., Akamatsu, C.T., Hunter, C., Krugh, K., & Ng, W. (1989). *Consistent linguistic input in the signing behavior of teachers: Modified Signed English* (Occasional Paper No. 127). East Lansing: Michigan State University, Institute for Research on Teaching.

Stewart, D.A., Akamatsu, C.T., & Bonkowski, N. (1988). Factors influencing simultaneous communication behaviors in teachers. *The ACEHI Journal (La Revue ACEDA), 14,* 43–58.

Stokoe, W. (1960). Sign language structure: An outline of the visual communication system of the American deaf. *Studies in Linguistics Occasional Papers No. 8.*

Stokoe, W.C., Casterline, D., & Croneberg, C. (1965). *A dictionary of American Sign Language on linguistic principles.* Washington, DC: Gallaudet College Press. (Reprinted 1976).

Stokoe, W., & Volterra, V. (Eds.) (1985). *SLR '83: Sign language research.* Silver Spring, MD: Linstok Press, Inc. and Rome, Italy: Istituto di Psicologia, CNR.

Stuckless, E.R., & Birch, J. (1966). The influence of early manual communication on the linguistic development of deaf children. *American Annals of the Deaf, 111,* 452–460.

Sugarman, S. (1978). Some organizational aspects of pre-verbal communication. In I. Markova (Ed.), *The social context of language* (pp. 49–66). New York: Wiley.

Vygotsky, L. (1986). *Thought and language.* (Translated and edited by A. Kozulin). Cambridge, MA: The MIT Press.

Weddell-Monig, J., & Lumley, J. (1980). Child deafness and mother-child interaction. *Child Development, 51,* 766–774.

Wilbur, R. (1987). *American Sign Language: Linguistic and applied dimensions.* Boston: College-Hill.

Wolk, S., & Schildroth, A. (1986). Deaf children and speech intelligibility: A national study. In A. Schildroth & M. Karchmer (Eds.), *Deaf children in America* (pp. 139–159). San Diego, CA: College-Hill.

Woodward, J. (1972). Implications for sociolinguistic research among the deaf. *Sign Language Studies, 1,* 1–17.

▶ 3

Cognitive Development and Deafness

DAVID S. MARTIN
Gallaudet University

The intellectual potential of the deaf learner has puzzled educators, parents, and employers for centuries. While pieces of this intriguing puzzle are clearly falling into place, the larger puzzle is far from definitively solved and continues to engage the interest of many, including the deaf community itself.

Since 1960, efforts to improve the intellectual performance of deaf learners within educational and clinical settings have been noteworthy. Heightened sensitivity to the needs of deaf persons in schools, clinics, and in the workplace has coincided with this trend. Thus, the 1990s may constitute a unique era in education and human services for deaf persons—an opportunity not only to examine what we have learned about cognition and deafness but also to take some giant strides forward in both research on the subject and education of the public on the central issues concerning the thinking processes of deaf people.

In this overview of cognition and deafness, we shall begin by looking backward at views of the cognitive abilities of deaf persons in the historical periods before our century as well as in our time. We shall then look closely at the particular issues related to this topic within the research and educational communities, and then conclude with a set of recommendations and directions for future actions for all persons interested in a constructive life for deaf learners.

The author gratefully acknowledges the assistance in data collection for this chapter by Ms. Janis Ruoff, Gallaudet University.

HISTORICAL VIEWS OF COGNITION AND DEAFNESS

Pre-Twentieth Century

Deafness as a condition is as old as humanity. How hearing persons have viewed the cognitive abilities of deaf persons in their midst in many cases is historically a sad story because of centuries of bias and lowered expectations by hearing people toward deaf persons.

A review of deafness in history indicates that the attitudes of persons in the ancient world toward disabled people were ambivalent. The ancient Jews indicated a sense of charity toward deaf people, and the Book of Leviticus in the Bible admonishes against curing deaf people. This point suggests that at least some persons were acting in negative ways toward disabled persons (Moores, 1982). We also know that deaf persons were treated in a similar way to helpless and retarded persons in terms of legal rights.

Because of the high value placed on the spoken word throughout ancient history, ancient Egypt, ancient Greece, and then ancient Rome showed little improvement in attempts to educate deaf individuals. In addition, the Romans appeared to have treated deaf people more harshly than either the Egyptians or the Greeks (Moores, 1982).

The interaction between language and thought (see Chapter 2) was, and has continued to be, a topic of great interest and debate. In the ancient world, the Greek philosophers believed that spoken words were the necessary means by which a person conceived thought. Aristotle designated the ear as the organ of instruction and believed that hearing was the greatest contributor to intelligence, with the result that he has been accused of keeping deaf people in ignorance for two thousand years (Deland, 1931).

Through the centuries deaf people seem to have been considered by many as incapable of the same type of thought processes as hearing people or at least not as intelligent. Terminology used to describe them reflects this attitude, and just as the Greek word for "deaf" (sometimes translated "mute") implied reduced mental capacity (Moores, 1982), so did more recent terminology. The common term in the nineteenth century in this country was reflected in the name of the first school for deaf children in America, "The American Asylum for the Education of the Deaf and Dumb."

Twentieth Century

In the early twentieth century, some researchers reviewed the available information on the intelligence of deaf persons and, in spite of the sometimes contradictory results, concluded that deaf children had inferior intelligence (Pintner, Eisenson, & Stanton, 1941). In 1924-1925, the National Research Council reported that deaf people were between two and three years "retarded" in comparison to hearing persons in their responses to the Pintner Non-Language Mental Test. In the 1950s, other researchers attributed a "concrete" nature to the intelligence of deaf persons, indicating that deafness restricts the learner to a world of "concrete objects and things" (Myklebust & Brutton, 1953). The influence of this latter statement has been far-reaching in that educators and clinicians working with deaf persons have for many years regarded the deaf learner as less able to work with abstract ideas. Fortunately, subsequent research has proven this interpretation to be false. Nonetheless, Myklebust represented one step forward—he did report the deaf learner to be at least quantitatively equal to the hearing learner, although inferior qualitatively.

In the 1960s, forward progress was clear. Furth (1964) , a highly regarded researcher, concluded that the poorer performance of deaf persons on some cognitive tests could be explained either by a lack of experience or by the conditions of those tests that would favor a background of a spoken language. Also, he asserted that deaf persons can comprehend and logically apply concepts as well as hearing persons.

Two significant reviews of studies drew together the mounting evidence for the equality of deaf and hearing persons' thinking processes. One (Rosenstein, 1961) found no differences between deaf and hearing persons in conceptual performance when the linguistic elements presented were within the language experience of the deaf learner. The important conclusion was that abstract thought is *not* closed to deaf persons. Another comprehensive review of 31 research studies using more than 8,000 deaf children of ages 3–19 (Vernon, 1967), found that in 13 experiments, deaf subjects had superior success to either the test norms or control groups. In 7 studies, the scores were not significantly different, and only in the remaining studies did deaf subjects perform at an inferior level. The important conclusion was that deaf youth perform as well as hearing youth in a wide variety of tasks that measure thinking.

Thus, by the end of the 1960s there seemed to be a growing consensus that deaf persons are not intellectually deficient. Many people, however, still considered deaf people to be linguistically impoverished, primarily because sign languages were still considered to be inferior to spoken languages (Moores, 1982). Although much research still is needed in the area of sign language development in deaf children, the idea of the inferiority of sign language has been successfully challenged (see Chapter 2).

Specific Findings

Studies in the 1970s and 1980s have focused on deaf persons' performance in a variety of specific cognitive skill areas, thus making possible more specific conclusions rather than the many over-generalizations of the past. Let us summarize what some recent researchers have reported about specific cognitive skill performance in deaf subjects, skill by skill, and what actions benefit deaf persons' cognitive performance. This information may assist the clinician in analyzing the needs and improving the employment prospects of deaf clients.

Memory
Profoundly deaf subjects perform less well than hearing subjects on short-term memory tasks (Karchmer & Belmont, 1976). However, if deaf learners use strategies that fit well

with information-processing, their performance is similar to that of hearing learners who select their own strategies. Deaf children can better remember words that have a sign equivalent than words that do not. Thus, programs that stress the direct teaching of particular strategies for cognitive tasks have great promise (Meadow, 1980).

Concept Application
Deaf persons logically apply concepts as well as hearing persons (Furth, 1964), and learn concepts in the same sequence as hearing persons, but at a later time (Meadow, 1980). Some deaf learners have difficulty with the discovery of a concept, but not with understanding or using it (Furth, 1964).

Part–Wholes
No differences are found in the performance of deaf as compared to hearing learners in the ability to distinguish parts from the whole or to do analysis (Furth, 1964).

Opposites
Inferior performance among deaf subjects is found on this dimension.

Similarities
Deaf learners are equal to hearing learners here (Furth, 1964; Meadow, 1980).

Analogy
Deaf children have difficulty in this area (Meadow, 1980).

Classification
Little difference between deaf and hearing learners is found in this skill area (Meadow, 1980).

Spatial Reasoning
Research suggests that because deaf children depend primarily on visual and tactile senses to a greater degree than hearing children, they may develop a different concept of space (Hauptman, 1980). Deaf persons may be more field-dependent than hearing persons (Parasnis & Long, 1979). Thus a deaf client whose cognitive style preference is for spatial reasoning may have difficulty with nonspatial cognitive tasks.

Working with More than One Type of Data
Research indicates that deaf learners experience more difficulty on tasks requiring reference to two items of data than do hearing individuals. Ottem (1980) concluded that deaf persons have apparently been taught to communicate only about *single* events, causing a problem that hearing educators have imposed on deaf persons.

This brief summary of results of various research studies is not easily condensed into a general statement about what researchers have discovered about the cognitive abilities of deaf persons. The most general implication is that deaf persons have the same achievement potential as hearing persons under conditions which do not bias the results against those who cannot hear. An additional supposition about these results is that deaf learners in some cases do not perform as well as hearing learners because they have not had similar opportunities to develop certain skills.

These conclusions are reflected in the recent trend to actively intervene in the cognitive performance of deaf learners through efforts to improve thinking skills. These efforts indicate an encouraging philosophical point of view that maintains that the deaf population has the same range of intellectual potential as the hearing population and can achieve that potential if the environment, instruction, and materials are appropriate. The results of these efforts will be examined further in the section of this chapter on cognitive intervention.

The history of attitudes toward the cognitive potential of deaf persons has thus passed through several phases. Earlier biases and, in many cases, discrimination eventually gave way to studies which compared deaf and hearing learners on some more specific measures. These results, however, were over-generalized and over-simplified. Later, more systematic analyses still tended to equate language with thinking, two related but separate domains. Finally, a time arrived when the performance of deaf persons began to be analyzed on its own terms and with a better understanding of the particular conditions under which a deaf learner develops. This type of analytic approach continues today along with active efforts to improve the cognitive performance of deaf learners. Let us turn now to some current issues and what we know thus far about them.

CURRENT ISSUES

Organic versus Educational Cognitive Disabilities

An etiology which causes deafness may also cause other disabilities. Although the estimated percentage of deaf persons who have other disabilities varies widely from study to study because of differences in definition and methods of data collection, we do know that there are those deaf people who have neurological damage which affects their cognitive ability. These effects may be manifested in cognitive performance which could be labeled as learning disabilities or mental retardation.

Because the term "learning disability" most often refers to low academic performance when compared with intelligence measures, and because many deaf students are academically behind their hearing peers, the dual label of deaf and learning disabled is not uncommon. Educators still, however, may be faced with some deaf students who do not seem to process information in the same manner as other deaf students. Such processing difficulties are not related to the individual's deafness but may be critical in rehabilitation plans for the client.

Other deaf persons with neurological damage tend to be generally, rather than specifically, impaired (O'Connor & Hermelin, 1978). Depending upon the degree of this impairment, an individual may be primarily impacted by retardation rather than deafness. However, it is absolutely essential to differentiate between organically based *general* retardation in the deaf client and possible *educational* retardation which has a general *effect* but which may be related to a specific *sensory* deficit, that is, deafness. The rehabilitation professional must not assume without appropriate evidence that general retardation is necessarily the result of a neurological impairment, as opposed to a general effect from a sensory impairment, unless appropriate evidence is present from medical and psychological diagnoses.

If organic mental retardation is present in the deaf client, the widely accepted philosophy in the education of these multiply disabled individuals is that learners must be given every opportunity both to be motivated to learn and to have successful learning experiences. Thus, for the clinical professional, that philosophy would include emphasizing what the client *can* do rather than what he or she *cannot* do. The technique of repeated learning or "overlearning" is applicable here, as well as a continuing emphasis on helping the person to see ways in which instruction will transfer to real-life situations. Hence, the curriculum for this population needs to be specific, based on task expectations, and oriented toward the client's future.

Neuroscience

The fascinating topic of brain organization in the deaf learner has received much focus in recent years. It is tempting but wrong to say that most cognitive differences between hearing and deaf persons are the result only of differences in brain organization. But it is useful to look at what research has indicated about the organic aspect of these differences.

Research results on the specialization of the two brain hemispheres have been in some cases ambiguous because of difficulties with research methods. However, there is some evidence that deaf persons do not have the same specialization in the left hemisphere of the brain for language functions (Kelly & Tomlinson-Keasey, 1977). One conclusion from this work is that the difference in brain lateralization is *not* the result of auditory deprivation or deafness, but rather is the result of a lack of early language stimulation (Greenberg & Kusche, 1989) since the majority (about 90 percent) of deaf people come from hearing families and usually do not have fluent communication in their early years. In contrast, we know that deaf adults who have deaf parents and who have used sign language from an early age *do* show left hemisphere specialization for language (just as most hearing people do) and have right hemisphere processing for visual-spatial functions, again like most hearing persons (Bellugi, 1983). The implication of such findings is clear in terms of intervention at an early age with the deaf learner—we must work at reducing or preventing deficiencies in linguistic processing, memory, and reading.

The two fundamental cognitive areas of spatial and temporal processes have been thought to be associated with auditory perception, and spatial processes have been thought to be associated with visual stimuli. However, these associations are by no means absolute. *Visual input* can have *temporal* organization, and *acoustic* information may be arranged *spatially*. All perceptual modalities allow both sequential and simultaneous processing (Knobloch-Gala, 1989). One study found that a special paper-and-pencil thinking skills program (Instrumental Enrichment) can successfully improve verbo-sequential deficits in deaf persons (Craig, 1989).

Even though research has indicated that hemispheric differences do exist between hearing and deaf persons in processing both non-linguistic and linguistic stimuli, it is not clear whether these findings represent differences in brain organization or information-processing strategies, or both (Greenberg & Kusche, 1989). In addition, we must remember that the deaf population is by no means homogeneous in hemispheric specialization. Factors such as linguistic skill, proficiency in oral and sign language skills, genetic factors, and early environment are all important to the development of brain specialization (Greenberg & Kusche, 1989).

These sometimes contradictory findings in this area demand more extensive research. In the meantime, human services professionals, educators, and others working with deaf persons should watch closely as the research expands as the result of improved technology and wider interest among researchers themselves. Let us now investigate the general cognitive processes of deaf learners and their implications for human services providers.

Cognitive Style

Cognitive style is the way in which a person best learns, and it varies from person to person. An important dimension of cognitive style is the continuum of "field dependence." A person who is *field-dependent* tends to use external referents, to experience surroundings in a rather global fashion, and to conform passively to the prevailing context. On the other hand, a person who is *field-independent* tends to rely primarily on internal referents, to perceive her or his surroundings analytically, and to experience objects as separate from their backgrounds. We know that differences in development on this dimension are not attributable to the degree of hearing loss or the age of onset of hearing loss (Gibson, 1985).

Differences in cognitive style suggest that deaf persons (just as hearing persons) need to have their work expectations match their cognitive style. Thus, it is useful for professional counselors to assess deaf clients' cognitive style, and tests have been developed for this purpose. The implication here is that the human services professional who is prepared for working with deaf clients must be skilled at selecting, administering, and interpreting assessment measures related to individual cognitive style.

Nonverbal Cognitive Abilities

While we will explore the relationship between deafness and *language* development later in this chapter, the topic of *nonverbal* cognitive abilities is of equal importance.

We know that the nonverbal cognitive abilities of deaf and hearing learners have a similar structure (Ljubesic, 1986). We also know that general conversational and communicative skills are not related to reasoning and verbal IQ results (Lou, 1989), so we must be cautious, as always, in our use of IQ scores when discussing an appropriate vocation with a deaf client.

Language and Cognition

Aspects of this topic have been addressed in Chapter 2 and referred to earlier in this chapter. Now we will examine in some depth the specific implications of the relationship between language and cognition in the deaf learner, because linguistic experiences appear to have such an important impact on many areas of academic work and achievement in deaf persons.

Traditional Approaches

The critical area of language and cognition has been a source of debate among researchers and educators for many years. The general approaches in regard to this topic can be divided into many categories, but two would be the psycholinguistic and the sociolinguistic. Psycholinguists focus on the behavior underlying the development and use of language on a psychological level; the work of Vygotsky is an important example of work in this area. Sociolinguists, on the other hand, try to explain the relationship between language and thought using observations of the social use of language, distinguishing between language used in formal versus informal communication. These two broad approaches can be applied to language and cognition in deaf people also. Psycholinguists have looked at the apparent linguistic deficits of deaf persons in contrast to the cognitive abilities already discussed (see Furth, 1964). Sociolinguists have examined the nature of the most typical form of language in deaf adults—American Sign Language (see Chapter 2) and how ASL is used in the daily functioning or adaptive behavior of deaf people.

Two basic questions, therefore, have engaged research interest in the past in connection with these approaches:

1. Do quantitative or qualitative differences exist between deaf and hearing people in various aspects of cognitive functioning?
2. Is there is a relationship between language and thought, and, if there is one, what is its nature? (Quigley & Paul, 1984).

The first section of this chapter mentioned the view that prevailed well into the twentieth century that deaf persons were intellectually inferior to hearing persons. Since that time, however, as was pointed out earlier, that view has been proven insupportable. In addition, it has been demonstrated that most deaf individuals are not linguistically deficient; rather they are skilled in a *different* language.

In the field of linguistics, the argument about whether language determines thought or vice versa has been long-standing. Studies indicate that much perceptual and cognitive development takes place *prior* to language development. On the other hand, although language does not *dictate* thought, it nonetheless has a significant *influence* on it (Quigley & Paul, 1984). Thus, the nature of the early language skills of deaf persons is important when examining this topic.

Considerable research has indicated that prelingually, profoundly deaf persons rarely reach high levels of proficiency in spoken language structures (Rodda & Grove, 1987). The complex rule systems of English grammar pose extensive problems for developing deaf children. For example, deaf children tend to assume that expressions in English invariably follow the rule of subject-verb-object word order. This assumption leads them to systematic errors of interpretation in some contexts, such as passive constructions (Wood, 1984).

Current Approaches

Given the fact that the data indicate that the range of cognitive potential is the same for both deaf and general populations, but that many deaf learners are not achieving at appropriate levels in English, they would seem to be an excellent group with which to examine the issue of the relationship between thought and language. But we now know that language development occurs in numerous ways, and that for the deaf learner a manual (signed) form of communication may be essential for that development, although there are some deaf learners for whom oral methods seem to be successful. Complicating the issue even more is that some studies have found that, as a medium of reception of language with some deaf individuals, sign language alone is somewhat less effective overall than simultaneous communication (using signs and speech together) and much less effective than reading (Rodda & Grove, 1987). Much debate, however, surrounds the pedagogy of the classroom in regard to the appropriateness of ASL versus a signed version of English as the most appropriate medium of instruction. Clearly, research remains to be done on this issue.

If we accept that the language skills of deaf persons are not irrelevant to their thinking, and various approaches to teaching language to deaf children exist, we are left with the question about what communication system is best to facilitate cognitive skills. At this writing, not only does disagreement in the field continue about the effectiveness of oral communication versus some manual communication system, but there is also as yet no conclusive evidence to establish which particular modes of sign language are the most effective for deaf learners.

One area of the literature appears to indicate that English-based sign systems in the school environment produce superior results in terms of later use of English language skills, both receptively and expressively (Luetke-Stahlman, 1988a, 1988b, 1988c; Moeller, 1988; Parkins & Whitesell, 1985; Wodlinger-Cohen, 1986). On the other hand, there are also equally compelling arguments and evidence that a visually based language such as American Sign Language (see Chapter 2) provides the most appropriate basis for higher-level cognitive processing through the visual mode (Klima & Bellugi, 1979; Johnson, 1981). In the workplace and elsewhere, many argue, a policy of *bilingualism* should be followed to permit the use of English together with American Sign Language.

Assessment of Cognitive Performance*

Studies of cognition in the deaf population have also been numerous in recent years. After an initial focus on IQ, the center of attention now is on the processes involved in cognition and perception. It is now a well-accepted fact that deaf persons as a group fall into the normal range of intelligence when tested on the performance, rather than the verbal, subtests of various IQ instruments (Drever & Collins, 1982). The exception is those students who have neurological impairments in addition to their hearing losses. We also know that when the influence of age is controlled, statistical data on deaf children indicate strong relationships between their achievement test scores and variables such as age of onset of hearing loss, cause of loss, degree of loss, other disabilities, ethnic background, and type of special educational program (Jensema, 1975).

Therefore, another of the critical issues in the cognitive performance of deaf persons is the need for appropriate assessment of both performance and intellectual potential. At several points previously in this chapter, we have implied that assessment has resulted in some unfairness to deaf persons in the past, and we have also alluded to some of the varieties of measures that are being used at this time. Some traditional measures of intellectual performance sometimes include only an English-based verbal dimension, which in many cases is not an appropriate assessment for a deaf learner. However, some other instruments do employ both verbal and performance dimensions. Another approach to fairness involves presentation of the verbal materials of such measures by using sign-language versions during the presentation. For example, a signed presentation of the verbal scale of the WISC-R for testing profoundly deaf children produces a more complete profile of the deaf learner, and has demonstrated that non-signed versions can prevent the deaf learner from receiving the entire message from the tester (Miller, 1985).

The Learning Potential Assessment Device (Feuerstein, 1979) assesses cognitive potential through a system which first attempts to teach the cognitive skill to the learner and then tests for it, thus removing any effect of cultural disadvantage. Deaf subjects who took this test performed significantly better than a comparison group using traditional psychometric procedures (Keane, 1983).

Some testers of deaf clients choose to rely on only the performance scales of IQ tests in order to remove linguistic bias on the verbal scales. However, recent research indicates that the Performance IQ score tends to obscure important differences between clients who are hearing, clients who are deaf from hearing parents, and clients

*See Chapter 7 for a more detailed discussion of this issue.

who are deaf from deaf parents. Thus, it is necessary to develop and implement alternative forms of measurements (Braden, 1987).

Therefore, the state of the art in the appropriate assessment of deaf persons is still in a fluid stage. Professionals working with and on behalf of deaf persons must demand balanced assessment measures which can be interpreted on their own terms and in the context of the specific history of the deaf individual and her or his etiology. The next decade promises important improvements in the assessment of cognitive potential in deaf persons.

Intervention Strategies: Learning to Learn

Throughout this chapter the data that have been reviewed and the conclusions from the more recent studies have all led to a consistent picture: Not only are deaf learners capable of the same range of intellectual performance as their hearing counterparts, but it is also possible to *improve* the intellectual functioning and cognitive potential of deaf (and hearing) persons. Let us look at what has been learned from proactive attempts to raise the thinking levels of deaf learners.

The authors of one particular thinking and language skills program for deaf students have pointed out that thinking skills not only are essential to the development of reasoning and critical thinking, but also are fundamental to the child's total learning ability. These skills include the ability to recognize relationships, store and recall information, recognize logical order, evaluate information, do original thinking, adapt the known to new situations, do trial-and-error thinking, and acquire an understanding of different types of concepts (Pfau, 1975). No evaluation data are available on the program, but the principles of focusing on higher-order cognitive skills as a learning plan is well founded, as will be seen in the following material about other programs.

Another example of a specific intervention program uses the computer program LOGO to promote an understanding of geometric concepts by focusing both on turtle-graphics technology to explore designs and then on the more abstract non-graphic, list-processing abilities of that particular computer language (Dietz, 1985). Students reportedly became more persistent in dealing with difficult problems, more willing to explore on their own without continuous feedback from the teacher, and better in their planning behaviors.

The Philosophy for Children program (Lipman, Sharp, & Oscanyan, 1980), which is also appropriate for adults, was applied to deaf learners in the context of philosophical inquiry in a school for deaf students. The program, which emphasizes philosophical dialogue in inductive reasoning, tolerating ambiguity, and logical thought patterns, resulted in clearer expression by students of their ideas, more tolerance of the opinions of others, a strengthening of analysis skills in school subject areas, and greater patience in carrying out philosophical inquiry (Rembert, 1985).

Instrumental Enrichment (Feuerstein, 1980) requires teachers to use specific paper-and-pencil exercises to enhance such cognitive functions as comparison, analysis, classification, and sequence, and to mediate students' reflections on the cognitive strategies they have used (metacognition), and then help them to make applications (bridging) to the subject matter under study. Special in-depth teacher training is needed to implement the program. Results with deaf adolescents included significant improvements on tests of reading comprehension, mathematics computation, and mathematics concepts; improvement in logical reasoning; better organization; and greater precision in solving problem situations (Martin & Jonas, 1986; Craig & Gordon, 1988).

Deaf persons using special cognitive skills programs become more capable of using metacognitive problem-solving skill in the sense of being able to *explain* why certain strategies did or did not work. The results of these studies have also demonstrated that deaf adolescents after mediation will use symbols and operations that reflect symbolic relational thought—that is, formal operational thinking. The implications here are clear that special cognitive skills training by a properly trained leader with appropriate materials can prepare the deaf learner for greater success in the workplace.

The most promising approaches to planned cognitive intervention appear to be those which have (1) a strong theoretical basis; (2) a focus on teacher training or retraining in the specific methodology; (3) a comprehensive incorporation of several, rather than only a few, cognitive skills; (4) regular opportunities for students to apply these skills to subject matter; and (5) an explicit metacognitive focus in terms of helping students to become aware of and discuss the cognitive processes and strategies which they are learning and applying. Educational intervention is apparently beneficial in making improvements in the reasoning and problem-solving abilities of deaf learners.

CONCLUSION

As we look to the future, we ask, "What principles should guide the professional who is responsible for assisting deaf clients in today's changing world?" Based on all of the foregoing research and theories, we can conclude that the most appropriate course of action for professionals, then, would be to act on at least the following principles:

1. Provide the deaf client with all possible modes of communication;
2. Become proficient as a professional in as many of those communication modes as possible;
3. Actively encourage colleagues to do the same;
4. Maintain high expectations for the deaf person, since no evidence suggests anything other than the same range of intellectual potential for deaf persons as for hearing persons;
5. Support the continuation of carefully designed and executed research on cognitive development and processing in deaf persons;

6. Systematically educate employers and hearing colleagues of deaf workers as to how to maintain high cognitive expectations (as well as adaptations) which are appropriate for deaf persons;

7. Help employers of deaf persons to understand that frequently what employers perceive as a "cognitive" problem for a deaf employee very well may be a *communication* problem instead;

8. Actively support efforts to provide appropriate cognitive training for deaf persons preparing to enter the work force.

When considering programs that will maximize the opportunity for these principles to be implemented, one might be tempted to declare that such implementation is possible only with additional funding. Such a statement, however, would not be entirely true, since, although funding is a *necessary* condition, it is not a sufficient one. The sufficient condition is the continuing conviction, based now on clear evidence, that the deaf client can indeed achieve higher levels of cognitive performance, given appropriate conditions and dedication by professionals. That challenge is the one to which educators and other professionals working with and on behalf of deaf persons must now rise.

REFERENCES

Bellugi, U. (1983, August). *Brain organization: Clues from sign aphasia.* Paper presented at the Conference on the Development, Psycholinguistic, and Neurolinguistic Aspects of ASL. Seattle, WA.

Braden, J.P. (1987). An explanation of the superior performance IQs of deaf children of deaf parents. *American Annals of the Deaf, 132*(4), 263–266.

Craig, H.B., & Gordon, H.W. (1988). Specialized cognitive function and reading achievement in hearing-impaired adolescents. *Journal of Speech and Hearing Disorders, 53*(1), 30–41.

Craig, H. (1989). *Specialized cognitive function among deaf individuals: Implications for instruction.* Unpublished manuscript. Pittsburgh, PA: Western Pennsylvania School for the Deaf.

Deland, F. (1931). *The story of lipreading.* Washington, DC: Volta Bureau.

Dietz, C.H. (1985). Improving cognitive skills in deaf adolescents using LOGO and instrumental enrichment. In D.S. Martin (Ed.), *Cognition, education, and deafness.* Washington, DC: Gallaudet College Press.

Drever, J., & Collins, M. (1982). *Performance tests of intelligence.* Edinburgh: Oliver & Boyd.

Feuerstein, R. (1979). *The dynamic assessment of retarded performers: The learning potential assessment device, theory, instruments, and techniques.* Baltimore: University Park Press.

Feuerstein, R. (1980). *Instrumental enrichment.* Baltimore: University Park Press. (A thinking skills curriculum disseminated through Curriculum Development Associates, Washington, DC).

Furth, H. (1964). *Thinking without language.* New York: Free Press.

Gibson, J.M. (1985). Field dependence of deaf students: Implications for education. In D.S.

Martin (Ed.), *Cognition, education, and deafness.* Washington, DC: Gallaudet College Press.

Greenberg, M.T., & Kusche, C.A. (1989). Cognitive, personal and social development of deaf children and adolescents. In *Handbook of special education.*

Hauptman, A.R. (1980). An investigation of the spatial reasoning abilities of hearing-impaired students. *Directions, 1*(3), 43–44.

Jensema, C. (1975). *The relationship between academic achievement and the demographic characteristics of hearing-impaired children and youth.* Washington, DC: Gallaudet College, Office of Demographic Studies.

Johnson, J. (1981), April). *Hearing-impaired learners with special needs.* Paper presented at the Symposium on Media and the Hearing-Impaired, Lincoln, NE.

Karchmer, M., & Belmont, J. (1976, November). *On assessing and improving performance in the cognitive laboratory.* Paper presented at the meeting of the American Speech and Hearing Association, Houston, TX.

Keane, K. (1983). *Application of mediated learning theory to a deaf population: A study in cognitive modifiability.* Unpublished doctoral dissertation. New York: Columbia University.

Kelly, R.R., & Tomlinson-Keasey, C. (1977). Hemispheric laterality of deaf children for processing words and pictures visually presented to the hemifields. *American Annals of the Deaf, 122,* 525–533.

Klima, E.S., & Bellugi, U. (1979). *The signs of language.* Cambridge, MA: Harvard University Press.

Knobloch-Gala, A. (1989). *Cortical integration of hemispherical processes versus cognitive processes in the deaf.* Unpublished manuscript. Krakow: Jagiellonian University.

Lipman, M., Sharp, A., & Oscanyan, F. (1980). *Philosophy in the classroom.* Philadelphia: Temple University Press.

Ljubesic, M. (1986). A contribution to the study of the structure of cognitive abilities of the deaf. *International Journal of Rehabilitation Research. 9*(3), 290–294.

Lou, M. (1989). *Cognitive development and its relationship to language for deaf adolescents.* Unpublished manuscript. Berkeley: University of California.

Luetke-Stahlman, B. (1988a). A description of the form and content of four sign systems as used in classrooms of hearing-impaired students in the United States. Submitted to *American Annals of the Deaf.*

Luetke-Stahlman, B. (1988b). SEE2 in the classroom: How well is English grammar represented? In G. Gustason (Ed.), *Signing English in total communication: Exact or not*? Los Alamitos, CA: Modern Signs Press.

Luetke-Stahlman, B. (1988c). Instructional communication modes used with Anglo hearing-impaired students: The link to literacy. Submitted to the *Journal of Speech and Hearing Disorders.*

Martin, D.S., & Jonas, B.S. (1986, December). *Cognitive modifiability in the deaf adolescent.* Washington, DC: Gallaudet University. (ERIC Document Reproduction Service No. ED 276 159).

Meadow, K. (1980). *Deafness and child development.* Berkeley: University of California Press.

Miller, M. (1985). Experimental use of signed presentations of the verbal scale of the WISC-R with profoundly deaf children: A preliminary report. In D.S. Martin (Ed.), *Cognition, education, and deafness.* Washington, DC: Gallaudet College Press.

Moeller, M.P. (1988, November). *Language skills of deaf students using manually coded English.* Presentation at the Convention of the American Speech-Language-Hearing Association, Boston, MA.

Moores, D.F. (1982). *Educating the deaf: Psychology, principles, and practices* (2nd edition). Boston: Houghton Mifflin.

Myklebust, H., & Brutton, M. (1953). A study of visual perception in deaf children. *Acta Oto-Laryngologica, Supplementum,* 105.

O'Connor, N., & Hermelin, B. (1978). *Seeing and hearing and space and time.* New York: Academic Press.

Ottem, E. (1980). An analysis of cognitive studies with deaf subjects. *American Annals of the Deaf, 125,* 564–575.

Parasnis, I., & Long, G.L. (1979). Relationships among spatial skills, communication skills, and field dependence in deaf students. *Directions, 1*(2), 26–37.

Parkins, S., & Whitesell, K. (1985). *Evaluating the communication skills of prospective teachers and currently employed teachers of hearing-impaired children in two hundred and fifty-four schools/programs for hearing-impaired children in the United States.* Submitted to the North Carolina Council for the Hearing-Impaired.

Pfau, G.S. (1975). *Final report for project LIFE.* (Contract No. OCE 0–73–0608). Washington, DC: U.S. Office of Education.

Pintner, R., Eisenson, J., & Stanton, M. (1941). *The psychology of the physically disabled.* New York: Crofts & Company.

Quigley, S., & Paul, P. (1984). *Language and deafness.* Austin, TX: College-Hill Press.

Rembert, R.B. (1985). Philosophical inquiry among hearing-impaired students: Promoting the development of thinking skills through the use of Philosophy for Children programs. In D.S. Martin (Ed.), *Cognition, education, and deafness.* Washington, DC: Gallaudet College Press.

Rodda, M., & Grove, C. (1987). *Language, cognition and deafness.* New Jersey: L. Erlbaum Associates.

Rosenstein, J. (1961). Perception, cognition and language in deaf children. *Exceptional Children, 27*(3), 276–284.

Vernon, M. (1967). Relationship of language to the thinking process. *Archives of Genetic Psychiatry, 16*(3), 325–333.

Wodlinger-Cohen, R. (1986). *The manual representation of speech by deaf children, their mothers, and their teachers.* Paper presented at the Conference on Theoretical Issues in Sign Language Research, Rochester, NY.

Wood, D. (1984). The assessment of linguistic and intellectual abilities of hearing-impaired school children. (Special issue: Hearing-impaired children—Their assessment and education.) *Association of Educational Psychologists Journal 6*(5), 31–39.

▶ 4

Affective and Social Development

MICHAEL STINSON
National Technical Institute for the Deaf

This chapter addresses three broad questions concerning the affective and social de-velopment of deaf people. The first one is, How do deaf people develop affectively and socially? This question concerns the effects of communication difficulties, of the family, and of educational programs as the deaf individual develops from infancy to adulthood. In part, this question pertains to the socialization of children; how they learn to become accepted members of society, and how they learn to get along with other people. The question also has to do with how children develop their own person-alities, sense of self, and individual nature (Damon, 1984).

The second major question is, How do deaf people function? Consideration of this question will include research findings that describe personal characteristics of deaf children and adults and their mental health, adjustment to work, and functioning in everyday life.

The third question is, What is the nature of the communities in which deaf people function? The reaction of general society to deaf people, social interaction between deaf and hearing individuals, and participation in the deaf community are among the issues relevant to this question.

A major focus of the chapter is to identify factors associated with optimal psy-chological and social development of individuals. Such factors would include certain rearing practices, educational experiences, possession of particular personality char-acteristics, as well as certain responses by society to deafness. Definition of terms such as "optimal development," "well-integrated personality," and "healthy person-ality" are probably somewhat value-laden, but there are certain concepts that have frequently been associated with these terms in the developmental literature. These include being competent, being sociable, having a sense of altruism, being emotionally responsive, having good feelings about one's self, having a sense of control over one's destiny, and being able to perceive the world and self correctly (Damon, 1984; Erikson, 1968). It is assumed that in many cases the same factors are associated with optimal development in deaf individuals as in hearing ones. At the same time, the manner in which desirable practices are carried out may be different for deaf individuals. For example, the use of sign language is very beneficial for the development of a great majority of deaf children, even though this means communicating differently with the child than with a hearing one. However, while the mode is different, the role of communication in personal and social development remains the same. Effective communication, with free interchange of ideas, permitting a democratic childrearing style, is associated with development of children with strong, healthy personalities regardless of communication mode and hearing status of the child.

Another important consideration is the significant individual differences among deaf people. Although much research has been produced which assigns particular attributes to deaf persons as a group, there are great differences between deaf persons in their personalities, skills, and backgrounds. They are individuals shaped by their experiences, just like hearing people.

Limitations of Research on Affective and Social Development

The research literature regarding affective and social development of deaf individuals must be treated with caution due to (1) the failure of some research to take into account the considerable diversity of the population, (2) measurement difficulties, and (3) recent extensive changes in educational practices and in the social climate. The diversity of the deaf population makes it easy for a researcher to overlook confounding variables. Contradictory results may be obtained when the same variables are measured for two subpopulations of deaf children under similar conditions. For example, one subgroup might include many rubella-deafened children, who often have additional disabilities, while the other subgroup includes few such children (Meadow, 1980; Moores, 1987).

Another problem area is the difficulty of obtaining reliable and valid research measurements with deaf subjects. Many measures in the affective and social domain are paper-and-pencil instruments, and the language of such measures is commonly at a level that is difficult for most deaf subjects to understand because of limited proficiency in English (Moores, 1987; Lane, 1989). Other measures, such as the Rorschach and the Thematic Apperception Test (TAT), require substantial communication between the examiner and the subject. Very few examiners have the communication skills, including knowledge of American Sign Language (ASL), and the extensive testing experience with deaf people required to administer such measures appropriately (Vernon & Andrews, 1990). In addition, the communication skills of the deaf subjects, especially children in schools, may sometimes be so limited that they have difficulty understanding the test questions and providing answers regardless of the communication skills of the examiner. Thus, if the questions are difficult for the subject, it is not clear to what extent the responses reflect understanding of the instructions and questions, and the affective or social characteristic under study.

An additional concern is that research conducted on deafness in the past may have limited generalizability to deaf individuals now being educated and rehabilitated because of significant, recent changes in education and in social attitudes towards deafness. Greenberg and Kusche (1989) have delineated five major recent changes: First, prior to 1970 almost all children were educated solely with oral communication. Since that time use of sign language has grown steadily and is now included in instruction for the vast majority of deaf children. Second, there has been an enormous increase in educational services for deaf children under three years of age. Third, there has been a sizable increase in the number of children attending classes in local public schools, and a corresponding decrease in the number attending residential schools. Fourth, there has been a growing acceptance of ASL as a language in its own right, and, fifth, there has been greater recognition of the deaf community and deaf culture. Thus, deaf children now being educated are clearly different from those studied by researchers in the past. Deaf youth receiving rehabilitation services or entering the job market in the early 1990s may have had more similar experiences to those of populations that were studied in the past, but these youths have probably also been influenced by the recent changes. Studies published in the 1980s and conducted with young deaf children probably best reflect the changes; however, not many such studies exist, and consequently, this chapter is only able to include a few of them. The reader is advised to bear in mind that the conclusions of the relatively older studies presented in this chapter have greater relevance to adult rehabilitation clients and have limited generalizability to the cohort of deaf children currently being educated.

AFFECTIVE DEVELOPMENT

Sensory and Linguistic Deficiencies

When a child is born with a severe hearing impairment, the absence of auditory stimulation generally causes delay or absence in the development of spoken language (Quigley & Paul, 1984). This delay in development of spoken language has been hypothesized to influence affective development (Harris, 1978). Some researchers have also hypothesized that the absence or limitation in auditory stimulation may itself directly influence affective development (Altshuler, Deming, Vollenweider, Rainer, & Tendler, 1976), although this suggestion has been challenged (Harris, 1978). These deficiencies in auditory stimulation and spoken language have been offered as explanations for certain personality characteristics that have been associated with deafness. These supposed characteristics include impulsivity, emotional immaturity, lack of understanding of the dynamics of interpersonal relationships, and an egocentric life perspective (Schlesinger, 1978).

In actuality, it is virtually impossible to isolate effects on affective development due to the absence of sensory stimulation and delays in spoken language from a third influence, the effects of the social environment. This third influence is the responses that deafness elicits from significant others in the environment—parents, teachers, and peers—and the consequent effects of these responses upon the deaf child's development.

Schlesinger (1978) and Liben (1978), on the basis of Piagetian theory, have suggested that early stimulation influences the development of curiosity. Extensive, varied sensory input is desirable for fostering curiosity. When the auditory input is markedly reduced, the infant is deprived of the opportunity to learn as much about how actions and objects produce sound. This reduction in stimulation may limit the child's interest in exploring these sound-producing objects and actions. Although this hypothesis has not been confirmed, the idea that early sensory stimulation is important should be taken seriously. Early use of hearing aids can increase auditory input, and additional interesting visual material may provide compensation for deficits in auditory stimulation (Liben, 1978).

One dimension of affective development that has been thought to be susceptible to auditory deprivation and linguistic deficiency is impulsiveness. Although auditory input has been hypothesized to be related to control of impulsivity (Altshuler et al., 1976), the issue may really revolve around *inner language*. Language deficiencies may influence affective development because language plays a role in self-regulation or self-control, which influences behavior, and because it influences ability to self-analyze one's feelings and to analyze life's events (Greenberg & Kusche, 1989; Meadow, 1980). In regard to self-regulation, language is important in helping the child develop inner controls which replace the outer controls that parents exercise with very young children (Schlesinger, 1978). According to this interpretation, deaf individuals may be impulsive because they do not have the language to tell themselves not to engage in the impulsive act. Also, with language, one can free him- or herself from the need for immediate gratification by simply telling oneself that it is possible to do or have it later. This language does not need to be spoken; signed language appears to work perfectly well (Harris, 1978).

Language is also important for being able to develop positive social relationships. There is a vocabulary necessary for self-analysis of internal events that includes cognitive words such as "thinking," "knowing," and "guessing," and also feeling words such as, "sad," "happy," "excited," and "frustrated" (Meadow, 1980). This vocabulary is important for sensitive analysis of how one's self is thinking and feeling in the social situation, for sharing thoughts and feelings with others, and for accurately interpreting the actions and comments of others (Greenberg & Kusche, 1989). Again, it is important to remember that this language may be either signed or spoken.

The way that language deficiencies exert the greatest influence on the child's personal and social development is through the consequences of the limited communication between the child and others. Schlesinger (1978) has suggested that toilet training is an example of how parent-child communication is intricately connected to the affective development of the child. Through language it is possible for parents to be flexible and reassuring in instituting this training. Schlesinger also points out that as the child grows older, communication is perhaps even more important because it becomes possible to state rules clearly to children, the reasons for the rules, and the consequences of breaking them. Research has indicated that these are effective discipline techniques for teaching children self-control.

Home Environment

For the deaf child, as well as the hearing one, the childrearing style of the parents has profound effect upon the child's affective development. Parents bear much of the responsibility, along with schools, for ensuring that children acquire the values and norms of society (Damon, 1984). When the child is deaf, parents need to accept their child's differences, they need to find effective ways to communicating with their child (which is often quite difficult), and they need to exercise special flexibility in order to match childrearing appropriately to the deaf child's needs. Parents who can successfully meet these demands are most likely to rear children who are competent, mature, and sociable. In more than 90% of the families with a deaf child both parents are hearing (Meadow, 1980), and most of the discussion and studies in this section will pertain to such parents. Deaf parents of deaf children will receive attention because of their ability to communicate with their deaf children and research indicates they have been especially successful in rearing these children.

Adaptation to Deafness by Parents

As discussed in Chapter 1, the establishment of the diagnosis of deafness is often an agonizing, prolonged process for parents. Once the child has been identified as deaf, parents often undergo a difficult adjustment to the fact. Doctors are rarely prepared to help parents deal with the feelings and emotions they experience when learning the diagnosis. At first parents may feel relieved that they at least now know what is wrong. But parents also often experience feelings of grief, anger, guilt, or sorrow. In addition there may be feelings of helplessness, of not knowing what to do, because the child is different.

Bodner-Johnson (cited in Greenberg & Kusche, 1989) conducted a study which provides evidence that the adaptation of the parents to the child's deafness is related to the development of academic competence. She found, for a sample of 125 deaf children 10–12 years of age, that the family's adaptation to deafness was significantly related to the children's reading achievement. One reason that these children of parents who made a better adaptation to deafness showed higher reading achievement may have been that the adaptation to deafness facilitated establishment of effective childrearing practices, such as having high, but realistic, expectations for their children's achievement. In turn, these practices may have promoted development of a sense of competence and a positive motivational orientation in the children which helped foster reading achievement.

Parent-Child Communication

The development of optimal communication between parents and children is critical in the affective development of the deaf child (Meadow, 1980; Greenberg & Kusche, 1989). Damon (1984) points out that for all children, good communication is essential for democratic childrearing. Such childrearing is characterized by a high level of verbal contact between parent and child, by the parent's soliciting the child's opinion when family decisions are made, and by the provision of reasons when punitive or restrictive measures are instituted. Research indicates that this style of childrearing is desirable in fostering children who are curious, assertive, and creative (Damon, 1984).

Communication is also critical for helping children develop a sense of trust in the world. If communication is restricted to immediate objects and actions, the child may become overly anxious because parents cannot communicate well enough with the child to provide explanations about things or to discuss the probable course of events (Meadow, 1980). This lack of communication about topics that do not have an immediate visual reference has been found for families with deaf children. In a study by Schlesinger (1972) that included only hearing parents, only 5 percent of the deaf children and their parents had conversations about topics without a visual reference; in contrast, 45 percent of the parents of hearing children made comments that referred to a nonvisible object. Research by Schlesinger and Meadow (1972) has demonstrated that the limitations in communication ability, as well as other demands on parents of having a deaf child, affect the quality of the parent-child interaction. Mothers of deaf preschool children were rated as significantly less permissive, more intrusive, more didactic, less creative, and less flexible when compared to mothers of hearing preschool children. In addition, the parents of deaf children used a more limited range of discipline techniques and used more spanking.

Research with deaf children also indicates that when parents can communicate with their children relatively effectively, their childrearing style tends to be more similar to that of parents with hearing children. Schlesinger and Meadow (1976) also collected data for their longitudinal study when the children were three years older. Interactions between parents and deaf children rated high in communication competence were quite similar to those between hearing parents and their children, but the parent-child interactions were less relaxed, creative, and effective for children with low communication competence (Schlesinger & Meadow, 1976). Greenberg (1980) compared interactions of parents using simultaneous communication (sign language and speech together) and those using oral communication with preschool children. When parent and child were using simultaneous communication, there was greater cooperation, and interactions tended to be longer and more complex.

Pacing of Demands for Development

Another critical issue for parents of deaf children is to pace their demands appropriately for the children's development. It is important for parents to give children sufficient independence, to have high expectations for them, and to not be overly intrusive, while simultaneously providing support and encouragement. Having relatively high expectations for the child and making high demands for mature behavior has been associated with rearing of hearing children who are competent, nonagressive, sociable, and altruistic (Damon, 1984). Parents of deaf children do not want to expose their children unnecessarily to situations where the lack of hearing could create dangers for them (e.g., not hearing a car when chasing a ball into the street). In order to keep experiences challenging for children there needs to be differentiation between areas where they are more capable and those where they are less capable and to adjust expectations and behaviors accordingly.

Research indicates that mothers of deaf children who are able to support the child without being too protective or demanding are likely to rear children demonstrating greater competence. Schlesinger and Meadow (1976) found that mothers rated as more encouraging and flexible with their children were more likely to have children with greater pride in mastery. Flexibility was characterized as the extent mothers modified the implicit and explicit rules for teaching, controlling, and relating to the child in accordance with the requirements of the situation. In addition, Stinson (1978) found that different patterns of maternal help and reward on a relatively easy task and on a more difficult task were associated with different achievement-oriented behaviors in deaf children. For the difficult task, relatively frequent help and reward were associated with achievement-oriented behavior, but for the easy task, frequent help and reward were not associated with achievement-oriented behavior. Thus, the mother's flexibility and her style of giving help and reward are related to the achievement behavior of the deaf child.

Deaf Parents of Deaf Children

Deaf parents have been effective in rearing deaf children who are competent. Deaf children of deaf parents, compared to deaf children of hearing parents, have been shown to demonstrate better academic performance, greater proficiency in English, a more positive self-image, and less impulsivity (Harris, 1978; Meadow, 1968; Meadow, 1969). Meadow (1980) interpreted the higher self-image of deaf children of deaf parents as being related to the following factors: (1) providing the child with a positive role model who is likewise deaf; (2) ease of parent-child communication as a result of early use of sign language; and (3) provision of an environment in which the child could experience pride in using sign language and in participating in the deaf community.

Deaf parents appear to be especially skillful in establishing effective communication with their children so that parent-child interaction is more similar to that of hearing parents with hearing children. Maestas y Moores (1980; Moores, 1987) studied the interaction of deaf parents with their children, both deaf and hearing, from birth to 18 months of age. Parents established communicative interaction with their children from birth. They used strategies for orienting the child's attention that were important for establishing effective communication, which presumably bears greater resemblance to communication between hearing parents and hearing children. For example, for children over six months, the mother would place her hand on the child's body or tap his or her shoulder in order to gain attention before speaking or signing. Parent-child interaction during free play was examined for deaf parents with deaf children in preschool, hearing parents with deaf children, and hearing parents with hearing children in a study by Meadow, Greenberg, Erting, and Carmichael (1981). The interactions of the deaf children with deaf parents were more similar to those of the hearing children with hearing parents than to those of the deaf children with hearing parents. In particular, the interactions of the deaf children with deaf parents were more complex and reciprocal than were those of the deaf children with hearing parents. Further study of the childrearing styles of deaf parents with deaf children may suggest ways that hearing parents can establish more effective communication and rapport with their deaf children. For example, ways that deaf parents orient the child to attend visually to messages could be adopted by hearing parents.

School Environments

As discussed in Chapter 1, the two predominant educational settings, residential schools and special classes in regular schools, have a number of distinguishing features, such as the extent of contact with hearing peers. Thus, children may undergo somewhat different socialization experiences in the two settings.

Residential Schools and Influences of Institutionalization

In order to understand how residential schools might influence affective and social development, it is useful to begin with a description of the schools' educational and social environments. Although there is much diversity in residential schools for deaf children, in the prototypical school a majority of the elementary students commute from home on a daily basis, while more of the secondary students reside at the school. The school generally uses a system of simultaneous communication at both the elementary and secondary levels (see Chapter 1). There is generally an excellent range of special services, such as audiologists, counselors, and psychologists. There is an extensive array of academic and vocational courses, and a wide range of athletic and social programs.

The presence of a large number of deaf peers and many activities supports positive social and emotional growth. Deaf adolescents in residential schools appear to have high levels of self-esteem, greater maturity, and more positive social and emotional adjustment compared to deaf students in regular schools (Farrugia & Austin, 1980).

On the other hand, deaf adolescents who attend residential schools may lack certain social skills compared to hearing peers, and this may be due to restrictions in the social environments of residential schools, such as lack of freedom to leave campus (Evans, 1975). Such restrictions are not unique to residential schools for deaf children, but are found in many residential institutions for special populations (Meadow, 1980). Quigley and Kretchmer (1982) have suggested, however, that many residential schools have recently become less restrictive.

In the Mainstream

Students who are mainstreamed attend classes in regular public schools that enroll predominantly hearing students. These children may be placed in special classes which are attached to the regular school, and the number of deaf students in these special programs varies from a few to over a hundred. Alternatively, one or two deaf children may attend a local public school. There is considerable variation in these mainstream programs. For example, in some programs virtually all students attend special classes and simultaneous communication is generally used for instruction. In others there is more flexibility, and a choice is provided between instruction in the simultaneous communication and oral modes (Moores, 1987).

A number of educators have expressed concern regarding the appropriateness of the mainstreamed environment for positive affective development of many deaf children. For example, the report of the recent Commission on Education of the Deaf stated that too many students are being mainstreamed without adequate educational and social support (Recommendations 3 to 9, 1988). The research on social relationships of mainstreamed deaf students with hearing peers also gives some cause for concern, as it suggests that these students often experience difficulty in social relationships (Davis, 1986). For example, Greenberg and Kusche (1989) summarized several descriptive studies of hearing-deaf child interactions in integrated settings when only oral communication was used. The deaf children interacted more frequently with other deaf children or with their teachers than they did with hearing children. Furthermore, Foster (1988) reported that graduates of the National Technical Institute for the Deaf described their high school mainstream experiences as including much loneliness, rejection, and social isolation. Mertens (1989) interviewed students at Gallaudet who had been mainstreamed, and they reported having similarly negative experiences. One caution in regard to the Foster (1988) and Mertens (1989) studies is that these students' descriptions of their mainstreaming experiences may possibly have been biased in the sense that they chose to continue their studies in institutions intended for education of deaf students rather than more integrated colleges.

Another concern is that mainstreamed deaf students may perceive a double message with respect to their status in the hearing world (Emerton, Hurwitz, & Bishop, 1979). On one hand, placing deaf students in "normal" education environments conveys the impression that they are expected to compete with hearing peers. On the other hand, deaf people sometimes perceive hearing peers as having negative attitudes towards deafness (Schroedel & Schiff, 1972). This perception by deaf students may lead them to think that hearing students do not view deaf students as capable of competing with hearing ones (Stinson, 1984).

An additional issue pertains to the development of identity. Glickman (1986), who has had much experience counseling deaf youths, suggests that it is important for them to find answers to the questions of Who am I? and How do I fit into the deaf and hearing worlds? Furthermore, orally trained students from mainstream programs, who have had little prior experience with deaf culture, may undergo internal conflict as they discover sign language and the deaf community. They may struggle in their efforts to clarify their affiliations to the deaf and hearing worlds.

There is, also, however, some evidence that deaf students can have positive, or at least non-negative, social experiences in the mainstream setting. Ladd, Munson, and Miller (1984) studied the interpersonal experiences of deaf adolescents placed in occupational education programs with hearing peers. Special efforts were made to establish a climate that supported positive interaction between deaf and hearing peers, and the results indicated that such positive interaction and friendship occurred. Additionally, Mertens (1986) did not find consistent differences between the social development of students who were mainstreamed for at least some of their classes and those who were always in self-contained classes.

Effect of Multiple Disabilities upon Personal Development

There is an association in deaf people between presence of an additional handicap and having behavioral problems, especially if the handicap is indicative of possible damage to the central nervous system. In the 1982–83 Annual Survey of Hearing-Impaired Children and Youth, 30 percent had one or more additional handicaps (Wolff & Harkins, 1986). The rate of behavioral problems for children with at least one additional handicap is approximately three times greater than that for children for whom there are no additional handicapping conditions (Jensema & Trybus, 1975). There is considerable variation in the rates of behavioral problems in accordance with the particular additional handicapping condition. The handicapping conditions associated with higher rates of behavioral problems are those more closely related to possible damage to the brain, such as perceptual-motor disorders (Meadow & Trybus, 1979).

Rubella-caused deafness has also been associated with a higher incidence of behavioral problems (Meadow, 1980; Wolff & Harkins, 1986). This is important because a significant number of young people with rubella-related deafness have recently entered the job market, or are about to enter. Chess, Korn, and Fernandez (1971) examined the frequency of psychiatric diagnosis among 243 rubella children. They found that 41.7 percent of the children with hearing defects alone were diagnosed as having a psychiatric disorder and that 76.2 percent with both a hearing and a visual defect had a psychiatric disorder.

While the evidence suggests that potential brain dysfunction is associated with behavioral problems, Meadow (1980) has urged that extreme caution be exercised in ascribing the label of "brain damaged" to children. She notes, "These terms have become catch phrases disguised as diagnoses and have been used to describe impairments in language, motor or sensory functioning, and intellectual abilities, all supposedly related to impairments of the central nervous system" (p. 121). Experts who have conducted research which includes groups with possible brain dysfunction have stressed the importance of relying upon "hard" signs such as current motor handicaps of central nervous system origin, or epilepsy (Meadow, 1980).

Another reason deaf persons with additional handicaps are likely to demonstrate behavioral problems is that these individuals face additional difficulties in life. Having additional handicaps may result in more life experiences that engender frustration and feelings of failure. Furthermore, people in general may be more rejecting toward those who have multiple handicaps (Meadow & Trybus, 1979).

PERSONALITY AND BEHAVIORAL CHARACTERISTICS

Review of Research Findings

Given the effects of the deaf individual's experiences in the family and at school and the possible influence of additional handicaps, what kinds of personality and behavioral characteristics are they likely to develop? The research on the characteristics discussed below has been divided into five areas: social maturity, rigidity and impulsivity, social-cognitive ability, self-esteem, and locus of control. As we consider these characteristics, it is particularly important to be sensitive to the substantial variation in personality characteristics of deaf people.

Social Maturity

Social maturity refers to the extent people can take care of themselves, be independent, and act responsibly (Meadow, 1976a). Earlier studies with deaf people most often used the Vineland Social Maturity Scale (Doll, 1965) which assesses children's progress toward being able to care for themselves. These studies generally found deaf children to be less socially mature than their hearing peers. Greenberg and Kusche (1989) criticized these studies because the Vineland Scale contains items for which oral language skills are required. Greenberg (1983) found that when a measure of social maturity that relied less on oral language was employed, the developmental ages of deaf and hearing children were similar.

Effective communication is important for development of social maturity. (Greenberg, 1983; Schlesinger & Meadow, 1971, 1972). Deaf preschool children rated high in communicative competence have been found to show higher social maturity than those rated low in communicative competence (Schlesinger & Meadow, 1971).

Relatively frequent contact with parents (at least for deaf children with hearing parents) also appears to play a role in development of social maturity. Quarrington and Solomon (1975) found that for deaf students attending a residential school, more frequent visits home were associated with greater social maturity.

Rigidity and Impulsivity

Two other personality characteristics that have been associated with deafness are rigidity and impulsiveness (Meadow, 1980; Greenberg & Kusche, 1989). Rigidity refers to a tendency to be unchanging when changes in the situation mean that other behaviors are desirable. It can also refer to a tendency to apply a rule indiscriminately (Meadow, 1976a). Impulsivity refers to tendencies to make fast decisions, many errors, and to show little forethought (Altschuler et al., 1976; Harris, 1978). These two traits have been associated with low educational achievement in deaf children (Levine & Wagner, 1974). The hearing status of deaf children's parents is related to the amount of impulsivity observed, with deaf children of deaf parents being less impulsive (Harris, 1978). These relationships point to the conclusion that effective early communication, manual communication in the case of deaf parents, contributes to development of adequate impulse control (Levine & Wagner, 1974).

Social-Cognitive Ability

The recent work on social-cognitive ability, which includes emotional understanding, role-taking, social problem-solving, and decision-making skills has been reviewed by Greenberg and Kusche (1989). In general, deaf subjects have not scored as high on measures of these dimensions as hearing controls; however, the extent of discrepancy between the performance of deaf and hearing subjects depends on the nature of the task. Deaf subjects perform similar to hearing ones when information transmission requirements are reduced. In addition, a brief training period can dramatically increase skill in perspective taking.

Social-cognitive ability also varies systematically in relation to other personal characteristics (Greenberg & Kusche, 1989; Young & Brown, 1981). For example, deaf children's ability to interpret emotional states and situations has been associated with higher nonverbal intelligence, low scores on impulsivity, higher reading comprehension, and parent and teacher ratings of fewer behavior problems.

Self-Concept and Self-Esteem

The self-concept is a broad construct that includes knowledge about one's own experience in the world, one's position in social relationships, personal characteristics, and one's own unique personal identity (Damon, 1984). Self-knowledge pertaining to appraisal of personal competence has been referred to as self-esteem.

Self-esteem is associated with academic success for both normally hearing and deaf students (Joiner, Erickson, Crittenden, & Stevenson, 1966; Walberg & Uguroglu, 1979). Joiner et al. (1966) found that deaf students in a residential high school with relatively high self-esteem tended to have high grade-point averages. Koelle and Convey (1982), studying a similar population, found that self-esteem was positively related to performance on the Stanford Achievement Test for Hearing-Impaired Students. These findings are important in demonstrating the association between self-esteem and competent performance. They are also examples of how personality characteristics of deaf people vary in the same way as those of hearing people.

Evidence regarding effects of the educational setting on self-esteem has been mixed. Some studies indicate that mainstreamed students tend to have lower self-esteem than residential students (Farrugia & Austin, 1980). Other studies have found no differences in self-esteem of students in residential and mainstream settings for children with hearing parents (Craig, 1965; Schlesinger & Meadow, 1972).

The self-concept includes self-knowledge of past successes and of competence relative to others (Damon, 1984). As with hearing people, this self-knowledge may well vary in terms of different areas of experience. For deaf individuals, it is probably in the areas of reading, writing, and using speech that this self-knowledge is most likely to translate into lack of confidence. Meath-Lang, Caccamise, and Albertini (1982) collected essays in which students were asked to describe their feelings about learning English. Most of these descriptions were markedly negative, revealing perceptions of limited proficiency and frustration in trying to master the language. For example, one comment was, "I realize that deaf school have 'limited' English while hearing school have 'unlimited' English."

Locus of Control
Locus of control is concerned with the extent that people perceive events as under their personal control. People classified as having an *external locus of control* tend to attribute the outcomes of events they are involved in to forces beyond their control, such as luck or task difficulty. Persons classified as having an *internal locus of control* tend to attribute outcomes to personal skill and effort.

The research on locus of control suggests that deaf individuals are more externally oriented than hearing ones (Bodner & Johnson, 1977; Dowaliby, Burke, & McKee, 1983). Given the childrearing styles of some parents, the strict structure in some special education settings, and the lack of acceptance of deafness by general society, the external locus of control of many deaf people may be a realistic view of how their lives are run by others.

A point of perhaps greater importance is that deaf persons with a more internally oriented locus of control have demonstrated greater achievement than those with a more external orientation. Koelle and Convey (1982) found that high school students attending a residential school who had more internality performed better on the Stanford Achievement Test than did those with more externality. In another study, deaf students at one college who were enrolled in mainstream programs, which were generally more challenging, had greater internality than did students in non-mainstream programs (Dowaliby & Saur, 19484).

A critical link between achievement and locus of control may be the individual's sense of responsibility and work habits. Dowaliby, Burke, and McKee (1983) reported that externally oriented deaf college students were more likely to avoid taking responsibility, to view the teacher as a powerful other person, and to have poor study habits compared to internally oriented students.

Measures versus Daily Function

Four types of research have been reviewed regarding the personality of deaf individuals: (1) effects of the social milieu, or environment, upon personality development;

(2) experiments which compare deaf people's performance in different situations; or which evaluate the effects of a special training procedure or information; (3) studies of individual differences of deaf persons in various cognitive and affective dimensions and interrelations between them; and (4) comparisons between deaf and hearing persons in regard to personality characteristics. Results of this fourth type of research (4) are regarded as the most suspect.

In most cases the measures used for comparison were designed to assess adjustment to life by hearing persons (Furth, 1973; Moores, 1987). It is questionable whether a different mean score on such measures implies a discrepancy in the quality of adjustment. In addition, many deaf persons may not understand or interpret items in the same manner as hearing people generally would. For example, when Garrison, Tesch, and DeCaro (1978) found that deaf college students showed lower self-esteem than hearing ones, the authors concluded that the reason for the difference was misinterpretation of the items rather than a real difference in self-esteem. Moreover, when measures have been developed especially for deaf individuals, deaf-hearing differences in performance are often reduced or disappear, such as when role-taking ability was assessed by a task in which the communication demands were reduced, there were no differences in role-taking ability.

In view of these considerations, it is clearly not appropriate to interpret the deaf-hearing differences obtained in certain studies as an indication that auditory loss in itself has a detrimental effect upon personality development. Furthermore, even if the research involving deaf-hearing comparisons had used measures of unquestioned reliability and validity, which of course has often not been the case, how helpful is this knowledge to providing education, rehabilitation, and mental health services? Such research offers little, if any, information on the optimal characteristics of deaf people and on the best ways to facilitate their development.

There is substantial variation in affective and social development among deaf people, just as there is among hearing ones. This variation is related to the interaction of the extent of communication with others, adaptation by the family, support at school, understanding of the community, exposure to deaf role models, opportunity to develop pride as a deaf person, and many other factors. Each deaf individual is unique and there is no one optimal way of functioning for all. Given the frequent communication difficulties and the limited understanding of the special subcultural status of deaf people in society, deaf individuals show strengths and weaknesses that any other group which has undergone similar experiences would be expected to have (Greenberg & Kusche, 1989).

Personality, Vocational Development, and Rehabilitation Counseling

The personality dimensions which have been discussed in regard to deaf people also have implications for vocational development. Self-esteem is related to occupational choice and satisfactory work adjustment. Individuals tend to prefer occupations that provide outcomes that they, themselves, value positively (Vroom, 1964; Betz, 1977). The extent that the values an individual holds influence vocational choice depends in part upon his or her expectations that it is possible to be successful in various occupations (Vroom, 1964). Individuals who are confident they can be successful in many different occupations will choose the one they most prefer; their choices should be highly predictable from their values. On the other hand, those who are less confident will tend to restrict occupations in accordance with lower self-estimates of ability. People with favorable self-images more frequently make vocational decisions in favor of high status, difficult to attain occupations (Osipow, 1973; 1975).

No studies on the relationship between self-esteem and occupational choice of deaf youths were found in the literature. Results have been mixed in regard to the question of whether deaf youth have different occupational expectations than hearing ones. Lerman and Guilfoyle (1970) reported that the occupations a group of adolescent deaf girls planned to enter were lower in prestige than the ones of a comparison group of hearing peers. In contrast, Joiner, Erikson, and Crittenden (1966) did not find a difference in planned occupational choices of deaf and hearing adolescents with respect to the occupation's prestige.

Once a person has entered the work force, self-esteem plays a role in successful functioning and adjustment. Levinson (1984), a deaf person who achieved a high position in a large corporation, has emphasized the importance of the deaf individual being perceived by colleagues as competent, as opposed to helpless, as self-confident and willing to take risks. Furthermore, it is important for deaf workers to maintain a positive attitude even when difficulties are encountered.

Foster (1987) interviewed deaf graduates of the National Technical Institute for the Deaf who were in technical and professional positions. Underlying their comments is the need for genuine self-confidence in confronting the difficulties in communication and the lack of understanding of deafness. This comes through, for example, when deaf workers were asked about opportunities for promotion at work. "Several believed it was possible to be promoted but added they did not want the responsibility. When asked to elaborate they said they were unsure of whether they could handle the level of social interaction and communication which would be required of them in a managerial or supervisory position" (Foster, 1987, p. 9).

The NTID graduates' comments also point to the important of taking responsibility. Workers felt that if they were going to be successful, they needed to work harder than their hearing co-workers. If they were experiencing difficulty at work, such as difficulty in understanding information presented at meetings, they were responsible for taking the steps to resolve the matter. They also felt the deaf person was primarily responsible for "breaking the ice" to make hearing co-workers comfortable in interacting, and they were responsible for introducing and encouraging the use of sign language so far as possible (Foster, 1987).

The importance of such perceptions of personal responsibility in the productivity of workers has been noted by Georgopoulos, Mahoney, and Jones (1957). These perceptions are, of course, related to the dimension of locus of control. Workers who perceive productivity as related to the attainment of personal goals are more likely to be productive (Andrisani & Nestle, 1976). A study by Guilfoyle, Schapiro, Katz-Hansen, and Lerman (1973) suggests that perceived personal control may be a determinant of occupational success for deaf workers. They found that workers rated as relatively independent, a characteristic associated with sense of responsibility and maturity, were employed a larger percentage of the time and enjoyed greater increases in salary.

Being able to exercise a certain amount of flexibility is also important for successful adjustment. For example, the NTID graduates who expressed the greatest satisfaction in managing difficult situations at work were those who used a range of strategies. These workers were able to evaluate different situations and then select the most appropriate strategy. For example, in certain situations, such as the need for greater written communication, the deaf worker might directly confront the supervisor about the problem. On the other hand, if the worker had found that repeated attempts to participate in coffee breaks with a group of hearing employees had produced little satisfactory interaction, the deaf worker might resort to simply bringing something to read during the break (Foster, 1987).

Levinson (1984) has commented on the need for another type of flexibility for deaf workers: being able to change one's mind regarding an issue or position when it appears that co-workers support a different one. At the same time, however, it is important to know when not to "give in."

What implications does research on affective development have for rehabilitation counselors who work with deaf clients? In regard to social maturity, there is as wide variation among deaf people as among hearing ones, and the counselor should not expect clients to show less social maturity and independence simply because they are deaf. The research suggests that clients with relatively weak communication skills, oral and/or manual, are the ones who are most likely to need encouragement to develop independence and do things for themselves. For example, certain clients may be reluctant to use the telephone for themselves. They can be shown how to use a Telecommunications Device for the Deaf (TDD), and to make contact with the telephone relay operator who can relay messages between the TDD user and the hearing person who is using voice phone (see Chapter 11). Counselors may also need to help some clients learn to manage certain facets of everyday life that are prerequisites for independent functioning, such as balancing a checkbook, using public transportation, and dealing with medical services, before they can be expected to assume conventional, full-time jobs (Meadow, 1976a). Mastery of these skills often leads to an increased sense of self-efficacy and self-esteem.

One step counselors can take to promote self-esteem is to help clients set specific goals for themselves. A specific goal identifies the task to be accomplished and level of proficiency be attained. For example, one way of providing a specific goal is to set a higher performance goal than that of previous work (Covington & Berry, 1976).

CULTURAL ISSUES

A critical aspect of understanding affective and social development of the deaf lies in the concept of deviance from "the norm" and stigmatization. Deafness has, with few exceptions (see Groce, 1985), historically been viewed by hearing society as a deviant condition. It is regarded as such because deaf people cannot do certain things that people should "normally" be able to do, in this case, hear, and speak with a certain voice quality. The process by which society discredits those who have a physical difference, such as homosexuality, has been referred to in sociological theory as stigmatization (Higgins, 1980). There is a discrepancy between the expectation that a person be whole and unblemished and the perception that the person is, in fact, deformed and blemished. Along with the perception of this discrepancy is the expectation that the individual should "right" him- or herself by attempting to approximate "normality" as far as possible (Bartel & Guskin, 1980; Goffman, 1963). The stigmatizing characteristic, deafness, is emphasized to the exclusion of other characteristics. The person is seen as deaf first and as a person second (Higgins, 1980).

The long history of mistreatment of deaf persons by society can be interpreted as consistent with stigmatization theory. Higgins (1980) gives a few examples from the many instances. Romans gave no legal rights to deaf people who could not speak. They could not make wills or grant freedom from slavery, and guardians were required to watch over their affairs. The Christian church from the time of St. Augustine to the Middle Ages believed that deaf people could not go to heaven because they could not say the sacraments. In the 1880s, persons in New York who were born deaf and could not speak were not allowed to vote. In many states, deaf persons were not permitted to make business contracts.

Stigmatization and Attitudes toward Deafness

The condition of deafness has little visibility until the deaf person begins to communicate with others, either deaf or hearing. In communicating with a hearing person, the difficulty the deaf person has in understanding the hearing person's speech is one indicator of deviance; another is that the deaf person's own speech may be unintelligible, or of an unusual vocal quality. As Meadow (1980) notes, "Many deaf persons do not use their voice because they have found that hearing people respond with fear or distaste to their vocal quality" (p. 164). Another way that deaf people reveal their condition is by using sign language, which is of special importance as the communication mode used by most deaf adults. Concern that deviance will be "revealed" to others sometimes underlies reluctance to use adaptive devices and a full range of communication modes.

What has research found in regard to the expressed attitudes of hearing persons towards deafness? Surveys conducted in the 1950s and 1960s found that the general hearing population was basically "indifferent" to deaf persons and knew virtually nothing about them (Meadow, 1980). These findings have been interpreted as a reflection of the fact that most of the general population has had very little or no contact with people who have profound, prelingual deafness. Furthermore, because deafness is an invisible disability, deaf people tend not to suffer from being objects of pity, as blind, cerebral palsied, and certain other disabled individuals often are (Vernon & Andrews, 1990). Children may have somewhat more negative attitudes towards individuals with disabilities than adults. Non-handicapped children become aware of physical handicaps in other children at about the age of four. Children tend to have negative attitudes toward persons with disabilities, and older children have more negative attitudes. Integration of children and youths with and without disabilities does not necessarily reduce the negative attitudes (Meadow, 1980). Deaf people themselves are aware of these negative attitudes, and, in fact, may think that hearing persons have even more negative attitudes toward deafness than they actually do. Attitudes of hearing people towards deafness may be changing because sign language and deafness are more frequently presented in the media, such as in the movie "Children of a Lesser God," and there are more general awareness programs presented at schools, etc., to promote understanding of disability.

These stigmatizing attitudes of larger society are important because they impact on the extent and manner in which deaf people can participate in society (Groce, 1985). They also influence psychological and social development. For example, one's self-concept is partly a reflection of experiences with others (Damon, 1984), and if general society has negative, patronizing attitudes toward deaf individuals, then their self-images are more likely to be negative. Finally, the attitudes of society probably influence the extent to which deaf people can feel pride in identifying with the deaf community. As deaf culture becomes more widely accepted and admired by all of society, it becomes correspondingly easier for deaf people to embrace it wholeheartedly.

Moores (1987) has pointed out that professionals who work with deaf individuals have taken two different views regarding their development and functioning. The first perspective is that deafness is a deviation. Until recently this perspective has been the predominant one among professionals involved in deafness. The focus is on the identification of ways in which deaf people fail to meet the norms or expectations of hearing society. There is special concern regarding the extent to which deaf persons can be made to conform to the verbal capacities of hearing persons, and the medical aspects of deafness are emphasized (Moores, 1987; Rosen, 1986). The physical dimensions of the hearing impairment are described in detail and other aspects of the deaf individual, notably the social and cultural aspects, are interpreted as consequences of the physical dimensions (Padden & Humphries, 1989).

The second perspective focuses on the identification of factors associated with healthy, optimal development of deaf persons. There is recognition of valid differences in the way that deaf people manage to lead successful lives, such as the use of American Sign Language (ASL) by many. At the same time, there is the assumption that deaf individuals have the same needs as any other people, and it is the ability to meet these needs that is important. There is greater recognition from this perspective of the disabling effects of deafness due to the limited understanding and acceptance of deafness by the general society (Rosen, 1986). This second perspective emerged first among professionals concerned with mental health and social adjustment, and is becoming increasingly prevalent among others. For example, Rohland and Meath-Lang (1984) recently considered the applicability of this perspective in audiology.

Along with changes in the perspectives of professionals, there has been increasing assertiveness and self-confidence among deaf people themselves (Rosen, 1986). Deaf people have worked for greater availability of sign language interpreters and for greater understanding and acceptance of sign language, including more sign language classes for the general public. They have also successfully campaigned for increased availability of captioned television and of telephone relay services to permit communication between TDD and voice telephone users (see Chapter 11). Deaf people have become more involved in decisions regarding all aspects of their lives. For example, the majority of members, including the chairman, of the recent Commission on Education of the Deaf, which made recommendations directly to Congress were deaf (Commission on Education of the Deaf, 1988).

Legislation, especially section 504 of the 1973 Vocational Rehabilitation Act, has increased rights to community services, education, and employment. For example, accessibility to higher education has dramatically increased largely because providers have become legally obligated to provide adequate support services such as interpreters (Rosen, 1986) (see Chapter 10).

Perhaps the most important effect of these changes has been the increased self-confidence and sense of power of deaf people themselves. They have become more comfortable and confident in asking for accommodation, appropriate programming, and educational and vocational opportunity (Rosen, 1986). It should be noted that while individuals closely associated with the deaf community have been the most active in convincing society to understand and address their needs, other hearing-impaired people have recently become more assertive. The recently formed organization, Self Help for Hard-of-Hearing People, has emerged as a vigorous information and advocacy organization. While deaf and hard-of-hearing people appreciate these recent social changes, they are by no means satisfied, given the attitudinal and discrimination barriers that remain.

Cultural Standards of Deaf People

Many, but by no means all, deaf adults identify themselves as members of the deaf community. In this highly cohesive community, members find mutual support and a "way of life." Belonging to this community is not based on extent of hearing impairment alone, but upon social and linguistic considerations as well. The following factors are associated with membership:

1. *Identification.* Members identify with the deaf community and deaf culture. They perceive themselves as belonging to the community and have positive views towards other members. This is perhaps the most important factor (Baker & Cokeley, 1980; Glickman, 1986; Higgins, 1980).

2. *Audiological.* Although the possibility of hearing people being members of the deaf community has been recognized, the vast majority of members have a significant hearing impairment. Persons with hearing impairment tend to identify with the community more deeply and accept its values more rapidly (Baker & Cokely, 1980).

3. *Political.* This refers to the extent an individual is involved in political activities that affect the deaf community. A person holding a state-level position in the National Association of the Deaf would be an example of political involvement (Baker & Cokely, 1980).

4. *Linguistic.* Persons with greater fluency in American Sign Language are more accepted by the deaf community than those with less fluency (Baker & Cokely, 1980).

5. *Social.* This refers to the extent the person participates in the social functions of the community. There are many organizations within the deaf community, including clubs, churches, school alumni associations, and sports groups. Social participation also refers to the extent of involvement in the informal social activities of the community (Baker & Cokeley, 1980; Higgins, 1980; Rosen, 1986). One piece of evidence of the social commitment is the high degree of intermarriage among deaf persons, about 87 percent (Schein & Delk, 1974).

6. *Shared Experience.* This refers to the extent the person shares common experiences with other members of the community. These include the frustrations in communicating with hearing persons, negative attitudes of some hearing persons, difficulties in participating in family activities as a child when all other members were hearing, being educated in a special class for deaf children, etc. Another shared experience, especially among older deaf adults, is attendance at a state residential school (Higgins, 1980).

Perhaps the most central feature of the deaf community is its sign language. Recently ASL has been viewed as a language of its own rather than as a form less grammatical than English (see Chapter 2). With the recognition of ASL, practitioners have taken greater pride in its use (Padden & Humphries, 1989; Rosen, 1986). Members of the deaf community have viewed use of the language as an indication of acceptance of deafness and commitment to the deaf world. Use shows willingness to expose to the hearing world one's personal commitment to the deaf culture, rather than trying to hide it; to be skilled, one must use it regularly, which generally means extensive association with other deaf people (Higgins, 1980).

The culture of the deaf community includes a "vocabulary" or set of symbols for describing the commonalties among members of the community and the relationship between it and hearing society. Some of these words are either unfamiliar to most hearing persons or are used in completely different ways. Padden and Humphries (1989) provide numerous examples of this. One example is the term, "hard-of-hearing."

"Little" and "very" hard-of-hearing have different meanings than the medical ones predominant in hearing society in the social context of the deaf community. From the deaf culture perspective, "little hard-of-hearing" means being "more deaf" than "very hard-of-hearing," which means being socially more oriented to the hearing culture. Thus, the deviation is in terms of what is different from being culturally deaf, rather in terms of what is different from being hearing.

Interaction between Deaf and Hearing Persons

It is difficult to generalize about interactions between deaf and hearing persons because the nature and outcome depend on the characteristics of the deaf and of the hearing individuals involved and the setting. Characteristics of deaf persons that affect the outcome include knowledge of sign language, intelligibility of speech, lip-reading ability, use of residual hearing, knowledge of conventions and expectations of hearing society, and assertiveness. Characteristics of the hearing person include clarity of mouth movement and patience. In general, hearing persons rarely understand deafness or know sign language or fingerspelling. In addition, deaf persons generally do better in one-to-one than in group settings, and if the deaf person makes use of residual hearing, communication is more difficult in a noisy environment.

When there are difficulties in the encounter, they occur largely because the deaf person must lipread the hearing person's speech and because the hearing person has difficulty understanding the deaf person's speech. There are additional factors, however, that impact considerably upon the encounter. Much strain is due to the failure of assumptions and routine practices that the persons generally use for successful interaction. (Higgins, 1980). For example, it is perfectly acceptable for hearing persons to avoid eye contact when communicating with each other, but this makes communication considerably more difficult for the deaf person. For instance, at a ticket counter, the clerk will generally look at the ticket and talk simultaneously rather than looking at the traveler's face. Another assumption is that the receiver of a message should be able to "get it" quickly, and thus, requests of a deaf person that a message be repeated may be met with little understanding or patience (Higgins, 1980; Vernon & Andrews, 1990). In addition, hearing persons may be distracted by the deaf person's voice quality or just the fact that he or she is deaf. These distractions may interfere with the hearing person's concentration and hinder understanding of the deaf person's speech. The strained interaction that often occurs between deaf and hearing persons has been compared to encounters between foreigners and natives (Higgins, 1980).

In interacting with hearing people, the deaf person may use a coping strategy which does not reveal the condition of deafness, or one which does. An example of a strategy which does not reveal the deafness is pretending to understand, such as smiling and nodding the head when the grocery store clerk gives a greeting. Strategies that reveal the deafness include telling the person to speak more slowly, using paper and pencil, and having an interpreter (Higgins, 1980). In general, it is desirable for the deafness to be disclosed when more than a brief encounter is required, and failure to do so may make the interaction even more strained.

Implications Relative to Work

When interaction between deaf and hearing persons is strained and impersonal, it may encourage negative attitudes toward deafness among hearing persons and lowered expectations of successful interaction in the future. Certain steps can reduce the extent of negative encounters: (1) The hearing persons can be provided information on deafness, ideally before meeting the deaf person; (2) the deaf individual can provide suggestions for positive interaction; and (3) for situations where communication is especially important, an interpreter can be used. The deaf person's place of employment is particularly appropriate for carrying out these steps, given the limited number of hearing co-workers and their long-term contact with the deaf person.

Information for hearing persons about deafness may help break down stereotypes about deafness that focus on disability and point out the competencies of the workers. Information may be presented regarding the high value deaf persons have attached to work, their excellent safety records, and the favorable impressions they make on hearing co-workers (Bolton & Brown, 1973; Vernon, 1981; Steffanic, 1983). In addition, information about what deaf people can specifically accomplish in a particular job may foster more positive attitudes because employers often underestimate the variety of tasks deaf workers can skillfully perform, as well as their safety records and dependability (Phillips, 1976). Information on communication strategies might include such items as the importance of getting the deaf person's attention before starting communication, likely ways the deaf person will communicate, situations of greatest communication difficulty, and encouragement of the learning of sign language (see Chapter 11).

Deaf persons may also be helped to function more effectively at work through information sharing and discussion. Although it is certainly appropriate for many deaf people to center their social lives around the deaf community, there is a need for an appreciation of the importance of satisfactory interaction with hearing co-workers. Garretson (1969) suggested that deaf workers who value interactions with hearing co-workers are more likely to adjust successfully to work than individuals who shun such interaction. It is also desirable for deaf workers to have realistic self-estimates regarding the nature (paper-and-pencil, speech, etc.) and level of communication that can be achieved. If self-estimates of communication skill are below actual communication proficiency, the worker may be unwilling to communicate with hearing co-workers in some situations where successful interaction is possible; on the other hand, if self-estimates of communication skills are too high, the deaf person may use an inappropriate communication strategy and experience frustration and despair (McKee, Stinson, & Blake, 1984).

Many deaf workers have reported at least one incident where they felt they were treated unfairly (Foster, 1987). In order to confront such situations appropriately, deaf workers would benefit from information regarding their rights as workers and strategies for addressing perceived discrimination.

MENTAL HEALTH ISSUES

Emotional Disturbance in the Deaf Population

Most of the literature on the prevalence of emotional disturbance among deaf individuals has dealt with children. Prevalence has ranged from six to eight percent in the Annual Survey of Hearing-Impaired Youth to 20 to 30 percent in studies of small populations (Greenberg & Kusche, 1989; Meadow, 1980; Wolff & Harkins, 1986). The analysis of Annual Survey data for the years 1982–83 was based on a population of 53,899 and found that 5.8 percent were classified as having emotional or behavioral problems (Wolff & Harkins, 1986).

Are the rates of emotional disturbance for deaf children higher than those for hearing ones? Research bearing on this question has yielded contradictory findings. Several studies have concluded that deaf children are not as emotionally well-adjusted as hearing children (Meadow, 1980; Wolff & Harkins, 1986); a few other studies, however, have concluded that there is no difference in the emotional adjustment of the two groups (Meadow, 1976b; Meadow, 1984). One important consideration here is whether the study used a measure originally developed for hearing children or one specially developed for deaf ones, because measures developed for hearing children may inappropriately identify certain behaviors of deaf children as indicative of disturbance. In this context, the study by Meadow (1984) is to be noted because it employed a measure that was specially developed to assess the socio-emotional adjustment of deaf preschoolers. Teachers' ratings of the extent of behavioral problems among deaf preschool children three to six years of age were compared with those of hearing peers. Teachers assigned similar ratings to the two groups.

Another question pertaining to emotional disturbance is whether deaf and hearing children show a different set of behavior problems. Research studies tell us that, with few exceptions, deaf children seem to show the same behavioral problems as hearing children (Greenberg & Kusche, 1989; Hirschorn & Schaittjer, 1979; Reivich & Rothrock, 1972). In general, these exceptions have to do with communication difficulties. For example, disturbed deaf children may avoid eye contact in order to refuse to communicate, or make disturbing noises, such as screeching (Meadow, 1976b). Such actions, however, appear to make up only a small proportion of the problem behaviors of deaf children.

Hospitalization for Mental Illness

In the late 1950s when inpatient mental health services for deaf people were first established in New York state, the rate of hospitalization for mental illness was three times greater for the deaf than for the hearing population. Because staff could not communicate with the patients, there was frequent misdiagnosis, such as "psychosis combined with mental deficiency." In addition, many patients remained hospitalized for long periods. Following appropriate treatment of deaf patients, the number requiring hospitalization was reduced to a level comparable to that for hearing people (Altshuler & Abdullah, 1981).

The deaf population is also comparable to the population at large with respect to the prevalence of schizophrenia. Altshuler and Rainer (1963) found that 52 percent of their deaf psychiatric patients were suffering from schizophrenia compared to 56 percent of hearing patients in New York psychiatric hospitals. They also reported that the proportion of deaf persons hospitalized for schizophrenia in New York State (2.5 percent) was only slightly higher than that for hearing persons (1 to 2 percent). In a further study, Altshuler and Sarlin (1963) compared the likelihood of schizophrenia for families with a deaf member who was schizophrenic with that for families with a hearing schizophrenic and found that the risk of having the disorder was similar for both groups. Thus, deafness per se did not increase the risk of schizophrenia.

Altshuler and Abdullah (1981) have described the following types of mental illness as most frequently requiring hospitalization of deaf patients. Schizophrenia was most prevalent—it is also the most common diagnosis for hearing patients requiring hospitalization for emotional disturbance. Depressive and manic depressive psychoses followed in prevalence. It is important to note that severe depressions generally manifest themselves somewhat differently in deaf patients. Among hearing patients there is often a slowing of movement and delusions of guilt; in contrast, severe depressions in deaf patients "are more likely to show a good deal of anxious agitation, activity levels near or above normal, and often somatic bodily preoccupations" (Altshuler & Abdullah, 1981, p. 102).

Persons characterized by Altshuler and Abdullah (1981) as having "immature, underdeveloped personalities" were also among the hospitalized deaf. These patients have generally had very limited life experiences and may be extremely dependent upon their parents. They may have been kept at home and severely restricted from participating in everyday life experiences that would have facilitated maturation.

Childhood behavior disorders account for additional hospitalizations and frequently stem from difficult family relationships that are possibly intensified by the individual's having an additional disability. These children may be difficult to discharge following hospitalization because families may not want them back.

The final group described by Altschuler and Abdullah (1981) was comprised of persons experiencing situational maladjustments which require hospitalization because of an unusually stressful set of life circumstances that temporarily exceeds their ability to cope.

Treatment Issues

Important features of therapy for seriously disturbed clients include psychotherapy and drugs for those with schizophrenia or manic depressive psychoses. Therapy is individually tailored to the patient (Altshuler & Abdullah, 1981). Direct communication between the therapist and patient is important. For patients who use sign language, the therapist must be sufficiently skilled in the modality so that the patient can express him or herself freely, and the therapist must have some understanding of the world view of the patient in order to empathize (Stewart, 1981). It is also important to prepare the patient to transfer back to the community outside the hospital. It is desirable if the rehabilitation counselor can become part of the mental health team while the patient is still under treatment. It may be helpful to explore the patient's vocational skills and interests and to begin vocational skills training prior to discharge. Training in communication and academic skills is also frequently helpful. A halfway house may be useful as an interim living arrangement (Altshuler & Abdullah, 1981; Rainer & Altshuler, 1970; Moores, 1987).

Deaf individuals with less severe problems, such as high anxiety or difficulty in coping with a particularly stressful situation, should be able to receive specialized outpatient treatment. Families with deaf children frequently have problems with adaptation to deafness and communication, and if these can be dealt with successfully, development of more serious difficulties later may be prevented (Meadow, 1980). The research evidence reviewed earlier in this chapter clearly indicates that successful adaptation and establishment of good communication is important for development of competence in deaf children. Deaf people also sometimes need help in coping with certain situations, such as handling sexuality, adapting to a new school, or a change in work setting, that in combination with deafness, are quite stressful (Rayson, 1987). Assistance from a professional who is knowledgeable in the developmental effects of deafness and who can communicate effectively is likely to result in greater subsequent health.

Healthiness of Most Deaf People

In thinking about the mental health aspects of deafness, it is important to keep in mind the essential healthiness of most deaf individuals. There may be more frequent behavior problems among deaf than hearing children, which may reflect difficulties in communication, frustration in learning English, problems in adaptation to deafness by the child's family, and the general lack of understanding of deafness by society. In addition, Furth (1973) and Lane (1989) have suggested that since identification of behavioral problems is often based upon ratings by teachers, the higher incidence figures may also reflect teachers' strain from difficulty in instructing deaf children. Furthermore, the group of children identified as having behavioral problems constitutes a rather small proportion of deaf children. Turning to adults, there appears to be rather limited data on the continuum of emotional adjustment from psychoses to "normal" mental health. The available data indicate that the rates of psychoses and hospitalization for mental illness are no greater for deaf than for hearing persons.

One interpretation of these results is that whatever obstacles the deaf child may have faced in growing up, they do not generally produce permanent, disabling effects upon personal and social functioning as adults. The fact that deaf people function so well in society in spite of these communication difficulties and misunderstandings is testimony to their strength and resilience. Terms such as dependency and impulsiveness often seen in the literature on deafness and mental health have frequently been based on impressions of persons seen for treatment of behavior problems, and use of these terms may have been overly generalized to other deaf persons (Moores, 1987).

Deaf individuals function in everyday life in much the same way as hearing people do (Moores, 1987). They show low crime rates and few driving violations. They show high rates of marital stability and adjustment. They have a high degree of job stability. A high percentage of deaf people vote and attend church or synagogue. Most deaf people live active, outgoing lives. They are fond of social activities, travel, and gossip. They usually have close friends and actively participate in clubs (Furth, 1973).

CONCLUSIONS

This chapter has selectively reviewed research findings on the affective and social development of deaf people. Much attention has been devoted to factors associated with optimal psychological functioning and to findings that demonstrate the importance of individual differences. The most important points raised were the following:

1. Readers should be sensitive to the difficulties in conducting research on the affective and social development of deaf individuals. Major problems are the diversity of the research population, methodological difficulties, and recent changes in educational practices and social climate.

2. While the absence of auditory input and delay in acquisition of spoken language may influence affective development to some extent, it is very difficult to disentangle these influences from the predominant one: that of the social environment—parents, teachers, and peers. For example, the way that language deficiency exerts its greatest influence on the child's personal and social development is through the consequences of limited communication between the child and others.

3. For parents, rearing a deaf child requires new perspectives, new communication skills, and much adaptability. It is important for parents to accept their child's deafness and differences. It is desirable that they find means to communicate effectively with their child; such communication often includes using sign language. In addition, parents who are able to challenge their deaf child and to hold high expectations, while at the same time providing needed support and encouragement, are more likely to rear motivated, competent children.

4. Deaf parents have been effective in rearing deaf children, in part due to their ready acceptance of the child and establishment of effective communication.

5. The two predominant educational settings for deaf children are residential schools and classes in regular schools. Although residential schools have certain limitations, such as possible restrictions in social independence compared to hearing students, they offer presence of a large number of deaf peers and opportunities to participate in many activities. In contrast, there is concern that students in mainstream programs do not always receive adequate educational and social support. However, if students have the necessary skills and receive adequate support, they may benefit from the mainstream setting.

6. Personality characteristics that have been the focus of research for deaf people include social maturity, social-cognitive ability, self-esteem, and locus of control. For all of these characteristics there are as great, if not greater, individual differences among deaf children and youths as among hearing ones. Individual differences in these characteristics are related to adjustment and achievement. For example, individual differences in self-esteem and locus of control have been associated with various measures of competent performance, including scores on standardized achievement tests, grades, and successful adjustment at work.

7. Comparisons between deaf and hearing persons on measures of personality characteristics are often of questionable value. In most cases the measures were developed for hearing persons and different mean scores for the two groups do not necessarily imply a discrepancy in the quality of adjustment.

8. Deaf people face a number of barriers to participation in general society. Historically, deafness has been viewed as a deviant, undesirable condition. In numerous instances this has meant that deaf people have been deprived of various rights, such as that to vote and to conduct business transactions. Current difficulties include communication barriers between deaf and hearing persons, the lack of understanding of deafness by hearing persons and the tendency of hearing persons to unsuccessfully use some of the same practices in interacting with deaf persons that they would with hearing persons, such as not always looking directly at the "listener."

9. Most deaf people belong to the deaf community in which members find mutual support and a "way of life." Belonging to this community is based upon attitudinal, audiological, political, linguistic, social, and experiential factors.

10. While behavior problems may possibly occur a little more frequently among deaf children than among hearing ones, the rates of psychoses and hospitalization for mental illness among deaf adults are not greater than those for hearing persons. The vast majority of deaf individuals make a successful adaptation to their disability and live normal lives in much the same way as hearing people do.

The extent to which deaf individuals have experienced optimal affective and social development is relevant to successful vocational rehabilitation. The likelihood of individuals succeeding in rehabilitation programs, and subsequently on the job, depends not only on the quality of the program, but also on the self-perceptions, motivations, competencies, and other personal resources that they can draw upon. For this reason, all the parental, educational, and social influences that shape individuals' character are relevant to their rehabilitation and vocational adjustment. For this reason also, an understanding of affective and social development is important to rehabilitation counselors as they help their clients to make the most of their abilities.

REFERENCES

Alpern, G.D., & Boll, T.J. (1972). *The developmental profile.* Indianapolis: Psychological Development Publications.

Altshulter, K.Z., & Abdullah, S. (1981). Mental health and the deaf adult. In L. Stein, E. Mindel, & T. Jabaley (Eds.), *Deafness and mental health.* New York: Grune & Stratton.

Altshuler, K.Z., Deming, W.E., Vollenweider, J., Rainer, J.D. & Tendler, R. (1976). Impulsivity and profound early deafness: A cross-cultural inquiry. *American Annals of the Deaf, 121,* 331–345.

Altshuler, K.Z., & Rainer, J.D. (1963). Distribution and diagnosis of patients in New York State mental hospitals. In J. Rainier, K. Altshuler, F. Kallman & W. Deming (Eds.), *Family and mental health problems in a deaf population.* New York: Columbia University Press.

Altshuler, K.Z., & Sarlin, M.B. (1963). Deafness and schizophrenia: A family study. In J. Rainer, K. Altshuler, F. Kallman, & W. Deming (Eds.), *Family and mental health problems in a deaf population.* New York: Columbia University Press.

Andrisani, P.J., & Nestle, G. (1976). Internal-external control as contributes to an outcome of work experience. *Journal of Applied Psychology, 61,* 156–165.

Baker, C., & Cokeley, D. (1980). *American sign language: A teacher's resource guide on grammar and culture.* Silver Spring, MD: T.J. Publishers.

Bartel, N.R., & Guskin, S.L. (1980). Handicap as a social phenomenon. In W. Cruickshank (Ed.), *Psychology of exceptional children and youth.* Englewood Cliffs, NJ: Prentice-Hall, Inc.

Betz, E.L. (1977). Vocational behavior and career development, 1976: A review. *Journal of Vocational Behavior, 11,* 129–152.

Bodner, B., & Johnson, J. (1977). Personality and hearing impairment: A study in locus of control. *Volta Review, 79,* 362–372.

Bolton, B., & Brown, K. (1973). The development of an instrument to assess work attitudes of deaf rehabilitation clients. *Journal of Rehabilitation of the Deaf, 4,* 18–24.

Chess, S., Korn, S.J., & Fernandez, P.B. (1971). *Psychiatric disorders of children with congenital rubella.* New York: Brunner-Mazel.

Commission on Education of the Deaf (1988). *Toward equality: Education of the deaf.* Washington, DC: Government Printing Office.

Covington, M.U., & Berry, R. (1976). *Self-worth and school learning.* New York: Holt, Rinehart and Winston.

Craig, H.B. (1965). A sociometric investigation of the self-concept of the deaf child. *American Annals of the Deaf, 115,* 79–85.

Damon, W. (1984). *Social and personality development,* New York: W.W. Norton & Co.

Davis, J. (1986). Academic placement in perspective. In D. Luterman (Ed.), *Deafness in perspective.* San Diego, CA: College Hill Press.

Doll, E.A. (1965). *Vineland social maturity scale: A condensed manual of directions.* Circle Pines, MN: American Guidance Service.

Dowaliby, F., Burke, N., & McKee, B. (1983). A comparison of hearing-impaired and normally hearing students on locus of control, people orientation, and study habits and attitudes. *American Annals of the Deaf, 128,* 53–59.

Dowaliby, F.J., & Saur, R. (1984). *Locus of control characteristics of mainstreamed students.*

Paper presented at the annual meeting of the New England Educational Research Organization, Rockport, ME.

Emerton, G., Hurwitz, A., & Bishop, M. (1979). Development of social maturity in deaf adolescents and adults. In L. Bradford & W. Hardy (Eds.), *Hearing and hearing impairment.* New York: Grune & Stratton.

Erikson, E.H. (1968). *Identity: Youth and crisis.* New York: W.W. Norton.

Evans, A. (1975). Experiential deprivation: Unresolved factor in the impoverished socialization of deaf school children in residence. *American Annals of the Deaf, 120,* 545–552.

Farrugia, D., & Austin, G. (1980). A study of socio-emotional adjustment patterns of hearing-impaired students in different educational settings. *American Annals of the Deaf, 110,* 456–478.

Foster, S. (1988). Life in the mainstream: Reflections of deaf college freshmen on their experiences in the mainstreamed high school. *Journal of Rehabilitation of the Deaf, 22,* 37–56.

Foster, S. (1987). Employment experiences of deaf college graduates: An interview study. *Journal of Rehabilitation of the Deaf, 21,* 1–15.

Freeman, R., Malkin, S.F., & Hastings, J.O. (1975). Psychosocial problems of deaf children and their families: A comparative study. *American Annals of the Deaf, 120,* 391–405.

Furth, H. (1973). *Deafness and learning: A psychosocial approach.* Belmont, CA: Wadsworth Publishing Co.

Garretson, M.D. (1969). Social adjustment of deaf school learners in the United States. *Journal of Rehabilitation of the Deaf, 2,* 42–50.

Garrison, W., Tesch, S., & DeCaro, P. (1978). An assessment of self-concept levels among postsecondary deaf adolescents. *American Annals of the Deaf, 123,* 968–975.

Georgopoulos, B., Mahoney, G., & Jones, N. (1957). A path-goal approach to productivity. *Journal of Applied Psychology, 41,* 345–353.

Glickman, N. (1986). Cultural identity, deafness and mental health. *Journal of Rehabilitation of the Deaf, 20,* 1–10.

Goffman, E. (1963). *Stigma: Notes on the management of spoiled identity.* Englewood Cliffs, NJ: Prentice-Hall, Inc.

Greenberg, M.T. (1980). Social interaction between deaf preschoolers and their mothers: The effects of communication method and communication competence. *Developmental Psychology, 16,* 465–474.

Greenberg, M.T. (1983). Family stress and child competence: The effects of early intervention for families with deaf infants. *American Annals of the Deaf, 128,* 407–417.

Greenberg, M.T., & Kusche, C.A. (1989). Cognitive, personal, and social development of deaf children and adolescents. In M. Wang, M. Reynolds, & H. Walberg (Eds.), *Handbook of special education: Research and practice.* New York: Pergamon Press.

Groce, N.A. (1985). *Everyone here spoke sign language.* Cambridge, MA: Harvard University Press.

Guilfoyle, G.R., Schapiro, F.H., Katz-Hansen, L., & Lerman, A. (1973). *The evaluation of vocational development of deaf young adults.* Final Report to Social and Rehabilitation Services, Department of Health, Education, and Welfare. Lexington School for the Deaf, New York.

Harris, R.I. (1978). Impulse control in deaf children: Research and clinical issues. In L. Liben (Ed.), *Deaf children: developmental perspectives.* New York: Academic Press.

Higgins, P.C. (1980). *Outsiders in a hearing world.* Beverly Hills, CA: Sage Publications.

Hirschorn, A., & Schaittjer, C.J. (1979). Dimensions of problem behavior in deaf children. *Journal of Abnormal Child Psychology, 7,* 221–228.

Jensema, C.J., & Trybus, R. (1975). *Reported emotional/behavioral problems among hearing-impaired children in special educational programs: United States 1972–1973.* Series R, Number 1, Washington, DC: Office of Demographic Studies, Gallaudet College.

Joiner, L.M., Erickson, E.L., & Crittenden, J.B. (1966). Occupational plans and aspirations of deaf adolescents. *Journal of Rehabilitation of the Deaf, 2,* 20–26.

Joiner, L.M., Erickson, E.L., Crittenden, J.B., & Stevenson, V.M. (1966). Predicting the academic achievement of the acoustically impaired using intelligence and self-concept of academic ability. *Journal of Special Education, 3,* 425–431.

Koelle, W.H., & Convey, J.J. (1982). The prediction of achievement of deaf adolescents form self-concept and locus of control measures. *American Annals of the Deaf, 127,* 769–779.

Kusche, C.A., Garfield, T.S., & Greenberg, M.T. (1983). The understanding of emotional and social attributions in deaf adolescents. *Journal of Clinical Child Psychology, 12,* 153–160.

Ladd, G.W., Munson, J.L., & Miller, J.K. (1984). Social integration of deaf adolescents in secondary level mainstreaming programs. *Exceptional Children, 50,* 420–429.

Lane, H. (1989). Is there a "Psychology of the deaf?" *Exceptional Children, 55,* 7–19.

Lerman, A.M., & Guilfoyle, G.R. (1970). *The development of prevocational behavior in deaf adolescents.* New York: Teachers College Press.

Levine, E.S., & Wagner, G.E. (1974). Personality patterns of deaf persons. *Perceptual and Motor Skills.* (Monograph Supplement 4–V39).

Levinson, K. (1984). Job mobility for the hearing-impaired: The next challenge in mainstreaming. *Volta Review, 86,* 85–98.

Liben, L. (1978). Developmental perspectives on the experiential deficiencies of deaf children. In L. Liben (ed.), *Deaf children: Developmental perspectives.* New York: Academic Press.

McKee, B., Stinson, M., & Blake, R. (1984). Perceived versus measured communication skills of hearing-impaired college students. *Journal of Rehabilitation of the Deaf, 18,* 19–24.

Maestas y Moores, J. (1980). Early linguistic environment. *Sign Language Studies, 26,* 1–13.

Meadow, K.P. (1968). Early manual communication in relation to the deaf child's intellectual, social and communicative functioning. *American Annals of the Deaf, 113,* 29–41.

Meadow, K.P. (1969). Self-image, family climate, and deafness. *Social Forces, 47,* 428–438.

Meadow, K.P. (1976a). Personality and social development of deaf persons. In B. Bolton (Ed.), *Psychology of deafness for rehabilitation counselors.* Baltimore, MD: University Park Press.

Meadow, K.P.(1976b). Behavioral problems of deaf children. In H. Schlesinger & K. Meadow (Eds.), *Studies of family interaction, language acquisition and deafness.* San Francisco: University of California S.F. Final Report, Office of Maternal and Child Health, Bureau of Community Health Services.

Meadow, K.P. (1980). *Deafness and child development.* Berkeley, CA: University of California Press.

Meadow, K.P. (1984). Social adjustment of preschool children: Deaf and hearing: With and without other handicaps. *Topics in Early Childhood Special Education, 3, 4,* 27–40.

Meadow, K.P., Greenberg, M.T., Erting, C., & Carmichael, H.S. (1981). Interactions of deaf mothers and deaf preschool children: Comparisons with three other groups of deaf and hearing dyads. *American Annals of the Deaf, 126,* 454–468.

Meadow, K.P., & Trybus, R.J. (1979). Behavioral and emotional problems of deaf children: An overview. In L. Bradford & W. Hardy (Eds.), *Hearing and hearing-impairment.* New York: Grune & Stratton, Inc.

Meath-Lang, B., Caccamise, F., & Albertini, J. (1982). Deaf persons' views of their English language learning. In H. Hoemann & R. Wilbur (Eds.), *Interpersonal communication and deaf people,* 295–329. Washington, DC: Gallaudet College.

Mertens, D. (1986). *Social development for hearing-impaired high school youth.* Paper presented at the annual meeting of the American Educational Research Association, San Francisco, CA.

Mertens, D. (1989). Social experiences of hearing-impaired high school youth. *American Annals of the Deaf, 134,* 15–19.

Moores, D.F. (1987). *Educating the deaf: Psychology, principles, and practices* (3rd edition). Boston: Houghton Mifflin Co.

Moores, D., & Kluwin, T. (1986). Issues in school placement. In A. Schildroth & M. Karchmer (Eds.), *Deaf children in America.* San Diego, CA: College-Hill Press.

Osipow, S.H. (1973). *Theories of career development* (2nd edition). Englewood Cliffs, NJ: Prentice-Hall, Inc.

Osipow, S.H. (1975). The relevance of theories of career development to special groups: Problems, needed data, and implications. In S. Picou & R. Campbell (Eds.), *Career behavior of special groups.* Columbus, OH: Charles E. Merrill.

Padden, C., & Humphries, T. (1989). *Deaf in America,* Cambridge, MA: Harvard University Press.

Phillips, G.B. (1976). An exploration of employer attitudes concerning employment opportunities for deaf people. *Journal of Rehabilitation of the Deaf, 9,* 1–9.

Quarrington, B., & Solomon, B. (1975). A current study of the social maturity of deaf students. *Canadian Journal of Behavioral Science, 7,* 70–77.

Quigley, S.P., & Frisina, D.R. (1961). Institutionalization and psychoeducational development of deaf children. *Council for Exceptional Children Research Monographs,* Series A, No. 3.

Quigley, S.P., & Kretchmer, R.E. (1982). *The education of deaf children: Issues, theory and practice.* Baltimore: University Park Press.

Quigley, S.P., & Paul, P.V. (1984). *Language and deafness.* San Diego, CA: College Hill Press.

Rainer, J.D., & Altshuler, K.Z. (1970). Expanded mental health care for the deaf. *Rehabilitation and Prevention.* New York: New York State Psychiatric Institute.

Rayson, B. (1987). Emotional illness and the deaf. In E. Mindel & M. Vernon (Eds.), *They grow in silence: Understanding deaf children and adults* (2nd edition). Boston, MA: College-Hill Press.

Recommendations 3 to 9 from report of Commission on Education of the Deaf (1988, April). *The Special Educator, 3,* (18), 5–20.

Reivich, R.S., & Rothrock, I.A. (1972). Behavior problems of deaf children and adolescents: A factor-analytic study. *Journal of Speech and Hearing Research, 15,* 93–104.

Rohland, P., & Meath-Lang, B. (1984). Perceptions of deaf adults regarding audiological services. *Journal of the Academy of Rehabilitative Audiology, 17,* 130–150.

Rosen, R. (1986). Deafness: A social perspective. In D. Luterman (Ed.), *Deafness in perspective.* San Diego, CA: College-Hill Press.

Schein, J.D., & Delk, M.T. (1974). *The deaf population of the United States.* Silver Spring, MD: National Association of the Deaf.

Schildroth, A.N. (1988). Recent changes in the educational placement of deaf students. *American Annals of the Deaf, 133,* 61–67.

Schlesinger, H.S. (1972). Meaning and enjoyment: Language acquisition of deaf children. In T. O'Rouke (Ed.), *Psycholinguistics and total communication: The state of the art.* Washington, DC: American Annals of the Deaf.

Schlesinger, H.S. (1978). The effects of deafness on childhood development: An Eriksonian perspective. In L. Liben (Ed.), *Deaf children: Developmental perspectives.* New York: Academic Press.

Schlesinger, H.S. (1987). Effects of powerlessness on dialogue and development: Disability, poverty and the human condition. In B. Heller, L. Flohr, & L. Zegans (Eds.), *Expanding horizons: Psychosocial interventions with sensorily disabled persons.* New York: Grune & Stratton.

Schlesinger, H.S., & Meadow, K.P. (1971). *Deafness and mental health: A developmental approach.* San Francisco: Langley Porter Neuropsychiatric Institute.

Schlesinger, H.S., & Meadow, K.P. (1972). *Sign and sound: Childhood deafness and mental health.* Berkeley, CA: University of California Press.

Schlesinger, H.S., & Meadow, K.P. (Eds.) (1976). *Studies of family interaction, language acquisition, and deafness.* San Francisco: University of California, S.F. Final Report, Office of Maternal and Child Health, Bureau of Community Health Services.

Schroedel, J.G., & Schiff, W. (1972). Attitudes towards deafness among several deaf and hearing populations. *Rehabilitation Psychology, 19,* 59–70.

Steffanic, D. (1983). *Reasonable accommodations for deaf employees in white collar jobs.* Silver Spring, MD: National Association of the Deaf.

Stewart, L. (1981). Counseling the deaf client. In L. Stein, E. Mindel, & T. Jabaley (Eds.), *Deafness and mental health.* New York: Grune & Stratton.

Stinson, M.S. (1978). Deafness and motivation for achievement: Research with implications for parent counseling. *Volta Review, 80,* 140–148.

Stinson, M.S. (1984). Research on motivation in educational settings: Implications for hearing-impaired students. *Journal of Special Education, 18,* 178–198.

Vernon, M. (1981). Employment, deafness and mental health. In L. Stein, E. Mindel, & T. Jabaley (Eds.), *Deafness and mental health.* New York: Grune & Stratton.

Vernon, M., & Andrews, J. (1990). *Psychology of deafness: Understanding deaf and hard-of-hearing people.* New York: Longman.

Vroom, V.H. (1964). *Work and motivation.* New York: Wiley.

Walberg, H.J., & Uguroglu, M.E. (1979). Motivation and educational productivity: Theories, results, and implications. In L. Fyans, Jr. (Ed.), *Achievement motivation: Recent trends in theory and research.* New York: Plenum.

Wolff, A.B., & Harkins, J.E. (1986). Multihandicapped students. In A. Schildroth & M. Karchmer (Eds.), *Deaf children in America.* San Diego, CA: College-Hill Press.

Young, E.P., & Brown, S.L. (1981). *The development of social-cognition in deaf preschool children: A pilot study.* Paper presented at the Annual Meeting of the Southeastern Psychological Association, Atlanta, GA.

▶ 5

The Post-Secondary Transition: From School to Independent Living

HELEN B. CRAIG
Center On Deafness: Western Pennsylvania School for the Deaf

ROSEMARY P. GARRITY
Center On Deafness: Western Pennsylvania School for the Deaf

"Transition," as the bridge between secondary school and post-school life, has become a national priority for youth with disabilities, with sustained employment as the targeted destination. This span, toward independent living, personal, social, and community adjustment, has proved difficult enough even for persons with no disabling conditions. For young people with hearing loss, the chasm to be bridged is frequently greatly magnified, enlarged not only by communication misunderstandings but by critical deficiencies in the essential literacy skills required in the workforce today. For many, the process of leaving school requires a vast experiential leap—from comfortable interactions with teachers and peers to unpredictable communication demands; from concerned service provision to impersonal competition; from scheduled consistency to the chaos of choice. These young people, whether seeking immediate employment or competitive post-secondary education, need concentrated assistance in building their own bridges toward self-sufficiency. This chapter describes the increasing number of options available to assist in this transition.

AN HISTORICAL PERSPECTIVE

Historically, post-school transition is a relatively recent concern, precipitated in part by the Industrial Revolution and its aftermath. Prior to 1900 and the child labor laws, the separation between schooling and work, or between work and everyday family living, was much less distinct than it is today. Communities were agrarian and small; work roles were relatively well defined; and children assumed adult responsibilities at an early age. Increased specialization, the demand for greater preparation, and, in part, a need to keep surplus (child) labor out of the workforce, led to a longer custodial or learning period, a greater delay between childhood and adult roles (Grant, 1988). For some, this transitional period has been used to prepare for improved opportunities, for skilled and effective employment, to learn new roles and responsibilities. For others, it has become instead a period of "floundering" (Osterman, 1980), with limited opportunities, insufficient guidance, increased discouragement, diminished status, and lowered self-esteem.

In 1989, 87 perecent of all 16- to 24-year-old non-disabled school leavers had at least completed high school (National Center for Education Statistics, 1989), and the transitional route reported for over half (56 percent) of these young people was post-secondary education (Wagner, 1989). However, of students who were deaf, 48 percent nationwide were reported to leave high school without receiving a diploma, 29 percent of these dropping out and 19 percent obtaining a certificate instead (Allen, Rawlings, & Schildroth, 1989). Both this substantial dropout rate and the diploma deficit have alarming implications for post-school placement of deaf youth, especially when employment conditions are requiring more—not less—preparation and literacy.

Education as Transition

The history of transitional incentives for deaf students in the United States may be dated from the establishment of Gallaudet College in 1864. This liberal arts college was the first post-secondary educational option specifically designed for deaf persons—a very vital option for deaf students who could qualify for college work and who could afford to move away from home, but no option at all for those who could not. Except for a few very scattered local incentives, Gallaudet remained the only such alternative until 100 years later.

In the century between 1864 and 1964, several proposals were made which addressed post-school transition for deaf persons, even though "transition" was not yet the catchword for discussion. Although not fulfilled at the time, these proposals laid the groundwork for future action, identifying the post-school problems which deaf persons could be expected to encounter and proposing solutions to prevent or remediate such problems and to make the most of the transitional period. As early as 1888, a plea was raised for a "Polytechnic Institute for Deaf-Mutes," suggesting that "higher intellectual education [as taught at Gallaudet] . . . would be well, were it not for the fact that many deaf-mutes have to earn their living as soon as they leave school" (Rogers, 1888, p. 184). In 1893, the Conference of Principals and Superintendents of American Schools for the Deaf resolved that a Technical Department should be added to the existing National College (Gallaudet) (Fay, 1892), but no action resulted (Scouten, 1984). This recommendation was repeated almost 30 years later (Morrison, 1920, p. 223), again with no action.

In 1940, a formal proposal was made for a separate "National School of Trades, Agriculture, and Technical Training for the Deaf" (Barnes, 1940a), a "cooperative job training center" which, foreshadowing the current transition initiative, would enlist the cooperation of employers from a wide variety of industries in providing actual work experience and training situations. In addition to this national post-secondary school, it was suggested that extensive "cooperative job training" be provided at the individual schools, during the high school years, enlisting the help of local employers and coordinating actual job experiences with related subject matter (Barnes, 1940b).

However, it was not until over twenty years later, as part of the increasing awareness of human rights and the federally funded "Great Society" movement of the 1960s, that these earlier visions began to be realized. The Babbidge Report to the Secretary of Health, Education and Welfare, on *Education of the Deaf* (1965), proposed not only a "national technical institute exclusively for the deaf" but also suggested the need for "federally supported regional vocational education schools" (p.50). Similar recommendations were made by the Conference of Executives of American Schools for the Deaf at their Riverside convention (CEASD, 1964), and at a National Workshop on Improved Vocational Opportunities for the Deaf, held in Knoxville, Tennessee (Schunhoff, 1964).

Legislation facilitating these recommendations was provided by P.L. 89-36, leading in 1968 to the establishment of the National Technical Institute for the Deaf at the Rochester Institute of Technology; and by P.L. 88-164 and P.L. 89-333, which authorized grants to establish Regional Postsecondary Education Programs for the Deaf. As a result of the latter grants, three regional post-secondary programs were initiated at existing junior colleges and vocational schools—Delgado Community College in New Orleans, St. Paul Technical-Vocational Institute, and Seattle Community College (Craig & Burrows, 1969). A fourth program, at California State University at Northridge, was also federally funded at this time, building on existing services for deaf persons at that university. The four regional programs are now reauthorized every five years on a competitive grant cycle; in this process, the Delgado program was replaced in the southern region in 1983, by a post-secondary education consortium centered at the University of Tennessee.

Additional legislative incentives were provided by Section 504 of the Rehabilitation Act of 1973, mandating that colleges and universities provide accessible facilities and support services for persons with handicaps (see Chapter 10), and resulting in a surge of support programs within colleges nationwide. In 1869, 36 deaf students were enrolled in the only post-secondary program available for them (Pratt & Fay, 1870); by 1988, over 6,000 were enrolled full-time in post-secondary programs with services not only available but designated especially for students with hearing loss

(Rawlings, Karchmer, & DeCaro, 1988). Not all programs are of equal quality; not all are appropriate for all students; however, all but one, Gallaudet University, represent completely new options for transitional learning, regionally accessible opportunities which did not exist prior to 1960.

Rehabilitation for Transition

Historically, the establishment of transitional rehabilitation facilities and services was even more delayed than the educational, especially for more severely affected "non-degree bound" deaf and other disabled youth. One year before Gallaudet College was established, the Hospital for the Ruptured and Crippled opened in New York, the first such program to recognize the vocational needs of crippled children (McGowan & Porter, 1967). Deafness was not mentioned here at all, and, in fact, the special needs of deaf persons within hospital settings were not recognized until the 1960s. Early rehabilitation incentives were frustrated in large part by a widespread Social Darwinism movement in the late 19th century and a related eugenics push, for selective human breeding, in the early 20th century. An emphasis on survival of the fittest and on segregation/sterilization of retarded and disturbed persons did not enhance rehabilitation efforts for disabled persons, and even residential training schools for retarded individuals were custodial only—not at all transitional. Other forces, including the Social Gospel and the American Charity Organization movements, did work toward a more rehabilitative approach, but focused on curing the "moral roots" of poverty and disability, providing advice by "friendly visitors" rather than material relief (Rubin & Roessler, 1978, p.15).

Governmental responsibility for rehabilitative efforts was first declared in 1908, by the President's Committee of the One Hundred on National Health, and money to fund these efforts was made available when the federal income tax legislation was enacted in 1913. In 1920, the first Vocational Rehabilitation Act (Smith-Fess Act) specified that vocational guidance, training, adjustment, and placement services should be provided for disabled civilians, and a series of subsequent laws increased the federal funding role.

With expanded funding came an increase in comprehensive rehabilitation centers, but most still seemed to assume that all their clients had normal hearing. The Hot Springs Rehabilitation Center in Arkansas, for example, was opened in 1961, but, because it provided no special considerations for clients who were deaf, these clients "were not helped to a great extent" (Blake, 1968). Soon, an awareness developed about the special problems of preparing deaf clients for work, and a number of projects were initiated to provide and evaluate this special support. Included among these early projects were two at Hot Springs, one in Boston, the St. Louis Jewish Vocational Services program, and Chicago Jewish Vocational Services (Bolton, 1975). The documented success of these specialized services led to an increase of funding through both the federal and state offices of vocational rehabilitation.

Theoretical Models of Transition

The transitional focus for persons with disabilities became even more sharply defined in the 1980s, as part of the federally sponsored transition model proposed by the Office of Special Education and Rehabilitative Services (OSERS) (Will, 1984). The OSERS model, used to promote and fund transitional programming initiatives, recognized two key points or "foundations" for transition—high school and employment—moving toward the sustained employment goal (and, eventually community integration) over one of three different bridges: (1) "transition without special services," using only the generic services available to anyone; (2) "transition with time-limited services," vocational rehabilitation, post-secondary vocational education, or job training; and (3) "transition with ongoing services," such as supported employment.

The OSERS model, with its focus on employment as the sole transitional target, was challenged as too narrow (Halpern, 1985). Instead, a three-pillared target was suggested, including "employment" as described in the OSERS model, but also "residential environment," including a person's home, neighborhood, safety and community services, and "social and interpersonal networks," with emphasis on communication, self-esteem, and support from family and friends (Halpern, 1985, p. 481). For young adults who are deaf, especially with the concomitant impairment in communication skills, the latter focus on community and interpersonal networks is extremely critical. It is this model which provides the focus for the current chapter.

TRANSITIONAL NEEDS AND OBJECTIVES

What then are the specific transitional needs and objectives for deaf persons? In actual practice, the needs of each will be unique, depending on such variables as degree of hearing loss, age of onset, additional handicapping conditions, intelligence level, hearing status and educational level of parents, and appropriateness of instructional program. However, basic problems and objectives may be identified which will impact upon most deaf students as they strive to reach the three targets of transition—sustained employment, social/interpersonal networks, and effective community/living environments.

The first of these needs is to strengthen and reinforce the literacy foundation, so that it can underlie, rather than undermine, the whole bridge to self-sufficiency. Second is the need to enrich and expand the cluster of psychosocial, interactive, and informational experiences which lead to development of employability, independent living, and personal/social skills. Finally, and basic to all, is the need for extended education, attuned not only to individual student needs but to each of the changing transitional targets. Each of these needs, and its corresponding objectives for intervention, is discussed below. Unfortunately, as Halpern (1985) has noted, success in achieving any one of these targets does not guarantee success in the other areas; although failure in one may very well preclude sustained success in the others.

Literacy and Communication Needs

In the transition from school to work, one of the major problems for deaf students, as identified by professionals in rehabilitation and education, is the "lack of language and reading skills [which] limit their opportunities for successful training and job placements" (Melton, 1987). In numerous studies during the past half century, the average literacy achievement of deaf students has been found to be significantly lower than that of their normally hearing peers. The frequently quoted median grade equivalent on reading comprehension, for example, is still only at the third- or fourth-grade level for deaf students nationwide, even by high school graduation (Trybus & Karchmer, 1977; Allen, 1986, p.168). Clearly, this is not true for all deaf students; but for those at or below the median point, this deficit can create overwhelming problems in making the transition to employment and independent living. Recent research on literacy with individuals with normal hearing nationwide notes that "roughly 95 percent of young adults read at or surpass the level of reading typical of the average fourth grader—the fourth grade being the standard adopted by the military almost half a century ago" (Kirsch & Jungeblut, 1989). Further, "80 percent of young adults are estimated to read as well or better than the average eighth grade student and more than 60 percent . . . as well or better than the average eleventh-grade student" (Kirsch & Jungeblut, p. 63).

The current increase in the literacy standard, as required for employment and everyday living skills today, can only exacerbate the problems for deaf students, especially those reading below the fourth-grade median. The earlier definition of "functional literacy" focused on the "surface" reading skills of letter identification, recognizing Stop signs, and writing one's own name. However, literacy has been redefined to include not only reading and writing, but also the ability "to reason effectively about what one reads or writes" (Applebee, Langer, & Mullis, 1987). In the increasingly complex workplace, with job parameters changing at least once every seven years (Applebee et al., 1987), this emphasis on the reasoning dimension of literacy becomes especially germane. In practical terms, this also raises the minimum literacy standard required in today's society and workplace to a level between eighth and eleventh grade (Skagen, 1986, p 17). For many deaf persons, another critical literacy problem can occur in their daily interactions with supervisors or peers, the "through-the-air" literacy essential both for conveying work-related information and for the casual conversations which enhance workplace satisfaction (see Chapters 2 and 11).

To meet these increasing literacy needs, programs for deaf persons are continually striving to increase the levels of both literacy and interpersonal communication. However, these have been standard objectives among programs for deaf students for many years, with little documented improvement nationwide. These objectives may, in fact, require extended and continuing education if they are to be realized.

Employability, Independent Living, and Psychosocial Needs

Literacy or academic skills, however, are not the only transitional needs of deaf students. In fact, the underlying theme of the Grant Foundation Commission's report, *The Forgotten Half* (1988), is that the non-academic, nonverbal skills of half the population in the United States are being neglected in the push for college education—especially when college is not a reasonable or desired expectation for the entire population. More flexible opportunities are recommended, an "added chance" to develop the skills and talents of tomorrow's workers (Grant, 1988).

Even for those who are college bound, certain employability skills—job-seeking, job-getting, and job-keeping—are frequently ignored in the high school curriculum. This lack is especially devastating for students who are deaf and who do not pick up critical information relating to career possibilities or to desirable/undesirable work habits—information usually conveyed through incidental conversations and interactions, or by "overhearing" parents and their colleagues. As a consequence, deaf young people, as they enter the labor force, "often . . . display poor work behavior and habits, they do not understand the value of work and they are unaware of most career fields and occupations" (Melton, 1987, p 315). They need opportunities to sample and explore career options; and they need to be taught the nuances of work—not only to read a work schedule but how to contact the employer when they cannot be at work. They need to be taught to be aware of and to look for the subtle indicators of approval or disapproval, such as facial expressions, when they miss the auditory intonation patterns. They need practical pointers in the differing language use and behavioral affect appropriate for interactions with employers versus peers, with close friends versus casual acquaintances (see Chapter 7).

As noted above, the major literacy needs for employment and effective living skills today include not only the surface reading of content but the ability to reason, to think about and act upon what is read. In this vein, the unique communication problems caused by early and profound loss of hearing can become especially critical, severely damaging the communication flow between the child and his or her parents or with other "mediating agents" who, in the normal care-giving process, help to organize "the world of stimuli for the child" (Feuerstein, 1980). Through this process, the child ordinarily acquires learning sets and develops the capacity to focus on salient aspects of the environment—to select, organize, and learn from a variety of internal and external sources. Many a deaf child is thus cut off not only from ease of language learning but also from the interactions which establish cognitive relationships and from the whole realm of incidental or informally transmitted learning, about other people, about jobs, about appropriate work and social behaviors and all the pragmatic nuances so essential for living and working in a community.

In like manner, loss of hearing can delay learning of the independent living and survival skills necessary for successful post-school transition. These skills, too, are learned in large part through incidental conversations and through experiences usually mediated by one's family members. Shared activities, accompanied by explanations, verbal chatter, and elaborations, are, in fact, early "minicourses"—in household management, from making the bed to remodeling the kitchen; in finance, from budgeting an allowance to purchasing blue jeans; and in use of leisure time, from planning a picnic to attending the World Series. They may include experiences with public transportation, with libraries, policemen, supermarkets, and hospitals. The child who misses out on such opportunities, especially the verbal elaborations which help to clarify experience, may well have problems in adjusting to the post-school community and will need specific training—transitional minicourses—in these areas.

Also within this cluster of needs are the personal and interpersonal skills required for interactions with others, again, both in the workplace and the community/living environment. Included are a wide range of skills to be developed, including: personal responsibility for actions; personal hygiene, grooming, and care of living space; interpersonal problem-solving and adjustment patterns, relating to peers and authority figures; recognition of and ability to follow established rules and policies; organization, planning, and participation in group activities; recognition of appropriate avenues for stress reduction; and pragmatic skills involving interpersonal dialogue, persuasion, and cooperation.

For some deaf students, supportive interactions with parents and instructors may have provided a sufficient "mediated learning experience" to accommodate these psychosocial needs—as well as the employability and living skill needs included in this cluster. For many others, in particular the students identified for extra transitional training, such mediation has not occurred. These students are unable to adapt to situations in flux. They exhibit behaviors such as passivity, lack of responsibility, and inability to problem-solve which are associated with an external instead of internal locus of control (Quigley & Kretschmer, 1982; see Chapter 4 for further discussion of these data). This cluster of behaviors, rather than or in addition to academic deficiencies, frequently presents *the* major problem for deaf students, one which must be addressed during any truly transitional program.

Extended Educational Needs

Because of all the needs and problems discussed above, one further need—that for long-term education—becomes even more critical. The deaf dropout figure of 29 percent (Allen et al., 1989), although lower than that for most other students with disabilities (Wagner, 1989), is especially devastating with regard to literacy levels, for unless the student has learned to read with some competency and has established a "reading habit," basic literacy learning will cease as soon as he or she leaves school (Hammermeister, 1971). Unfortunately, for some groups of deaf students, the reported dropout rate is much higher (Allen et al., 1989), increasing to 37 percent for those attending regular/local schools which provide academic integration for deaf students, and even to 54 percent for those attending a regular school but without academic integration. (It is lower [17 percent–23 percent] for those students who attend a special facility, are integrated part-time in academic classes or are non-integrated respectively.) The dropout rate is much higher for deaf students with two or more additional handicaps (57 percent), those who are Hispanic (36 percent), and for females (33 percent).

Of the deaf students who do complete high school, with either a diploma or certificate, from 30 percent to 53 percent now go on to some form of post-secondary transitional education (Allen et al., 1989), ranging from vocational or trade schools, to technical colleges, two-year colleges, four-year colleges, and graduate school. However, results from five sets of follow-up surveys, given to deaf graduates at 1, 2, 5, 10, and 20 years after graduation, and from 24 secondary school programs for deaf students nationwide, indicate that only 17 percent of the students who enrolled in post-secondary programs continued to degree completion (MacLeod-Gallinger, 1984). Further, the majority of degrees attained (72 percent) were at a sub-bachelor's level. In the general population, only 29 percent of the college degrees awarded in 1980 were Associate's or other two-year degrees (U.S. Bureau of the Census, 1981).

The significance of the problems noted above—the literacy deficits that extend even beyond graduation, the dropout rate, and the sub-bachelor's level of degrees achieved—becomes especially clear with a look at employment and earning statistics which are related to degree of schooling and literacy.

- In March 1986, only 55 percent of all dropouts under age 20 were employed, and of these only one in five was able to work full time (Grant, 1988, p. 23).
- Among female dropouts under age 20, only 1 in 7 dropouts held full-time jobs (Grant, p. 23).
- Regardless of race or ethnicity, the more years spent in education, the greater the annual earnings. In 1986, real mean annual earnings of 20- to 24-year-old civilian males who were dropouts was $6,725, compared to $10,720 for high school graduates and $13,502 for college graduates (Grant, pp. 21–22).
- For the one-half of youth who don't enroll in post-secondary education, the typical "first real job" is almost always in the secondary labor market, one that requires few skills, offers low pay and few or no benefits, little training, slim opportunity for advancement, and little significant contact with adults (Grant, p. 26; for example, fast food jobs).
- Youth whose reading and mathematics scores are in the bottom fifth of their class, compared with their peers in the top half, are "8.8 times more likely to leave school without a diploma, 8.6 times more likely to have a child out of wedlock, 5 times more likely to have an income below the poverty line, 2.2 times more likely to . . . [be] arrested" (Grant, p. 4).
- By 1990, three out of four jobs will require some education or technical training after high school (Applebee et al., 1987, p.3).
- Only 27 percent of all new jobs will fall into low skill categories, compared to 40 percent of jobs today (U.S. Department of Education & U.S. Department of Labor, 1988, p. 4).

- Even the average newspaper today requires an eighth or ninth grade reading level (C. Chandler, American Newspapers Publishers Foundation, personal communication, September, 11, 1989).
- Further, without continued reinforcement, literacy gains tend to lapse, even for "graduates" of literacy programs (Skagen, p. 19).

PLANNING FOR TRANSITION: THE HIGH SCHOOL YEARS AND BEFORE

How do we identify the parameters of this transition? Does post-school transition begin on graduation day? In high school? Or in kindergarten? Does it refer only to work-related skills? Or does it also include preparation for independent living, for interactions within the community as well as at work? Does it involve only educators and employers? Or does it include parents and various community members? For students who are deaf, it can very logically refer to the broadest of definitions, including each of the parameters below.

School-Based Services: K–12

The development of school-based services to prepare for the transition to post-school years was first pursued in the 1960s and 1970s, both in education at large and in education for deaf students (Dwyer, 1985), and has since expanded to include nationwide conferences and in-service training programs, both for educators and parents. One of the earliest major career education efforts was a three-year demonstration project by 12 programs for deaf students in New York State, Cooperative Research Endeavors in the Education of the Deaf (CREED), developing both methods and materials for use and dissemination (Munson & Egelston, 1975). A Comprehensive Career Education Model (CCEM), developed at Ohio State University, became the foundation for many career education programs, including the MSSD/NTID National Project on Career Education (NPCE) and the Arizona Career Education Matrix, later selected as a theoretical model for career education for deaf students (Dwyer, 1985). This three-dimensional model included: (1) the elements of self-awareness, educational awareness, career awareness, economic awareness, decision making, beginning competency, employability skills, attitudes and appreciations; (2) three different learning environments (home, school, and community); and (3) developmental stages for each, from birth through post-secondary education, from awareness through exploration, preparation, and specialization (Egelston-Dodd, 1980). In 1980, the Conference of Executives of American Schools for the Deaf approved a position paper confirming that "Career Education must be a comprehensive and appropriately infused part of every educational program serving hearing impaired students" (CEASD, 1985).

One example of early career infusion is that of a third-grade teacher who persuaded several community members "from the mayor to the manager of the local

McDonald's shop—to allow each of her students to spend a working day with them," shadowing them in daily aspects of the job and providing "a memorable experience of the world of work" (McHugh, 1975, p.8). Another example emphasizes potential out-of-school roles in the progression toward vocational maturity. Thus, a first step may be payment from parents for chores done, the weekly allowance. After this, "a major transitional step occurs when the youngster first works for someone other than his parents . . . mows the neighbor's lawn, delivers papers, babysits . . ." (Bolton, 1975).

Preparation for Post-Secondary Education Options

Included among the more recent projects preparing in-school for the transition to post-secondary education were: (1) the Career Awareness Summer Program, a joint venture of NTID and Gallaudet (O'Brien, Egelston-Dodd, & Lenard, 1983); (2) "Explore Your Future," a one-week summer program at NTID for deaf high school juniors, which provided "hands-on learning experiences revolving around outdoor education, field trips, and career exploration labs" designed to enhance awareness of self and of technical career options (Egelston-Dodd, O'Brien, & Bondi-Walcott, 1987); and (3) the Scranton State School for the Deaf "College Awareness Program for Hearing-Impaired Youth" (1985), a week-long summer program to link secondary and post-secondary programs serving deaf students in northeastern Pennsylvania. In the latter program, deaf high school students met with college counselors to discuss potential problems they might encounter, and they attended college classes to experience first-hand the academic requirements and procedures.

A related option is to offer full semester "samplers" of college course work to deaf students in their junior or senior years of high school, providing the challenge and experience of taking one or two community college courses while offering additional preparation and support by the students' own high school teachers. This option, provided to students at the Western Pennsylvania School for the Deaf, proved to be a highly successful experience in reality training—alerting students to gaps in their own independent study habits, providing motivation for improvement, and then enhancing their self-esteem, their confidence that they could compete at the college level (Craig, 1980). Funded by the National Science Foundation, with the express goal of encouraging exploration of careers in science, this project also enhanced awareness of new career options, in chemistry, biology, geology, and computer science, and demonstrated to the students themselves that, with concentrated effort, they could succeed in these areas.

In preparing deaf students for college enrollment, secondary schools not only must comply with the academic requirements of the selected colleges and universities, but also must address the rapid expansion of personal freedom and responsibility which students will encounter in the college environment. Most deaf students, as a pre-condition for acceptance into a particular college, will meet the academic requirements set for admission. Many, however, are unable to handle the behavioral independence which is thrust upon them after graduation. Many are not emotionally

prepared to deal alone with roommate problems, unsupervised study hours, or independent assignments, let alone to resist the peer pressures for drug and alcohol consumption. Unable to establish priorities, to develop productive study habits, or to
cope with the pressures of independence, many students become frustrated, cut
classes, and eventually, quit or are dismissed from college. The very low rate of
degree completion for deaf students, as cited earlier, attests to the problems they are
failing to overcome.

Preparation for Direct Employment and Non-Degree Options

Similarly, deaf young people who are not academically able to go on to college, or
who choose not to go, must also deal with the issues of instant independence and the
pressures of life after school—usually with neither the economic security nor sense of
responsibility that would optimally accompany independent living. In preparing non-
college-bound students who are still at the high school level for this transition, educators of deaf students have especially tough decisions to make. More and more
educators of students with normal hearing, both disabled and non-disabled, are suggesting that substantial work experience during the high-school years is an essential
factor in out-of-school success. Not only pre-vocational training but actual apprenticeships are being recommended (Grant, 1988). Unfortunately, the very significant
literacy problems of deaf students may mitigate against meaningful apprenticeships
before high school graduation, or at least reduce the time available for this experience.
Without functional literacy, as currently defined, including the reading, writing, and
mathematics skills necessary for most jobs, plus the reasoning skills to deal with
problem solving and change, job training alone may be unrealistic. Training for any
specific job also becomes a less and less satisfactory alternative when the job itself
may change entirely or be eliminated within six or seven years. Retraining, too, may
be offered verbally—without visual or hands-on support—requiring continued literacy skills. At the high school level, an added complication comes from the increasingly strict curriculum mandates from state departments of education concerning
courses which are required for graduation. There may not be time within the standard
12-year, 9-month-per-year, school program to meet all the needs expressed.

However, and this is a very powerful argument, work experience (especially paid
work experience) is consistently documented as *the* major factor in later employment
success for youth with normal hearing (Hasazi, Gordon, & Roe, 1985), and lack of
work experience as one of the major problems for deaf young adults in rehabilitation
programs (Bolton, 1975). One option is that schools could, "as part of their curriculum, provide opportunities for vocational exploration after school, on weekends, and
during vacations . . . not only allow but encourage their students to take part-time or
volunteer jobs during their adolescent years" (McHugh, 1975). Another option is to
provide paid work or training allowances for special in-school student projects or
employment ventures—e.g., a weekly salad bar luncheon for staff, a nightly snack bar

for students, a candy company for holiday sales (Iurlano, 1983). On the job, students not only learn good work habits and attitudes, plus purchasing, money exchange, and record-keeping skills, but they learn the rewards of a job well done, the pride of accomplishment.

Most schools for deaf students and public high schools with vocational program offerings do provide some vocational coursework as part of the high school curriculum. Other "career infusion" may take place at any level from kindergarten upward. The amount, however, varies from area to area and from state to state. Even for those whose schooling within the high school program is extended, the problems are not solved. Students who stay in high school until age twenty-one may very well feel they should be ready to start work immediately. In many cases they will not yet be prepared. Other students may get out of school and find that Supplemental Security Income (SSI) payments are more attractive (and lucrative) than working for a minimum wage. Additional follow-up by a team from the student's secondary school may then be needed to help prevent post-secondary attrition.

In response to these situations, school staff members should not only prepare all graduating students for post-secondary placements, but also track them after graduation, engaging in such activities as interviews at the colleges and training sites each year until students complete the program entered. Adjustment problems and academic difficulties should be discussed and addressed, with intervention provided whenever necessary.

One such program, the Drop Out Intervention Team (DOIT) was established at the Western Pennsylvania School for the Deaf (Fell, 1988). Since this program began in 1986, only 10 percent of graduates have failed to complete their programs, compared with incompletion rates of 70 to 83 percent on a national level (Walter, Foster, & Elliot, 1987; MacLeod-Gallinger, 1984).

The federal government has mandated systematic and cooperative planning for disabled students as they enter the transitional process with the ITSP, the Individualized Transitional Service Plan (see Chapter 10). An example of this initiative is a plan developed by an intermediate unit task force in Pennsylvania (Allegheny Intermediate Unit, 1987). "Process" meetings are conducted which include the parents, rehabilitation counselors, and school representatives. Career exploration, assessments, work opportunities, educational options, and realistic career goals for the young adult are discussed at length; and all participants agree on a concrete plan to ease the transition from school to eventual employment.

Assessment as an Aid to Transitional Planning

To plan more systematically for the transition period, to help in establishing realistic career goals, and to schedule students during high school for courses which will optimally assist them upon graduation, a concentrated vocational/career assessment program is essential. Among the measures available for this assessment and used in programs for deaf secondary students and young adults (Fell, 1987) are the following:

1.   *MESA (Microcomputer Evaluation and Screening Assessment)* (MESA, 1982). The MESA is a computerized vocational screening system which includes vocational interest and awareness assessment; physical capacities and mobility evaluation; work sample skill screening; perceptual screening; and computer exercises which screen for visual acuity, eye-hand and eye-hand-foot coordination, memory, reasoning, and academic skills.

2.   *Valpar Component Work Sample Series.* The Valpar series currently consists of 19 individual assessment units or work samples. These are used selectively in the vocational evaluation, based on results of measures such as the MESA and intake interviews. The work samples are designed to evaluate job-related motor and thought process skills specifically related to the job function (Valpar, 1979). They have been normed for deaf individuals.

3.   *Specialized work samples.* Some individual work samples may be selected from commercially available units, such as Singer (1973), CHOICE (1980), and CHEC (1979). Areas such as Building Maintenance Services, Bench Assembly, Housekeeping Services, Data Entry, Bookkeeping, Electrician Service, Masonry, Plumbing and Pipefitting, Insulation Services, Telephone and Cable TV, Welding, and Metal Working allow clients to explore specific work options in more detail.

4.   *Other Measures.* Other informative measures include: the Wide Range Interest-Opinion Test (WRIOT)(1979), to assess career interests and attitudes; and the Jewish Employment Vocational Service Work Sample System (JEVS)(1973), which provides further data on job interests, performance and skill levels. During an optimal evaluation period, students will also receive career counseling and have access to numerous career exploration materials.

PROGRAMMING THE TRANSITION ITSELF: THE POST-SECONDARY YEARS

For many deaf graduates—even with preparation during the high school years—the leap to life after school proves too great. In trying to make it unaided, they fail, and they establish a pattern of failure which becomes more and more difficult to escape. This is especially unfortunate for the many students who might be classified as "late bloomers"—those whose primary disability (hearing loss) has been accompanied by developmental delay, by emotional disturbance, or by educational misplacement, and who "age-out" of high school before they are developmentally ready to assume adult roles and responsibilities. For these and other students systematic transitional programs are needed, ones which will provide initial tools and support services and then, through phased reduction, encourage the individual to become architect of his or her own independence—to choose, compete, and move within today's work force.

Among the post-secondary options available for facilitating this transition are: (1) full degree-granting programs—colleges and technical-vocational schools; (2) non-degree training or rehabilitation programs, including those which provide job preparation and adult and workforce literacy; and (3) pre-college and/or pre-vocational training programs—providing transitional services and instruction to facilitate further education or training. The program components for these three options will be discussed below, concluding with a working model of the third, most recent, option, with strategies specifically geared to the individual transitional needs of young adults who are deaf.

Degree-Granting Transitional Programs: College and Technical

The college and career programs currently available offer a multitude of new opportunities for deaf persons, opening career doors from data processing to biotechnology, from commercial art to economics, from elementary education to gerontology. The 156 degree-granting options identified in the 1988 survey of post-secondary programs for deaf students in North America (Rawlings et al., 1988) include vocational/technical, liberal arts, and graduate/professional study, with 119, 132, and 55 programs respectively listing these options. Sixty of these colleges reported the degrees actually awarded to deaf students in the prior (1986–87) school year, with the following results: 478 certificates or diplomas, 266 Associate degrees, 232 Baccalaureates, 137 Masters, 11 Professional Certificates, and 2 Doctoral degrees (Rawlings et al., 1988).

In the 1988 survey, 6,041 full-time and 1,342 part-time deaf students were reported as enrolled in these programs. By far the largest number of students, with well over 1000 each, were in the two programs responsible by law for serving deaf students nationwide, Gallaudet University and Rochester Institute of Technology: National Technical Institute for the Deaf (NTID). In the other federally funded regional programs, California State University at Northridge had over 200 deaf students, St. Paul Technical College approximately 140, Seattle Community College 87, and the colleges affiliated with the Tennessee Consortium almost 200 full and part-time deaf students. Of the remaining programs nationwide, only 7 had an enrollment of over 50 deaf students, and 57 had only 1 to 10 enrolled. These figures represent only those colleges identified and responding to the 1988 survey. This would include all the larger programs, although there are, undoubtedly, other community college and university programs which have some deaf students enrolled.

Special supportive options for deaf students are provided by most of these programs, in accordance with section 504, including one or more services such as interpreters, note-takers, tutors, special classes (remedial mathematics or English), assistive devices (TDDs, TV decoders, amplified phones, real-time captioning), speech and hearing services, personal and/or vocational counseling, placement services, faculty/staff training, and supervised housing. The quality of these services may vary widely, from certified paid interpreters to volunteers; from counselors who use manual communication to those who neither have sign language skills nor interpreters (Rawlings et al., 1988). With the passage of the Americans with Disabilities Act of 1990, all public facilities will be required to make "reasonable accommodation" (p. 9) for people with disabilities and to provide "auxiliary aids and services" (p. 5), a mandate which should further increase the services actually available. One particular concern of the Commission on Education of the Deaf (COED) (1988) was that, in many college programs claiming to provide support for deaf students, the range of services offered was far less than required for full 504 compliance. The COED Report then suggests a "critical mass" concept—that it is "easier and more cost effective to provide support services when there is a minimum number of deaf students" enrolled in a program (p. 57).

Clearly, deaf students have many more options for post-secondary training today than they did even ten years ago, but with the options come decisions and responsibility for these decisions. Does the deaf person go to a program specifically for deaf students, where there will be more deaf peers and, usually, more intensive support services available, or to another program which may provide training in a specific area of interest or offer more opportunities for interaction with normally hearing peers, but less support? The choice is now available.

Not all deaf students are able or eager to go to college—for academic, financial, family, or emotional reasons, or just because they are not yet ready. Many colleges will deny admission to any student not scoring at a standard criterion on an entrance examination. NTID, for example, requires an overall Stanford Achievement Test score of eighth grade or higher (Rawlings et al., 1988), and Gallaudet's requirements are similar. Therefore, these college options, as well as most other four-year college programs, are closed to well over half of deaf secondary school graduates.

Some deaf students choose to go first to a community college, selecting a one- or two-year job-preparatory major, or transferring afterward to a four-year college once their academic skills have improved. Most community colleges have open admissions policies, but students must maintain a certain level of performance, such as a 2.0 grade average, to transfer or to get a degree. Because deaf students choosing this route may encounter several college courses requiring reading comprehension, mathematics, and written language skills well beyond their entering literacy level, remedial English classes or special tutoring and counseling, as well as skilled interpreters and notetakers, will frequently prove essential.

Another degree option is at a vocational/technical school, providing training in a specific vocation for which the student shows both interest and potential skill. At St. Paul Technical College, for example, majors are determined after a period of vocational exploration and evaluation in a Preparatory Program which also offers Independent Living Skills training and courses in mathematics, reading, or science (Rawlings et al., 1988). Deaf young adults live in apartments off campus and attend classes geared toward vocational training in a specific area—from business and office occupations or graphic arts to machine tool processing, welding, or truck mechanics. These technical offerings may be one-, two-, three-, or four-year programs, with St. Paul, among others, now offering college credits for some courses, as well as certificates and diplomas. Not all job skill training options will lead to academic degrees or recognition, but they may be tied to successful performance on job-related criteria.

If these college or technical programs are to have optimum value, deaf students must not only get into the programs, they must also be able to stay, to perform, and ideally to graduate with a diploma or degree which documents their readiness for the requirements of work. DiLorenzo and Welsh (1981) reported that, on the average, deaf students require almost four years to complete a two-year Associate degree, making degree completion at the Baccalaureate level or beyond a real test of perseverance.

Non-Degree Training Programs

Although the recent influx of post-secondary education options for deaf persons is very encouraging, as many as 60 percent of all deaf high school graduates or dropouts will not be able to benefit from post-secondary education (COED, 1988, p.69). "Many . . . enroll in college because it is their only option—then fail" (p.70). There are others who left school several years ago but whose literacy skills have not kept up with the current, escalating literacy requirements of the workplace. What are the options for these deaf adults?

In 1989, 47 rehabilitation centers with residential facilities were listed as providing placements for deaf adults (NICD, 1989). However, federal funding for such programs has diminished considerably since the 1970s, when the Rehabilitation Services Administration (RSA) provided substantial support for comprehensive centers in 14 different states (COED, 1988, p. 69). Programs available today, operating with state, federal, and private monies, are estimated to serve only 700 clients nationwide, although "an estimated 100,000 deaf people of all ages are unemployed or seriously underemployed due to additional handicapping conditions, such as deficiencies in language performance, and related psychological, vocational, and social underdevelopment" (COED, p. 69). One of the major COED recommendations was that "The Congress should establish one comprehensive service center in each of the ten federal regions of the United States . . ." (p. 71). Such centers would rewrite "the long history of inadequate funding and inappropriate programming for thousands of deaf individuals . . . who do not qualify for formal post-secondary education" (p. 71).

Comprehensive rehabilitation centers serving deaf clients should include services such as evaluation, personal and vocational counseling, vocational training in various areas, interpreting, tutoring, job readiness, advocacy, supervised housing, and recreation. One such facility, the Hiram G. Andrews Center in Johnstown, Pennsylvania, serves over 500 clients with disabilities, including approximately 30 in the Deaf Services Unit. It offers the above services, including vocational training in 30 different areas. The center's Associate degree programs in areas such as accounting and drafting are for four 16-week terms, whereas preparation for other occupations, such as woodworking, jewelry, food service, health support, and building maintenance require less time—one or two terms. The funding for this Center comes primarily through payments by the Pennsylvania Office of Vocational Rehabilitation for services rendered.

Another type of program, privately funded, is the Job Development Program for

Deaf Adults, operated by the Lutheran Friends of the Deaf in Mill Neck, New York. This community-based program was established in 1986 both "to fill the void created by the termination of secondary school programs" and to "bridge the gaps with industry commonly thought to hinder employment of people who are hearing impaired" (Keenan, Fangmeier, & Oddo, 1989). It provides aid for deaf adults in finding, getting, and keeping employment, through a concentrated series of services including pre-employment contacts, job interviews, job counseling, on-site job training with a job coach, communication on-the-job, and follow-up services, including supported work contacts where needed. In the first 1½ years, 110 deaf adults were served, with a mean age of 22 years but a range from 19 to 77 years. Over half had one or more secondary disability. At entry, 61 percent were unemployed, and those who were employed were having work-related problems. In contrast, following the Job Development services, 81 percent were employed and remained employed one to three years later (Keenan, 1989, pp. 6, 14).

A third type of program that is needed would be geared more specifically toward the literacy problems of deaf adults. The provision of adult literacy classes is an effort receiving strong state and federal encouragement. Students in such programs may be provided both with small-group instruction, by a teacher certified to teach deaf students, and with individualized reinforcement and tutoring. The latter may be done by volunteers who are first trained by the teacher. Emphasis should be on pragmatic reading skills, those needed to perform both at work and as part of the community.

One example of such a program is that at the Center On Deafness (COD) at the Western Pennsylvania School for the Deaf. COD initiated an Adult Literacy Program for Hearing-Impaired Adults in 1987. The highly encouraging results of this program have led to its continuation in each ensuing year. Results from the first two years, with 78 deaf adults enrolled, showed a consistently high (87 percent) attendance rate and significantly improved performance in reading skills. In only 25 three-hour sessions per program period, these deaf adults, with incoming reading scores at the 0–4 grade level, gained from one-third of a year to a full year's grade equivalent on standardized achievement tests of reading comprehension—essentially the same gain that would be anticipated for normally hearing and normally literate individuals who were in school on a daily basis (Craig, 1988, 1989; Schecter-Connors, 1989). Workforce Literacy training was added to this program in 1989 to address the literacy demands of specific jobs, of job retraining, and of the ongoing communication needs of both the deaf employees themselves and their supervisors and co-workers.

Pre-College and Pre-Vocational Transitional Instruction

In addition to long-term programs directed specifically toward college or career education, and shorter-term programs for job or literacy training, there has emerged a need for instructional programs geared specifically toward the transition itself. These "transitional-instructional" programs can address the psychosocial, cognitive, and interpersonal communication skill needs of many deaf students prior to their attempting specific career preparation—or following failure in such attempts.

Of the previously cited college and career programs, several provide preparatory periods prior to full enrollment in their own programs. Gallaudet University, for example, has its Postsecondary Enrichment Program (PEP), in which students who are not fully prepared academically are given a one-year opportunity to attend pre-college-level classes, concentrating on academic preparation in reading, language and math (Gallaudet, 1989). A "Vestibule" program at NTID provides similar preparation for students who have been admitted to that school; and St. Paul TVI has its Preparatory Program to enhance independent living, as well as reading, mathematics and science skills (Rawlings et al., 1988).

A transitional program with somewhat broader goals is the Program for Hearing Impaired (PHI) at Northern Illinois University (NIU), which includes both Pre-Vocational and College Preparatory sections, plus a Cooperative Alternative Secondary Program (CASP). Each of these is a 9-month program, preceded by a 6-week Summer Diagnostic session to determine individual levels of functioning and to select the most appropriate option. Students eligible for PHI, in addition to having hearing loss, must be in the 16–24 age range, single, and have a minimum Performance IQ of 80. If the option chosen is Pre-Vocational, the students participate in academic classes for one-half of a day and a work experience for the other half. In the College Preparatory program, the classes are designed to help prepare the student for college-level work, with special emphasis on reading, writing, and study skills, and with required enrollment in at least one college level course. The third option, CASP, is designed as an alternative way to meet requirements for a high school diploma. All PHI students receive regular counseling services, and all live in a NIU residence hall. This program is an integral part of the Department of Communicative Disorders at NIU, working in cooperation with the Illinois Department of Rehabilitation Services (Northern Illinois University, 1981).

Transitional Programming: A "Working" Model

One relatively new type of programming—devoted solely to post-secondary transitional instruction and not affiliated with any college or university program—is offered regionally or statewide in conjunction with a few "Center Schools" for deaf students. A 1990 survey by the authors located three programs clearly of this type: one coordinated by the Texas School for the Deaf in Austin; a Transitional Living Center in Oklahoma City, affiliated with the Oklahoma School for the Deaf; and the Transitional/Instructional Program in Pittsburgh (TIPP), a part of the Center On Deafness at the Western Pennsylvania School for the Deaf. (The survey did locate several Center schools which provide "transitional" vocationally oriented programs at the high-school level, sometimes in cooperation with local community colleges, but no others providing instructional services to students once they had graduated from secondary school.) Because the Transitional/Instructional Program in Pittsburgh was a pioneer in post-secondary transitional programming and can provide a functional model which has been proven effective with deaf students, it is described in some detail below.

Begun in 1986, the TIPP provides individualized programming for young adults with a wide range of abilities and interests, including those whose placement on completion of the transition may be college, technical/vocational training, employment, or even sheltered workshop. The major criteria for entrance are that the students: (1) have an educationally significant hearing loss; (2) have a clearly identified need for extra transitional instruction and experience; and (3) have a reasonable chance, through this program, to improve their employability, their independent living skills, or their opportunities for continuing education. As shown in Figure 5–1, referrals may come from residential or day schools for deaf students, from public school intermediate units or school districts, from the district rehabilitation counselors, or from other sources such as parent referral. The program is funded primarily through fees for service from the Pennsylvania Office of Vocational Rehabilitation (OVR), although students throughout the mid-Atlantic region are eligible for admittance, funded through vocational rehabilitation offices within their own state of residence. Designed with a structure similar to the PHI program in Illinois, the TIPP includes: (1) a one- to three-week Diagnostic Session, followed by (2) one to four 16-week Training Sessions—either "Pre-College" or "Pre-Vocational"—depending on clients' needs, skills, and preferences.

The *Diagnostic Session*, offered three times a year, provides intensive evaluation of vocational, academic, psychological, cognitive, and communication aptitudes and skills. The vocational evaluators and counselors use this assessment to identify the client's specific aptitudes and problem areas, especially with regard to possible post-secondary options. They then use the results as the basis for transitional program planning and placement, and for both individual and group counseling relating to potential career alternatives.

The *Pre-College* instruction is intended to bridge from secondary level to college or advanced technical training, whereas the *Pre-Vocational* training is intended to bridge from secondary level education either to more specific vocational training options or directly to competitive employment. Both options have several components in common, as shown in Table 5–1, although the actual classes and experiences will be geared to different levels of functioning and to different career goals. Additional instructional and counseling activities provided as part of the Pre-College program are listed in Table 5–2; additional activities within the Pre-Vocational option are listed in Table 5–3. Upon completion of the Pre-Vocational option, the TIPP students also have access to Job Placement and Workforce Literacy services at the WPSD Center On Deafness to further ease the transition into the workplace and to provide follow-up services as needed.

One very unique component of the this transitional program is that it offers highly individualized "mediated" instruction and counseling for all students, geared to the development of the cognitive and metacognitive skills necessary for indepen-

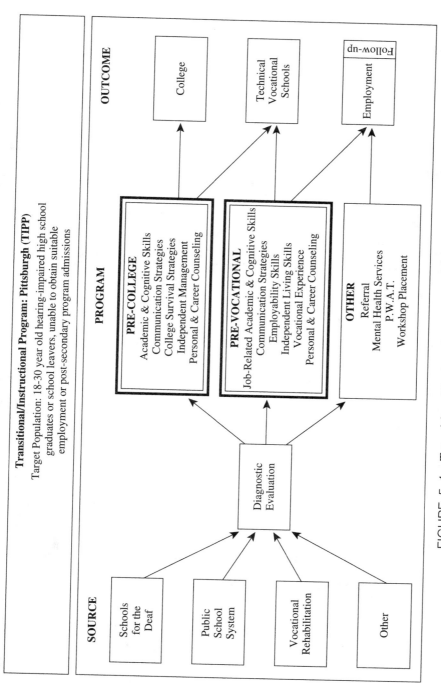

Transitional/Instructional Program: Pittsburgh (TIPP)

Target Population: 18-30 year old hearing-impaired high school graduates or school leavers, unable to obtain suitable employment or post-secondary program admissions

SOURCE

Schools for the Deaf

Public School System

Vocational Rehabilitation

Other

Diagnostic Evaluation

PROGRAM

PRE-COLLEGE
Academic & Cognitive Skills
Communication Strategies
College Survival Strategies
Independent Management
Personal & Career Counseling

PRE-VOCATIONAL
Job-Related Academic & Cognitive Skills
Communication Strategies
Employability Skills
Independent Living Skills
Vocational Experience
Personal & Career Counseling

OTHER
Referral
Mental Health Services
P.W.A.T.
Workshop Placement

OUTCOME

College

Technical Vocational Schools

Employment

Follow-up

FIGURE 5-1 **Transitional/Instructional Program: Pittsburgh (TIPP)**

TABLE 5–1   **Courses in Common for Pre-College and Pre-Vocational Components: Transitional/Instructional Program: Pittsburgh (TIPP)**

- *academic coursework and tutoring:*
    computer literacy and word processing
    cultural literacy
    deaf culture

- *cognitive and metacognitive training*—oriented to:
    academic coursework
    employment and community living situations

- *communication courses, tutoring, and individual practice:*
    situational vocabulary and language for interactions (educational, workplace, and
        community settings)
    speech, speech reading, sign language
    technical communication aids
    reading and writing notes/memos
    pragmatic language for dialogue, debate, and questioning

- *independent living skills*—coursework and practice:
    financial and household management
    scheduling daily activities
    community mobility
    personal management

- *employability skill training:*
    seeking, getting, and keeping a job
    job application and interview strategies
    work habits, values, and responsibilities

- *individual and group counseling*, re:
    personal responsibility and self care
    problem solving; coping strategies
    interpersonal relationships
    group participation; cooperation
    stress management; anger control
    developing self esteem

- *career counseling:*
    job exploration and job "shadowing"
    information search re: career options, financial benefits, job requirements

- *regularly scheduled seminars:*
    speakers on timely topics (AIDS, SSI, self-defense)
    interactions with successful deaf adults—providing opportunities for student
        questions, discussions

dent living, study, employment, and social interactions. The capacity to think clearly, to analyze work and life choices is essential for graduates who are moving into new and independent arenas of employment or post-secondary schooling. They will have new stimuli to select or discard, new habits and skills to develop, and new expecta-

TABLE 5–2 **Additional Components for the TIPP Pre-College Option**

- *academic coursework and tutoring:*
  English: composition and grammar
  reading
  mathematics and algebra

- *college survival strategies:*
  independent study habits
  outlining and note-taking
  time management
  use of support services (interpreters, note-takers, advisors, counselors, health
    services, library)

- *career exploration:*
  visits to and from diverse college programs
  interviews with college personnel and employees in targeted job areas

- *mainstream college experience*, where appropriate

TABLE 5–3 **Additional Components for the TIPP Pre-Vocational Option**

- *academic coursework and tutoring:*
  vocational English and reading
  vocational mathematics

- *vocational experience/cooperative work-study programs*
  with local employers (12–20 hours per week)
  work orientation and work sampling
  self appraisal re: work potential
  payment (for most) on a biweekly basis
  budgeting: pay checks and living expenses

tions to accommodate. Successful adaptation to this change requires not only information on the new work options and environment, but also the ability to explore options systematically, to make decisions based on evidence, to plan ahead in ordered steps, to exhibit sensitivity to others, and to demonstrate confidence in one's self. To help transitional program students develop these essential cognitive skills, the TIPP program includes intensive, three-hour-per-week training in Feuerstein's Instrumental Enrichment program (IE) (1980) (see Chapter 3), in tandem with weekly counseling or therapy, following a Cognitive Behavioral model (Meichenbaum, 1977) (see Chapter 8).

Feuerstein's IE, a comprehensive program of cognitive mediation and training, offers the opportunity to overcome the lack of early mediating experience already identified as a major problem for deaf students in this transitional period. The IE program provides highly interactive instruction toward the systematic development of 14 cognitive skills, such as selecting critical cues, analyzing wholes and parts, giving and following logical instructions, recognizing temporal, numerical, and hierarchial relationships, and making predictions based thereon. Research both with normally hearing and deaf adolescents, including the Transitional students in the Pittsburgh program, provides support for this thinking skills program (Feuerstein, 1980; Savell, Twohig, & Rachford, 1986; Martin & Jonas, 1986; Craig, 1987; Craig & Gordon, 1989). Like Feuerstein's instructional model, Meichenbaum's (1977) therapeutic model of Cognitive Behavior Modification emphasizes mediational techniques—self-instructional training, thinking aloud, and self-talk—and uses these techniques to develop the personal/social strategies most needed by these Transitional students.

The living arrangements in the Pittsburgh program also are designed to reinforce the school-time mediated learning experiences. The Transitional Program dormitory space has immediate access to a student lounge, kitchenette, laundry facilities, reading room, recreational/fitness areas, the computer room, communication practice units, and career exploration modules. Regular after-school field trips are also scheduled to provide experiences with public transportation, shopping, banking, cultural, and recreational opportunities. These arrangements are designed to provide hands-on experience with household and financial management, personal mobility, and scheduling of study and recreation times—with supervised "mediation" available to assure a gradual and planned passage into more fully independent living.

In its first eight years of operation, the TIPP program has served a total of 152 young men and women from Pennsylvania, Ohio, and West Virginia, ranging in age from 18 to 33 years, and with hearing losses ranging from moderate to profound (with a mean better-ear average of 94 dB). Both intelligence test and entry achievement scores have shown quite a wide spread. For example, entry-level grade equivalents (GE) in Reading Comprehension on the Stanford Achievement Test (SAT) (Gardner, Rudman, Karlsen, & Merwin, 1982) ranged from 1.3 to 10.4. Achievement gains on the SAT, from program entry to completion, have been significant beyond the 0.001 level in both reading and mathematics, with an average 0.7 GE gain in Reading Comprehension and a 1.2 GE gain in Mathematics Computation. By way of contrast, nationwide studies have documented an average yearly gain for deaf students of slightly less than 0.3 GE for SAT Reading Comprehension (Trybus & Karchmer, 1977).

Of the 58 Pre-College students so far completing the Transitional/Instructional Program, 91 percent have now entered the college of their choice and two-thirds of these have either graduated from college (21 percent) or are still enrolled (45 percent). Of the Pre-Vocational students completing the program (all of whom were previously unemployed), 64 percent have become directly employed and are remaining on the job, and 26 percent have gone on to other vocational training programs. Only 12 percent of all students enrolled in the TIPP have left prior to program completion. Initial experience with the students in this transitional program thus offers encouraging signs that a concentrated and targeted transitional option may indeed provide an effective boost for deaf young adults who are at risk for post-school disappointment. Although this and similar programs are still in the formative stage, the high rate of program completion and of productive outcomes by TIPP "graduates" indicates the enhanced opportunities for success which one or two years of transitional training can provide—opportunities which may become increasingly important with the continually rising cognitive and literacy requirements of the workplace today.

SUMMARY, CONCLUSIONS, AND IMPLICATIONS FOR PRACTICE

Transitional programming for deaf youth is a process which may begin in the preschool years and continue through a variety of post-secondary education and training options. The ultimate purpose of such programming is to prepare the young person for post-school life, for an optimum transition into the workforce and independent community living. Preparation for transition is important for any young person. For those whose communication opportunities with individuals with normal hearing have been reduced by severe to profound deafness, the extension of education into the transitional years may prove especially critical.

Historically, both the impetus and the opportunities for transitional programs are of relatively recent vintage, primarily within the past 30 years. The impetus has been the rapid acceleration in the complexity of society, and the informational and literacy demands of the workplace. Opportunities for post-secondary transitional training began with the establishment of Gallaudet College in 1864, as a liberal arts college specifically for deaf students. However, not until 100 years later did transitional options broaden to include both post-secondary technical/vocational training and school-based, K–12, preparation for the post-school period. These possibilities, proposed as early as 1888, first began to be realized with legislative efforts in the 1960s, establishing both the National Technical Institute for the Deaf and four federally supported regional post-secondary education programs. In the late 1960s, opportunities were further broadened with federal support for comprehensive rehabilitation centers, providing for the first time specialized services to assist in preparing deaf clients for work. In the 1980s, "transition" itself became the major federal focus, with a three-tiered high-school-to-employment model proposed by the Office of Special Education and Rehabilitation Services (OSERS).

The transitional needs of each deaf person will be different, depending on a multitude of factors, ranging from degree and onset of hearing loss to occupational interests and aptitudes. Several basic needs, however, will impact upon most deaf students, especially those with severe to profound loss of hearing. The communication problems which they have in common not only affect their ability to read and write the English language, but also reduce their ability to interact freely with significant others in developing concepts about the world of work and the community in which they will live. Especially with the recent increase in literacy requirements and in information needed for today's workforce, deaf young people will need (1) improved and continuing literacy skills, (2) enhanced development of employability, independent living, and personal/social skills, and (3) expanded education and counseling to meet the above needs. For students whose informal sources of information are frequently limited or misunderstood, the development of these skills may well require formal training—not only during the K–12 school years, but also beyond high school and before the more standard post-secondary routes.

In planning for transitional options, school-based services may be provided, using as a foundation a Comprehensive Career Education Model, as developed in the 1970s, and infusing career education throughout the instructional years. Such a model includes self-awareness, knowledge of educational and career options, decision-making ability, and employability skills and attitudes. At a later stage, preparation for post-secondary options may be provided in summer career awareness programs, in samplers of college course work during the junior or senior years, and/or in paid work-experience programs during vacations or as part of the high school curriculum. One essential part of planning for transition is comprehensive assessment of vocational awareness, interests, and aptitudes, including a variety of work samples and career counseling opportunities.

In facilitating the transition itself—the years following secondary school—several post-secondary options are now available. These include over 150 different college and technical schools which provide special services for deaf students, several non-degree programs providing short-term job preparation or adult and workforce literacy, and specifically transitional programs, both pre-college and pre-vocational, which concentrate on transitional skills per se, as needed either on the job or in further post-secondary education environments. A model of the last of these has been discussed in some detail to demonstrate both the programming options which can be offered and the positive results to which these options can lead.

Clearly, post-school transitional opportunities for deaf young adults have expanded significantly, especially in the past three decades. Even more clearly, the need for such options has also accelerated—just to keep up with the increased literacy and cognitive demands of today's workplace, the increased complexity and pressures of community living. New and expanded transitional initiatives may well be required, building on these past and present options, as a bridge to even greater vocational maturity and more viable and challenging post-school opportunities in each of the years to come.

REFERENCES

Allegheny Intermediate Unit. (1987, June). *Transitional planning for disabled students: A parent manual.* (Available from the Exceptional Children's Program of the Allegheny Intermediate Unit, Pittsburgh, PA 15219–1178).

Allen, T.E. (1986). Patterns of academic achievement among hearing-impaired students: 1974 and 1983. In A. Schildroth & M. Karchmer (Eds.), *Deaf children in America* (pp. 161–206). San Diego, CA: College-Hill Press.

Allen, T.E., Rawlings, B.W., & Schildroth, A.N. (1989). *Deaf students and the school-to-work transition.* Baltimore, MD: Paul H. Brooks Publishing Co.

Americans with Disabilities Act (1989, May). Senate Bill #933, An Act: To establish clear and comprehensive prohibition of discrimination on the basis of disability. 101st Congress, 1st Session. Washington, DC.

Applebee, A., Langer, J., & Mullis, I. (1987). Learning to be literate in America. *The Nation's Report Card,* Report No. 15–RW–01. Princeton, NJ: National Assessment of Educational Progress (ANEP) at Educational Testing Services.

Babbidge, H., & Advisory Committee on Education of the Deaf. (1965). *Education of the deaf: A report to the Secretary of Health, Education and Welfare.* Washington, DC: Office of the Secretary.

Barnes, H.B. (1940a). A co-operative job training center for the deaf—if! *American Annals of the Deaf, 85,* 347–350.

Barnes, H.B. (1940b). The need for separating advanced vocational training from the elementary school atmosphere. *American Annals of the Deaf, 85,* 449–451.

Blake, G. (1968). How the program for the deaf developed at the Hot Springs Rehabilitation Center. In G. Lloyd (Ed.), *International research seminar on the vocational rehabilitation of deaf persons.* SRA, Department of Health, Education and Welfare. Hot Springs, AR.

Bolton, B. (1975). Preparing deaf youth for employment. *Journal of Rehabilitation of the Deaf, 9,* 11–16.

CEASD, Career Development Committee. (1985). Career education: The position paper of the Conference of Educational Administrators Serving the Deaf. *American Annals of the Deaf, 130,* 74–78.

CEASD. (1964). *Proceedings of the thirty-sixth regular meeting of the Convention of Executives of American Schools for the Deaf.* Riverside, CA.

CHEC: Consumer and Home Economics Careers Program. (1979). Salt Lake City, UT: Utah State Office of Education.

CHOICE: Carrels for Hands-On Career Education. (1980). Salt Lake City, UT: Career Research Corporation.

Commission on Education of the Deaf. (COED) (1988). *Toward equality: A report to the President and the Congress of the United States.* Washington, DC: U.S. Goverment Printing Office.

Craig, H.B. (1980). *College level samplers of science coursework for deaf high school students.* Technical description of projects and results. National Science Foundation. (Project #SPI–79–08721).

Craig, H.B. (1987). Instrumental Enrichment: Process and results with deaf students. *Thinking Skills Newsletter, Spring-Summer,* 28–30.

Craig, H.B. (1988). Results of the 1987–88 adult literacy program at Center On Deafness. *1987–88 Adult Literacy Program Data Form.* PDE–3066AL. Harrisburg, PA: Dept. of Education, Division of Adult Basic Education.

Craig, H.B. (1989). Results of the 1988–89 adult literacy program at Center On Deafness. *1987–88 Adult Literacy Program Data Form.* PDE–3066AL. Harrisburg, PA: Dept. of Education, Division of Adult Basic Education.

Craig, H.B., & Gordon, H. (1989, July). Specialized cognitive function among deaf individuals. Presentation to: The Second International Symposium on Cognition, Education and Deafness. Gallaudet University, Washington, DC.

Craig, W.N., & Burrows, N.L. (1969). *Improved vocational, technical and academic opportunities for deaf people: Research component.* RSA Grant No. RD–2723–S–68. Pittsburgh, PA: University of Pittsburgh.

DiLorenzo, L., & Welsh, W. (1981). *How long to receive a degree?* (Concept Paper: Follow-Up Report No. 1). Rochester, NY: National Technical Institute for the Deaf, Institutional Planning and Research.

Dwyer, C. (1985). Career education: A literature review. In M. Bullis & D. Watson (Eds.), *Career education of hearing-impaired students: A review,* (pp. 3–25). Little Rock, AR: Rehabilitation Research and Training Center on Deafness and Hearing Impairment.

Egelston-Dodd, J. (Ed.) (1980). *Trainer's manual, career education and planning skills.* MSSD/NTID National Project on Career Education. Rochester, NY: National Technical Institute for the Deaf.

Egelston-Dodd, J., O'Brien, E., & Bondi-Walcott, J. (1987). Explore your future: An NTID parent transition workshop. In G. Anderson & D. Watson (Eds.), *Innovations in the habilitation and rehabilitation of the deaf* (pp. 84–98). Little Rock, AR: Rehabilitation Research and Training Center on Deafness and Hearing Impairment.

Fay, E.A. (Ed.) (1892). Report of the committee on a technical school. *American Annals of the Deaf, 37,* 279–280.

Fell, B. (1987). Vocational evaluation: What we have to offer. *Dimensions, 2*(1), 3–4.

Fell, B. (1988). DOIT. *Western Pennsylvanian, 96*(3).

Feuerstein, R. (1980). *Instrumental enrichment. An intervention program for cognitive modifiability.* Baltimore, MD: University Park Press.

Gallaudet University Pre-College Programs. (1989). Post-secondary enrichment program (PEP). Model Secondary School Transitional Program Brochure. Washington, DC: Gallaudet University.

Gardner, E.F., Rudman, H.C., Karlsen, B., & Merwin, J.C. (1982). *Stanford Achievement Test.* New York: Harcourt Brace Jovanovich.

Grant, William T. Foundation Commission on Work, Family and Citizenship. (1988). *The forgotten half: Non-college youth in America.* Washington, DC: The William T. Grant Foundation Commission on Work, Family and Citizenship.

Halpern, A.S. (1985). Transition: A look at the foundations. *Exceptional Children, 51,* 479–486.

Hammermeister, F. (1971). Reading achievement in deaf adults. *American Annals of the Deaf, 116,* 25–29.

Hasazi, S.B., Gordon, L.R., & Roe, C.A. (1985). Factors associated with the employment status of handicapped youth exiting high school from 1979 to 1983. *Exceptional Children, 51,* 455–469.

Iurlano, A. (1983). Working 9–5: Special studies candy company. *Western Pennsylvanian, 91*(2).

JEVS. Worksample Evaluation Sample. (1973). Philadelphia: Jewish Employment and Vocational Service, Vocational Research Institute.

Keenan, R.J., Fangmeier, R., & Oddo, C. (1989, June). Transitional employment: Yes, it works. Paper presented at Waves of the Future: CAID/CEASD Convention. San Diego, CA.

Kirsch, I., & Jungeblut, A. (1989). *Literacy: Profiles of America's young adults.* Report #16–PL–02. Princeton, NJ: The National Assessment of Educational Progress at Educational Testing Service.

MacLeod-Gallinger, J. (1984). *Secondary school graduate follow-up program: Annual report.* Rochester, NY: Division of Career Opportunities, Rochester Institute of Technology, NTID.

Martin, D., & Jonas, B. (1986). Cognitive modifiability in the deaf adolescent. *Resource in Education,* Document ED276159.

McGowan, J., & Porter, T. (1967). *An introduction to the vocational rehabilitation process.* Washington, DC: U.S. Government Printing Office.

McHugh, D.F. (1975). A view of deaf people in terms of Super's theory of vocational development. *Journal of Rehabilitation of the Deaf, 9*(1), 1–11.

Meichenbaum, D. (1977). *Cognitive behavior modification: An integrated approach.* New York: Plenum Press.

Melton, W. (1987). Trends and directions in vocational rehabilitation and their influence upon the education of deaf people. *American Annals of the Deaf, 32,* 315–316.

Morrison, J. (1920). Industrial training: What shall we subtract and what shall we add in the new century of education of the deaf? *American Annals of the Deaf, 65,* 213–225.

Munson, H.L., & Egelston, J.C. (1975). Career education for the deaf: A program model and materials. *Journal of the Rehabilitation of the Deaf, 9*(2), 24–35.

National Center for Education Statistics: Analysis Report. (1989). *Dropout rates in the United States: 1988.* U.S. Department of Education, Office of Educational Research and Improvement.

National Information Center On Deafness (NICD). (1989). Rehabilitation centers with residential facilities. Resource List. Washington, DC: Gallaudet University.

Northern Illinois University. (1981). *Program for Hearing Impaired (PHI).* Transitional Program Brochure. DeKalb, IL: Northern Illinois University.

O'Brien, E., Egelston-Dodd, J., & Lenard, J. (1983, June). The NPCE parent career education workshop. Paper presented at the biennial meeting of the Convention of American Instructors of the Deaf, Winnipeg, Manitoba.

Osterman, P. (1980). *Getting started: The youth labor market.* Cambridge, MA: MIT Press.

Pratt, L., & Fay, E.A. (Eds.) (1870). Institutions for instructing the deaf and dumb in the US. *American Annals of the Deaf, 15,* 63–64.

Quigley, S., & Kretschmer, R.E. (1982). *The education of deaf children: Issues, theory, and practice.* Baltimore, MD: University Park Press.

Rawlings, B., Karchmer, M., & DeCaro, J.J. (Eds.) (1988). *College and career programs for deaf students.* Gallaudet University, Washington, DC & NTID, Rochester Institute of Technology.

Rogers, D.S. (1888). A plea for a polytechnique institute for deaf-mutes. *American Annals of the Deaf, 33,* 184–185.

Rubin, S., & Roessler, R. (1978). *Foundations of the vocational rehabilitation process.* Baltimore, MD: University Park Press.

Savell, J., Twohig, P., & Rachford, D. (1986). Empirical status of Feuerstein's 'Instrumental Enrichment' (FIE) technique as a methodology of teaching skills. *Review of Educational Research, 56,* 381–409.

Schecter-Connors, M. (1989, June). Model literacy program for hearing-impaired adults. Presentation to: Literacy Conference, Gallaudent University, Washington, DC.

Schrodel, J. (1987). The educational and occupational aspirations and attainments of deaf students and alumni of post-secondary programs. In G. Anderson & D. Watson (Eds.), *Innovations in the habilitation and rehabilitation of the deaf* (pp. 117–149). Little Rock, AR: Rehabilitation Research and Training Center On Deafness and Hearing Impairment.

Schunhoff, H. (Ed.) (1964). Needed expansion of vocational training program. *Proceedings of a national workshop on improved opportunities for the deaf, The University of Knoxville* (pp. 16–24). Washington, DC: U.S. Department of Health, Education and Welfare.

Scouten, E.L. (1984). *Turning points in the education of deaf people.* Danville, IL: Interstate Printers & Publishers, Inc.

Scranton State School for the Deaf. (1985). College awareness program for hearing-impaired youth in conjunction with the Pennsylvania Office of Vocational Rehabilitation Program announcement. Scranton, PA: Scranton State School.

Singer Vocational Evaluation Systems. (1973). Rochester, NY: Singer Educational Division, Career Systems.

Skagen, A. (Ed.), 1986). *Workplace literacy.* New York: American Management Association (AMA) Membership Publication Division.

Texas School for the Deaf. (1989). A transition to the future: Texas school for the deaf transitional post-secondary program. Program brochure. Austin, TX: Texas State School for the Deaf.

Trybus, R., & Karchmer, M. (1977). School achievement scores of hearing-impaired children: National data on achievement status and growth patterns. *American Annals of the Deaf, 122,* 62–69.

U.S. Bureau of the Census (1981). *Statistical abstract of the United States* (102d edition). Washington, DC: U.S. Government Printing Office.

U.S. Department of Education & U.S. Department of Labor. (1988). *The bottomline: Basic skills in the workplace.* Washington, DC: U.S. Government Printing Office.

Valpar Component Work Sample Series Manual. (1979). Tucson, AR: Valpar Corporation.

Wagner, M. (1989, March). *The transition experience of youth with disabilities: A report from the national longitudinal transition study.* Menlo Park, CA: SRI International.

Walter, G., Foster, S., & Elliot, L. (1987, July). Attrition and accommodation of hearing-impaired college students in the U.S. Paper presented at the Tenth National Conference of the Association of Handicapped Student Service Programs in Post-Secondary Education, Washington, DC.

Will, M. (1984). *OSERS programming for the transition of youth with disabilities: Bridges from school to working life.* Office of Special Education and Rehabilitative Services.

WRIOT: Wide Range Interest—Opinion Test. (1979). Wilmington, DE: Jastak Associates, Inc.

▶ 6

The Assessment of Deaf Individuals in the Context of Rehabilitation

THOMAS E. ALLEN
Gallaudet University

STEVEN R. SLIGAR
Georgia Sensory Rehabilitation Center

The assessment of deaf individuals represents one of the most complicated issues facing counselors, teachers, and other professionals who work with this segment of the population. Despite the virtual explosion onto the market of tests purporting to measure a wide variety of characteristics (Buros Institute of Mental Measurement, 1988; Traxler, 1989), it is a sad fact that, because of cultural, communication, and linguistic factors, many of these published tests have limited utility when used with deaf clients. Vocational evaluators must be aware of the psychometric limitations of available instrumentation and be prepared to design, implement, and subsequently justify evaluations using techniques that may have little psychometric support.

Client evaluation is crucial to many activities associated with education and rehabilitation: the determination of appropriate rehabilitation services, planning appropriate educational or vocational programming, establishing program accountability, assuring nondiscrimination, and justifying allocation or reallocation of resources to ensure that those most in need will be adequately served (Halpern & Fuhrer, 1984a). Referrals for vocational evaluation may range from a high school graduate seeking a general career direction to an adult seeking employment in a specific industry to a multi-handicapped deaf person having problems adjusting to a new living arrangement. Given these wide-ranging needs, the lack of psychometric support for many of the published evaluation strategies for use with deaf clients is an extreme problem.

Much of the psychometric research has considered individual instruments and their reliability and validity with deaf individuals. While important, these studies typically look at instruments in isolation and fail to take into account the broad range of evaluative activities undertaken by vocational evaluators when making recommendations about clients. Nadolsky (1971) provides useful distinctions among three levels of vocational assessment: micro, macro, and encounter.

Psychometric studies deal, almost exclusively, on the *micro* level. The micro level is concerned with the assessment of single traits. In micro level assessment, the evaluator obtains an in-depth sample of a narrow band of abilities or traits, and then synthesizes these to form the basis of recommendations. This clinical approach usually adheres to test protocols involving standardization, validation, and other psychometric procedures.

The *macro* approach to assessment involves a more active assessment of client traits, e.g., through rehabilitation workshop evaluations, on-the-job tryouts, selective placements, vocational class tryouts, and techniques for evaluating persons in supported employment situations. It utilizes observational techniques and places emphasis on work productivity, and/or the work personality of the client. Industrial or workshop standards are used as the primary criteria for assessment and serve as the basis for making recommendations.

The *encounter* approach involves the use of simulated work samples. These provide an opportunity to analyze the client's relationship to his or her work environment. Both specific traits and global behaviors are assessed in a clinical setting within the vocational evaluation area. These, along with considerations of specific job characteristics and the client's interests, form the basis for recommendations.

A full understanding of the role of assessment in the rehabilitation process requires both a knowledge of the specific psychometric properties of tools that are on the market and a perspective on how various approaches toward assessment fit into the broader context of the evaluation process. This chapter will discuss vocational assessment from both these points of view. The first part will describe the theoretical and psychometric context of assessment. Definitional issues will be addressed, the legal context will be described, and selected studies from the psychometric literature will be summarized. In the second part, a broader, more practitioner-oriented context will be described. This part will consider the basic objectives of evaluation, which are: 1) to provide a judgment or prognosis of rehabilitation potential; 2) to identify direct vocational assets; 3) to identify vocational barriers and limitations; and 4) to provide recommendations for subsequent planning (Shiels, 1986). The first part portrays a "gloom-and-doom" picture that has been presented by theorists, lawyers, and psychometricians, while the second part demonstrates that there are promising options. At the conclusion of the chapter, three case studies will be presented in which systematic evaluations led to successful rehabilitation planning and outcomes for deaf clients.

THE THEORETICAL CONTEXT

A Definition of Assessment

A concise definition of assessment is difficult, since assessment occurs in many contexts and for many reasons. In rehabilitation, unlike medicine, our concern is to determine how an individual functions in the world. While medical tests can assess the amount of damage sustained by a particular organ of the body, the results of those tests convey only limited information about the consequences of this damage on the functioning of the individual in society. Thus, assessment in the context of rehabilitation is better served by the definition of "functional assessment" provided by Halpern and Fuhrer (1984b). It states, "Functional assessment is the measurement of purposeful behavior in interaction with the environment, which is interpreted according to the assessment's intended uses" (p. 3).

Three aspects of this definition are worth highlighting. First, it stresses that the behavior being assessed, be it the manifestation of an intellectual or vocational ability, must be purposeful. Our goal in rehabilitation is to observe the client engaged in purposeful activities and to make predictions about how the client will perform in other work, training, or living settings. Second, the definition emphasizes the interaction between the individual and the environment. Too often, assessments are presumed to inform us about abilities without consideration of environmental factors. One serious impediment to the predictive validity of many tests is the failure to consider the environmental contexts of either the testing situation, the work or training situation, or both. Finally, the definition recognizes that assessments are performed for "intended uses." Failure to specify clearly the intended use of a test score will almost guarantee that it will be sued inappropriately.

Many of the validity problems that have been encountered in the testing of deaf individuals can be traced to a lack of clarity in their relationships to any of the three major components of the Halpern and Fuhrer definition. Either the purposeful nature of the assessed behavior is not clearly described, environmental requirements of either the test itself or the work or training experience to which the test pertains are not adequately accounted for, or the intended use of the assessment results are not adequately specified or are inappropriate.

In the three levels of assessment categories described above, it should be noted that the functional relevance of assessments increases as we move from the micro to the encounter levels. However, the levels of standardization, reliability, and objectivity decrease at the same time. Thus, optimal evaluations are those which employ a combination of strategies involving both standardized and non-standardized experiences.

The Classification of Individuals and the Assessment of Disadvantage

Inevitably, assessments serve to categorize or classify individuals. Applicants are deemed either qualified for a job or for acceptance into a vocational training program or they are not. Clients are deemed eligible for a particular kind of assistance or they are not. Yet problems pertaining to classification and the use of classification schemes have been present in the rehabilitation literature for many years.

Reschly (1987) notes that confusion over medical and social models of classification has resulted in widely varying classification schemes. Walberg and Wang (1987), for example, view hearing impairment as a medical classification and one in which there is "little controversy." However, audiological results, by themselves, have only limited value in predicting whether an individual will be able to function in a particular job. Returning to our definition mandating the study of purposeful behavior within an environmental context for a specific use, we can see that the classification of persons with hearing impairments using purely medical or audiological classifications may very well lead to considerable controversy.

One approach for describing the sources of an individual's disadvantage in society has been proposed by the World Health Organization (Halpern & Fuhrer, 1984b; World Health Organization [WHO], 1980). Known as the International Classification of Impairments, Disabilities, and Handicaps (ICIDH), this scheme holds potential for reducing some of the confusion faced by service providers who perform assessments and desire to make meaningful classifications of disabled students or clients. This scheme segregates the various consequences of disease and injury into three hierarchical levels which progress from purely medical considerations to purely social ones. At each step, rehabilitation practitioners must consider the potential consequences of assessments on the function of the individual at tasks which are higher in the hierarchy.

The *impairment* level of assessment pertains to a direct evaluation of the loss of organ function that is the result of disease, injury, or genetic factors. The *disability* level of assessment refers to the determination of the skills or lack of skills that an individual exhibits while interacting with the environment. Much of the assessment that occurs within the context of rehabilitation is at this level. The *handicap* level refers to the disadvantages experienced by individuals while attempting to perform social roles that are generally available to other people.

The distinction between the disability level and the handicap level is crucial. The fact that a hearing-impaired client can demonstrate the ability to operate a computer does not guarantee employment as a computer operator. At the handicap level, disadvantage accrues from society's unwillingness to accommodate the particular needs of individuals with impairments, regardless of their abilities to perform work-related tasks successfully.

The Legal Context

The law addresses the issue of the use of assessment devices with individuals with disabilities quite directly. Standards related to the fair use of tests have derived both from the U.S. Constitution and from recently enacted Federal legislation. Under the Constitution, the Equal Protection Clause of the Fourteenth Amendment protects against intentional unjustifiable classification by state and federal governments. Thus, state laws that result in the classification of individuals on the basis of a test are subject to federal scrutiny, and there have been numerous court cases that have alleged linguistic or racial discrimination when tests have been used to classify minority students (Wigdor & Garner, 1982).

As regards federal legislation, the regulations for implementing Public Law 94-142, the Education for All Handicapped Children Act (EHA), mandate that tests and other evaluation materials not be culturally discriminatory, that these materials be presented in the child's native language and mode of communication, that no single test serve as the sole criterion for determining educational programming, and that all test materials are to be validated for the specific purpose used (Education for All Handicapped Children Act Regulations [EHA], 1977).

Finally, Section 504 of the Rehabilitation Act of 1973 mandates the fair use of tests with individuals with disabilities and the need for establishing the reliability and validity of any test used in making any important decisions about these individuals (Section 504 of the Rehabilitation Act of 1973, 1973; Wigdor & Garner, 1982).

In spite of these regulations, it is evident that the use of tests with unproven validity and reliability is widespread. A recent survey of educational programs providing school-to-work transition services for deaf high school students, conducted by the Center for Assessment and Demographic Studies at Gallaudet University, revealed that 88 percent of deaf high school students had been administered some type of achievement test; 68 percent had been administered some type of vocational test; and 40 percent had been administered some type of socio-emotional test for the purpose of making an educational placement or tracking decision (Traxler, 1989). What was particularly alarming about the findings of this research was the number of different vocational tests reported being used. A total of 59 individual vocational instruments were reported in use with this population. Of these, only 4 tests were used with a substantial number of students, while 55 different tests were administered, each to an average of only 1 percent of the population. For most of these, validity with respect to the deaf student population had not been demonstrated (Traxler, 1989). The results of this research suggests a pervasive lack of consensus regarding the relative merits of instruments used to assess deaf individuals.

In 1979, the National Research Council (NRC) was requested by the Office of Civil Rights to study testing practices with individuals with disabilities and to make policy recommendations. In the final report of the NRC's Panel on Testing of Handicapped People (Sherman & Robinson, 1982), they state:

> Almost since the promulgation of Section 504 regulations, it has been clear that there exists insufficient information to allow the demonstrably valid testing of handicapped people, as required in the regulations. Information on standardized and modified tests taken by handicapped people, that is data on their reliability and validity, and on the effects of modifying test administration procedures, is essential (p. 141).

One inescapable conclusion that can be drawn from a study of the federal regulations, the deliberations of this special panel empowered by the Office of Civil Rights to study the implementation of these regulations, and by research examining test use among the deaf population, is that a considerable amount of testing is performed on shaky legal grounds. Yet testing, particularly among the student population, cannot be abandoned. P.L. 94-142 mandates the creation, for each student receiving federally funded special educational services, of an individual educational program (IEP). Often evidence from standardized testing is relied upon heavily in determining the features of the IEP for individual students. Thus, in spite of warnings about the possible sources of invalidity in standardized tests available on the market, the net impact of the federal regulations—particularly those associated with P.L. 94-142—will be to increase, rather than decrease, the use of such tests.

PSYCHOMETRIC CONSIDERATIONS ON THE USE OF PUBLISHED INSTRUMENTS WITH HEARING-IMPAIRED CLIENTS

General Comments

When interpreting deaf individuals' test scores which have been derived from standardized tests developed for hearing individuals, two broad categories of errors are likely to be encountered. The first occurs because the standardization samples typically do not include deaf individuals; thus, the norms inappropriately assign scores which identify the relative position of deaf persons in a population in which they are not represented.

The second error derives specifically from biased test items, which hearing-impaired students are likely to get wrong, because their acculturation is different from that of the individuals comprising the standardization samples. Examples of biased items would be: (1) a preference inventory where "listening to records" might be listed as an alternative; or (2) a reading comprehension item based on a paragraph glorifying "the sounds of spring." These types of items occur frequently in published tests. In tests such as these, the raw scores obtained by deaf test-takers are not true reflections of their interests or abilities, because of biased item content.

One common solution proposed for adapting tests for hearing-impaired persons is to translate English paper-and-pencil versions into signed modes of communication. However, signed versions of tests developed with hearing populations typically fail for two reasons: First, despite the modality change, the acculturation differences are not accommodated, even if the modality change (written to signed) is accompanied by a language change (such as English to American Sign Language); and second, such radical adaptations to the presentation of test items tend to invalidate the norms (Gerweck & Ysseldyke, 1979). New tests in which the background experiences of

deaf individuals are taken into account, and which are subjected to rigorous psychometric evaluations, are sorely needed.

In the following sections, research pertaining to the use of specific instruments
when administered to deaf individuals will be described. The intent is to demonstrate
the results of psychometric research and to show specific problem areas in the use and
interpretation of particular tests. As such, each of the instruments mentioned is only
briefly described. Fuller descriptions, publisher, and price information for these and
other tests commonly used with deaf individuals are available in several compendia
of test reviews and descriptions. The *Mental Measurement Yearbook: Online Database* (Buros Institute of Mental Measurement, 1988) is an excellent source of test
information and test reviews. Also, the reader is referred to a resource list at the end of
this chapter for a listing of publications with descriptions of tests commonly used with
deaf and other disabled persons.

Personality and Social Skills Instruments

Quite often, research reveals that typical deaf subjects show pathological responses to
personality tests (Vestberg, 1989). For example, Levine (1956), based on administering Rorschach ink blots to 31 deaf female adolescents, concluded that deaf girls
demonstrated: (1) underdeveloped mental capacity; (2) emotional underdevelopment; (3) a lag in understanding dynamics of interpersonal relationships; (4) egocen-
tricity; (5) constricted life area; and (6) rigid adherence to book-of-etiquette code
rather than to inner sensibility as a standard for behaving. Levine attributed these
results to the deaf subjects' delayed language acquisition. Unfortunately, she failed to
consider the strong possibility that the results might have been an artifact of the
instrument. Other studies (e.g., Myklebust, 1964) have similarly noted pathological
responses to personality measures by deaf individuals, but have failed to consider
whether the tests used were valid.

Studies conducted more recently have recognized the possibility that these aber-
rant test results may be artifacts of the tests rather than reflections of the students.
Evidence has been presented which evaluates the psychometric properties of instruments used to assess the social and personality characteristics of deaf individuals. For
example, Acree (1987) studied the relationship of two commonly employed measures
of self-concept: the Meadow Pictorial Scale of Self Image (MPSSI [Meadow, 1967])
and the Tennessee Self-Concept Scale (Fitt, 1965), as adapted for deaf people. He
found no correlation between the two tests. In a related study he found only low
correlations between MPSSI and the Meadow-Kendall Social-Emotional Assessment
Inventory for Deaf Students (MKSEAI [Meadow, 1980]). Thus, even when evaluating two instruments measuring similar constructs either developed or adapted for
hearing-impaired students, low correlations were obtained.

The lack of reading ability often confounds the results of published tests of personality and social skills. However, some studies indicate low reliability even when

samples are limited to deaf students with adequate levels of skill in reading English. Jacobs (1987) administered the Sixteen Personality Factor Questionnaire, Form A (16PF-A [Cattell, Eber, & Tatsuoka, 1978]) to deaf college students who had demonstrated the seventh-grade reading level required for using this instrument. In spite of overall comparability with norms for college students in the general population, the authors computed extremely low reliability coefficients for many of the 16 factors. Thus, even when samples of hearing-impaired students are limited to those with demonstrated ability in English, the reliability of the 16PF is questionable.

The use of more projective personality tests does not improve the reliability or validity. Ouellette (1988) reports on various psychometric tests of the validity of the House-Tree-Person (H-T-P [Buck, 1948]) projective test of personality. She concludes that the H-T-P was both valid and reliable for only three of eight traits evaluated for deaf clients: aggressiveness, impulsivity and immaturity.

Other common evaluation techniques involve the use of a behavioral checklist, where a third party, typically a parent or a teacher, checks a list of behaviors that are typical for the person being evaluated. Quarrington and Solomon (1975) asked both mothers and house parents of students in residential schools to complete the Vineland Social Maturity Scales (Doll, 1965). Comparing the ratings, the authors found differences; house parents rated the students as being more socially immature. The researchers question the validity of such techniques when information is provided by persons who are not familiar with aspects of the student's (or client's) behavior.

Some research has been reported in which published measures of personality and social factors have been adapted to accommodate the needs of hearing-impaired clients. These adaptations have met with varying success. Dwyer and Wincenciak (1977) report on a version of the 16PF-E presented in American Sign Language (ASL) on videotape. While there were no significant differences in overall results when this ASL adaptation was compared to the traditional paper-and-pencil version, interscale correlations for individual factors between the two modalities were poor; in fact, *one factor showed a significant negative correlation for the ASL and paper-and-pencil presentation.* This indicated that, for this one factor, persons who scored high via the paper-and-pencil version tended to score low via the ASL version. Obviously, the validity of the ASL procedure, based on this study has to be seriously questioned.

Intellectual Assessment

Research geared toward the development of appropriate measures of intellectual abilities has proceeded along two separate paths: that which has sought to develop an adequate assessment of IQ, and that which has sought a valid measure of academic achievement. Unfortunately, virtually all of this work has been done with deaf children. Given the importance of literacy to the attainment of meaningful employment for adults in today's society, this lack is particularly troublesome. Nevertheless, a review of the major efforts to develop valid assessments of both IQ and achievement levels for deaf children is instructive in the current context. Conclusions can be drawn which may hopefully guide test development efforts in the future.

IQ

By far, the most widely used IQ measure with deaf children is the Wechsler Intelligence Scale for Children-Revised, Performance Factor (WISC-R-P [Wechsler, 1974]), partly due to the existence of norms computed on the deaf population (Ray, 1982). It has subscores associated with tasks called Block Design, Picture Completion, Picture Arrangement, Object Assembly, and Coding. Validity studies with this instrument have been mixed. Evans (1980) noted high correlations between the WISC-R-P with Raven's Coloured Progressive Matrices (Raven, 1976) for hearing-impaired children in Britain, attesting to the validity of this device. In an American study, Hirshoren, Hurley, and Hunt (1977) noted a very high correlation between the WISC-R-P and the Hiskey-Nebraska Test of Learning Aptitude (H-NTLA [Hiskey, 1966]), a test which also has norms computed for deaf individuals. However, in a subsequent analysis, Hirshoren, Hurley, and Kavale (1979) evaluated the predictive validity of the WISC-R-P by looking at correlations with subtest scores of the Stanford Achievement Test, 6th Edition (The Psychological Corporation, 1974). While some statistical evidence for predictive validity was noted, the authors were skeptical about the practical significance of the correlations.

Other studies have led to similar conclusions. Wilson, Rapin, Wilson, and Van Denburg (1975) administered the WISC-R-P, the H-NTLA, and Raven's Colored Progressive Matrices to a sample of deaf children with normal brain functioning. While they noted median scores on the aggregated indices for all three instruments comparable to hearing children of the same age, they also found that patterns of subscale scores for the various subtasks differed radically from those shown by typical hearing students. They concluded that deaf students may handle complex cognitive tasks in ways that are radically different from those demonstrated by hearing children.

To summarize these studies, the existence of norms computed on samples of hearing-impaired children and some validity studies that have demonstrated high intercorrelations among nonverbal measures of IQ have led to widespread use of these measures, particularly the WISC-R-P and the H-NTLA. However, the nonverbal nature of these tests, which is seen as a virtue, results in the situation where they have shown limited predictive validity when the criterion measure has been a test of academic achievement which requires verbal skills with the English language. Thus, the utility of these instruments has yet to be described in terms of current educational practice.

Furthermore, psychometric evaluations of these instruments have typically revealed subtest score patterns that deviate significantly from those demonstrated by hearing test takers, in spite of comparability in the aggregated scores. To the extent that these findings represent valid differences in the cognitive approaches that deaf and hearing individuals take to solving complex tasks, they may have implications for efforts designed at restructuring job descriptions and demands for deaf workers.

Academic Achievement

By far, the greatest amount of work in the assessment of the academic achievement levels of hearing-impaired students has been carried out by Gallaudet University's Center for Assessment and Demographic Studies (CADS) using the Stanford Achievement Test (The Psychological Corporation, 1974, 1982, 1989). As noted by Traxler (1989), a national study conducted by CADS revealed that 91 percent severely and profoundly deaf high school students administered any achievement test for the purpose of tracking or course placement were administered the Stanford Achievement Test.

A wealth of psychometric information has been published about the use of the Stanford with hearing-impaired students. Allen (1986) has reported that both internal consistency and parallel forms estimates of the Stanford (7th edition) subtest reliability are adequate. Also reported are the results of a content validity study in which teachers were asked to rate Stanford (1982) items in mathematics computation and reading comprehension in terms of the opportunities that their students had to learn the content represented through actual instruction. The results indicated a high level of alignment between the Stanford (1982) mathematics computation and reading comprehension subtests and the curriculum in use by educators of deaf students throughout the country.

In spite of these optimistic psychometric properties, the existence of norms representing the performance of deaf students, and the overwhelming level of use enjoyed by this test throughout the United States, much of the published literature which describes analysis of the Stanford data argues for restraint in its use and interpretation. Many of the findings related to the WISC-R-P (1974), described above, in which unusual patterns of subtest scores undermined the successful interpretation of the aggregated index of IQ, are echoed in various item analyses that have been reported for Stanford data.

With test item data from the 6th edition standardization with hearing-impaired students, Rudner (1978), using a statistical technique which allowed for the identification of biased test items, demonstrated systematic bias for certain items. Evidence for similar bias has been provided using item data from the 7th edition standardization with hearing-impaired students (Allen, Holt, Bloomquist, & Starke, 1987; Allen, Holt, Hotto, & Bloomquist, 1987; Bloomquist & Allen, 1987). The existence of statistical basis in the Stanford (1982) items raises problems for interpreting the normed scores.

This familiar finding, i.e., a differential pattern of test results, was found in a separate study of readability by LaSasso (1980). She administered a Cloze test of reading[1] to a group of 95 profoundly deaf residential school students who had scored between 4.0 and 7.6 grade equivalents on the Stanford Reading Comprehension subtest (1974). In her test, she selected passages determined by commonly employed readability formulas to be at the third, fifth, and seventh grade levels of difficulty. The

---

[1]The Cloze procedure used in this study was one in which every fifth word of a 250-word reading passage was deleted and replaced by a blank line. The student's task was to fill in the missing words based on contextual cues.

students in her sample found the fifth-grade passage the easiest to read (as indicated by the highest percentage of correct responses), followed by the seventh-grade passage. *The third-grade passage was the most difficult for the deaf students.*

A way to characterize these achievement tests would be to say that they yielded consistent results, and are thus reliable; however, the scores have limited utility in providing information about the specific subtask areas which make up the composites.

Vocational Assessment

In the area of vocational assessment, very little psychometric research on existing instruments, as administered to deaf individuals, has been reported. Few studies have supported using paper-and-pencil measures, rating scales, work samples, and situational assessments. For example, in a study of students enrolled at the National Technical Institute for the Deaf (NTID), White and Slusher (1978) found low correlations between scores on a variety of commercially available career maturity tests and measures of actual student career awareness and aspirations, although, individually, the instruments yielded acceptable reliability coefficients. These researchers conclude that commercially available tests are not very useful in obtaining this kind of information for deaf clients.

One instrument used widely with deaf adolescents is the Wide Range Interest and Opinion Test (WRIOT [Jastak & Jastak, 1979]). In fact, among deaf students in a national study of school to work transition, it was the second most widely used vocational assessment instrument (Traxler, 1989). Its primary advantage for the deaf population is that it does not require reading ability: The items are presented pictorially. However, the WRIOT has been challenged for its lack of psychometric support. Traxler (1989) notes, "the WRIOT has received much criticism from test reviewers" (Hsu, 1985; Manuele, 1985; Zytowski, 1978). These reviewers noted that the test stimuli were ambiguous and that, for special populations such as persons with hearing impairment, no evidence of reliability or validity is presented.

In spite of this generally bleak picture with respect to the assessment of vocational skills and attitudes of hearing-impaired clients, recent efforts at developing tools specifically for use with deaf youth in transition from school to work have been encouraging. Reiman and Bullis (1988) have reported on a pilot study to develop an assessment of the transitional needs of hearing-impaired youth. These authors begin with some fairly straightforward assumptions: (1) Assessment procedures should be directly related to the content and skills that deaf students should know and perform; (2) results from traditional psychometric procedures provide only tangential information and are of minimal utility for instructional programs; and (3) there is a need to develop functional, transition-oriented assessment instruments to reflect content which is relevant to the deaf population.

Reiman and Bullis (1988) have identified three broad domains of outcomes: (1) employment, (2) independent living, and (3) social and interpersonal skills. Specifically targeted to hearing-impaired individuals with low achievement levels who have no serious secondary impairments and who are seeking employment directly after high school, they have developed a set of competencies and a corresponding set of items for the employment and independent-living domains, based on a survey of experts in the field. To date, they have prepared both signed and written versions of their competency battery, called the Transition Competency Battery, and have pilot tested it with a small sample of mainstream and residential high school juniors and seniors.

The Reiman and Bullis project provides a model for assessment development. They have identified domains of importance; they have sought expert advice from the field in order to specify competencies and create test items; they have prepared multiple versions of their instruments in written as well as sign communication modalities. Furthermore, they have specified clearly the population for which the test is to be used, i.e., low-achieving deaf school leavers without additional handicaps who desire jobs immediately after leaving school. The clarity with which these components are specified should ensure the eventual publication of one instrument that has good utility for workers in the field.

THE PRACTICAL CONTEXT

Components of the Evaluation Process

In contrast to the previous section, which focused on aspects of psychometrics and the difficulties encountered by researchers attempting to establish validity and reliability, this section begins with an overview of evaluation in rehabilitation, which can be viewed as a five-step process. This section considers vocational assessment in a more global evaluative context.

Step 1: Review of Background Information
The first step involves a review of relevant client characteristics including demographic (age, sex, ethnic, etc.), medical (hearing loss and other handicapping conditions), educational, vocational, and psycho-social information. Also, a review of the client's communication history is important at this step (Watson, 1976; Cheung, 1983). The evaluator must determine which variables, including those related to the client's deafness, may have the greatest impact on the subsequent evaluation.

The skilled evaluator must also be aware of the referral source. Is the referral made by a rehabilitation counselor for deaf people, or is the referral from a general vocational rehabilitation counselor who may not be attuned to many of the cultural variables which should have been investigated prior to the referral?

Step 2: Developing an Individual Written Evaluation Plan (IWEP)
All clients receiving a vocational evaluation must participate in the development of their evaluation plan. The IWEP should specify questions and areas in need of assess-

ment. These areas may have been suggested in the referral, identified by the client, or determined by the vocational evaluator as a result of the review process. A well-written IWEP includes all of these areas, as well as specifications of the types of behaviors to be observed, the data to be gathered, the vocational interests to be identified, and the timeframe for conducting the assessments. Assessment areas might include: intellectual capacity, educational achievement, work skills and work tolerance, communication skill and language preference, job-seeking skills, interests and attitudes, knowledge of occupational information, and other areas (Commission on Accreditation of Rehabilitation Facilities [CARF], 1989).

Step 3: Implementing the IWEP

Step 3 involves carrying out the assessments specified in the IWEP. Cheung (1983) describes the process of vocational evaluation of severely disabled deaf adults; it includes the review of background and referral information, a client orientation and interview, and an evaluation of physical abilities, basic skills (usually via paper-and-pencil tests), and job readiness. Cheung concludes that client evaluations should focus on the client's potential for learning new tasks and developing good work habits rather than on determining specific job categories. Both Cheung (1983) and Shiels (1986) state the need to plan carefully the order of administering psychometric tests, and recommend alternating between paper-and-pencil tests and work samples so that individuals who may excel in one type of evaluation and do poorly in other types will not become overly discouraged if presented with too many tests of the latter type. Finally, the vocational evaluator should be sensitive to how the client will respond to the evaluation battery. For example, if a client is highly motivated to attend college and wants to participate in paper-and-pencil testing, then this type of assessment should occur early in the process. However, if the client has had numerous unsuccessful evaluations or a poor record of academic performance, a paper-and-pencil measure of school achievement would be an inappropriate place to begin an evaluation.

An important aspect to the implementation phase is the process through which the client gives and receives feedback to and from the evaluator. For many clients, face-to-face interviews are held frequently throughout the evaluation. These interviews may take many different forms, including specific interviewing related to future plans or solicitation of feedback regarding particular tasks or work samples. Some interviews might be simulations of meetings with hearing employers. Finally, exit interviews are used to review and clarify what has occurred throughout the process and to discuss what specific recommendations will be made.

The implementation phase needs to include the client's perceptions of the worth or validity of the tests or work samples that have comprised the evaluation battery. This is referred to as the "face validity" of the evaluation and involves the client's perception of the relationship between the tasks at hand and the client's goals.

The following example illustrates how different modes of evaluation purporting to measure similar constructs might lead to different recommendations, depending upon the client's needs. The Minnesota Clerical (Number and Name Comparison

[1979]), the VALPAR Component Work Sample #5 (CWS [Valpar Corporation, 1989]), Clerical Perception (mail sorting and filing), and a facility-developed workstation that includes some on-the-job activities are all designed to determine the client's ability to sort and file. The Minnesota Clerical utilizes a strictly standardized approach to measure a specific trait. The VALPAR CWS #5 samples similar traits but takes into account more global work factors, such as the client's like or dislike of the work. Lastly, the facility-developed workstation is a sample of an actual job which the client can experience. In each case the client performs similar tasks, but the evaluation environment varies. This may affect the client's performance, depending on his or her interests and goals. As was noted earlier, the failure to specify the environmental components in the assessment of a client's "purposeful activity" may subvert the assessment process.

Step 4: Analyzing the Results of the Assessment
Step 4 involves reviewing all data gathered during the evaluation process and translating them into vocationally meaningful terms. The goal of this step is to generate a composite of all available background, observation, and test data. The purpose of the composite is to show the impact each element, individually and combined, will have on the client's ability to be employed. The evaluator asks questions relating to specific recommendations and then determines if sufficient data has been generated. For example,

1. Has the client's school provided sufficient information about careers to enable the client to select a college major?
2. Is the client a sign language user and able to use an interpreter in pursuit of a college degree?
3. Will the client's family risk his or her going to work, potentially placing the client in a dangerous situation?
4. Has the client matured to a level where he or she can state, "I like to do this type work" or "I don't like to do that type work"?

Based upon the reasons for the client's referral and the data generated during the evaluation process, the evaluator will have to answer questions such as these. Frequently, these questions have been asked specifically at referral. At other times, they arise during the evaluation. It is then incumbent on the evaluator to chart the evaluation and gather appropriate information.

The evaluation process generates a massive amount of information ranging from test scores to descriptions of hygiene habits to job coach ratings of production. The evaluator must then select the relevant information and relate it to the client's readiness to work in a given job field. The job-related criteria for entry to a specific occupation could include actual industry requirements, local job analysis information, computer-based job matching programs, *Dictionary of Occupational Titles*

(D.O.T. [U.S. Department of Labor, 1977]) qualifications profile, and other relevant information. The evaluator for deaf persons must constantly be aware of artificial barriers to employment, such as jobs coded as needing hearing when this is not a critical aspect of the job. More subtle barriers can be achievement level requirements, method of on-the-job training, the manner in which work instructions are administered, and discriminatory hiring practices.

Step 5: Report and Recommendations

In the final step, the evaluator provides a summary of all the observational and test data and utilizes this as a basis for making recommendations. It is the vocational evaluator's responsibility to provide a clear definition of the client's needs, based on the data. Recommendations for a deaf client may target specific inappropriate behaviors (such as teasing co-workers), may result in a direct job placement or placement in a specific training program, or may include the need for independent living skills training, job-seeking training, interpreting, sign language training, the purchase of a telecommunications device for the deaf (TDD), or other services.

THREE CASE STUDIES

Three case studies which illustrate the five evaluation steps will be presented. The three emphasize the different approaches (micro, macro, and encounter) defined at the beginning of this chapter. Each case study is based on composites of actual clients who have received services at the Georgia Sensory Rehabilitation Center. The vocational evaluator is an expert in the field of deafness and is a skilled signer.

Case No. 1: Mary Micro

Reason for Referral

"Determine if client should pursue a career in deaf education or consider other options." Mary was referred by an experienced general caseload counselor with no deafness background.

Background

Mary is a 24-year-old single female of average height and weight. She has a severe to profound bilateral sensorineural loss and medical limitations of asthma and heart murmur which cause shortness of breath from exertion. A cardiologist's report indicates that jobs requiring physical demands above light work must be approved by a physician. She lives at home with her supportive middle-class parents in Smalltown, USA, and she has had no other residence.

Mary graduated from a regular public high school without specialized support for hearing-impaired students. She attended Smalltown Community College as a sub-freshman. She did not pass Developmental Studies[2] after three quarters and discontinued. She has never been employed.

Behavioral Observations
Mary was neat and well-groomed. She was punctual in following her schedule, and she co-operated with her supervisor. She communicated fluently and expressively through oral means. She demonstrated some skill with the manual alphabet and used English signs, albeit somewhat awkwardly. Her speech was clear and usually understandable, although some words and consonants are slurred. She interacted with both orally and manually communicating peers in a friendly and appropriate manner. She was attentive to all work instructions and understood them readily. She expressed a fear of living on her own; however, it was her goal to do so.

Data
Mary is considered to be in the high/average range of intelligence. Since she had good English skills, she was administered a battery of instruments that are not typically employed with hearing-impaired clients. On the Raven Standard Progressive Matrices (Raven, 1958) she scored in the 75th percentile. On the Wechsler Adult Intelligence Scale-Revised (Wechsler, 1981) she received a verbal score of 108, a performance score of 120, and a full-scale score of 114. Academically, she is above the high school level in the areas of reading comprehension, vocabulary, spelling, and grammar, but is only at the seventh-grade level in mathematics computation. In the area of practical problem solving she scores at the ninth-grade level. These scores are from The Adult Basic Learning Examination.

Vocational Interests/Aptitudes
Mary's stated vocational goal is to become an elementary or secondary teacher of deaf students. Tests used were the Holland Self-Directed Search (Holland, 1985), which indicated primary interest areas as artistic, social, and conventional; and the Wide Range Interest and Opinion Test, which shows high interest in music, drama, art, social service, and protective service. Work samples show average abilities in numerical skills, finger and manual dexterity, and fine and gross motor skills. Above average skills in form, spatial, and clerical perceptions were noted.

Recommendations
Based on the evaluations, the following recommendations were made.

1. Remedial mathematics through developmental studies at Big City College which has a special program for hearing-impaired students.

[2]In the state Mary was from Developmental Studies is a group of courses including reading, English, and math designed to raise a student's skill level to be able to compete in a college setting.

2. Support services during college to include tutors, note takers, FM audio loop system, and oral interpreters.
3. Continuing career guidance and counseling during college developmental program to gain greater awareness of jobs in which she is interested, to establish a specific vocational goal, and to select appropriate education or training site. It is recommended the *Guide for Occupational Exploration* (GOE) groupings of Editing, Creative Writing, Teaching and Instructing, General, and Library Services be a springboard for career exploration.
4. VR sponsorship in college or vocational technical training in a career related to areas of interest, i.e., art or social services.
5. Provide independent living skills evaluation at client's residence with follow-up training as indicated to facilitate the transition to independent housing.

Outcomes
Client completed the Developmental Studies program at Big City Community College which necessitated moving out of parents' home. She has since enrolled in a regular degree program at Big City Community College, with the support services of a note taker and an oral interpreters, and she is pursuing a college degree in education.

Discussion: Case No. 1
The referring counselor presented sufficient background data. As Mary has basically been in the hearing culture, the counselor was able to develop and manage the case as was customary for a Smalltown caseload. Whereas Mary had been able to succeed in public high school with support from her friends, family, and teachers, she was unable to do so in a college setting, and she failed in her first attempt at Developmental Studies.

Given her vocational goal, there were no medical limitations. The evaluator noted the asthma and heart murmur but did not allow their presence to pose a significant barrier. Many deaf clients will present a wide array of other medical problems and it is necessary to apply vocational requirements to limitations as stated by the physician.

Observational data yielded appropriate socialization skills. The primary expressive and receptive language was through an oral mode with secondary skills in sign language noted. The determination of language preference was gleaned from observation in both formal (interview and testing) and informal (breaks and non-test times in the unit) situations.

Test data were from two sources. The intelligence testing was performed by a local Ph.D. psychologist without an interpreter. The test results were interpreted cautiously, given the problems of test validity and reliability that have been noted earlier in this chapter. The academic information was obtained in the rehabilitation unit.

Vocational interest tests were also administered and interpreted with caution due to her lack of exposure to the work world. Given her lack of work experience, the test results were suspect. However, they did provide information on her desire to socialize with or around others in a clean environment, and they confirmed her stated vocational objective. Physical capacities and clerical work samples were administered to allow for observations. They helped to determine if Mary had basic work skills (filing, task completion, etc.) necessary for college work.

Recommendation #1 was based on low mathematics computation scores. The Big City College program would provide support services as listed in recommendation #2. The third recommendation identified areas for counseling. The GOE, which provides a cross section of jobs within the same occupational interest area, was selected to form the basis of ongoing career exploration.

Recommendation #4 specifies a need for VR to sponsor Mary's training. This statement was based on her evaluation which demonstrated clearly that Mary had the potential to benefit from VR-supported training activities.

The final recommendation was based on her need to move to Big City. She demonstrated potential for acquiring independent living skills on her own; however, without support, she might be limited in her ability to succeed.

Case No. 2: Mac Ro

Reason for Referral
"Client referred to determine feasibility for employment and if continuation of rehabilitation services is appropriate." Mac was referred by a rehabilitation counselor for the deaf at the client's request.

Background
Mac is a 21-year-old male from Rural, GA. He graduated from a state school for the deaf with a vocational certificate of attendance and has been living at home with his parents for the two years since graduation. Neither Mac's non-working parents nor younger siblings have any sign communication skills and Mac's sign skills are regressing. The family expresses concern about his deteriorating vision and fears his leaving the protective environment of their home. He has a profound, congenital, sensorineural hearing impairment of unknown etiology. A secondary disability of retinitis pigmentosa is also present. Six months ago, a low vision evaluation indicated the need for low vision aids for reading standard print, for assistance in distance vision, and for controlling glare. The vision field was estimated at 70 degrees. During the vocational evaluation, however, the client did not use glasses or low vision aids except those provided in the unit. Mac describes himself as being blind at night and is afraid to travel alone after dark.

The school psychologist reported that several standardized tests were attempted with the client, but the results were not valid. Therefore, other sources of evidence—interviews with teachers and supervisors, classroom observation—were employed to determine Mac's level of intellectual functioning. Based on those qualitative sources, the school psychologist estimated that Mac functions in the moderate range of intelligence, and recommended that work information should be presented slowly, sequentially, and only a few steps at a time.

While a senior in high school, the client had received a short-term vocational evaluation at a rehabilitation center for the deaf. Results of this evaluation indicated that continuing observation and assessment would be necessary after high school.

Behavioral Observation

Mac dresses appropriately for his small 5'3", 150-pound stature. The previous evaluation noted that he was punctual reporting to and leaving work. However, unless specifically instructed to return to work, he was 15 to 20 minutes late returning from breaks. No other problems were noted. He communicates through American Sign Language and is very slow in responding to questions until he is familiar with the other signer. Mac also requires a short adjustment period to position himself so that he is able to view the signs. As he becomes familiar with the environment and other signers, the level of spontaneous communication increases. In his previous work site, he interacted appropriately with a signing supervisor, but did not interact with non-signing co-workers. Interpersonal skills were demonstrated with those workers who attempted to utilize sign language, but were not demonstrated with those who would not attempt to sign. Mac was able to package foods when hands-on demonstration was provided and when he was allowed to practice with a model for a short period of time. No problems were noted with his physical abilities to perform these tasks. His overall work demeanor was described as cooperative, but timid.

Data

No specific tests were administered. It was noted that he was able to meet production standards after approximately one week on the job. This is about twice the average time for a sighted, hearing worker and about as fast as hearing, sighted, developmentally disabled persons performing the same task. Mac works at one station and is responsible for placing various pre-packaged items (crackers, cookies, condiments, etc.) on trays moving down a conveyor belt. He is the only person with a disability on this line. His supervisor has knowledge of 50 work-related signs and has supervised one other deaf person. Mac was observed to be eager to report to work and stay on task the entire time. Problems of reporting back late from break, which were observed in the first vocational evaluation, were not observed in the long term assessment. Mac indicated that he enjoyed the work, the money, and the opportunity to have a job.

Recommendations

Based on the evaluations, the following recommendations were made.

1. Mac should continue his employment with ABC Food Packaging Company as a food packager. He is in need of ongoing support for those times when he will have to change jobs, or if a new supervisor without sign skills enters the area. He has demonstrated the interest and aptitudes to perform this type of work. He will

be able to function with only minimal support, provided that supervisor or work duties do not change.
2. Independent Living Skills evaluation and training is indicated.
3. Medical monitoring and follow-up ophthalmologist exam is strongly recommended.

Outcomes
Mac continues today as a food packager, lives in nearby subsidized housing, and transports himself to and from work on public transportation. He is independent in his day-to-day activities and follows a highly structured schedule. Any changes of his daily routines, e.g., banking and grocery shopping, require additional support.

Discussion: Case No. 2
The referral information was complete and adequate with respect to Mac's audiological and communication limitations, but lacking with respect to his cognitive functioning. Background information contained several significant items. First, the vocational certificate indicating failure to complete high school degree requirements is a "red flag." This type of certificate is frequently used to "graduate" deaf persons with minimal language skills. The inability of family members to sign may be indicative of social isolation. The family's expressed fears may be genuine, or they may mask other motives (dependence on SSI payments or use of client as babysitter).

The retinitis pigmentosa diagnosis was first made in school, and Mac's vision has since deteriorated. The previous psychological and vocational evaluation results and the professional opinion of the school psychologist with respect to Mac's cognitive functioning were considered useful.

The information on how the client positions himself to communicate is vital for work instructions, so that social interactions among co-workers are facilitated. The work environment needs to contain persons who have some knowledge of sign language.

The primary source of assessment data was production standards. Job placement was determined by the availability of a previously developed integrated site and also by the availability of a job within his range of abilities. Public transportation was also a factor. Mac's positive attitude toward his job was also an important consideration in formulating recommendations.

This evaluative approach was utilized because referral information was reliable, standardized tests were deemed invalid, a job site was available, and the client was highly motivated to work. Bypassing traditional clinical approaches saved time and possible client frustration.

The first recommendation is based on his successful performance of the job. The need for continuing support is requested to ensure eligibility for a supported work program. Independent living training is clearly indicated. The final recommendation provided for the client to receive services necessary for his deteriorating vision.

Case No. 3: Sam N. Counter

Reason for Referral

"Needs to establish a vocational objective and increase his readiness for work." Sam was referred by a rehabilitation counselor for deaf clients.

Background Information

Sam is a 26-year-old single male from Big City, GA, who graduated from Big City High School six years ago. This is a large mainstream program with support services for deaf students.

He is in good physical condition with a severe to profound bilateral sensorineural hearing loss present since birth. Etiology is unknown. Currently he lives with his parents. Previously he lived on his own for two years in another state while employed for a major recreation theme park. At this park he performed janitorial and food service duties. He has also worked for a large department store in Big City as a stock clerk (1 year). He states he liked both jobs "ok" but quit to get "other job-better." His first job after high school was for the Internal Revenue Service as a file clerk. He was discharged after 6 months due to a misunderstanding with another employee. Case records received from the Big City High School Deaf Program indicate that, at the time of graduation, the client was functioning at a normal level of intelligence and at approximately a third- to fifth-grade level of overall academic achievement.

Observations

Sam is of average height and weight. His well-trimmed hair and clean clothes indicate acceptable hygiene. He was very friendly and stated an interest in meeting other deaf persons who were attending the rehabilitation center. He arrived early for his evaluation the first day, but after meeting other deaf persons, he wanted to leave early for breaks and would not return unless the evaluator sought him out. He was usually found socializing with other persons in the lounge area. He accepted all assignments given him, and when questioned about his performance on or interest in them stated they were "all right."

During interviews Sam indicated he missed the freedom he had while in the other state and did not like the "rules" of his parents.

Vocational Interest/Aptitudes

Sam's three expressed vocational goals were to work as a file clerk, computer operator, or metal lathe operator. His stated areas of interest were art and operating different kinds of machines. A work sample battery was administered. The VALPAR Component Work Sample (VCWS) and the Vocational Interest Temperament Aptitudes System (VITAS) were administered. These batteries showed Sam to be above average in finger and manual dexterity, bi-manual coordination, eye-hand-foot coordination, color perceptions, and electrical circuitry and print reading. The VCWS and

VITAS showed Sam to be average in form and spatial perception. He scored below average in numerical aptitude and clerical perception.

Recommendations

Based on the evaluations, the following recommendations were made.

1. Vocational counseling regarding job possibilities in machine operations, production work, and related fields to establish a specific vocational goal, and to follow-up with appropriate training.
2. Work adjustment services at nearby rehabilitation center to observe behavior in an integrated hearing/deaf environment and to receive supportive counseling services from rehabilitation counselor.
3. Independent living skills evaluation to determine potential problems during placement and post-placement.

Outcomes

Client is currently employed as an electronic assembler for a small computer assembly plant. While paying rent to his parents, he remains at home in order to save money to purchase a better car, and furnishings for his own apartment. He completed training at a local vocational technical school with an interpreter and other support services. This occurred after a 60-day work adjustment program.

Discussion: Case No. 3

The client's participation in a large mainstream program had allowed him to sample both the hearing and deaf cultures. His work history indicates he is able to find jobs but has difficulty keeping them.

Work samples were selected for use with Sam because they would allow him to experience the requirements of different work tasks. The evaluator was able to observe his work behavior and attitudes more closely and gain greater insight into his inability to keep a job. Sam was able to select work samples and to relate some of them to work he would like to do.

It was quite apparent that Sam had the ability to perform most of the tasks assigned him, but he still needed to develop a stronger "work" personality. His work sample scores were average or above, yet he preferred the company of friends to the challenges of his job assignments. His motivation to regain his independence and his intelligence proved to be the biggest factors in his successful rehabilitation.

The work samples provided an opportunity for Sam to complete successfully different work related "tests." The work sample results supported his expressed interest to make tangible products with his hands.

The first recommendation is supported by his work sample performance and displayed interests. The follow-up training will be necessary to ensure at least entry level placement in the Big City area. The vocational counseling will be combined with recommendation #2, short-term work adjustment. The specific rehabilitation center was chosen because it is a facility offering community placement sites as well as the more traditional "in-house" adjustment workshop. Sam was rotated through an off-site stocking job and in-house electric salvage operation. He preferred the off-site location.

Sam stated he was willing to attend school for a short time, but he preferred to work. This was used to justify the technical program he attended.

The independent living skills evaluation indicated the need for some money management training, but no problems were identified that required long-term training.

SUMMARY

Vocational evaluation of persons who are deaf is a process through which specific assets and rehabilitation problems are identified using various tools and techniques. The results of evaluation serve as a basis for rehabilitation planning.

This assessment process can occur within any of the three levels (micro, macro, and encounter) discussed in this chapter. Due to these differing levels, the many contexts in which evaluations can occur, the legal requirements mandating unbiased and valid assessment, and the lack of empirical evidence demonstrating validity for the large majority of tests that are currently in use, this process is almost always confusing. Added to this confusion are all of the compounding problems presented by a deaf person (etiology, communication preference, linguistic and cultural factors, etc.).

By defining vocational evaluation as functional assessment, vocational evaluators can focus on determining how deaf individuals function in their work environment. The International Classification of Impairments, Disabilities, and Handicaps offers this perspective. It views different aspects of the client's milieu as part of an integrated system. The notion that the characteristics of the individual may interact with the characteristics of the environment to exacerbate or lessen the experience of disadvantage has to be clearly understood when making recommendations about the future paths for deaf clients based on test results, and evaluation procedures must be judged as to their functional relevance.

From a legal standpoint, the mandate for fairness in testing is clear and unambiguous. The onus of responsibility is on the test publisher and the test user to demonstrate that the use of a particular test gives results which have been demonstrated to be both valid and reliable for students with particular characteristics, such as deafness. Unfortunately, many tests are administered and interpreted on shaky legal grounds. The preponderance of research into the validity of particular instruments has led researchers to question the validity of the tools under their scrutiny. Nonetheless, assessment using commercially available instruments is widespread. It is somewhat ironic that the same legislation which mandates fairness in testing also mandates the establishment of IEPs for individual students; out of necessity, IEPs, in turn, rely on the results of standardized testing.

A review of the literature yields a bleak picture of the state of the art. It is quite clear that tests developed for hearing individuals can very rarely be simply administered to deaf individuals reliably and validly. The verbal nature of most tests precludes their successful use with deaf individuals. Nonverbal tests are therefore popular; however, these tests have little validity for predicting success on tasks which, themselves, require mastery of English. Evidence for this conclusion was provided in domains covering the assessment of social and personality factors, intellectual factors, and vocational factors.

A cursory look at the evaluation process for deaf clients shows it is the same for this group as for any other. Yet the evaluator must be aware of the impact that deafness has on each facet of evaluation. Only skilled evaluators who understand deafness and are able to communicate effectively with deaf clients are able to carry out effective evaluations.

Shiels (1986) noted the critical role the evaluator plays in the assessment process. The amount of training the evaluator has received in three specific areas is crucially important. The first is the evaluator's skills with respect to the different tools and techniques in the field of vocational evaluation. The second involves the evaluator's knowledge of deafness as a disability and the problems associated with varying degrees of hearing impairment, different types of educational backgrounds, and other associated issues. The final area involves the evaluator's proficiency at communicating in a variety of sign or oral systems.

It is unrealistic to assume that there will be an adequate number of individuals skilled both in areas of evaluation and in communication with deaf clients. Thus, in many cases, a qualified individual may serve a dual capacity as an interpreter and as an evaluation specialist. Within this context there is a need to minimize role confusion and to assure the individual does have both clinical and communication skills (see Chapter 11).

Vocational evaluation is a dynamic field that has developed both as a science and an art. Because of the complexities and the problems associated with assessment that have been described in this chapter, the evaluator will continue to play a crucial role in the process. The burden of using and adapting tests, work samples, rating forms, and the myriad of other techniques that are available, still rests with the evaluator. Since little psychometric evidence exists to support the selection of individual tools, the evaluator must exercise both caution and savvy in designing multifaceted evaluations.

Future Directions

Within the field of evaluation, there have been some recent encouraging developments; for example, there has been an increase in the use of computer technology. The evaluator now has the ability to access local labor market information, generate norms, use the computer as a test instrument, access electronic mail networks, and apply computer technology to a broad spectrum of other applications.

Additionally, the advent of supported employment programs has brought changes to the field of rehabilitation, broadening its traditional role. Also, an approach to assessment which emphasizes the work environment is becoming more and more prevalent. Such assessments involve a "dynamic holistic process that involves the assessments of individuals, environments, and their congruence" (Parker, Szymanski, & Hanley-Maxwell, 1989, p. 26). This approach differs from traditional evaluation, since it stresses viewing the client in terms of the environment where he or she will be working. This view is consistent with a definition of assessment that stresses function over impairment. Menchetti and Rusch (1988) point out that one of the steps in vocational evaluation for those potentially in need for supported employment services is to determine the clients' transportation, medical, and economic needs as well as their vocational skills. This broader approach is being utilized to an increasing degree by vocational evaluators.

In conclusion, the future, with advanced technology combined with changes in philosophy and techniques, will provide more accurate and beneficial evaluations. In spite of these developments, however, the evaluator will remain the catalyst in a process designed to include the client as a partner.

RESOURCE LIST

- DeStefano, Linn, and Markward. (1987). Review of student assessment instruments and practices in use in secondary/transition projects.
- Sligar. (1983). Commercial/vocational evaluation systems and deaf persons.
- Spragins, Blennerhassett, and Mullen. (1987, March). Reviews of five types of assessment instruments used with hearing-impaired students.
- Traxler. (1989). The role of assessment in placing deaf students in academic and vocational courses.
- Zieziula. (1982). Assessment of hearing-impaired people: A guide for selecting psychological, educational, and vocational tests.

REFERENCES

Acree, M.C. (1987). Assessing the self-image of deaf adolescents. In G. Anderson & D. Watson (Eds.), *Innovations in the habilitation and rehabilitation of deaf adolescents* (pp. 208–223). Little Rock, AR: Rehabilitation Research and Training Center in Deafness and Hearing Impairment.

Allen, T.E. (1986). *Understanding the scores: Hearing-impaired students and the Stanford Achievement Test (7th edition)*. Washington, DC: Center for Assessment and Demographic Studies. (ERIC Document Reproduction Service No. ED 280 247)

Allen, T.E., Holt, J.A., Bloomquist, C.A., & Starke, M.C. (1987). *Item analysis for the Stanford Achievement Test, 7th edition, 1983 standardization with hearing-impaired students*. Washington, DC: Center for Assessment and Demographic Studies.

Allen, T.E., Holt, J.A., Hotto, S.A., & Bloomquist, C.A. (1987). *Differential item difficulty:*

Comparisons of p-values on the Stanford Achievement Test, 7th edition, between hearing and hearing-impaired standardization samples. Washington, DC: Center for Assessment and Demographic Studies.

Bloomquist, C.A., & Allen, T.E. (1987, April). *Comparison of Stanford Achievement Test item responses by hearing and hearing-impaired students.* Paper presented at the meeting of the American Educational Research Association, Washington, DC.

Buck, J.N. (1948). *House-tree-person projective technique.* Brandon, VT: Clinical Psychology Publishing Company.

Buros Institute of Mental Measurement. (1988). *Mental measurements yearbooks: Online database* [Distributed by Bibliographic Retrieval Services Information Technologies, Scotia, NY]. Lincoln, NE: Buros Institute of Mental Measurement.

Cattell, R.B., Eber, H.W., & Tatsuoka, M.M. (1978). *Sixteen Personality Factor Questionnaire.* Champaign, IL: Institute for Personality and Ability Testing, Inc.

Cheung, F.M. (1983). Vocational evaluation of severely disabled deaf clients. In D. Watson (Ed.), *Vocational evaluation of hearing-impaired persons: Research and practice.* Little Rock, AR: University of Arkansas, Rehabilitation Research and Training Center on Deafness and Hearing Impairment.

Commission on Accreditation of Rehabilitation Facilities. (1989). *Standards manual for organizations serving people with disabilities.* Tucson, AZ: Author.

DeStefano, L., Linn, R., & Markward, M. (1987). *Review of student assessment instruments and practices in use in secondary/transition projects* [Revised edition]. Champaign, IL: Board of Trustees of the University of Illinois.

Doll, E.A. (1965). *Vineland social maturity scale.* Circle Pines, MN: American Guidance Service, Inc.

Dwyer, C.L., & Wincenciak, S.L. (1977). A pilot investigation of three factors of the 16PF Form E comparing the standard written form with an Ameslan videotape revision. *American Annals of the Deaf, 10,* 17–23.

Education for all Handicapped Children Act, 20 U.S.C, Paragraph 1401, et seq., Public Law 94–142. Regulations at 45 C.F.R. Paragraph 121 (1977).

Evans, L. (1980). WISC performance scale and coloured progressive matrices with deaf children. *British Journal of Educational Psychology, 50,* 216–222.

Fitt, W. (1965). *Tennessee self-concept scale.* Nashville: Counselor Recordings and Tests.

Gerweck, S., & Ysseldyke, J. (1979). Limitations of current psychological practices for the intellectual assessment of the hearing impaired: A response to the Levine study. *Volta Review, 77,* 243–248.

Halpern, A.S., & Fuhrer, M.J. (1984a). *Functional assessment in rehabilitation.* Baltimore: Paul H. Brookes.

Halpern, A.S., & Fuhrer, M.J. (1984b). Introduction. In A.S. Halpern & M.J. Fuhrer (Eds.), *Functional assessment in rehabilitation* (pp. 1–10). Baltimore: Paul H. Brookes.

Hirshoren, A., Hurley, O.L., & Hunt, J.T. (1977). The WISC-R and Hiskey-Nebraska Test with deaf children. *American Annals of the Deaf, 122,* 392–394.

Hirshoren, A., Hurley, O.L., & Kavale, K. (1979). Psychometric characteristics of the WISC-R Performance Scale with deaf children. *Journal of Hearing and Speech Disorders, 44,* 73–79.

Hiskey, M.S. (1966). *Hiskey-Nebraska test of learning aptitude.* Lincoln, NE: Author.

Holland, J. (1985). *Self-directed search.* Iowa City: Psychological Assessment Resources, Inc.

Hsu, L.M. (1985). Wide Range Interest-Opinion Test. In J.V. Mitchell (Ed.), *The ninth mental measurements yearbook* (pp. 1737–1739). Lincoln, NE: Buros Institute of Mental Measurement.

Jacobs, R. (1987). Use of the Sixteen Personality Factor Questionnaire, Form A, with deaf university students. *Journal of Rehabilitation of the Deaf, 21*(2), 19–26.

Jastak, J.R., & Jastak, S. (1979). *Wide range interest and opinion test.* Wilmington: Jastak Associates, Inc.

LaSasso, C. (1980). The validity and reliability of the Cloze procedure as a measure of readability for prelingually, profoundly deaf students. *American Annals of the Deaf, 125,* 359–363.

Levine, E.S. (1956). *Youth in a soundless world.* New York: University Press.

Manuele, C.A. (1985). Wide Range Interest-Opinion Test. In J.V. Mitchell, Jr (Ed.), *The ninth mental measurements yearbook* (pp. 1739–1740). Lincoln, NE: Buros Institute of Mental Measurement.

Meadow, K.P. (1967). *The effect of early manual communication and family climate on the deaf child's development.* Unpublished doctoral dissertation, University of California, Berkeley.

Meadow, K.P. (1980). *Meadow/Kendall social-emotional assessment inventory for deaf students: Manual.* Washington, DC: Gallaudet University, Pre-College Programs. (ERIC Document Reproduction Service No. EC 150 681)

Menchetti, B.M., & Rusch, F.R. (1988). Vocational evaluation and eligibility for rehabilitation services. In P. Wehman (Ed.), *Vocational rehabilitation and supported employment.* Baltimore, MD.

Myklebust, H.R. (1964). *The psychology of deafness: Sensory deprivation, learning, and adjustment* (2nd edition). New York: Grune & Stratton.

Nadolsky, J.M. (1971). *Development of a model for vocational evaluation of the disadvantaged.* Auburn, AL.

Ouellette, S. (1988). The use of projective drawing techniques in the personality assessment of prelingually deafened young adults: A pilot study. *American Annals of the Deaf, 133,* 212–218.

Parker, R.M., Szymanski, E.M., & Hanley-Maxwell, C. (1989). Ecological assessment in supported employment. *Journal of Applied Rehabilitation Counseling, 20*(3),1989.

The Psychological Corporation. (1974, 1982, 1989). *Stanford achievement test* (6th through 8th editions). San Antonio: Author.

Quarrington, B., & Solomon, B. (1975). A current study of the social maturity of deaf students. *Canadian Journal of Behavioral Sciences, 7,* 70–77.

Raven, J.C. (1958). *Standard progressive matrices.* New York: The Psychological Corporation.

Raven, J.C. (1976). *Coloured progressive matrices.* San Antonio: The Psychological Corporation.

Ray, S. (1982). Adapting the WISC-R for deaf children. *Diagnostique, 7,* 147–157.

Reiman, J., & Bullis, M. (1988). *Assessing the school to community transition skills of deaf adolescents and young adults.* Monmouth, OR: Oregon State System of Higher Education.

Reschly, D.J. (1987). Learning characteristics of mildly handicapped students: Implications for classification, placement, and programming. In M.C. Wang, M.C. Reynolds, & H.J.

Walberg (Eds.), *Handbook of special education: Research and practice: Vol. 1. Learner characteristics and adaptive education.* Oxford, England: Pergamon.

Rudner, L.M. (1978). Using standard tests with the hearing impaired: The problem of item bias. *The Volta Review, 80*(1), 31–40.

Section 504 of the Rehabilitation Act of 1973, 29 U.S.C., Paragraph 794. Regulations at 45 C.F.R. Paragraph 84 (1977).

Sherman, S.W., & Robinson, N.M. (1982). *Ability testing of handicapped people: Dilemma for government, science, and the public.* Washington, DC: National Academy Press.

Shiels, J.W. (1986). Vocational assessment. In L. Steward (Ed.), *Clinical rehabilitation assessment and hearing impairment: A guide to quality assurance.* Little Rock, AR: University of Arkansas, Rehabilitation Research and Training Center on Deafness and Hearing Impairment.

Sligar, S. (1983). Commercial vocational evaluation systems and deaf persons. In D. Watson (Ed.), *Vocational evaluation of hearing-impaired persons: Research and practice.* Little Rock, AR: University of Arkansas, Rehabilitation Research and Training Center on Deafness and Hearing Impairment.

Spragins, A.B., Blennerhassett, L., & Mullen, Y. (1987, March). *Reviews of five types of assessment instruments used with hearing-impaired students.* Paper presented at the annual convention of the National Association of School Psychologists. New Orleans.

Traxler, C.B. (1989). The role of assessment in placing deaf students in academic and vocational courses. In T.E. Allen, B.W. Rawlings, & A.N. Schildroth (Eds.), *Deaf students and the school-to-work transition* (pp. 141–188). Baltimore: Paul H. Brookes.

U.S. Department of Labor. (1977). *Dictionary of occupational titles* (4th edition). Washington, DC: U.S. Government Printing Office.

VALPAR component work sample #201–205. (1989). Tucson: Valpar Corporation.

Vestberg, P. (1989). *Beyond stereotypes: Perspectives on the personality characteristics of deaf people* (Working Paper 89–2). Washington, DC: Gallaudet Research Institute.

Walberg, H.J., & Wang, M.C. (1987). Effective educational practices and provisions for individual differences. In M.C. Wang, M.C. Reynolds, & H.J. Walberg (Eds.), *Handbook of special education: Research and practice: Vol. 1. Learner characteristics and adaptive education.* Oxford, England: Pergamon.

Watson, D. (1976). Introduction and overview. In D. Watson (Ed.), *Deaf evaluation and adjustment feasibility: Guidelines for the vocational evaluation of deaf clients.* New York University School of Education.

Wechsler, D. (1974). *Intelligence scale for children-revised.* San Antonio: The Psychological Corporation.

Wechsler, D. (1981). *Adult intelligence scale-revised.* New York: The Psychological Corporation.

White K., & Slusher, N. (1978). *Measuring career development among postsecondary deaf students* (paper #25). Rochester, NY: National Technical Institute for the Deaf.

Wigdor, A.K., & Garner, W.R. (1982). *Ability testing: Uses, consequences, and controversies* (Pt. II: Documentation Section). Washington, DC: National Academy Press.

Wilson, J.J., Rapin, I., Wilson, B.C., & Van Denburg, F.V. (1975). Neuropsychologic function of children with severe hearing impairment. *Journal of Speech and Hearing Research, 18,* 634–665.

World Health Organization. (1980). *International classification of impairments, disabilities,* and handicaps: A manual of classification relating to the consequences of disease. Geneva: Author.

Zieziula, F.R. (1982). *Assessment of hearing impaired people: A guide for selecting psychological, educational, and vocational tests.* Washington, DC: Gallaudet College Press.

Zytowski, D.G. (1978). Wide Range Interest-Opinion Test. In O.K. Buros (Ed.), *The eighth mental measurements yearbook* (pp. 1641–1643). Hyland Park, NJ: Gryphon Press.

Author Notes: In the review of the literature for this chapter, the authors made extensive use of the publication, *Research on assessment procedures with individuals with severe hearing impairments: An annotated bibliography,* by John Reiman and Michael Bullis (Not Dated).

▶ 7

Vocational, Career, and Work-Adjustment Counseling

NANCY M. LONG
Northern Illinois University

DEAF PEOPLE IN THE WORKFORCE

Historical Perspective

The rate of unemployment and underemployment for persons who are deaf represents perhaps the greatest challenge to the field of deafness rehabilitation. Christiansen (1982) reported that the rate of employment among hearing-impaired persons, eligible for participation in the workforce, has lagged, historically, in comparison with the general population. In terms of underemployment, Lunde and Bigman (1959) found about 83 percent of deaf workers were employed in manual labor jobs (compared to approximately 53 percent of hearing workers). In fact, the 1965 Babbidge Report, drawing on the data available at the time, concluded that deaf people, in addition to being underrepresented in the workforce, were employed considerably below their basic aptitudes (Educational Testing Service, 1990). This trend has continued throughout the 25 years that have elapsed since the Babbidge Report came out. Passmore (1983) described the picture of underemployment of deaf persons who gain entry into the workforce. He reported that most of these people were employed in the skilled, semi-skilled, and unskilled jobs found predominantly in the manufacturing industries. The jobs were characterized by low job security, low wages, and little chance for advancement. In a more recent report, Walter, MacLeod-Gallinger, and Stuckless (1987) found deaf high school graduates participated in the labor force at a rate that was 10 percent lower than hearing graduates. As expected, the majority of deaf workers identified in this study were employed in the manufacturing sector.

The Workplace of the Future

The overrepresentation of deaf people in manufacturing sector jobs is a serious problem considering the trends reported for employment in the future. The United States, riding the crest of a technological revolution, will be relying less on manufacturing and more on the information processing and service industries (Johnston & Packer, 1987).

At the same time, the picture is changing with regard to where workers will work. Trends reported indicate that a greater number of small to medium-sized companies will exist by the year 2000. By that time, the majority of job opportunities are predicted to rest with smaller companies (fewer than 100 employees) (Myers & Scott, 1989). This trend is already occurring. Large companies are aggressively retrenching, refocusing, and downsizing. At the same time, a larger number of entrepreneurs are taking risks and striking out on their own. In 1965 there were 204,000 business start-ups in the United States; in 1988 the number reached close to 700,000 (Cole, 1989). These events impact deaf workers as they compete for jobs at smaller companies that, by virtue of size, may not be in a position to be aware of appropriate accommodations. In the past, primarily large companies had the finances to develop exemplary accommodations programs for workers with disabilities.

Implications for Vocational Rehabilitation (VR) Counselors

Vocational rehabilitation has long played a significant role in assisting deaf persons to secure and maintain employment. To continue this successful system of service delivery, vocational rehabilitation counselors serving deaf clients will have to sharpen their skills in the area of vocational guidance and counseling. The VR counselor will need to be apprised of and current with changes in labor market needs. This information should then be transformed into interventions and directions to be used in making plans with and serving hearing-impaired clients. The "jobs of the future" will have to be identified nationally, regionally, and locally so that vocational advisement and training will reflect the changing needs of the workplace.

VOCATIONAL COUNSELING

Jobs for the Future

To provide effective vocational guidance and counseling, the successful vocational rehabilitation counselor will need to know employment trends. The jobs of today and future are being found primarily in the information processing and service industries.

These include retail trade, education, health care, government, finance, insurance, and real estate. Also included are food services, wholesale trade, transportation, public utilities and business services (Johnston & Packer, 1987).

While it is clear that employment growth will see large increases in the information and service sector, certain manufacturing industries with a direct link to the information processing and service industries listed above will continue to grow in similar fashion. These industries include printing and publishing, drugs and pharmaceutical products, computers (hardware and software), plastic products, and the instrument industries (Long, 1990).

As our society becomes increasingly "disposable" and dependent on the exchange of information, the trends presented here do not come as a surprise. Computers and robotics will be in use in many workplaces by the year 2000. Some have predicted that computers with human intelligence will be commonplace within the next 50 years, thus further refining the types of employment needed and available (World Future Society, 1989). VR counselors will be required to anticipate these trends and work with their clients to help prepare for changes in the work environment and in work requirements.

Vocational Preparation

To prepare clients better for the jobs of the future, the vocational rehabilitation counselor must first have an accurate assessment of that client's skills and abilities in the areas of reading, writing, and mathematics. Increasingly, employers seek applicants with general basic skills. The job duties and roles are becoming so specific that employers prefer to do their own specialized and advanced training. What they are concerned with is getting an applicant who can be trained. Basic reading, writing, and math skills are essential in preparing deaf clients for the jobs of the future.

While it is true that the basic skills described here should be taught in school settings, it is clear that deaf people are not graduating with the fluency that employers desire, and therefore they are not competitive in the job market. Allen (1986) compared achievement scores of deaf high school students to hearing cohorts. For reading, deaf students' mean comprehension score on the Stanford Achievement Test in 1983 was approximately the third grade level. This compared to a hearing sample score of tenth grade for the same year. Math scores were slightly higher with deaf students achieving a mean computation score of approximately seventh grade as compared to a mean score for hearing students at tenth grade.

Vocational rehabilitation counselors should access local training opportunities in continuing education for their deaf clients to assure that reading comprehension levels are brought up to at least the sixth to eighth grade level (the level at which most daily news periodicals are written). College level reading comprehension is the ideal, although this is often not realistic when teaching literacy to adults for whom English is not a first language. Local Councils on Literacy may offer programs that can be adapted or accommodated for deaf people. Some state residential schools for deaf students offer community education programs throughout their states. Public high schools and community colleges with mainstream programs for deaf students are often a valuable resource for accomplishing this directive. In addition, the Gallaudet University Regional Centers offer a variety of Continuing Education Programs. The Regional Center nearest to a certain location can be identified by writing: Office of Continuing Education, Gallaudet University, 800 Florida Ave., NE, Washington, DC 20002.

In addition to basic skills, workers are increasingly being required to have skills in basic computer use. The availability and affordability of the personal computer has made it a standard fixture in most offices. By the year 2000, 95 percent of all jobs may be in service industries, and the jobs available will call for workers who are familiar with computers and other information-processing technologies (World Future Society, 1989). Workers will need to be comfortable with computers and will have to have some working knowledge of several popular word processing programs and database management programs. Several programs have sprung up across the nation to respond to this need. An exemplary model program began operation in 1990, in California. Goodwill Industries in Long Beach developed and implemented a "Computer and Clerical Skills" training program for deaf and hard-of-hearing persons. This program focuses on basic office and computer skills including Office Procedures, Data Entry, General Accounting, Word Processing, Database Spreadsheets, Computer Graphics, Database Management, and Desk Top Publishing. By developing a computer lab setting where trainees can learn and practice on the state-of-the-art software being used nationally in offices, this program hopes to provide opportunities for hearing-impaired persons to acquire more marketable skills for the labor force. A large local manufacturer has already approached Goodwill about referrals for employment based on the availability of this training. Vocational rehabilitation counselors attempting to guide their clients into personally fulfilling and financially rewarding occupations should consider seeking and accessing training programs like this.

CAREER COUNSELING

Career Information

When the deaf VR applicant is first interviewed, the VR counselor will obtain a history of previous work experience and/or training. In addition, the counselor will explore the employment interests of the applicant. Once eligibility has been determined, the counselor and client will together discuss their options and make a plan. It is during this time that the team of client and counselor need to be aware of the options and possibilities available in the labor force. The counselor, as an informed professional, should have information about the availability of jobs, the training requirements, the educational requirements, and some sense of the possibility of advancement for particular occupations. It will then become his or her responsibility to share and discuss the information as it related to the client's Individualized Written Rehabilitation Plan (IWRP).

Career Education

For the most part, people begin to acquire information about jobs and careers in early childhood (Ginzberg, Ginsberg, Axelrod, & Herma, 1951). The fantasy play games of children serve a purpose in beginning to identify those careers of interest. Children, in acting out these fantasies, are role playing possible future career scenarios. As the child matures, information is gathered through formal means (e.g., school subjects and career classes) and informal means (e.g., incidental learning about the occupational requirements of parents and family).

Due to communication obstacles, the deaf person (typically born into a hearing family) will not have access to as much information as his or her hearing peers (Long, 1988). The typical deaf VR client will possess a somewhat sketchy background of information about jobs, careers, and related information. The responsibility of the VR counselor as part of the team is to "shore up" the informational deficits experienced by the deaf person in this area. In addition, the VR counselor must facilitate the deaf person's exploration of occupational information as related to personal interests and capabilities.

The elements of a successful program of a career education for deaf persons include the following:

1.   A description and discussion of the types of employment, divided into "sectors" (e.g., food services, assembly);
2.   A description of the variety of jobs found within each sector;
3.   A discussion of the entry level skills and education requirements for jobs discussed;
4.   A discussion of the day-to-day activities of people with a particular job title; emphasis placed on the skills needed to complete these daily responsibilities;
5.   A description of the typical working environment for a particular job;
6.   An exploration of clients' responses and interests in the jobs discussed, with attention given to the physical and mental abilities necessary to perform the job.

The successful and efficient VR counselor will locate and access an appropriate career education training program for deaf clients. This can often be found at comprehensive rehabilitation facilities such as the Southwest Center for the Hearing Impaired in San Antonio, Texas, or in community programs and organizations (e.g., Easter Seals, Goodwill). Where this is not available, VR counselors can adapt a system to fit into the daily routine of their VR office.

One way to address this need is to review the career education materials being developed for the classroom setting. Several excellent resources are available that might make a library of resources for clients. Making materials generally available for clients to explore allows for more independent activity on the part of clients and should assist in increasing their investment in the whole vocational process (see Long & Davis, 1986, for a discussion of the benefit of client involvement in the job-seeking process).

Recommended resources for the client and counselor include the *Occupational Outlook Handbook*—a publication of the U.S. Department of Labor, Bureau of Labor Statistics (1990). This routinely updated handbook describes occupations within industries. The Handbook provides information on individual occupations, e.g., the nature of the work, working conditions, and typical places of employment (Long, 1990). There is a companion publication to the Handbook, titled *The Guide for Occupational Exploration*, that assists the reader to utilize this resource in gathering information about jobs and careers. To obtain ordering information, one should contact the regional office of the U.S. Department of Labor, Bureau of Labor Statistics (usually found in the U.S. Government pages of the telephone book).

A second excellent resource that should be a fixture in VR offices is the *Directory of Occupational Titles*. This valuable resource is published by the U.S. Department of Labor, Employment, and Training Administration (1991) and describes job tasks and responsibilities for each of the occupations listed within nine occupational categories. The nine occupational categories include: professional/technical/managerial, clerical/sales, service, agricultural/fishery/forestry, processing, machine trades, benchwork, structural work, miscellaneous. A supplement is available containing new occupations and revisions of DOT entries to reflect the rapid changes in the workplace due to technology (Long, 1990). Again, one should contact the local Department of Labor Office to obtain ordering information.

For clients, deaf and otherwise, who might have difficulty with reading comprehension, less complicated packages are available. One good example is *The Job Box* (King, 1985). This package includes a small box ($9'' \times 6'' \times 5''$) filled with 56 attractive booklets, color-coded into seven major occupational categories, including automotive, building trades and construction, food services, industrial and retail, office and clerical, ranching, farming and horticulture, and trades and services. Each booklet provides brief but clear explanation of the occupation, the environment where one performs the occupation, the training needed, career ladder/advancement, and more. Using photographs to supplement the printed material, the information is provided in a clear, understandable fashion. Worksheets are provided to assist with independent career exploration. The worksheets help to determine the level of understanding of the occupation. They also serve as excellent teaching tools in that they assist the explorer in remembering the pertinent information given. "Job rating" exercises are included on each worksheet to assist the explorer in determining the level of interest in a particular occupation. This structured learning format is desirable regardless of the actual materials used to provide the career information, as it will help the counselor-client team in making decisions about employment and careers. To obtain additional information on this resource, contact the publishers, Fearon/Janus/Quercus, 500 Harbor Blvd., Belmont, CA 94002. Or, one may obtain *The Job Box* through a national distributor: JIST Works, Inc., 720 North Park Avenue, Indianapolis, IN 46202. The JIST Works is a clearinghouse of career education and job-seeking information for learners with special needs. The personal experience of this author is that many materials designed for this population often serve as excellent starting points for professionals attempting to develop materials for use with deaf persons needing VR services. This is especially true with deaf people who have additional disabilities.

Career Advancement of the Deaf Employee

Critical to the career advancement of the deaf workers is career counseling and guidance. The term "career" implies a forward and upward movement through jobs in an occupation. Too often, deaf people have been guided (or misguided) by significant others into entry level jobs within an occupation. Lack of information on the part of parents, educators, and VR counselors themselves have, on occasion, caused them to steer deaf people to low expectations and dead-end jobs. Young deaf people, because of informational deficits, often perceive very few occupations as available to them (Egelston-Dodd, 1977). The resulting low aspiration on the part of deaf adolescents has been found to be severely limiting to their occupational choices and movement (Christiansen & Barnartt, 1987). The ideal situation for the client-counselor team to effect career movement is to do so while the client is working. However, because of federal regulations, most rehabilitation cases are closed after the client has demonstrated successful employment (60 days after initial hire). This limits the counselor's ability to maintain involvement and provide guidance and training to facilitate the client's/employee's advancement up the career ladder.

The counselor can address the concept of career advancement in a limited fashion while the clients are in the evaluation and training phases of their rehabilitation plans. The client should receive instruction on accessing employee training programs and should be provided with the opportunity to learn and practice appropriate ways to deal with supervisors about promotions and seeking advanced training. This instruction may also occur during the 60 days after initial hire. The counselor may also work with the client to learn the particular employer's system for dealing with training and promotions. At the same time, and equally as important, the counselor should take advantage of the opportunity to work with the employer about the career advancement of the client/employee.

With the passage of the Americans with Disabilities Act in 1990, employers are required to address the employment and advancement needs of persons with disabilities. The creative VR counselor will take advantage of this opportunity to forge positive relationships (if not partnerships) with employers to assist them in meeting their needs. Employers will require information about reasonable accommodations and awareness and sensitivity training in order to integrate workers with disabilities into their worksite. While specific case closure will depend on time limits, counselors are afford some flexibility in their employer-development activities. The successful VR counselor will work with employers not for one initial entry level placement, but for a series of placements whereby new clients/applicants fill slots vacated by the promotions of previously placed clients.

WORK-ADJUSTMENT COUNSELING

Content and Format

Work-adjustment counseling with deaf people has typically focused on two content areas. The first area includes information relative to new employment. This content centers on understanding terminology (e.g., benefits, vacation time, deductions). In addition, common workplace rules are described and discussed (e.g., the rules surrounding break time). The second content is perhaps best described as social skills training. In this domain, clients are assisted in developing appropriate interactive styles with co-workers and supervisors. Interpersonal problem-solving skills are typically addressed as part of this emphasis.

The conduct of work-adjustment counseling typically takes place in one of two forms. The first format is usually a part of some classroom-type training in which a group of clients participate in group meetings. These meetings focus on the information as listed above. Typically, they are characterized by basic forms of instruction, exercises, worksheets, modeling of appropriate behaviors, role-play practices, discussion, feedback, and homework. Many times this type of training and counseling will take place as part of a job-seeking skills training program. This approach has its strengths and weaknesses. The obvious strength is in its efficacy. A classroom situation allows several people to be addressed at the same time in a cost-efficient and time-efficient manner. A major weakness in this type approach, however, is seen in the low likelihood for generalization of skills beyond the classroom situation. One remedy is to make the role-play situations as real as possible for the client. Utilization of employers from a Business Advisory Council to participate in role-plays and provide feedback has been found by this author to be a powerful approach.

The second format remedies the shortcomings of the classroom situation. In this format, the work-adjustment training takes place while the client is working. This approach has been used with multiply disabled deaf people in sheltered workshop settings where inappropriate social and interpersonal behavior could be dealt with directly and efficiently at the time it occurs. Some deaf people are sent to workshop training specifically for this work-adjustment training with the intent of moving them into competitive employment when training is deemed complete. This is the approach used by the Southwest Center for the Hearing Impaired in San Antonio. At this national facility, work-adjustment training is provided to address the content areas mentioned earlier. Workshop training occurs with clients performing in a Center-operated sheltered workshop setting. When training is completed, clients are returned to their home states or locales where the Center hopes they will obtain competitive employment. For a multiply disabled population in particular, the advantages of this approach are seen in its direct applicability to the clients. For more information on this program, contact the Director, SCHI, 6487 Whitby Rd., San Antonio, TX 78240-2198.

In recent years, the U.S. Department of Education Rehabilitation Services Administration implemented a special "supported employment" initiative. In this initiative, persons with disabilities severe enough that they would be otherwise deemed unable to become employed in competitive employment are moved into the workforce through the use of a job coach. The responsibility of the job coach is to work at the site with the client/employee to assure that the worker is successful in his or her employment efforts. Job coach responsibilities may include assisting workers to engage in appropriate interpersonal behavior and helping them to stay on task.

The best approach to work-adjustment counseling seems likely to include both sets of content information and to utilize both formats as much as possible. Classroom situations are a time-efficient and cost-efficient means for providing information. While generalization of social skills may present some problems, this approach is not without its benefits. Followed by in-vivo work-adjustment counseling, the classroom training can provide a base on which to build. This proved true with a social skills training program researched on deaf adults by this author (Long, 1988). The teaching package consisted of nine lessons assisting deaf people to consider the needs and feelings of other people, to assess situations accurately, and to choose socially acceptable (i.e., not offensive to others or self) solutions to problems. While formal evaluation showed little improvement in clients' skills, feedback from the staff working with the deaf VR clients in other facility settings reported that drawing on the lesson content proved efficient and beneficial in the clients' dealing with individual problem behaviors at the worksite.

CHALLENGE FOR THE FUTURE

The world of work is changing. Manufacturing jobs, where deaf people have been over-represented in the past, are on the decrease. The flood of workers moving out of manufacturing adds to the competition for jobs in the service sectors. The role of vocational rehabilitation in successfully addressing its responsibility in facilitating employment of deaf people has never been as important as now. Employers are facing an aging workforce. They are being forced to consider applicants that they have not had to consider before, including women, immigrants, minorities, and persons with disabilities (Johnston & Packer, 1987).

These changes, in concert with the changes that will be required as a result of the passage of the Americans with Disabilities Act, put vocational rehabilitation in a position to be envied. Vocational rehabilitation has something that employers want. Vocational rehabilitation counselors have knowledge about accommodations that employers want; VR counselors have access to trained applicants that employers want.

Counselors owe it to their clients to improve their knowledge about the skills and abilities required by employers and then to assure that these are adequately addressed in the training programs developed with clients. At the same time, VR counselors must work closely with employers to assure that they look to persons with disabilities to fill their employment needs. Counselors seeking information on career education and exploration should seek resources such as the University of Arkansas Rehabilitation Research and Training Center on Deafness and Hearing Impairment. Federally funded by the U.S. Department of Education-National Institute on Disability and Rehabilitation Research (NIDRR) since 1981, this Center has earned a reputation for development of intervention materials that are readily applicable for use with deaf persons. For more information, contact: Research and Training Center for Individuals who are Deaf or Hard of Hearing, 4601 West Markham St., Little Rock, AR 72205.

A second viable resource, recently funded by NIDRR (begun in 1990), is the Northern Illinois University Research and Training Center on Traditionally Underserved Persons Who Are Deaf. This Center's core projects address the needs of those deaf people typically considered "low functioning" in the areas of employment and independent living. This Center's address is: Research and Training Center on Traditionally Underserved Persons Who Are Deaf, Department of Communicative Disorders, N.I.U., DeKalb, IL 60115.

Counselors working with deaf clients must be fully versed in the assistive devices available and useful to hearing-impaired persons. VR counselors working with this population must also be flexible and able to work with employers concerning other accommodations that might be necessary to integrate workers who are deaf into the worksite (see Chapter 11).

Vocational rehabilitation counselors serving deaf people must also actively develop and pursue networking opportunities with other professionals. The American Deafness And Rehabilitation Association (ADARA) is an excellent resource for counselors. This professional organization conducts a national conference every other year and is a major sponsor of at least one other national conference a year. Conference proceedings are published for all conferences and the organization published a professional journal (quarterly) and newsletter (bi-monthly). Special interest sections allow members with particular needs and interests to network for further information sharing. The Placement/VR special interest section provides opportunities for people to gather additional resources on the topics addressed in this chapter. To obtain membership information, contact ADARA at PO Box 251554; Little Rock, AR 72225.

The opportunities presented to the profession of deafness rehabilitation have never been as promising as during this last decade of the 20th century. The responsibilities of the VR system in career education, career advancement, and related career counseling as well as vocational counseling and work-adjustment training are clear. Deaf people, as all people, must be well prepared for the information and service jobs that will dictate employment in the future. Vocational rehabilitation, in providing its services, will need to address these needs to continue its successful course of service delivery.

IMPLICATIONS FOR PRACTICE

The world of work is rapidly changing. Rehabilitation counselors working with deaf clients must be prepared to assist their clients to anticipate the changes in nature of work through vocational guidance, career counseling, and work-adjustment counseling. Counselor practices should reflect the needs of clients as well as to make allowances for increased employment trends in the service industries. To assist deaf clients to meld into the workplace of the future, vocational rehabilitation counselors, through their planning and working with clients, must assure that clients possess basic reading and writing skills. Career counseling must focus on the skills needed and the opportunities presented in emerging industries. Work-adjustment counseling should focus on reinforcing the skills needed to maintain and advance in employment situations.

REFERENCES

Allen, T.E. (1986). Patterns of academic achievement among hearing-impaired students: 1974 and 1983. In A.N. Schildroth & M.A. Karchmer (Eds.), *Deaf children in America*. San Diego, CA: College Hill Press.

Christiansen, J.B. (1982). The socioeconomic status of the deaf population: A review of the literature. In J.B. Christiansen & J. Egelston-Dodd (Eds.), *Socioeconomic status of the deaf population*. Washington, DC: Gallaudet University.

Christiansen, J.B., & Barnartt, S.N. (1987). The silent minority: The socioeconomic status of deaf people. In P. Higgins & J. Nash (Eds.), *Understanding deafness socially*. Springfield, IL: Charles C. Thomas, Publisher.

Cole, D. (1989, June). The entrepreneurial self. *Psychology Today, 60*–64.

Educational Testing Services. (1990). *Progress in education and rehabilitation of deaf and heard of hearing individuals*. Princeton, NJ: ETS.

Egelston-Dodd, J. (1977). Overcoming occupational stereotypes related to sex and deafness. *American Annals of the Deaf, 122*, 489–491.

Ginzberg, E., Ginsberg, S.W., Axelrod, S., & Herma, J.L. (1951). *Occupational choice: An approach to a general theory*. New York, NY: Columbia University Press.

Johnston, W.B., & Packer, A.H. (1987). *Workforce 2000: Work and workers for the 21st century*. Indianapolis, IN: Hudson Institute.

King, C.L. (1985). *The job box* (2nd edition). Belmont, CA: David S. Lake Publishers.

Long, N. (1988). Assertiveness training with deaf rehabilitation clients. In S. Boone & G. Long (Eds.), *Enhancing the employability of deaf persons: Model interventions*. Springfield, IL: Charles C. Thomas, Publishers.

Long, N. (1990). *Managing employer development: A resource manual*. Little Rock, AR: University of Arkansas Rehabilitation Research and Training Center on Deafness and Hearing Impairment.

Long, N.M. (1988). Self-directed job seeking skills training: Utilization in a Projects With Industry program for deaf persons. In D. Watson, & B. Heller (Eds.), *Mental health and deafness: Strategic perspectives*. Little Rock, AR: American Deafness And Rehabilitation Association.

Lunde, A.S., & Bigman, S.K. (1959). *Occupational conditions among the deaf.* Washington, DC: Gallaudet University (NARIC No. AN 79–03–X00488–1033).

Myers, J.R., & Scott, E.W. (1989). *Getting skilled, getting ahead: Your guide for choosing a career and a private career school.* Princeton, NJ: Peterson's Guides.

Passmore, D. (1983). Employment of deaf people. In D. Watson, G. Anderson, N. Ford, P. Marut, & S. Ouellette (Eds.), *Job placement of hearing-impaired persons: Research and practice.* Little Rock, AR: University of Arkansas Rehabilitation Research and Training Center on Deafness and Hearing Impairment.

Walter, G., MacLeod-Gallinger, J., & Stuckless, R. (1987). *Outcomes for graduates of secondary education programs for deaf students: Early findings of a cooperative national longitudinal study.* Rochester, NY: Rochester Institute of Technology, National Institute of the Deaf.

U.S. Department of Labor, Bureau of Labor Statistics. (1990). *Occupational outlook handbook: 1990–1991 edition.* Washington, DC: Author.

U.S. Department of Labor, Employment and Training Administration. (1991). *Dictionary of occupational titles* (4th edition). Washington, DC: Author.

World Future Society (1989). *Outlook '90 and beyond.* Bethesda, MD: World Future Society.

▶ 8

The Use and Application of Cognitive-Behavioral Psychotherapy with Deaf Persons

PAUL A. LOERA
*Center On Deafness: Western Pennsylvania
School for the Deaf*

INTRODUCTION: HISTORY AND GENERAL CONCERNS

It has now been 35 years since the first mental health program for deaf persons was established. Many advances have taken place during this time, based largely on the efforts of rehabilitation personnel who work with this population. These efforts are summarized in an historical overview by Adler (1978) and include the pioneering work done by Kallman, Rainer, and Altshuler at the New York Psychiatric Institute, the opening of the St. Elizabeth's program for deaf patients in Washington, DC in 1963, and the University of California Center On Deafness with its focus on mental health. Thirty-five states and the District of Columbia now have programs listed in the American Deafness and Rehabilitation Association's Directory of Mental Health Services for Deaf Persons (Long, High, & Shaw 1989). However, there are still large discrepancies between the service ideal and the service rendered to deaf persons with mental health problems.

Acknowledgement: Special thanks is given to Dr. Donald Meichenbaum for reviewing this chapter, as well as for his continued interest in the application of cognitive-behavioral psychotherapy with hearing-impaired persons.

The Center On Deafness at the Western Pennsylvania School for the Deaf conducted a survey of Pennsylvania Rehabilitation Counselors for the Deaf (RCD) (Loera, 1988). The survey gathered information on the counselors' perceptions of mental health service needs for hearing-impaired clients of the Office of Vocational Rehabilitation. With a 75 percent response rate to the survey, representing a caseload of over 1000 Pennsylvania deaf clients annually, at least 17 percent of the clients were considered to have mental health problems and 12 percent had confirmed mental health diagnoses. Seventy-five percent of the counselors cited major problems with the inaccessibility of mental health services. The discrepancy between the service ideal and the service rendered to deaf persons is highlighted by a response from a counselor whose comments encapsulate the need for improved mental health service for individuals who are deaf:

> This population has been largely ignored by the present mental health and mental retardation system. Deaf clients are either given inappropriate treatment or no treatment at all. I, as an RCD, have received many calls from the local MH/MR units, and the psychiatric units of local hospitals, asking my assistance with deaf MH patients. Further, successful rehabilitation closure does not necessarily mean the client has succeeded. A client needs only to "hang-on" to employment for two months to be "successfully closed." The deaf MH client may last two months and a day and then reapply for OVR services and begin the whole process again. However, what typically happens is that the case is never closed. It may remain open for years while the client is placed in one program after another. His mental health problems are usually *not* dealt with, and he never succeeds.

The comments provided by the counselor, combined with the overall survey results, reflect an ongoing problem with available and accessible community-based mental health services for deaf people.

Referrals to the Center On Deafness mental health program include many persons who have a history of rehabilitation failures and chronic mental health or adjustment problems. These individuals are faced with the dilemma of having their vocational rehabilitation services interrupted or stopped if they do not obtain mental health services to resolve problems impeding rehabilitation progress. This scenario is analogous to the findings of Joyce and Mathay (1986) in their study of deaf rehabilitation cases closed unsuccessfully after entering the vocational rehabilitation process. They found that deaf clients with a secondary disability, in addition to deafness, were eligible for and provided with vocational rehabilitation services only to have cases closed unsuccessfully due to difficulties arising from the severity of the disabilities.

Beene and Larson (1979) completed a study ". . . to estimate the frequency of misdiagnosis in rehabilitation and counseling settings with hearing-impaired clients" (p. 14). The authors defined misdiagnosis as ". . . the erroneous original assessment of a client" (p. 11), and they found misdiagnosis to be a frequent problem in rehabilitation settings serving this population—a problem which impedes effective program planning. Craig, Craig and Loera (1990) surveyed Pennsylvania rehabilitation counselors for the deaf to determine the extent and strength of current need for RCD training in the area of mental health. A 100 percent response, representing 19 Pennsylvania RCDs, answered the survey questions. The combined caseload for all 19 counselors represents 1829 severely/profoundly deaf clients served in the past year. A strikingly high percentage of this caseload—550 clients or 30 percent—were identified as having mental health problems, either formally diagnosed or rated as "very probable" by the RCD. In this survey it was also estimated that the cases for 41 percent of these dually impaired clients were being closed unsuccessfully. At least 28 percent of unsuccessful closures for Pennsylvania vocational rehabilitation deaf clients were attributed specifically to their mental health problems. The responding RCDs rated deaf clients with mental health problems as having significantly greater problems with the rehabilitation process than did other deaf clients (4.4 on a scale of 1 to 5—with 1 representing "same difficulty" and 5 representing "considerably greater difficulty"). These clients were also rated considerably more difficult for the RCD to work with effectively (4.0 on a scale of 1 to 5). Severe problems with accessibility of county-based mental health services were also cited, with 78 percent of the RCDs indicating a lack of available referral sources for diagnosis and treatment. Specific accessibility problems cited in this survey included the resistance of some county mental health/mental retardation systems to serve deaf clients, lack of knowledge within the MH/MR system when dealing with deaf clients, and misdiagnosis by practitioners unfamiliar with deafness. These problems reflect the need for practitioners and service providers, in both rehabilitation and mental health agencies, to work cooperatively to (1) diagnose client problems, (2) implement a service plan for helping the client manage and reduce problems, and (3) refer hearing-impaired clients to agencies where direct services are available and accessible, e.g., in terms of language and communication.

The various issues discussed thus far raise specific concerns about the quality of rehabilitation and mental health services available to hearing-impaired persons. A nationwide survey of agencies serving the deaf reports that a shortage exists for every rehabilitation personnel role, with the greatest need existing for mental health counselors and psychologists (Danek, 1988).

The role played by the RCD is key to facilitating successful rehabilitation case closure with hearing-impaired clients. Yet, it is clear that inadequate staffing and the inability of many professionals to distinguish between problems related to deafness and those due to true mental health needs are frequent reasons given by rehabilitation agencies for being unable to offer the services needed by this population (Myers & Danek, 1989). The RCD may view his primary role as that of a counselor, a service coordinator, or in a role which combines both skills (Thoreson & Tully, 1971). Regardless of the preferred role, certain procedures can be used by the RCD to help the hearing-impaired client learn and use skills which can lead to a higher competence level and self-efficacy.

Identification of Mental Health Needs

A 1982 report to the Pennsylvania Office of Vocational Rehabilitation on mental health services for deaf persons (Loera, 1982a) emphasized the need for the Office of Vocational Rehabilitation and the Office of Mental Health to initiate a cooperative effort to address the mental health treatment needs of deaf individuals at the community level in order to reduce inappropriate treatment service and restrictive institutional placements. In 1986 the Center On Deafness surveyed RCDs in western Pennsylvania to rate the quality of mental health services for hearing-impaired persons, their impressions of treatment outcomes, and the mental health service needs. Over 75 percent of the respondents rated MH services as fair to poor, including intermediate, long-term, and follow-up/follow-along services. The counselors combined responses estimated an immediate mental health service need for 150–200 hearing-impaired persons in western Pennsylvania alone.

A more recent Center On Deafness survey of all OVR districts in Pennsylvania (Loera, 1988) sought to determine exactly where the rehabilitation process breaks down for deaf individuals with mental health problems. The majority of RCDs (80 to 100 percent) identified a substantial number of problems in each of the following areas:

1. Lack of involvement of clients in the rehabilitation process, including passive participation, inability to set goals, lack of desire for achievement, difficulty maintaining recommended treatment goals;
2. Problem-solving difficulties, such as difficulty recognizing/defining problems, difficulty planning and selecting strategies for effective problem solution, inability to implement or follow through on plans, and inability to evaluate the success of problem-solving strategies;
3. Stress management problems, to include general impulsivity and age inappropriate response to internal or external stress;
4. Interpersonal relationship problems, to include egocentric behaviors, difficulty expressing wants/needs/thoughts, and difficulty getting along with others (e.g., rehabilitation counselor, employer, teachers, family members); and
5. Problems with representational thinking, including inability to conduct "if-then" thinking essential to problem solving, inability to transfer strategies from one situation to another, and lack of ability to move from concrete to abstract relationships and thoughts.

These commonly identified problems reflect a need for the deaf mental health client to gain experience with the means to modify thoughts and behaviors which impede adjustment and interfere with rehabilitation planning and goal attainment. The process of modification also requires the counselor to develop familiarity with models of treatment and effective techniques for facilitating change in the way the client views and responds to life events.

COGNITIVE-BEHAVIORAL PSYCHOTHERAPY

One treatment approach, Cognitive-Behavior Psychotherapy (Meichenbaum, 1977), has been used successfully at the Center On Deafness with deaf clients who present problems similar to those identified in the survey of RCDs. This treatment approach provides a systematic model of intervention for helping the client assume a more active, responsible, and competent role in problem-solving, personal management, and goal attainment. Cognitive-behavioral interventions have already demonstrated effectiveness with diverse populations (Meichenbaum, 1985; Meichenbaum & Jaremko, 1983; Meichenbaum & Cameron, 1974). Recent attention has also focused on how cognitive-behavioral techniques can enhance treatment cooperation, adherence, and follow-through for a number of client population groups (Meichenbaum & Turk, 1987).

While very little has been written on the use of cognitive-behavioral strategies in a psychotherapeutic situation with hearing-impaired persons, researchers (Greenburg, Kusche, Gustafson, & Calderone, 1984; Kusche, Greenberg, Calderone, & Gustafson, 1987; O'Brien, 1987; Harris, 1978; Greenberg, 1985) have found that the use of cognitive-behavioral strategies with deaf children and adolescents holds promise for enhancing the prevention of mental health problems. In academic settings, increasing attention has been placed upon studying the cognitive processes of deaf individuals in the developmental stages (Martin, 1984; 1988), and research is beginning to suggest that the use of specific approaches for teaching thinking skills and metacognitive processes to deaf students can have significant and positive effects on intellectual growth. The use of cognitive-behavioral psychotherapy at the Center On Deafness, with deaf individuals who present mental health and rehabilitation problems, has led us to believe that this approach does provide an effective treatment modality with deaf individuals who, as described by Brauer (1981), have less than effective life-problem coping skills, an external locus of control, a passive approach to problem solution, and difficulty with managing stress and anxiety.

The focus upon a cognitive-behavioral approach does not preclude the use of alternative therapeutic interventions as more or less effective. A review of the literature on counseling approaches used with deaf people illustrates the diversity in orientations being used, to include reality therapy (McCrone, 1983; 1985), provocative therapy (Quedenfeld & Farrelly, 1983), community counseling (Zieziula, 1980), Adlerian counseling (Farrugia, 1985), and behavior modification (Lennan, 1981). The interested reader will also find an overview on counseling the hearing-impaired client (Scott, 1978), cross-cultural issues in counseling the hearing-impaired person (Anderson & Rosten, 1985; Glickman, 1983), as well as a diversity of personal views. Yet, a number of unanswered questions continue to be voiced by professionals, particularly those new to counseling hearing-impaired persons. The recurring questions may include, What special techniques are useful for helping a minimal language skilled deaf client understand cause-effect relationships? Or, What means are particularly effective for confronting client resistance?

The therapist working with hearing-impaired persons must combine clinical training and experience with special training related to hearing impairment in order to maximize treatment effectiveness. The choice of a theoretical and therapeutic orientation is important for guiding meaningful interaction and appropriate intervention. Snyder and Thomsen (1988) provide three probable rationales used by therapists for adhering to a particular theoretical orientation in the absence of conclusive evidence which supports prominence of any one approach over another. The first source of support is frequently from peers and colleagues who share a belief in a specific approach. The second source is derived from published professional articles about a particular form of therapy. The final source is the clinical experience of therapists which ". . . may constitute a particularly powerful and highly persuasive source of evidence that bolsters therapists' beliefs in the validity of their own approaches" (p. 126).

Clearly, this chapter's focus upon a cognitive-behavioral approach is based upon these three sources of support. While there is scarce information on the use of cognitive-behavioral psychotherapy with hearing-impaired persons, the large and available literature on the use and effectiveness of this approach supports the hypothesis that it can be used with hearing-impaired persons when appropriate and creative means are used to modify the procedures for effective use with this population.

This chapter will provide a review of the use of cognitive-behavioral psychotherapy with hearing-impaired persons. This review will include individual and group methods which can be appropriately modified to use with low and high functioning deaf persons who require both rehabilitation and mental health intervention. A case study is provided in the appendix to demonstrate how cognitive-behavior psychotherapy can be applied. Reference will be made to the case study at various points in the chapter.

Individual Cognitive-Behavioral Psychotherapy

This decade has seen a rapid growth in the use of cognitive and cognitive-behavioral therapies for the treatment of mental disorders. Mahoney and Gabriel (1987) indicate that there is a marked increase in the popularity and use of these approaches by U.S. clinical and counseling psychologists in therapy. Specifically, they cite seventeen distinct cognitive approaches for therapy which have wide applicability to a number of clinical groups. These approaches have been used for the treatment of personality disorders (Beck & Freeman, 1990; Freeman & Leaf, 1989), depression (Beck, Rush, Shaw, & Emery, 1979), anxiety disorders and phobias (Beck & Emery, 1985), impulsivity in children (Kendall & Braswell, 1985; Meichenbaum & Goodman, 1971), for the development of metacognitive and problem-solving skills (D'Zurilla, 1986; Pellegrini & Urbain, 1985; Butler & Meichenbaum, 1980; Meichenbaum & Asarnow, 1979), anger control (Feindler & Ecton, 1986; Novaco, 1979), schizophrenia (Meichenbaum & Cameron, 1973; Meichenbaum, 1969), pain and behavioral medicine (Turk, Meichenbaum & Genest 1983), substance abuse (Marlatt & Gordon, 1985; Marlatt, 1979), stress and anxiety (Meichenbaum, 1985; Meichenbaum &

Jaremko, 1983), problems in development which can lead to mental health disorders (Guidano, 1987), and for the facilitation of adherence to treatment regimens (Meichenbaum & Turk, 1987).

Meichenbaum and Gilmore (1982) define their cognitive-behavioral intervention as an ". . . active, time-limited, and structured form of treatment . . . designed to help the client identify, reality test, and correct maladaptive distortions, conceptualizations and dysfunctional beliefs" (p. 134). The major goal of therapy is to provide clients with the skills necessary not only for immediate problem reduction, but also to enhance the client's ability to apply newly acquired skills to a variety of situations in an adaptive manner. The various cognitive and behavioral strategies used with this theory teach the client to develop new skills, self-monitor progress, modify distorted thinking processes, and reduce the stress and anxiety which may arise when facing difficult situations.

Cognitive-behavioral psychotherapy incorporates investigative strategies throughout the treatment process for the purpose of identifying as many factors as possible which might impede progress and increase client resistance to change. Diverse procedures can be used to help the client alter the meaning and impact of maladaptive thought processes which guide and influence behavior. A sampling of cognitive-behavioral procedures available to the therapist include: (1) self-monitoring—teaching the client how to self-observe thoughts and behaviors, and then record the automatic thoughts which precede, accompany and follow problem situations; (2) role-rehearsal—using coaching, modeling, shaping, and performance feedback; (3) cognitive restructuring—helping the client to understand the relationship between thoughts, feelings, and behavior, working collaboratively to help the client identify faulty or self-defeating thoughts, and then replace these cognitions with coping thoughts and behaviors; (4) imagery rehearsal—teaching the client more effective problem-solving skills which can be generalized to a wide range of problems and situations by utilizing images of problems and situations the client has experienced; and/or (5) graded in-vivo exposure assignments—slowly exposing the client to real problem situations in order to facilitate the transfer of skill from the therapy session to the client's environment. The therapist engages the client in an ongoing evaluation of "core organizing principles," i.e., the beliefs, principles, and rules that govern the client's behavior and provide meaning to his or her experience. The therapeutic process includes intervention at the cognitive level to change maladaptive thoughts and perceptions while using behavioral principles to guide and influence behavior change.

Phase I: The Conceptualization of the Problem

Cognitive-behavioral psychotherapy is a three-phase process of change. Phase I, the conceptualization of the problem, is an information-gathering process aimed at understanding the nature of the client's perspective on his or her presenting problems. Since clients frequently do not view their own thinking processes and behavior as sources of disturbance (Meichenbaum, 1975), the therapist must actively work with the client in a collaborative role to develop a common understanding of the client's presenting problem. Turk et al. (1983) stress that the effectiveness of any treatment, and the individual's adherence to any treatment plan, is ". . . in part mediated by the closeness of fit of the treatment with the patient's understanding of the problem and how it can be treated" (p. 7). The client is asked to become an observer of his or her thoughts, feelings, and behaviors. An analysis is made of the client's presenting problems to include the nature and severity of the problem, conditions which intensify or alleviate the problem behavior, and the antecedents and consequences of the behaviors. Most importantly, attention is given the cognitions which occur in problem situations. A variety of assessment procedures are used for evaluating the role that the client's maladaptive thoughts and beliefs play in contributing to the problem situation. Formal assessment procedures (such as the structured clinical interview, Beck Depression Inventory) are combined with other methods for understanding the client's problems. An attempt is made to have the hearing-impaired client reveal recurring problems which have an effect upon adjustment in social, interpersonal, training, and/or work situations.

A situational analysis may be conducted with questions directed toward gathering information on recurring problems, the client's typical response for managing or resolving problems, as well as the private thoughts which may result from the client's attempts to problem solve. A client may lack awareness of everyday events which precipitate problems, particularly if the client lacks insight into his or her behavior. The success of treatment intervention depends, in part, upon helping the client develop an understanding of the presenting problems. This can be accomplished through the use of homework assignments. Initially, homework assignments involve having the client gather information related to problem situations, the client's response (behavior) to the situation, and the thoughts/emotions experienced at the time the problem occurs. It is important for the therapist to gain the client's cooperation by presenting a rationale which emphasizes the importance of the therapist's and client's having a clear understanding of the problem(s) in order to select the most effective method(s) for treatment. The collaborative nature of the relationship when initiating homework assignments can increase the probability that the client will comply with later assignments, which will involve implementation of problem resolution strategies learned and practiced in individual sessions. The use of homework assignments must include a therapist check to verify that the client (1) understands what is to be done in the assignment, and (2) possesses the minimal repertoire of skills to complete the assignment successfully.

The example of Mr. X, presented in the appendix, provides a serious problem with interpersonal relationships. While Mr. X is able to describe problem situations with exacting detail, he lacks insight into how his behavior affects interpersonal relationships. Figure 8–1 provides an example of Mr. X's typical response to a common problem, his perception of the consequences resulting from his problem response, and the recurring thoughts he frequently experiences. Mr. X's description of his problems provided the foundation for interventions which would follow from this first phase of therapy. In this example of Mr. X, the need for stress inoculation, problem-solving

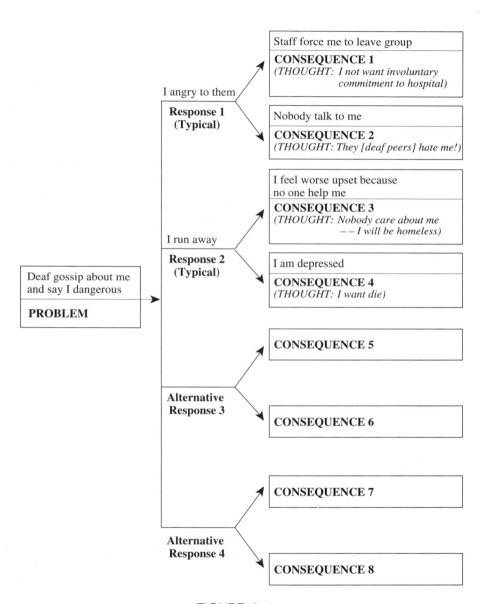

FIGURE 8–1

therapy, cognitive restructuring, and social skills training is evolving from the client's problem description.

The client is encouraged to discuss topics such as prior coping and problem-solving strategies, or family and social support networks. Mental imagery and role-play procedures can be used effectively for assessing how the hearing-impaired client typically responds to stressful situations, as well as for gathering information on the thoughts that the client may have about the problem situation. The mental imagery, problem reconstruction techniques, self-monitoring procedures, or homework assignments can be used to have the client gather additional information regarding problem behaviors, automatic thoughts, physiological reactions, and interpersonal behaviors which might typically occur to intensify problems, cause additional problems, or help reduce the problem. During Phase I, the client is not challenged with regard to his perception and beliefs about his problems. The information gathered through the in-session interview assessment and the various homework assignments helps to crystallize an understanding of the client's presenting problem which can lead to a formulation of an initial treatment plan.

A common problem encountered during this phase of cognitive-behavioral psychotherapy is that the client has difficulty expressing feelings and thoughts which lead to problematic actions and behaviors. Therefore, the therapist purposefully uses therapy sessions and structured homework assignments to help the client become increasingly aware of his or her thoughts and feelings. It is frequently helpful to use a facial line drawing depicting a person who is thinking (Figure 8–2). The client is continually invited to share the personal and private thoughts (internal dialogue) which influence and affect behavior. The line drawing becomes a common useful tool for helping the client attend more closely to thoughts, a procedure which takes on greater importance throughout the therapeutic process. The mouth on the facial line drawing is intentionally omitted for the purpose of having the client describe feelings which may accompany the thoughts. As the deaf client demonstrates increasing ease with the procedure, and a willingness to share the thoughts and feelings which precede, accompany, and follow problems, he or she is asked to describe the intensity of both the thoughts and feelings. A visual feeling and thought thermometer (Figure 8–3) is used to help the client rate the intensity of such thoughts and feelings. The visual format is used until such time that the client becomes accustomed to the procedure and can perform the rating without it. At this point in the therapeutic process the aim is to facilitate information gathering. The plan is to avoid premature intervention and remediation by first organizing information directly connected to the treatment goals the client hopes to achieve. As Meichenbaum (1975) states, ". . . a motivating factor for a number of clients is the need to make sense of their behaviors, to understand what is happening and why, to receive assurances that they are not going to 'lose their minds,' and that something can be done to help them change" (p. 363). Through the process of developing a common view of the presenting problem, a variety of therapeutic interventions can be used to help the client begin the process of change and adjustment.

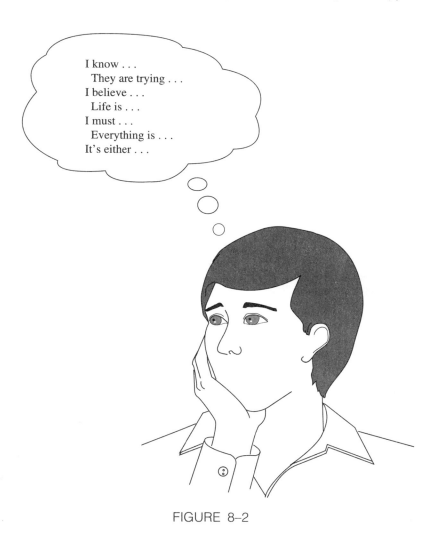

FIGURE 8-2

Phase II: The Reconceptualization Process

The second phase is the reconceptualization process, during which the client is helped to specify his problems and view them as "solvable." During this phase the client will acquire the skills needed to adapt, cope, modify self-statements, and produce new behaviors. The rationale for treatment is presented to the client, giving him or her the opportunity to learn and use new cognitions and behaviors that will reduce and eliminate the use of maladaptive behaviors. The client is given additional homework assignments to test the reality of situations and to listen to self-statements made during

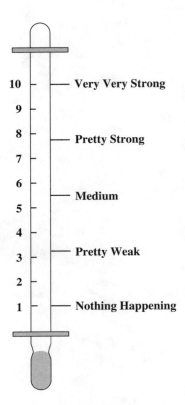

FIGURE 8–3

problem situations. Helping the client attend to self-statements (i.e., internal dialogue) made before, accompanying and following his or her behavior will ultimately have ". . . directive effects upon (1) what the individual attends to in the environment; (2) how he appraises various stimulants and events; (3) to what he attributes his behavior; and (4) his expectations about his own capacities to handle a stressful event" (Meichenbaum, 1977, p. 206). The information gathered during the first phase of therapy, i.e. problem conceptualization, provides necessary evidence to help the client understand the relationship between the thoughts and feelings which influence behavior. This information also provides predictive value with regard to what the client may think or do in diverse problem situations. As in the case of Mr. X, he presents problems as being caused by others, e.g., "she gossip that I am dangerous person so I angry to her." Mr. X views relationships in extremes, either idealized or denigrated, and he does not possess the rudimentary skills or experience to effectively manage normal conflicts which may occur with peers, family, professionals, or at work. The process of collaboratively gathering information provides the necessary evidence to support the treatment plan.

Individual treatment intervention procedures follow specifically from the problem reconceptualization because the therapist has carefully investigated successful and unsuccessful strategies the client uses for managing problems. The therapist increasingly emphasizes the "collaborative" nature of therapy by offering the client the opportunity to learn new and resourceful means to deal with his or her current problems in combination with the successful strategies already available in the client's skill repertoire.

The second phase of therapy with hearing-impaired persons can be quite effective in helping the client develop skills to cope and function more competently and independently. The use of problem-solving therapy, cognitive restructuring, stress inoculation, guided imagery exercises, modeling procedures, in-vivo experiments and a number of other procedures are essential means for helping the client change. As an example, Figure 8–4 provides a concrete means for Mr. X to conceptualize anger control. He quickly grasped the concept of the balloon exploding when too much air is blown into it as representing the escalating nature of his anger to the point where he explodes and becomes threatening to others. More importantly, Mr. X began to understand how the skills learned in therapy can be used to generate more effective ways to cope, manage, or resolve problems without losing control of his anger. Through such procedures, the client more accurately assesses the reality of situations while controlling negative and self-defeating internal dialogue which results in the use of automatic, maladaptive, and self-defeating behaviors.

The therapist-client collaborative work, combined with the therapist's Socratic questioning, homework assignments, and interpretive statements provide an educational component to the reconceptualization process. The hearing-impaired client is provided explanations for his or her problems through the collaborative data gathering process. The explanations are meant to help the client view the problem(s) as more manageable, thus offering hope that they can be reduced or solved. Socratic questioning provides the opportunity for the therapist to assume the role of an investigator asking questions to solve a complicated case. The questions are meant to have the client help the therapist (collaborative effort) understand his problems, the hidden thoughts associated with problems, and possible alternative solutions.

As an example, Mr. X frequently becomes anxious when interacting with peers and the anxiety often leads to conflict, anger, and confrontation. Questions are directed to explore the thoughts Mr. X has when interacting with peers and the interpretation(s) he may have about the behavior of others. The therapist also explores possible strategies Mr. X uses to manage his feelings, verify if his thoughts and perceptions are accurate, and control his behavior. A typical solution provided by Mr. X is that "I must ignore them." This appears to be common advice given to him in the past when problems occurred. However, Mr. X does not have the skill to "ignore" the actions of others. He is hypervigilant, and sufficient data has been gathered from Mr. X to prove that ignoring others does not work for him. At this time a number of more

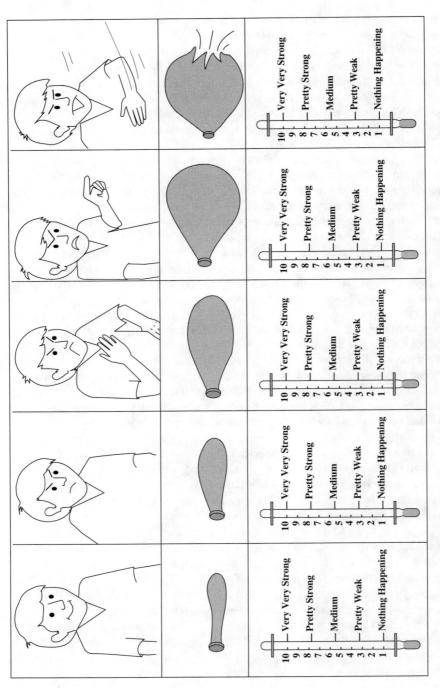

FIGURE 8–4

effective solution alternatives, and the means for acquiring the skill to use the alternatives, can be presented.

The second phase of therapy prepares the hearing-impaired client for change through training in areas where skill deficits are noted, using procedures such as D'Zurilla's (1986) problem-solving therapy, or Meichenbaum's (1985) stress inoculation training. In-session therapy utilizes modeling, role-play, and imagery rehearsal procedures to help the client develop and learn complex behaviors, better retain the procedural steps of training, and rehearse coping and problem-solving strategies which are essential to the final phase of treatment. Homework activities, such as graded in-vivo assignments, begin with achievable and manageable goals which allow for the building of self-confidence, strengthening a sense of self-control, and the experiencing of problems with the opportunity to correct difficulties the client will frequently face in his or her environment. Turk et al. (1985) recommend that (1) each homework assignment be discussed with the client, and that the client indicate which assignments he or she is willing to complete, and (2) each assignment include a "do" statement (specifying what the client should accomplish) and a "quantity" statement (specifying the frequency for the tasks to be accomplished). The client is also expected to provide a self-rating of the difficulty encountered and success experienced. These procedures help reduce resistance and non-compliant behaviors and increase a supportive and collaborative relationship for accomplishing the goals. It is important for the therapist to work intensely with the client to anticipate, subsume, and prepare to eliminate as many obstacles as the client may perceive as interfering with the successful completion of an assignment.

Phase III: The Use of Problem-Solving and Goal-Oriented Strategies

The final phase of therapy involves a more intense use of problem-solving and goal-oriented coping strategies. This phase of skill application and follow through is intended to help the hearing-impaired client produce ". . . constructive, incompatible self-statements and behaviors" (Meichenbaum, 1975, p. 360) which lead to a more adaptive and functional ways of living. Bandura (1977, 1982) stresses the role of cognitive processes in the acquisition and retention of new behavior patterns. He emphasizes the importance of increasing the client's (1) ability to judge whether a particular coping behavior will result in a favorable outcome (outcome expectancy), and (2) belief that he or she is capable of producing the desired behaviors successfully (self-efficacy expectancy). This is accomplished by organizing the hearing-impaired client's cognitive, social, and behavior skills to reduce the doubts an individual may have about his ability to cope effectively and resolve daily challenges.

Treatment intervention refinements may focus on changing the client's cognitive processes (problem-solving and coping skills, automatic thoughts), cognitive structures (beliefs, meaning system), and/or behavior by attending to the client's increased ability to use internal dialogue to problem solve and replace maladaptive behaviors with alternative coping responses. Meichenbaum (1977) states that ". . . if the change process is to be lasting, then one must not only teach new behavioral skills, alter internal dialogue, but also one must influence cognitive structures" (p. 226).

In the case of Mr. X, the process of skill application continues due to the severity and duration of his problems, which began in early childhood. Approximately 1½ years ago, the likely prediction was that Mr. X would return to a state-operated hospital for long-term care. Since that time Mr. X has needed hospitalization, but the decision to enter the hospital was voluntary and short-term. When I first began working with this person he was frequently out-of-control and feared hospitalization because (1) his past hospital treatments were perceived as very bad experiences, and (2) he believed that his peers and professionals were conspiring to have him returned to a state-operated hospital for long-term care. Mr. X's hospitalization during the past 1½ was voluntary and short-term. He is becoming better able to recognize when he needs more intensive help, and he is better able to view short-term hospitalization as an enabling process for him to return to the community and resume work on his goals. In fact, Mr. X is now working, and he demonstrates an increased ability to use the cognitive skills learned in therapy, i.e., to use adaptive responses rather than resorting to maladaptive behaviors.

While the ideal goal is to have the hearing-impaired client master the skills needed to function adaptively, reality leads the cognitive-behavioral therapist to employ strategies to increase coping ability. The therapist, by actively working with the client, can model appropriate coping cognitions, emphasize anticipatory problem solving, and use a myriad of useful techniques (such as imagery rehearsal or cognitive reattribution) to increase a generalization of behaviors which can be used effectively in a variety of circumstances.

Cognitive-behavioral psychotherapy shows promise of being successful with those deaf individuals who, as described by Brauer (1981), have less than effective life-problem coping skills, an external locus of control, a passive approach to problem solution, and difficulty with managing stress and anxiety. The use of cognitive-behavioral procedures provides an important step toward understanding ". . . the nature of the cognitive processes and imagery that sustain thinking and reasoning in a context of deafness" (Levine, 1976, p. 29).

GROUP COUNSELING

In individual counseling, the therapist serves as the primary source of help and information when working collaboratively with the client. In group therapy, members of the group serve as a source of feedback, role models, guides, and sources of support as the group works together to develop the coping skills to function adaptively both in and out of the group. Group counseling involves a process of interaction in which participants begin to define themselves in relation to others, a process which can enhance pro-social learning and behavior change. Yalom (1985) indicates that therapeutic groups are like a "social microcosm" in which each group member eventually begins to act out interpersonal problem strategies and behavior that exist in the individual's everyday life. Group counseling affords many opportunities for personal growth and learning, for developing new ways of managing situations through more adaptive coping mechanisms, and learning adaptive social behavior through the group process, combined with psycho-educational and behavioral rehearsal experiences to enhance growth.

The use of group counseling with a deaf population is a viable and recommended approach for selected settings and purposes (Rainer & Altshuler, 1966; Sussman, 1974; Degrell & Ouellette, 1981; Schein, 1982; Feinstein, 1983). Schein (1982) pointed to the lack of research on group counseling with hearing-impaired persons, and emphasized the need for such research in order to increase the professional's knowledge and understanding of group techniques. Professional articles, for the most part, describe group counseling and psychotherapy with (1) deaf adults who are placed in psychiatric hospitals (Swink, 1980; Robinson, 1966, 1978; Rainer & Altshuler, 1966, 1971; Geller, 1970; Collums, 1969), (2) deaf adolescents (Danek, 1985; Feinstein, 1983; Bonham, Armstrong & Bonham, 1981; Sarlin & Altshuler, 1968; Altshuler, 1967), and (3) deaf rehabilitation clients (Anderson, 1983; Bolton, 1979; Sussman, 1974).

Until recently, very little was known about group counseling processes with deaf persons or about the frequency with which group counseling methods are used with this population. Loera (1987) completed the first major survey research designed to study the use of group counseling methods with deaf adolescents enrolled in residential schools. Group counseling is the most frequently recommended and used approach with adolescents, regardless of hearing status. The survey research represents data gathered from 94 counselors and psychologists. Responses were received from 56 of 72 residential schools in the United States. The results provide in-depth information related to (1) the professional characteristics of residential school counselors, such as background and training experience in group counseling; (2) the characteristics of deaf adolescent counseling groups; and (3) the counselors perceptions about the value, problems, and need for a group counseling approach. The survey results are quite extensive and, therefore, only selected findings will be summarized. Sixty percent of the responding counselors reported current involvement with leading adolescent counseling group sessions. When asked to identify either individual or group counseling as the most effective approach with deaf adolescents, 35 (48.6 percent) users of group counseling chose individual counseling as the more effective treatment modality, 16 (22.2 percent) preferred a group counseling approach, and 21 (29.2 percent) viewed individual and group counseling methods as effective complementary processes with this population. The most common reasons given by counselors for preferring an individual approach included the ability to maintain confidentiality, as well as the group counselors' lack of training and experience with group counseling methods and procedures. The vast majority of respondents to the survey indicated a strong interest in learning more about the practice and technique of group counseling with deaf adolescents. Overall, the survey results in part reflect Sussman's (1974) experience leading a counseling group with late adolescents and young adults who were clients of vocational rehabilitation. He concludes that success of group counseling lies with the therapist in terms of group therapy training and experience, an ability to communicate at the deaf person's conceptual level, and a willingness to learn from the group members themselves.

Group counseling and, specifically, cognitive group counseling is an effective approach for helping people when the professional possesses the necessary background and training. Cognitive group counseling is receiving increased attention for a variety of problems, to include pain (Turk et al., 1983), stress (Meichenbaum, 1985), anger control problems (Feindler & Ecton, 1986; Novaco, 1979), problem solving (D'Zurilla, 1986, 1988), treatment of substance abuse problems (Marlatt & Gordon, 1985), and social skills training (Becker, Heimberg, & Bellack, 1987). Anecdotal records from the Center On Deafness indicate that cognitive group counseling can be very effective for providing learning and corrective emotional experiences, and direct feedback about a client's behavior.

Cognitive-Behavioral Group Counseling

The three phases of individual cognitive-behavioral therapy are applicable to cognitive group counseling. Cognitive group counseling provides the opportunity for each group member to re-evaluate beliefs and meaning systems (cognitive structures), change and/or modify thoughts and problem-solving skills (cognitive processes), and test out new ways of behaving while obtaining corrective feedback from the group's leader and members. Assessment plays an equally important role in cognitive group counseling, as it does in individual treatment. The therapist continually assesses client progress and movement toward completion of treatment goals. Success with cognitive group counseling is enhanced also by providing pre-therapy training to each potential candidate for a group. During the time the therapist is assessing the candidate's problems, prior to the formation of the group, the client is also prepared to understand the goals, purpose, and process of group counseling (Wessler & Wessler, 1989; Corey, 1981; Gazda, 1971). The use of pre-therapy training insures a collaborative relationship by increasing the bond between the group candidate and therapist, and decreasing the likelihood of premature termination from the group (Kaul & Bednar, 1986). Norms such as regular group attendance, active participation of each individual, and restraint of physical acting-out and aggressive behaviors should be discussed as part of the pre-therapy preparation (Yalom, 1975; Gauron & Rawlings, 1975). It is also essential to stress the importance of confidentiality regarding group content and membership if the group leader hopes to foster free interaction and self-disclosure. Maintaining confidentiality was a frequently cited issue raised by residential school counselors working with deaf adolescents (Loera, 1987).

Cognitive group counseling is based partly on an educational model emphasizing the remediation of deficits through didactic experiences, followed by the application of newly acquired skills to promote cognitive, emotional and behavioral change. The group leader initially takes a very active role to model and shape behavior. Through active listening and careful observation, the therapist routinely evaluates the nature of each member's problems and the circumstances which may influence inappropriate behaviors.

The use of a cognitive group counseling approach with hearing-impaired persons is very effective when it combines the use of psycho-educational, problem-solving, and affective-experiential group procedures discussed by Wessler and Wessler (1989). The psycho-educational approach uses teaching as a primary means to provide information group members should know to increase personal growth and development, such as in assertiveness training or stress inoculation.

The problem-solving approach also incorporates educational aspects for the purpose of preparing the client to self-monitor behavior. Group members are instructed on how to help each other through the therapist's use of guided imagery, role-rehearsal, modeling or psychodrama procedures. Written and behavioral homework assignments follow closely from in-session experiences to graded in-vivo assignments. The therapist must be prepared to deal with group resistance to carrying out homework assignments related to both individual and group goals. It is advantageous to have the group members identify tasks they would like to attempt and then collaboratively negotiate a reasonable assignment with the therapist.

The affective-experiential approach uses more indirect methods to help clients assimilate learning experiences through active means, i.e., games, exercises, guided fantasies. The use of action-oriented techniques allows not only the learning of new skills, but also the opportunity to understand the ". . . connections between cognitive appraisals and resulting emotions" (Wessler & Wessler, 1989, p. 574). The affective-experiential approach provides the hearing-impaired group members with the occasion to process their affect-laden experiences, while increasing both emotion-focused and problem-focused coping skills (Lazarus & Folkman, 1984).

Group counseling approaches can provide hearing-impaired clients with learning experience to enable them to function more adaptively. Yet there continues to be an absence of investigations to provide insight and direction to use the process more effectively. The success of group approaches is related to multiple variables such as the training and experience of the therapist, group composition and role expectations, communication and group interaction patterns, methods of conflict resolution, client pathology, pre-group preparation, and appropriate matching of clients and treatment modality (Loera, 1987). Yet, the majority of counselors who use a group approach with deaf adolescents report a preference for individual therapy and, in part, cite their lack of training and experience as influencing their preference. While group approaches are effective (Kaul & Bednar, 1986; Yalom, 1985; Seligman, 1982) and recommended for use with hearing-impaired persons (Loera, 1987; Danek, 1985; Anderson, 1983; Schein, 1982; Sussman, 1974), it is clear that more research, therapist training, and supervision is needed to meet the challenges of effectively using this potent form of therapy.

PRACTICAL INTERVENTION CONSIDERATIONS

Reducing Resistance to Treatment

Psychotherapy is a professional healing process aimed at helping an individual, the client, learn effective strategies to cope with or solve problems of living. Resistance to change is a natural and continuous part of this process, and it is expressed by the client and experienced by the therapist. Resistance from the client takes many forms, such as missed appointments, and may reflect the client's fear of change or lack of understanding about the therapeutic process. The therapist may experience and interpret client resistance in many ways, such as a personal failure or a worsening of the client's symptoms. Ultimately, the therapist must confront this resistance with the client in a way that leads to adaptation, ability to cope, and psychological well-being.

The process of psychotherapy is most like to be effective and lead to improved functioning when the client is exposed to anxiety-provoking situations in a setting which allows risk-taking behaviors, which lead to the development of mastery or coping skills that can be applied in a variety of life situations (Lambert, Shapiro, & Bergin, 1986). The effectiveness of the psychotherapeutic process and the amount of resistance to change will depend, in part, upon the nature of the client-therapist bond, the regularity and amount of time invested in therapy, the client's preparation for participating in therapy, and the client's willingness to work collaboratively with the therapist by sharing the responsibility for problem-solving (Orlinsky & Howard, 1986).

Resistance that is unchallenged can severely limit a client's willingness to adhere to a planned treatment program. Meichenbaum and Turk (1987) indicate the seriousness of treatment non-adherence and provide a useful 10 step cognitive-behavioral approach for reducing client resistance and increasing treatment adherence. These steps have proven very effective for working with deaf mental health clients referred to the Center On Deafness. The reader is encouraged to refer to the original source for a detailed explanation of the 10 treatment adherence steps recommended by Meichenbaum and Turk. Briefly, the 10 steps are: (1) anticipate nonadherence, e.g., what is the client's compliance history; (2) take the client's perspective and involve the client in treatment planning and goal setting; (3) foster a collaborative relationship; (4) be client-oriented by probing into the client's views, expectancies, and understanding of the problem(s); (5) customize treatment by adjusting and modifying treatment procedures to meet the needs and skills of the client; (6) enlist family support; (7) provide for continuity of care and an atmosphere of accessibility, sincerity, respect, and a non-judgmental attitude; (8) make use of other health care providers and community resources; (9) repeat everything to increase the likelihood of continued adherence generalization; and (10) don't give up—analyze problems, and correct barriers to adherence.

Identification of Qualified Counselors

The literature on counseling services for deaf individuals is replete with concerns and criticism of the current state of psychological services available to deaf people

(Loera, 1982b, 1987, 1988; Brauer, 1978; Brauer & Sussman, 1980; Degrell & Ouellette, 1981; Spragins, Karchmer, & Schildroth, 1981; Danek, 1987; Robinson, Sachs, & Sloan, 1978; Levine, 1977). Recommendations are urged for the training and development of needed therapeutic skills that psychological service providers must have to work effectively with deaf children, adolescents, and adults (Levine, 1977), and for the initiation of research which can help the psychological service provider become a better utilizer of counseling techniques and processes which can ultimately benefit the deaf person (Sussman, 1988; Loera, 1987; Levine, 1977).

Considerable support exists to insure that trainees and professionals who work with deaf people have the competency (training, experience, supervision) in the individual's respective field of practice, such as mental health, and also competency and knowledge of the deaf subculture, their language and mode(s) of communication, and of the special treatment techniques to use with this population (Schein, 1982; Levine, 1977; Robinson, 1978; Sussman & Stewart, 1971). Counselors and therapists are encouraged to recognize that (1) the individual needs of the deaf person are important for planning a treatment approach, and (2) the stereotypic views of deaf people (i.e., language limitations, lack of ability to reason on an abstract level, rigid personality structure) will only interfere with and prevent the establishment of a meaningful therapeutic relationship (Brauer & Sussman, 1980).

Sussman (1987) indicates that difficulties and failures in the provision of counseling services to deaf people are frequently associated with the therapist's clinical skills, personality, attitude, sign language competence, understanding of deafness, cultural sensitivity, and experiences with deaf clients. Langholtz and Heller (1987) report on a semi-structured interview with thirteen psychotherapists nominated by their peers as effective in their work with deaf clients. The summary report indicates that the therapists emphasized training in, and understanding of, developmental, cultural, educational, and linguistic aspects of deafness as a means for avoiding diagnostic and treatment mistakes. The clinicians all expressed the importance for therapists to possess strong clinical training, supervised clinical experiences, and specialization in deafness.

The need for strong clinical training and supervised clinical experiences is emphasized in the survey research previously discussed on group counseling with deaf adolescents (Loera, 1987). Over 75 percent of the survey respondents reported receiving group counseling training on a formal (e.g., university course) and/or informal (e.g., in-service) basis. Over 60 percent of the counselors indicated they received some form of academic, observational, experiential, and supervisory training as recommended by the American Group Psychotherapy Association and the Association for Specialists in Group Work. Nearly 90 percent of the group counselors indicated receiving no "formal" group supervision. An interesting finding was that the counselors rated their university training in these four component areas as less than useful as preparation to be a group counselor with adolescents, regardless of hearing status. A summary of the counselors' responses and ratings on the survey call into question the adequacy of university academic, observational, experiential, and supervision training provided to counselors as preparation to provide group counseling.

Two additional problems exist with regard to unethical services provided to deaf persons. Sussman (1990) describes the problem where

> . . . purveyors of psychological services with questionable and dubious cre-
> dentials and without appropriate training in the behavioral sciences and psy-
> chotherapy . . . [mental health] professionals who attempt to treat [deaf]
> clients for disorders that are beyond their level of training and compe-
> tence. . . . Likewise, not all professionals have the required competencies for
> evaluating diagnosing and treating mental, emotional, adjustment, or behav-
> ioral problems. . . . There are abuses and misrepresentations of another
> stripe. Proficiency in sign language, including ASL, is not to be equated with
> proficiency in psychotherapy with deaf people. Another facet of the sign
> language conundrum is the example of a hearing Ph.D. clinical psychologist
> who, in attempting to increase the number of clients in his private practice,
> takes a six-week beginner's sign language course and, upon completion,
> advertises himself as an expert on deafness and actively solicits referrals of
> deaf clients (pp. 24–25).

This quote is presented as a very real problem which must be addressed if deaf persons are to receive competent and appropriate services from ethical professionals.

The Spartansburg Conference (Levine, 1977) provides specific guidelines for the identification and selection of counselors who can provide direct psychological services to deaf persons. In addition to sound clinical training, the Spartansburg Conference identified a number of special competencies and knowledge necessary for providing psychological services to deaf persons. Counselors should possess the (1) ability to use and understand all modes of communication used in the deaf community, (2) ability to communicate at the language and conceptual level of the deaf client, (3) knowledge of the deaf individual, community, and subculture, (4) knowledge and understanding of the special techniques of psychological evaluation, and (5) special skills and knowledge of the techniques and application of psychotherapeutic intervention, to include individual, group, or family counseling.

Use of Interpreters in Psychological Situations

The use of interpreters in mental health situations is a controversial topic. Brauer (1978) indicates that the use of interpreters in such situations is not preferred because it (1) is a barrier between the client and therapist relationship, (2) is a threat to confidentiality, (3) is not preferred by most deaf people, and (4) removes responsibility from the mental health professional to provide direct service in the client's natural language. While direct mental health service provision is the ideal goal, the vital role of the interpreter must be considered in relation to the deaf population needs (Goulder, 1977) and the current inaccessibility of services. As Sussman (1987) states ". . . it is the sign language interpreter, despite reported pitfalls inherent in the triadic relationship, that is helping many deaf individuals gain access to the wide variety of therapies and therapists" (p. 8). The use of interpreters for mental health situations has gained increased importance for providing accessibility for deaf persons to the mental health system (Harvey, 1983, 1989; Long, Ouellette, Andrews, & Harvey, 1987; Maher & Waters, 1984; Taff-Watson, 1983; Williams, 1983; Schein, 1982).

When a deaf person is referred for mental health services, and there is no mental health and deafness specialist, then effort must be directed toward insuring that relevant information is available for the service agency or professional regarding the use of interpreters, contact procedures, service cost, and the recommended qualifications, functions, and proper use of the interpreter. A number of important issues should be clarified regarding the use of an interpreter in mental health situations, from the small but important detail of seating arrangements to the major concern for insuring confidentiality.

The therapist and interpreter will need to establish steps for dealing with procedural topics regarding psychological assessments, therapeutic approach and process, clinical procedures and techniques to be used, and understanding key terminology and concepts. These professionals should also develop a team approach which clearly defines therapist and interpreter boundaries, procedures for managing process problems, and steps for preparing the deaf client for understanding and differentiating the therapist and interpreter roles. The interested reader is encouraged to review the available professional literature which discusses the use of interpreters in mental health settings (Owens, 1989; Taff-Watson, 1983; Williams, 1983; Straub, 1976), as well as for individual therapy (Owens, 1989; DeMatteo, Veltri, & Lee, 1985), group therapy (Schein, 1982), and family therapy (Harvey, 1989; 1983).

CONCLUSION

This chapter presented a cognitive-behavioral approach for intervention with deaf persons who have mental health problems. This chapter also provides anecdotal support for the effectiveness of a cognitive-behavioral intervention which indicates that deaf people are able to benefit from a therapeutic approach emphasizing the ability to use and/or change one's cognitions for adaptive functioning. The anecdotal discussion of therapeutic effectiveness has been the most frequently used means for discussing therapy and therapy effectiveness with hearing-impaired persons (Anderson & Rosten, 1985; McCrone, 1983; Quedenfeld & Farrelly, 1983; Glickman, 1983; Stein, Mindel, & Jabaley, 1981; Brauer & Sussman, 1980). The experiences at the Center On Deafness at the Western Pennsylvania School for the Deaf indicate that this approach is effective with a wide range of mental health problems.

There is reason to believe that therapists use specific approaches and continue to adhere to their preferred approach, or brand of therapy, because personal experiences provide support and validation of the particular treatment effectiveness. Yet the field of mental health and deafness cannot afford to continue to rely upon anecdotal records. The need for process and outcome studies is apparent, but there are many variables which make the research process difficult. Despite the difficulty, it is believed that single-case experimental designs, as described by Kazdin (1982, 1986), do offer researchers the opportunity to provide data regarding the effectiveness of various treatment procedures with this population (Craig, Craig, & Loera, 1987). In addition to the need for research, there is a clear need to make mental health services more accessible to hearing-impaired persons at the community level.

While we may recognize the need for mental health services for deaf persons, it is also important to recognize that in the current economic environment, funding for these services will continue to fall short of the need. Alternatives to governmental funding must be identified in order to insure that not only in-patient care, but also emergency, partial hospitalization, outpatient, and consultation and education services, are made available and accessible to all without removing the hearing-impaired person from the mainstream of society.

In order to facilitate a more constructive approach for reducing the current problem, reasonable recommendations must be reviewed and implemented as a foundation for meeting the mental health needs of hearing-impaired persons. The state-managed mental health system should consider developing an action plan for providing statewide, regional, and local training for those professionals in administrative and direct service positions. This training should initially focus upon awareness issues related to the complexity and importance of providing mental health services to hearing-impaired persons. Additional training should be focused upon specific information needed by those professional (caseworkers, therapists, psychologists, psychiatrists) who will initiate and follow through on treatment for those seeking service. Very intensive and in-depth training should be provided to those mental health specialists who have the interest, motivation, and potential skills for providing more direct service to this population.

State mental health offices should also develop broad guidelines regarding the use of consultation service which can be used within the county MH/MR system. The guidelines should provide a basis for the county system to develop specificity with regard to agency, staff, and client consultation services. A list of qualified experts in deafness and mental health should be developed and distributed to all MH/MR programs and their service contractors. Specific consultation guidelines can allow an opportunity for local service providers to begin developing knowledge and experience with diagnostic, treatment, and referral services under the guidance of the consultant. A most important objective is to insure that supervision by a specialist trained in deafness and mental health be made available to direct appropriate treatment when the therapeutic process seems to break down.

Ultimately, the goal of these recommendations is to allow for an expansion of direct services to hearing-impaired clients within their community catchment areas. The ability of the county system to provide such services will depend on the availability of monies to (1) hire professionals who have the additional training in deafness, (2) train existing personnel who have the potential to develop special skills, and/or (3) hire certified interpreters to act as communication facilitators. State and county mental health offices should develop a long-range plan with short- and long-term goals to allow for a gradual growth in the number of county-based mental health workers who can provide services to this disability group.

The success of an action plan to provide quality mental health service to hearing-impaired persons rests, in part, on a means for (1) referring individuals into the mental health system, and (2) referring the hearing-impaired individual to a specialist in deafness when the local base service unit is unable to meet the individual's needs. A policy procedure is recommended that provides a decision-tree format to guide the mental health professional toward a decision to either provide direct service or to refer the hearing-impaired person to a mental health and deafness specialist.

APPENDIX: SAMPLE CASE STUDY USING COGNITIVE-BEHAVIORAL THERAPY

Case Study: Client X

Client X is a deaf male, in his mid-20's, referred for therapy by a community mental health center. Mr. X's developmental history includes early and severe child abuse, hyperactivity, aggression toward others, self-abuse, extreme mood changes, and one suicide attempt. As a child his behavior was hard to manage. His father rejected him and abandoned the family. By age four, his mother could not control him and she resorted to boarding up his bedroom windows and putting a lock on his bedroom door. He became a ward of the courts with placements in a number of foster homes. Mr. X is an individual deafened by rubella. He began his education at a residential school for the deaf. His academic achievement was marginal, yet his language and manual communication skills are good.

Mr. X has been hospitalized seven times, with four of the hospitalizations ranging from 1 to 1½ years each. He was also placed in a number of special schools for emotionally disturbed children as his behavior worsened. Hospital commitments became standard procedure, and the use of neuroleptic medications, anxioletics, and mood stabilizers became the most common treatment. Individual psychotherapy was attempted but discontinued numerous times. During the past 18 years, Mr. X's diagnosis has changed and included the following: conduct disorder, mixed personality disorder, explosive personality disorder, borderline personality disorder, dysthymia, adjustment disorder with mixed disturbance of emotion and conduct, and a bipolar disorder.

The therapeutic process with Mr. X has been difficult and challenging because of the severity and duration of his problems, his poor impulse control, and the extreme level of anxiety and hypervigilant behavior he experiences. A major problem has been his historical noncompliance with any therapeutic treatment plan. Attempts to have Mr. X define his problems typically led to an increase in his anxiety and/or anger. Most often he projected blame onto others for his problems. He seemed entirely unaware of the effects of his behavior on others, and he frequently perceived and interpreted the behavior of others as hostile or rejecting. His level of anxiety often was so acute that he had difficulty managing internal dialogue. For example, during times of anxiety and stress, his thoughts would race between a belief that certain people were blaming him for problems and trying to hurt him, to thoughts of past problems with his mother when he was abused.

Mr. X's severe problems and lack of trust in others made it particularly important to build and emphasize the *collaborative* nature of our work. Initial emphasis was placed upon *stress inoculation training. Imagery techniques and role rehearsal procedures* became important in-session tools for helping Mr. X gain skill with stress inoculation, *problem identification,* and *thought catching.* Mr. X was given *assignments* to attend to situations which repeatedly caused problems and to record the thoughts and feelings he experienced before, during, and after the situation. Mr. X frequently would not write such information. However, I found that recording increased significantly when we resorted to having him leave messages on my TDD answering machine. Throughout therapy I performed *comprehension checks* to make sure Mr. X understood what he was to do and that he had the necessary skills to *self-monitor.*

The second phase of therapy focused upon *cognitive restructuring procedures* as an extension of the initial *problem-solving training.* Particular attention was placed upon absolutistic thinking. As Mr. X developed more competence with these procedures, more attention was placed upon *problem-solving therapy* as well as *social skills training.*

The third phase of treatment emphasizes *generalization of skills and adherence* to newly developed skills, as well as continued use of stress inoculation, problem-solving, cognitive restructuring, *visual imagery and graded in-vivo assignments.*

Mr. X continues in therapy but he currently is employed. His last hospitalization occurred over one year ago, since I began working with him. While all his prior hospitalizations were involuntary commitments, his last hospitalization was a voluntary decision on his part to have his medications adjusted. He currently works and lives in an independent apartment.

REFERENCES

Adler, E. (1978). Mental health services to deaf people: A historical review. *Gallaudet Today,* 5–8.

Altshuler, K. (1967). The psychiatric preventive program in a school for the deaf. In J. Rainer & K. Altshuler (Eds.), *Psychiatry and the deaf* (pp. 11–24). New York: New York State Psychiatric Institute and the New York University Center for Research and Training in Deafness Rehabilitation.

Anderson, C., & Stewart, S. (1983). *Mastering resistance: A practical guide to family therapy.* New York: Guilford Press.

Anderson, G. (1983). A structured group counseling approach for delivering adjustment services to deaf individuals in rehabilitation settings. In D. Watson & B. Heller (Eds.), *Mental health and deafness: Strategic perspectives,* (pp. 20–23). Silver Spring, MD: American Deafness and Rehabilitation Association.

Anderson, G., & Rosten, E. (1985). Towards evaluating process variables in counseling deaf people: A cross-cultural perspective. In G. Anderson & D. Watson (Eds.), *Counseling deaf people: Research and practice* (pp. 1–23). Little Rock, AR: Arkansas Rehabilitation Research and Training Center, University of Arkansas.

Bandura, A. (1977). Self-efficacy: Toward a unifying theory of behavioral change. *Psychological Review, 84*(2), 191–215.

Bandura, A. (1982). Self-efficacy mechanism in human agency. *American Psychologist, 37*(2), 122–147.

Beck, A., & Freeman, A. (1990). *Cognitive therapy of personality disorders.* New York: Guilford Press.

Beck, A., Rush, A., Shaw, B., & Emery, G. (1979). *Cognitive therapy of depression.* New York: Guilford Press.

Beck, A., & Emery, G. (1985). *Anxiety disorders and phobias: A cognitive perspective.* New York: Basic Books.

Beckman, E., & Watkins, J. (1989). Process and outcome in cognitive therapy. In A. Freeman, K. Simon, L. Beutler, & H. Arkowitz (Eds.), *Comprehensive handbook of cognitive therapy* (pp. 61–82). New York: Plenum Press.

Becker, R., Heimberg, R., & Bellack, A. (1987). *Social skills training: Treatment for depression.* New York: Pergamon Press.

Beene, G., & Larson, J. (1979). Misdiagnosis in rehabilitation settings. *Journal of Rehabilitation of the Deaf, 13*(2), 11–15.

Bolton, B. (1979). Comprehensive rehabilitation of multiply handicapped hearing-impaired young adults. In L. Bradford & W. Hardy (Eds.), *Hearing and hearing impairment* (pp. 365–379). New York: Grune & Stratton.

Bonham, H., Armstrong, T., & Bonham, G. (1981). Group psychotherapy with deaf adolescents. *American Annals of the Deaf, 126*(7), 806–809.

Brauer, B. (1978). Mental health and deaf persons: A status report. *Gallaudet Today, 9,* 1–4.

Brauer, B. (1980). Perspectives on psychotherapy with deaf persons. *Mental Health and Deafness, 4,* 4–8.

Brauer, B. (1981). *Mental health research at Gallaudet College.* Paper presented to Scientific and Professional Issues Seminar, Gallaudet Research Institute, Washington, DC.

Brauer, B., & Sussman, A. (1980). Experiences of deaf therapists with deaf clients. *Mental Health and Deafness, 4,* 9–13.

Butler, L., & Meichenbaum, D. (1980). The assessment of interpersonal problem-solving skills. In P. Kendall & S. Hollon (Eds.), *Cognitive-behavioral interventions: Assessment methods* (pp. 197–225). New York: Academic Press.

Collums, L. (1969). Group psychotherapy. In R. Grinker (Ed.), *Psychiatric diagnosis, therapy and research on the psychotic deaf* (pp. 53–57). Washington, DC: Social and Rehabilitation Service, U.S. Department of Health, Education and Welfare.

Corey, G. (1981). *Theory and practice of group counseling.* California: Brooks/Cole Publishing Co.

Craig, W., Craig, H., & Loera, P. (1987). *A cognitive-behavioral model for mental health rehabilitation of deaf individuals.* Unpublished manuscript, Pittsburgh, PA: Center On Deafness.

Craig, W., Craig, H., & Loera, P.(1990). *Meeting mental health needs of deaf clients: Training for rehabilitation counselors of the deaf.* Unpublished manuscript, Pittsburgh, PA: Center On Deafness.

Danek, M. (1985). Structured group counseling with deaf adolescents. In G. Anderson & D. Watson (Eds.), *Counseling with deaf people: Research and practice* (pp. 235–249). Little Rock, AR: University of Arkansas.

Danek, M. (1987). Deafness rehabilitation needs and competencies: Results of a survey. In D. Watson, G. Long, M. Taff-Watson, & M. Harvey (Eds.), *Two decades of excellence: A foundation for the future* (pp. 183–193). Little Rock, AR: American Deafness and Rehabilitation Association.

Danek, M. (1988). Deafness rehabilitation needs and competencies: Results of a survey. In D. Watson, G. Long, M. Taff-Watson, & M. Harvey (Eds.), *Two decades of excellence: A foundation for the future* (pp. 183–193). American Deafness and Rehabilitation Association Monograph 14.

Degrell, R., & Ouelette, S. (1981). The role and function of a counselor in residential schools for the deaf. *American Annals of the Deaf, 126,* 64–68.

DeMatteo, A., Veltri, D., & Lee, S. (1985). Role of the sign language interpreter in psychotherapy. In *Registry of Interpreters 9th Annual RID National Convention,* San Diego, CA.

D'Zurilla, T. (1986). *Problem-solving therapy: A social competence approach to clinical intervention.* New York: Springer Publishing Co.

D'Zurilla, T. (1988). Problem-solving therapies. In K. Dobson (Ed.), *Handbook of cognitive-behavioral therapies* (pp. 86–135). New York: Guilford Press.

Farrelly, F. & Quedenfeld, C. (1985). Provocative therapy with the hearing-impaired client. In G. Anderson & D. Watson (Eds.), *Counseling deaf people: Research and practice* (pp. 187–210). Little Rock, AR: University of Arkansas.

Farrugia, D. (1985). Adlerian counseling and the deaf client. In G. Anderson & D. Watson (Eds.), *Counseling deaf people: Research and practice* (pp. 145–166). Little Rock, AR: University of Arkansas.

Feindler, E., & Ecton, R. (1986). *Adolescent anger control: Cognitive-behavioral techniques.* New York: Pergamon Press.

Feinstein, C. (1983). Early adolescent deaf boys: A biopsychosocial approach. In M. Sugar (Ed.), *Adolescent psychiatry: Developmental and clinical studies* (pp. 147–162). Chicago: University of Chicago.

Freeman, A., & Leaf, R. (1989). Cognitive therapy applied to personality disorders. In A. Freeman, K. Simon, L. Beutler, & H. Arkowitz (Eds.), *Comprehensive handbook of cognitive therapy* (pp. 403–434). New York: Plenum Press.

Freeman, A., Pretzer, J., Fleming, B., & Simon, K. (1990). *Clinical applications of cognitive therapy.* New York: Plenum Press.

Freeman, A., Simon, K. Beutler, L., & Arkowitz, H. (Eds.) (1989). *Comprehensive handbook of cognitive therapy.* New York: Plenum Press.

Gauron, E., & Rawlings, E. (1975). A procedure for orienting new members to group psychotherapy. *Small Group Behavior, 6,* 293–307.

Gazda, G. (1971). *Group counseling: A developmental approach.* Boston: Allyn and Bacon.

Geller, R. (1970). Reaching the deaf: Report of an in-hospital group. *Mental Hygiene, 54,* 388–392.

Glickman, N. (1983). A cross-cultural view of counseling with deaf clients. *Journal of Rehabilitation of the Deaf, 16*(3), 4–15.

Goulder, T. (1977). Federal and state mental health programs for the deaf in hospitals and clinics. *Mental Health In Deafness,* Experimental Issue #1, Fall, 13–17.

Greenberg, M. (1985). Problem-solving and social relationships: The applications of a stress and coping model for treating deaf clients. In G. Anderson & D. Watson (Eds.), *Counseling deaf people: Research and practice* (pp. 83–104). Little Rock, AR: University of Arkansas.

Greenberg, M., Kusche, C., Gustafson, R., & Calderone, R. (1984). The PATHS project: A model for prevention of psychosocial difficulties in deaf children. In G. Anderson and D. Watson (Eds.), *The habilitation and rehabilitation of deaf adolescents* (pp. 243–263). Proceedings of the National Conference on Habilitation and Rehabilitation of Deaf Adolescents, Wagoner, OK.

Guidano, V. (1987). *Complexity of the self.* New York: Guilford Press.

Harris, R. (1978). The relationship of impulse control to parent hearing status, manual communication, and academic achievement in deaf children. *American Annals of the Deaf, 123*(1), 52–67.

Harvey, M. (1982). The influence and utilization of an interpreter for deaf persons in family therapy. *American Annals of the Deaf, 127,* 821–827.

Harvey, M. (1988). An ecological perspective on deafness. *Journal of Rehabilitation of the Deaf, 21*(3), 12–20.

Harvey, M. (1989). *Psychotherapy with deaf and hard-of-hearing persons: A systemic model.* Hillsdale, NJ: Lawrence Erlbaum Associates.

Joyce E., & Mathay, G. (1986). A study of closed cases: Implications for the administration of deafness rehabilitation services. *Journal of Rehabilitation of the Deaf, 20*(1), 5–13.

Kaul, T., & Bednar, R. (1986). Research on group and related therapies. In S. Garfield & A. Bergin (Eds.), *Handbook of psychotherapy and behavior change* (pp. 671–714). New York: John Wiley & Sons.

Kazdin, A. (1981). Methodology of psychotherapy outcome research: Recent developments and remaining limitations. In J. Harvey & M. Parks (Eds.), *Master lecture series, Vol. I: Psychotherapy research and behavior change.* Washington, DC: The American Psychological Association (2nd printing, 1984).

Kazdin, A. (1982). Single-case experimental designs. In P. Kendall & J. Butcher (Eds.), *Handbook of research methods in clinical psychology* (pp. 461–490). New York: John Wiley & Sons.

Kazdin, A. (1983). Treatment research: The investigation of psychotherapy. In M. Hersen, A. Kazdin & A. Bellack (Eds.), *The clinical psychology handbook* (pp. 265–288). New York: Pergamon Press.

Kazdin, A. (1986). Comparative outcome studies of psychotherapy: Methodological issues and strategies. *Journal of Consulting and Clinical Psychology, 54,* 95–105.

Kendall, P., & Braswell, L. (1985). *Cognitive-behavioral therapy for impulsive children.* New York: Guilford Press.

Kusche, C., Garfield, T., & Greenberg, M. (1983). The understanding of emotional and social attributions in deaf adolescents. *Journal of Clinical Child Psychology, 12*(2), 153–160.

Kusche, C., & Greenberg, M. (1983). Evaluative understanding and role-taking ability: A comparison of deaf and hearing children. *Child Development, 54,* 141–147.

Kusche, C., Greenberg, M., Calderone, R., & Gustafson, R. (1987). Generalization strategies from the PATHS project for the prevention of substance use disorders. In G. Anderson & D. Watson (Eds.), *Innovations in the habilitation and rehabilitation of deaf adolescents* (pp. 263–304). Little Rock, AR: University of Arkansas Rehabilitation Research and Training Center On Deafness and Hearing Impairment.

Lambert, M., Shapiro, D., & Bergin, A. (1986). the effectiveness of psychotherapy. In S. Garfield & A. Bergin (Eds.), *Handbook of psychotherapy and behavior change* (pp. 157–212). New York: John Wiley & Sons.

Langholtz, D., & Heller, B. (1988). Effective psychotherapy with deaf persons: Therapists' perspectives. In D. Watson, G. Long, M. Taff-Watson, & M. Harvey (Eds.), *Two decades of excellence: A foundation for the future* (pp. 54–68). Little Rock, AR: American Deafness and Rehabilitation Association, Monograph 14.

Lazarus, R., & Folkman, S. (1984). *Stress, appraisal, and coping.* New York: Springer.

Lennan, R. (1981). Behavior-modification model in a residential setting for multi-handicapped deaf children. In L. Stein, E. Mindel, & T. Jabaley (Eds.), *Deafness and mental health* (pp. 85–98). New York: Grune & Stratton.

Levine, E. (1976). Psychological contributions. *Volta Review, 78,* 23–33.

Levine, E. (1977). The preparation of psychological service providers to the deaf. *Journal of Rehabilitation of the Deaf,* Monograph 4.

Loera, P. (1982a). *Mental health and deafness: Recommendations for the provision of mental health services to deaf individuals in Pennsylvania.* Unpublished manuscript, Pennsylvania Office of Vocational Rehabilitation.

Loera, P. (1982b). Mental health and deafness: The unmet needs of a special target population. In Pennsylvania Department of Public Welfare, Vol. II: *The 1982–83 Mental Health Plan and 1981–82 Annual Report.*

Loera, P. (1986). "now that we know the extent of the problems we should . . . ?": Going beyond assessment toward implementation of mental health services for Pennsylvania's hearing-impaired population. In Pennsylvania Department of Public Welfare, Vol. II: *The 1986–87 Mental Health Plan and 1985–86 annual report.*

Loera, P. (1987). Group counseling with deaf adolescents in residential schools: A survey of residential school counselors. University of Pittsburgh: Doctoral dissertation. *Dissertation Abstracts International.*

Loera, P. (1988). *The road to accessible mental health services for hearing-impaired persons is paved with good intentions.* Testimony presented to the Public Policy forums, Office of Mental Health, Pennsylvania Department of Public Welfare.

Long, B., High, C., & Shaw, J. (1989). *Directory of mental health services for deaf persons (2nd Ed.).* Little Rock, AR: ADARA Mental Health Section: American Deafness and Rehabilitation Association.

Long, G., Ouellette, S., Andrews, M., & Harvey, M. (1987). Families in transition: Issues for deaf adolescents and their families. In D. Watson, G. Long, M. Taff-Watson, & M. Harvey (Eds.), *Two decades of excellence: A foundation for the future* (pp. 2–15). Little Rock, AR: American Deafness and Rehabilitation Association.

Maher, P., & Water, J. (1984). The use of interpreters with deaf clients in therapy. *Journal of Rehabilitation of the Deaf, 17*(4), 11–16.

Mahoney, M., & Gabriel, T. (1987). Psychotherapy and cognitive sciences: An evolving alliance. *Journal of Cognitive Psychotherapy, 1,* 39–60.

Marlatt, G. (1979). Alcohol use and problem drinking: A cognitive-behavioral analysis. In P. Kendall & S. Hollon (Eds.), *Cognitive-behavioral interventions: Theory, research and procedures* (pp. 319–355). New York: Academic Press.

Marlatt, G., & Gordon, J. (1985). *Relapse prevention: Maintenance strategies in the treatment of addictive behaviors.* New York: Guilford Press.

Martin, D. (1984). Cognitive modification for the hearing-impaired adolescent: The promise. *Exceptional Children, 51*(3), 235–242.

Martin, D. (1988). Directions for post-secondary education of hearing-impaired persons. *Journal of the American Deafness and Rehabilitation Association, 22*(2), 36–40.

McCrone, W. (1983). Reality therapy with deaf rehabilitation clients. *Journal of Rehabilitation of the Deaf, 17*(2), 13–15.

McCrone, W. (1985). Reality therapy applications with hearing-impaired clients. In G. Anderson & D. Watson (Eds.), *Counseling deaf people: Research and practice* (pp. 167–186). Little Rock, AR: University of Arkansas.

Meichenbaum, D. (1969). The effects of instruction and reinforcement on thinking and language behavior of schizophrenics. *Behavior Therapy, 7,* 101–114.

Meichenbaum, D. (1975). Self-instructional methods. In F. Kanfer & A. Goldstein (Eds.), *Helping people change* (pp. 357–391). New York: Pergamon Press.

Meichenbaum, D. (1977). *Cognitive-behavior modification: An integrative approach.* New York: Plenum Press.

Meichenbaum, D. (1985). *Stress inoculation training.* New York: Pergamon Press.

Meichenbaum, D., & Asarnow, J. (1979). Cognitive-behavioral modification and metacognitive development: Implications for the classroom. In P. Kendall & S. Hollon (Eds.), *Cognitive-behavioral interventions: Theory, research and procedures* (pp. 11–35). New York: Academic Press.

Meichenbaum, D., Butler, L., & Gruson, L. (1981). Toward a conceptual model of social competence. In J. Wine & M. Smye (Eds.), *Social competence* (pp. 36–60). New York: Guilford Press.

Meichenbaum, D., & Cameron, R. (1974). The clinical potential of modifying what clients say to themselves. *Psychotherapy: Theory, Research and Practice, 11*(2), 103–117.

Meichenbaum, D., & Genest, M. (1980). Cognitive-behavior modification: An integration of cognitive and behavioral methods. In F. Kanfer & A. Goldstein (Eds.), *Helping people change* (pp. 390–422). New York: Pergamon Press.

Meichenbaum, D., & Gilmore, J. (1982). Resistance: From a cognitive-behavioral perspective. In P. Wachtel (Ed.), *Resistance in psychodynamic and behavioral therapies* (pp. 135–155). New York: Plenum Press.

Meichenbaum, D., & Goodman, J. (1971). Training impulsive children to talk to themselves: A means of developing self-control. *Journal of Abnormal Psychology, 77,* 115–126.

Meichenbaum, D., & Jaremko, M. (Eds.) (1983). *Stress prevention and management: A cognitive-behavioral approach.* New York: Plenum Press.

Meichenbaum, D., & Turk, D. (1987). *Facilitating treatment adherence.* New York: Plenum Press.

Myers, P., & Danek, M. (1989). Deafness mental health needs assessment: A model. *Journal of Rehabilitation of the Deaf, 22*(4), 72–78.

Novaco, R. (1979). The cognitive regulation of anger and stress. In P. Kendall & S. Hollon (Eds.), *Cognitive-behavioral interventions: Theory, research and procedures.* New York: Academic Press.

O'Brien, D. (1987). Reflection-impulsivity in total communication and oral deaf and hearing children: A developmental study. *American Annals of the Deaf, 132*(3), 213–221.

Orlinsky, D., & Howard, K. (1986). Process and outcome in psychotherapy. In S. Garfield & A. Bergin (Eds.), *Handbook of psychotherapy and behavior change* (pp. 311–384). New York: John Wiley & Sons.

Owens, P. (1989). *Handbook for interpreters in the mental health setting.* Olathe, KS: Johnson County Community College.

Pellegrini, D., & Urbain, E. (1985). An evaluation of interpersonal cognitive problem solving training with children. *Journal of Child Psychology and Psychiatry, 26*(1), 17–41.

Quedenfeld, C., & Farrelly, F. (1983). Provocative therapy with the hearing-impaired client. *Journal of Rehabilitation of the Deaf, 17*(2), 1–12.

Rainer, J., & Altshuler, K. (1966). *Comprehensive mental health services for the deaf.* New York: Department of Medical Genetics, New York Psychiatric Institute, Columbia University.

Rainer, J., & Altshuler, K. (1971). A psychiatric program for the deaf: Experiences and implications. *American Journal of Psychiatry, 127,* 1527–1532.

Rainer, J., Altshuler, K., & Kallman, F. (1963). *Family and mental health problems in a deaf population.* New York: Department of Medical Genetics, New York Psychiatric Institute, Columbia University.

Rehm, L., & Rokke, P. (1988). Self-management therapies. In K. Dobson (Ed.), *Handbook of cognitive-behavioral therapies* (pp. 136–166). New York: Guilford Press.

Robinson, L. (1966). Group psychotherapy for deaf psychiatric patients. *Current Psychiatric Therapies, 6,* 172–176.

Robinson, L. (1978). *Sound minds in a soundless world.* Washington, DC: National Institute of Mental Health, U.S. Department of Health, Education & Welfare.

Robinson, L., Sachs, B., & Sloan, M. (1978). The mental health needs of deaf Americans. *Mental Health and Deafness, Experimental Issue 2,* 6–13.

Sanderson, R. (1974). A personal theory of counseling. *Journal of Rehabilitation of the Deaf, 7*(4), 22–28.

Santostefano, S. (1985). *Cognitive control therapy with children and adolescents.* New York: Pergamon Press.

Sarlin, B., & Altshuler, K. (1968). Group psychotherapy with deaf adolescents in a school setting. *International Journal of Group Psychotherapy, 18,* 337–344.

Schein, J. (1982). Group techniques applied to deaf and hearing-impaired persons. In M. Seligman (Ed.), *Group psychotherapy and counseling with special populations* (pp. 143–162). Baltimore: University Park Press.

Scott, W. (1978). Counseling with deaf persons: An overview of literature dealing with definitions, situations, and types of approaches used. *Journal of Rehabilitation of the Deaf, 11*(4), 16–32.

Seligman, M. (Ed.) (1982). *Group psychotherapy and counseling with special populations.* Baltimore: University Park Press.

Snyder, M., & Thomsen, C. (1988). Interactions between therapists and clients: Hypothesis testing and behavioral confirmation. In D. Turk & P. Salovey (Eds.), *Reasoning, inference, and judgment in clinical psychology.* New York: Free Press.

Spragins, A., Karchmer, M., & Schildroth, A. (1981). Profile of psychological service providers to hearing-impaired students. *American Annals of the Deaf, 126*(2), 94–105.

Stein, L., Mindel, E., & Jabaley, T. (Eds.) (1981). *Deafness and mental health.* New York: Grune & Stratton.

Stewart, L. (1981). Counseling the deaf client. In L. Stein, E. Mindel, & T. Jabaley (Eds.), *Deafness and mental health* (pp. 133–160). New York: Grune & Stratton.

Stewart, L., & Watson, D. (1987). The quality of life of severely disabled former VR clients with impaired hearing: A survey of long-term adjustment. *Journal of Rehabilitation of the Deaf, 20*(3), 1–10.

Straub, E. (1976). Interpreting for the deaf in a psychiatric setting. *Journal of Rehabilitation of the Deaf, 10*(2), 15–21.

Sussman, A. (1974). Group therapy with severely handicapped deaf clients. *Journal of Rehabilitation of the Deaf, 8,* 122–126.

Sussman, A. (1987). Approaches in counseling and psychotherapy revisited. In D. Watson, G. Long, M. Taff-Watson, & M. Harvey (Eds.), *Two decades of excellence: A foundation for the future* (pp. 2–15). Little Rock, AR: American Deafness and Rehabilitation Association.

Sussman, A. (1988). Approaches in counseling and psychotherapy revisited. In D. Watson, G. Long, M. Taff-Watson, & M. Harvey (Eds.), *Two decades of excellence: A foundation for the future* (pp. 2–15). Little Rock, AR: American Deafness and Rehabilitation Association Monograph 14.

Sussman, A. (1990). Let the buyer beware: Psychotherapy and the deaf consumer. *Gallaudet Today, 20*(3), 22–29.

Sussman, A., & Stewart, L. (1971). *Counseling with deaf people.* New York: New York University.

Swink, D. (1980). Psychodrama: An action therapy for deaf people. *Mental Health in Deafness, 4,* 14–19.

Taff-Watson, M. (1983). Sign language interpretation in the mental health setting. In D. Watson & B. Heller (Eds.), *Mental health and deafness: Strategic perspectives* (pp. 183–196). Silver Spring, MD: American Deafness and Rehabilitation Association.

Thoreson, R., & Tully, N. (1971). Role and function of the counselor. In A. Sussman & L. Stewart (Eds.), *Counseling with deaf people* (pp. 87–107). New York: New York University Deafness, Research & Training Center.

Turk, D., Meichenbaum, D., & Genest, M. (1983). *Pain and behavioral medicine.* New York: Guilford Press.

Wessler, R., & Wessler, S. (1989). Cognitive group therapy. In A. Freeman, K. Simon, L. Beutler, & H. Arkowitz (Eds.), *Comprehensive handbook of cognitive therapy* (pp. 559–582). New York: Plenum Press.

Williams, F. (1983). Interpreting in mental health situations: Basic issues. In D. Watson & B. Heller (Eds.), *Mental health and deafness: Strategic perspectives* (pp. 177–182). Silver Spring, MD: American Deafness and Rehabilitation Association.

Yalom, I. (1985). *The theory and practice of group psychotherapy* (3rd ed.). New York: Basic Books.

Zieziula, F. (1980). An alternative approach in service to deaf individuals: Community counseling. *Journal of Rehabilitation of the Deaf, 14*(1), 1–5.

▶ 9

Systemic Rehabilitation

MICHAEL A. HARVEY
Private Practice

Systemic rehabilitation of deaf persons is an approach to rehabilitation that can be used constructively with families as well as individual clients. Conceptualizing cases according to the principles of systems theory often allows the vocational counselor to intervene more precisely and effectively in promoting vocational development and related psychological growth. In this chapter, we will examine the application of systemic rehabilitation in working with deaf clients.

The following example of a *nonsystemic* referral for individual therapy may help the reader to better understand the process. Richard was described as a 20-year-old, profoundly deaf young man who was depressed, was abusing alcohol and drugs, and had a history of vocational failures. The referral from the RCD contained a concise description of the problem and, by implication, the solution. The problem was depression "in" Richard, which caused his substance abuse, which, in turn, caused his irresponsible behavior on the job. The solution, therefore, would be to help Richard better understand the nature and origins of his thoughts, feelings, and dysfunctional behavioral patterns and then to guide him to make changes. This solution seemed simple enough, at least in theory.

Systemic thinking, however, makes things more complex. It teaches us, for example, that what we observe around us can be understood in different ways, because events can be seen in different contexts, each one giving different meaning to an event (Campbell, Draper, & Huffington, 1989). There is no one truth. For example, if we expand the context of Richard's behavior a bit, we notice that Richard's proclaiming his depression and irresponsibility enables him to stay home during the day and protect his mother from being a victim to his brother's physical abuse. In this context, Richard is not only depressed but is also a self-proclaimed sacrificial object. Expanding the context further, we notice that Richard lacks a peer group of deaf young adults and does not feel accepted by his hearing peers, except at the bar where he buys everyone drinks. Here, his drinking and depression represent his attempts to affiliate with others. Or Richard's responses may represent ways to distance himself from an ongoing turf struggle which had evolved between the VR agency and mental health clinic about who knows more about his case and has the "truth." The more Richard senses this conflict, the more he is bothered by loyalty issues, the more he drinks and acts depressed, the more his brother abuses his mother, and the more one agency accuses the other of incompetence. There are many possibilities to explain Richard's behavior. There are many "truths."

To see Richard for individual therapy would necessarily mean to demarcate him as containing the problem. A primarily individual focus would also limit the therapist's access to the larger contexts in which Richard functions, and therefore would minimize direct access to influencing key figures in Richard's life who could spark change. In contrast, the systemic, or family, therapist constantly limits and expands contexts within a client's relevant system. Although this perspective is more complex, it is also often more effective.

The application of systems theory principles to the rehabilitation of deaf persons has been a recent endeavor. The New York Mental Health Project for the Deaf was the first program to delineate the prevalence of psychiatric disturbance among a deaf psychiatric patient population, and to recommend a variety of treatment modalities, including family therapy (Rainer, Altshuler, & Kallman, 1963). Since that time, there has been much research on deaf-member families with respect to how the family impacts the deaf member's personality development (see Mindel & Vernon, 1971, 1987; Schlesinger & Meadow, 1972; Bodner-Johnson, 1986; Freeman, Malkin, & Hastings, 1975; Hoffmeister, 1985; Levine, 1981). Moreover, there has been increasing attention to describing systemic intervention strategies to treat deaf-member families (see Scott & Dooley, 1985; Greenberg, 1983; Luterman, 1979; Moses, 1986; Mendelsohn & Rozak, 1983; Robinson & Weathers, 1974; Shapiro & Harris, 1976; Long & Harvey, 1990; Harvey, 1982, 1984a, 1984b, 1989; Harvey & Dym, 1987, 1988).

As the field of family therapy has become more sophisticated, there has been a shift from assuming a priori that the family is the appropriate unit of intervention to acknowledging that the "relevant system" is the appropriate unit (Harvey & Dym, 1987). Briefly, the members of a relevant system are those individuals who influence, and are influenced by, the behavior of an individual. It typically includes a client's family, and may also include friends, professionals, and extended family. The "relevant system" of a deaf client is unique from that of hearing, non-disabled clients in that it often includes more people and is often characterized by internal conflict, for example, sign versus no sign, or ASL versus English-based sign (Harvey & Dym, 1987, 1988).

As an example of a relevant system, consider the case when an RCD is providing services to a deaf individual when that individual is also receiving psychotherapy. From the vantage point of the RCD, his or her interventions influence, and are influenced by, the individual, family, and clinician. These members comprise the relevant system. The RCD's interventions will be noticed by these members, and thus will influence all of them in some way. As a result, the client, family, and clinician will, in turn, influence the RCD's interventions. Similarly, from the vantage point of the clinician, his or her interventions influence, and are influenced by the individual, family, and RCD. In both of these cases, the RCD and the clinician must take into account the context, the relevant system, that includes the other in order to effectively promote change. Simply put, they must work in close collaboration with each other.

What if this collaborative relationship does not happen? The RCD may form a strong alliance with only the deaf individual and not work closely with the family and clinician. Here, the RCD may unwittingly support the identified patient's position against the family and clinician. As a result, the RCD may increase the resistance of the family and clinician to following appropriate rehabilitation interventions. Similarly, if the clinician does not work closely with the RCD, the individual and family may likely receive conflicting and/or confusing advice. Or the individual and/or family may attempt to alternately criticize and disqualify both the RCD or clinician. Whatever the scenario, both rehabilitation and clinical efforts too often lose their effectiveness.

It will be shown that using a systems theory framework can help ensure that rehabilitation efforts will be effective and supported by those individuals who are, like the RCD, involved in the deaf client's life. The RCD may be the sole provider of services; the RCD and a systems clinician may form a consultation relationship about a deaf client; they may provide services independently; or they may meet with the relevant system members together. There are many possibilities.

This chapter will present guidelines showing how an RCD and family therapist can work together in a systemic manner and present a beginning framework to enable an RCD to act as the sole provider of systemic intervention. This chapter will first define family therapy, or systems intervention; delineate the initial tasks of an RCD-family therapist team, such as establishing rapport with each other and expanding the locus of confidentiality beyond the individual client; describe the process of formulating a systemic understanding of the client's needs and difficulties; describe the "nuts and bolts" of setting up communication logistics during a session; and finally, will present a case study, with verbatim therapy transcripts, of an RCD working with a family therapist.

INITIAL TASKS OF AN RCD-FAMILY THERAPIST TEAM

Joining

The process of therapeutic "joining," or establishing rapport, between client and therapist has been extensively described (see Rogers, 1951; Minuchin, 1974). However, the concept and importance of professionals joining other *professionals* in their client's relevant system has only recently been described. Consider the following example of a pre-session between the RCD and myself when we were formulating therapeutic and vocational goals for a subsequent meeting with a 22-year-old deaf woman, Joan, and her parents (Harvey, 1989). In this case, the RCD and I had already worked together in a number of different contexts and clearly respected and trusted each other.

Therapist: (to RCD) I want to know together the history of how this family has interfaced, for lack of a better word, with rehab counselors in the past. I suspect that there will be a battle about how much involvement Mother and Father will have with you because that's been the issue during most of Joan's life. So I think you will probably be in the same position. So I'll probably start by saying that we have Neil Glickman here, . . . and that one option is for Neil and Joan to work together; and that I want to explore what each of you [Joan, Mother, and Father] would like to do with Neil; how all of you would like to be involved. And then you can explain how you think you can be helpful. Then Mom and Dad can ask questions of you. Then we can work towards separating our roles. How about that?

RCD: I've only had one session with Joan and her Mother. I had the feeling that Joan was dragged to my office and did not want to be involved. And we haven't really had the time yet to set up a plan, much less establish rapport. I think we will establish one relatively quickly though . . .

I got a sense from the Mother that they're not going to help Joan. She can go to school, great, but they're not going to give her transportation. They're not going to give her any money.

Therapist: So if that's the stance, we can play with that . . . what "help" Joan needs from parents via the rehab plan and then we'll explore conflicts.

RCD: That sounds fine. I'm not sure about Joan's motivation for school, for a job, for a license, for independence; I'm not sure of that. I could be effective in helping her do those things but she needs to want that.

Here, the RCD and I agreed on mutual goals and on a rough idea of how to achieve them: namely, to meet with Joan and her family together as well as providing services separately.

Expanding the Locus of Confidentiality

It is important to expand the boundaries, or field of confidentiality, to include the RCD, family, deaf member, therapist, and anyone else who is involved in maintaining the problem (and by implication, solving the problem). Continuing with the above example, the importance of the pre-sessions between the RCD and me, and our shared view of the problem and solution, became important in that we agreed that rigid boundaries around the RCD introduced a third option for parental involvement other than total involvement in the rehabilitation process (enmeshment) or no involvement (disengagement): namely, the option of "balancing confidentiality" between these two extremes. Let us continue with the transcript of the family meeting.

Therapist: [To RCD, with interpreter interpreting voice to sign] Well, to summarize for the family some discussions that you and I have had over some lunches about how many therapists and rehab counselors only work with the individual and ignore, if you will, the family . . . and how that doesn't make sense. But we need to have a *clear* sense of what you expect from the family and what the family expects from you.

RCD: [To parents, with interpreter interpreting voice to sign] I hear you both saying that you want to help Joan, and at the same time you want to have a sense of what's going on, especially in terms of making decisions. That makes sense. That has to be balanced with confidentiality. The fact is that, in almost all sessions between rehab counselor and client in the office—i.e., between me and Joan—I am not allowed to discuss what goes on in the session without Joan's permission. What I try to do, and in practice almost always works out, is to get her permission to discuss certain parts of our session with another person, such as parents. This is especially important when we're at the point of deciding on license, school, job, and how we're going to go about that. Especially when there are money issues involved, as there sometimes are. If Joan chooses not to give me permission to talk to you, I'm stuck.

Mother: I would say you are! Because at that point, I mean, every appointment she's ever going to have involves our lives. The two of us have to take off work, I mean, that's a direct involvement in our lives. So what is she going to come to me to say, 'You have to take me to your office but I'm not going to tell you what for!'?

Father: Well, we can't leap to that conclusion, Mother.

Mother: Well, starting off with the doctor appointments, we're going to have to transport her; and *that's* an involvement. (Appears angry at father).

RCD: That's right.

Therapist: Can I ask you [RCD] to talk to Joan about what she would like from you; and, in part, how she would like to establish boundaries between you two and her parents?

RCD:	[to Joan, with interpreter interpreting sign to voice] We just met about two weeks ago, and we hadn't really talked in depth about what we planned to do. I'm wondering how you feel I can help you.
Joan:	Well, I need a job so I can be able to support myself. I need to have money so I can...
RCD:	What I was also wondering is how can we get your parents involved? How do you want them to be involved?
Joan:	I have no idea.
RCD:	There is a rule about confidentiality, so I need to have your permission to talk with them. Do you want your parents involved? Do you not want your parents involved, or what?
Joan:	I don't know; it depends.
RCD:	Yeah, I agree. It sounds like we need to develop a plan that involves school, work, and getting a driver's license. These are all important decisions. Your parents need to know some of what's going on with that, if you're going to ask them maybe for some help. Do you think it's possible that maybe we could ask them to join us for a meeting and share your plans with them?
Joan:	Sometimes. Not all the time.
RCD:	Oh, I agree, not all the time. We're not talking about all the time. Most of our meetings will be one-to-one and confidential. But if you have specific plans for school, or job, or your license . . . you think it's important for your parents to be involved?
Joan:	All right. That's fine.

Thus, Joan agreed with the RCD's suggestion to "balance confidentiality" between the extremes of enmeshment and disengagement between the RCD and her parents. The question naturally comes up of what would have happened had Joan *not* agreed with his suggestion? However, it is more fruitful to ask *how did it happen that Joan did agree to the RCD's suggestion*? Joan's affirmative response was not random good luck; it was a function of the RCD and therapist having already joined with each other and with Joan during previous individual and family sessions.

FORMULATING A SYSTEMIC DIAGNOSIS OF THE PROBLEM AND GOALS

Spatial Dimension of the Relevant System: The Biopsychosocial Hierarchy

When a helping professional, such as an RCD, attempts to understand and assist a client, the problem is always too much data. Systemic thinking at first seems only to add to the overwhelming complexity of human behavior without offering a readable map to navigate change. The helper is often at first both humbled and immobilized by acknowledging the complex series of biological, psychological, and interpersonal interactions in which individual symptomatic behavior is embedded.

The biopsychosocial hierarchy is a useful map, or heuristic model, which the RCD and therapist can use to make sense out of this complexity. It serves as the framework for the RCD and clinician to make systemic diagnoses on which they can base their interventions. There are many levels of organization in human experience, from subatomic particle and living cell, to complex organs and organ systems, to whole persons, to families, communities, cultures and larger societies (Engel, 1955; Bronfenbrenner, 1979). These differing systems levels appear to be arranged hierarchically, with each level more complex than the one before and encompassing all those that come before it. Bronfenbrenner (1979) has depicted this hierarchy as "a set of *nested structures*, like a set of Russian dolls" which are inextricably linked with one another. The following is a brief discussion of those systemic levels, or nested structures, which are most relevant to the study of deaf people.

(1) Biological
Obviously, biological factors are important. Here we include the etiology of the hearing loss, the age of onset, the degree of hearing loss, the rate of loss, prognosis for continued hearing loss or gain, the configuration of the audiogram across the speech range, and the amount of residual hearing. Also important is the classification of the hearing loss (sensorineural or conductive) and the degree of hearing loss (see Chapter 1).

There may be related medical conditions in addition to hearing loss, depending on etiologic factors. For example, maternal rubella contracted during the first trimester of pregnancy is often associated with hearing loss, heart defects, cataracts, chorioretinitis, cerebral palsy, mental retardation, autism, delayed growth, diabetes mellitus, thyroid problems, and panencephalitis (Shaver, 1987).

(2) Psychological
The particular characteristics of an individual have a great influence on how he or she adapts to deafness and on how the deafness is viewed by his or her family, school, and greater society. While such children and adolescents may well pass through some common and identifiable stages of development, each will do so in a unique way which is determined by his or her personality (Palmer, 1970). This idea of personality can be further refined by discussing cognitive, behavioral, and emotional elements. For example, an individual with a hearing loss who is taught that being deaf or hard-of-hearing is severely limiting will develop differently than a child who does not.

(3) Family
The family is the main environment for the developing child, particularly the young child. Its behavioral patterns, concepts about hearing loss, emotional responses to the loss, interactions with the child, etc., all exert powerful influences on development. Furthermore, family development is powerfully influenced by the child and by the

demands of raising a deaf child. In this sense, the child influences everything, from the use of time and space to financial arrangements, travel patterns, patterns of communication among all family members, to the family's image of itself—as well or not well, competent or incompetent, nurturing or not nurturing. The deaf child or adolescent influences, and is influenced by, hearing siblings, grandparents, and extended family members.

(4) Professional
As with virtually all disabled or chronically ill people, many deaf clients have extensive and often intense relationships with numbers of professional systems, including school, medical, audiological, and other service agencies (Harvey & Dym, 1987, 1988). In this regard, it is important to note that *for each ramification of hearing loss, there is often a corresponding professional.* Professional systems can be more or less relevant at different stages of the client's life. For example, physicians tend to be important early on, with school systems later becoming the most influential.

The interpersonal patterns which emerge between parents and professionals may become so powerful that the boundary between these two systems virtually disappears. Therapeutic efforts to help the deaf individual and his or her family are frequently impossible unless the ways that professional systems reinforce family patterns, and vice versa, are also addressed. The "oral-manual debate" among professionals, that is, whether deaf students should exclusively use speech and speechreading or a signed language to communicate, is a well known example of how the professional level influences families and the child. For example, Moores (1982) stated that ". . . the centuries-old 'oral-manual controversy' has accounted for more confusion than any other question in the field, and it is not surprising that professionals on the periphery are not clear about the issues" (p. 8).

(5) Informal Networks
Informal networks made up of friends and acquaintances of both the child and parents can exert strong influences on family development and thereby on the development of the individual. The simple amount of support parents receive may determine how well they cope with the extra demands a deaf child may place on them. But networks may play more complex functions in much the same way that professionals do, i.e., supporting or opposing one kind of educational or rehabilitation programming over another, or supporting one parent over another. Networks, like professionals, reinforce functional and dysfunctional family patterns. Informal networks play an increasingly major role in the development of such individuals, particularly during adolescence.

(6) Cultural/Political
The way that a particular culture or subculture views being deaf and, through its political process, the way that a culture provides for such persons exert a major influence on the development of each child (Sussman, 1976; Higgins, 1980; Lane,

1987). With reference to deafness, Moores (1982) reported that "most of [deaf peoples'] problems are caused by the dominant society. Deaf people have survived and endured in the face of an indifferent world that must be dealt with daily" (p. 141). In contrast, the deaf community is a minority group with its own hierarchical social structure, culture, and language (Padden, 1980; Baker & Cokely, 1980; Woodward, 1982). It provides a vital supportive network for diverse human needs, such as the exchange of information, social/emotional support, and political action.

All of these systems levels comprise the context in which symptomatic behavior may be embedded. It is not enough to say that "it is a family problem" or "it is an individual problem;" for, as was described earlier, a "whole" is simultaneously a "part". Consequently, it is necessary to thoroughly understand the interactional patterns within and between each systems level in order to provide effective rehabilitation. As Bateson (1971) put it, "If you want to understand some phenomenon or appearance, you must consider that phenomenon within the context of all *completed* circuits which are relevant to it" (p. 244).

As an example, let us recall the earlier example of Richard who was depressed, abusing alcohol and drugs, and who had a history of vocational failures. His depression and irresponsibility enabled him to stay home during the day and protect his mother from his brother's abuse. He lacked meaningful affiliations with deaf and hearing peers, except at the bar. His depression also helped him distance himself from an ongoing turf struggle between the VR and mental health agencies. In this example, the following *spatial* levels of the biopsychosocial hierarchy were most directly involved in maintaining Richard's problem: *psychological* (depression, alcohol abuse), *family* (protecting his mother from brother), *informal network* (peers rejecting him except at bars), and *professional* (turf struggles between VR and mental health). In addition, we can certainly surmise influences from the biological and cultural levels in understanding Richard's difficulties.

Temporal Dimension of the Relevant System: The Recurrent Cycle

The preceding section described the spatial dimension of relevant levels, as depicted by the biopsychosocial field. In the case of Richard, described above, any change in one of several spatial levels of the biopsychosocial field serves as a catalyst to change another level. Perhaps Richard becomes depressed. His mother is the first to notice and attempts to support him. His brother becomes jealous, picks a fight with their mother, who, in turn, becomes overwhelmed and withdraws. Richard feels abandoned and goes outside in a vain search to hang out with peers. Finding nobody willing to talk with him, he goes off to the neighborhood bar. The next morning, he wakes up with a hangover and misses work. The RCD receives a call from his boss and schedules a meeting with Richard. During that meeting, the RCD gives him one more chance. Richard's mental health counselor, however, views the RCD as a "codependent enabler." The mental health counselor subtly communicates this sentiment to Richard, who, in turn, is caught between the advice of his RCD and mental health counselor. He sulks at home, becomes more depressed. His mother is the first to notice and attempts to support him. His brother becomes jealous, picks a fight with their mother who . . . and so on. The cycle repeats itself over and over again, that is, it is *recurrent*.

The concept of a *recurrent cycle* helps us to *track* the relationships occurring among the multiple levels of a biopsychosocial field. This happens, then that happens, then that happens, and so on. Recurrent cycles not only encompass space—that is, include persons within different biopsychosocial levels—but also encompass *time*. Changes in systems levels contained in a given recurrent cycle may be separated by only moments, or by hours, days, weeks, months, or even years. To return to the recurrent cycle which contains Richard's difficulties, we notice that mother notices his depression after only a few moments of his sulking. We also notice that Richard is typically able to tolerate loneliness for one solid month before getting drunk. We note that the mental health counselor becomes irritated with vocational rehabilitation's "attitude" only around the end of each fiscal year when the pressure to terminate clients is high.

A recurrent cycle is a sequence of events which gives the appearance of being repetitive and stable. We noticed that Richard *typically* drinks to avoid experiencing loneliness; his boss, sooner or later, *typically* becomes intolerant of Richard's tardiness, and so on. It becomes apparent, however, that the steps of a recurrent cycle actually can and do change. For example, although Richard's boss typically tolerates his tardiness for one month, Richard may show up late at work on a particularly "bad day" and then immediately get fired.

Within a systems theory framework, we must first delineate the recurrent cycle which contains the problem: namely, who is involved and what changes happen between which biopsychosocial levels over what period of time. Then, however, *we must notice when and how the recurrent cycle changes*. Certain systems levels contained in the recurrent cycle may be more unstable than others at any particular time, and therefore more likely to respond to rehabilitative or therapeutic interventions. An intervention, no matter how well formulated and implemented, may need to be implemented at a *particular time*; perhaps simultaneously with a shift in one or more spatial levels of the system, such as at the time when the client or another family member experiences a crisis, or when a member who serves to stabilize the system is absent (Dym, 1987). This framework clarifies some reasons why a brilliantly formulated and implemented intervention may sometimes prove successful and other times fall "flat on its face." *Whether or not a rehabilitative or therapeutic intervention is effective is a function of the interrelationships of systems levels at any given time.*

Essentially, the process of formulating a systemic diagnosis and a systemic rehabilitation intervention strategy largely involves a three-step process. First, an RCD and clinician need to figure out which level(s) of the biopsychosocial field are most relevant to a client's vocational and life difficulties; whether a client's difficulty results from predominantly a biological imbalance; intrapsychic cognitive or emotional factors; family dysfunction; peer or social factors; inappropriate assistance by professionals; and/or cultural influences. Secondly, the RCD and clinician must examine each of these "causes" of the problem and decide which one(s) need changing the most and, at the same time, predict which ones would likely be responsive to therapeutic intervention. For example, eliminating cultural discrimination against disabled people would certainly increase a disabled client's self-esteem, but a therapist cannot expect to change the world easily. Finally, the RCD and clinician must choose a particular intervention technique(s) and aim it toward the appropriate target.

For the reader versed in systems theory, the preceding "pragmatics of intervention" can be stated in its most technical form. Effective intervention requires the RCD and clinician to:

1. formulate a systemic diagnosis of the problem(s) which delineates the spatial and temporal dimensions of the recurrent cycle in which the problem(s) is embedded;
2. assess which spatial level(s) is most unstable and thus most amenable to change, relative to its temporal contiguity with other natural or clinically induced changes in other levels;
3. intervene accordingly with a particular treatment modality. (Harvey, 1989, p. 76)

In order to clarify these rather abstract concepts, a clinical vignette will be described which, for professionals who work with deaf clients, should have a familiar ring to it. The vignette describes the combined efforts of an RCD and myself, as family therapist, to provide brief, strategic intervention to assist a deaf 20-year-old young adult male, named "Frank." This is a Hispanic family consisting of Carl (51), Clara (48), and five siblings, ranging from 26 to 4 years old. All members of the family except Frank had normal hearing and spoke both English and Spanish at home. Frank communicated proficiently via American Sign Language and had minimal oral/aural skills with both English or Spanish; his family did not know sign language.

It should be noted that four years prior to this referral, I had accepted a request from Carl to provide, in his words, "father-son" therapy due to Frank's then argumentative behavior at home. During the initial session, I observed a common pattern of parent-adolescent conflicts over rules, and had scheduled subsequent meetings with the entire family. However, prior to the second meeting two weeks later, Carl suffered a heart attack, was hospitalized, and canceled subsequent meetings.

I had not heard from this family until an RCD initiated the referral to me, in response to a telephone call from Carl. According to Carl and the RCD, Frank was threatening both Carl and Carla with physical violence, was unemployed, and had failed to show up for several vocational rehabilitation appointments. Moreover, he had recently dropped out of college, after only six months, stating that "it was boring."

Upon re-examining the background and interviewing the referral sources, the following six-step recurrent cycle became clear. As with any recurrent cycle, we can begin at an arbitrary point. Frank becomes argumentative with his parents. Father disciplines Frank, while mother withdraws. Frank then threatens violence. Father, in turn, develops hypertension and cardiac symptoms and also withdraws. Father or mother opposes Frank, and suggests individual psychotherapy or more frequent meetings with the RCD. Frank instead becomes argumentative, and the cycle continues.

At this time, however, the family level contained in the recurrent cycle was clearly in flux, in that the father was not about to withdraw via sickness and both parents were amenable to meeting as a family as opposed to requesting that Frank be seen individually. Given that the recurrent cycle was destabilized a bit and therefore more likely to respond to rehabilitative or therapeutic interventions, it seemed vital to take advantage of this "window of opportunity" by introducing change: namely, by initiating a family meeting.

After a few meetings, detailed individual clinical assessment of Frank indicated that he was not likely to actually exhibit violence toward his parents. His rebellion was more via threats or passive aggressive behaviors, the latter exemplified by his opting not to attend subsequent family treatment meetings. At this juncture, I continued to prod both parents to "make it easier for Frank to grow up than not to grow up" by proposing the following plan:

1. Carl would visit the town courthouse and obtain information about restraining orders.
2. Carl and Clara would privately, "behind closed doors," make a specific list of rules for the house.
3. Carl and/or Clara, at their discretion, would attend the next therapy meeting with me and bring the list of rules. However, they would emphasize to Frank that *under no conditions* is he allowed to attend these two meetings. During that meeting, we would review the rules and discuss the mechanics of implementing the restraining order should he break any rules. We would also rehearse for the next meeting which would include Carl or Clara, Frank, the RCD, an interpreter, and myself.

The purpose of this plan was *not* necessarily to push Frank out of the house, a value that belongs to many white, middle class families and not necessarily to this Hispanic family (McGoldrick, Pearce, & Giordano, 1982). Rather, its purpose was to make it easier for Frank to grow up with the help of VR services than not to grow up; to re-establish the family hierarchy and more functional boundaries around the parents.

Carl and Clara agreed that Carl would attend the "planning meetings" with me. He had obtained information concerning a restraining order, and he and Clara had decided on a list of rules. We were ready for the final family meeting!

The participants of this meeting were Carl; the RCD; Frank; an interpreter; myself; and Frank's 24-year-old brother, Denis, whom the father had invited. During this session, Carl put on an impressive display of his authority by clearly delineating the new family rules and the consequences for breaking them. He also eloquently described Frank as too involved in being a bully around the house that he hadn't had time to grow up and get a job. Interestingly, at this point, Denis stepped in and attempted to redefine the problem simply as Frank not being afforded the opportunity by vocational rehabilitation of working. As is illustrated by the following transcript from this session, the RCD countered his frame quite effectively and in a way that I could not have done, as I did not have the necessary information. The frame that was finally agreed on was that Frank has not been "ready" to grow up.

Denis: I'd like to say something. Why can't you [RCD] get Frank started in his career, to get a job or go back to school, and we'd resolve the whole problem. That's the main problem right there . . . [to father] You don't have to talk about the rules, how to restrict him . . . [to RCD] The thing I'm saying is, just get Frank on a career, a job, school, keep his mind busy; and he'll start with his life, that's all.

Therapist: [to RCD] Would you respond?

RCD: Sure. I would say that after almost two years . . . the door has been open to Frank. Frank is very intelligent and has everything he needs to start a career or go to college or do almost anything he wants. But for some reason, Frank has been stuck for a long time.

The door to my office is open. The world is ready! But he is stuck. And I was concerned that Frank was depressed. A lot of times when people are stuck and sleep a lot, it's because something else is bothering them. And I felt like the something else that was bothering him has been bothering him for a long time. And for anybody to work with us, to start with their career, they have to follow a lot of rules. A person has to show up for their appointments all the time. I can't go chasing people. People have to chase me, because I see 80 people at a time. And if somebody follows rules and is responsible, and chases me a little, I'll go to bat for them. But see, Frank has been stuck; and I was concerned about that because I hate to see somebody wasting their potential.

So I think I would disagree with you [to Denis]. I would disagree with you that all Frank needs is a career. If that were true, it would have happened already. He would still be in college, or he would be in on-the-job training at an auto body shop, or doing any of the things that he could do with all of his talent . . . I would like to hear Frank's opinion.

Denis: So it's a matter of . . . it's really up to Frank.

RCD: It's really up to Frank; no one can push a person. A person has to be ready and I haven't felt that Frank is ready.

Denis: When is Frank ready?

RCD: That's for Frank to answer.

At this time, I asked Denis to find out from Frank the reasons for his missed appointments in order to assess how this dyad functioned. In retrospect, I might have instead asked Carl, for it would have been consonant with my goal of empowering him to parent his children.

Therapist: [to Denis] Would you find out from Frank? Help out?
Denis: [to Frank with interpreter interpreting voice to sign] What's wrong? Why don't you do something?
Frank: [to Denis with interpreter interpreting sign to voice] How am I going to get there, to her office? I can't get there.
Denis: There's trains. I traveled on trains to Boston.
Frank: That takes money. If I had work, I'd have money and I could go there. I got no money.

The RCD again stepped in and challenged Frank by reminding him that there was a VR office only a couple of miles from his home.

RCD: I have an answer to that problem, it's up to you; you have a choice. There is an RCD right near here, which would be much easier for you to get to. The office is in [town X].
Frank: Where? I didn't know that. I didn't know there was an RCD right in [town X]!
RCD: And there's a counselor . . .She would be willing to meet you in her office, and help you look for a job. It's up to you, you have a choice. So then the car would not be a problem.
Frank: I didn't know that. For two years I didn't know that.
RCD: I have to tell you; before I told you about the RCD in [town X] office . . .
Frank: I thought your office was the only office.
RCD: I don't remember it the same way . . . but that's okay. So you have a choice now, it's up to you.

Within two months from this session, Frank had met with the new counselor once and had obtained steady employment and had not broken any rules which would have necessitated his leaving home. However, he was saving his money to get an apartment of his own. He was still employed as of a year follow-up.

THE "NUTS AND BOLTS" OF SETTING UP COMMUNICATION LOGISTICS DURING A SESSION

Up to now, we have discussed and illustrated how an RCD-clinician team, or RCD, makes a systemic assessment of vocational problems that deaf clients present. However, we have not examined the actual "nuts and bolts" mechanics of how an RCD, clinician, or family members are to communicate verbally during a meeting(s), that is, whether to use vocal or manual communication. For an individual who has a profound, bilateral hearing loss of prelingual origin, it is likely that manual communication would be his or her primary means of verbal communication, of fully understanding discourse in the environment, particularly intrafamilial discourse (Mindel & Vernon, 1987; Schlesinger & Meadow, 1972). However, many hearing members of such families do not achieve a high degree of proficiency with manual communication (Rawlings, 1971; Mindel & Vernon, 1987). Therein lies "the communication problem." Consequently, an RCD and/or therapist is immediately faced with the task of establishing the verbal communication logistics of the treatment session.

Table 9–1, Logistics of Verbal Communication between RCD/Therapist and Client, lists six options for the RCD's or therapist's mode of communication with each family member.

As can be seen from Table 9–1, the first three options are implemented in conjunction with an interpreter: The therapist or RCD communicates either orally, via a visually coded English system without voice, or via American Sign Language (ASL) (naturally, without voice). Here, the interpreter voices for the benefit of the hearing

TABLE 9–1   **Logistics of Verbal Communication between Therapist/RCD and Client**

Persons with Whom the Therapist/RCD Communicates Directly	Therapist's/RCD's Mode of Communication	Interpreter's Mode of Interpreting for the Therapist/RCD
Option 1. Hearing family members	Oral (without sign language)	Voice to manual communication
Option 2. Deaf and hearing family members	Manually Coded English without voice	Manual to voice communication
Option 3. Deaf and hearing family members	ASL (without voice)	Manual to voice communication
Option 4. Hearing family members	Oral	No interpretation
Option 5. Deaf and hearing family members	Manually Coded English with voice ("sim-comm")	No interpretation
Option 6. Deaf family member	Manual communication without voice	No interpretation

members when the therapist or RCD signs without voice, and signs for the benefit of the deaf member when the therapist or RCD is voicing English without signing. The latter three communication options are implemented without interpretation: The therapist or RCD communicates orally, via a visually coded English system simultaneously with voice, or via ASL. Naturally, the mode of communication that the therapist or RCD chooses will, in part, depend on his or her proficiency. For example, a hearing or deaf RCD who is not skilled in ASL would not opt to use Option 3, ASL (without voice). Similarly, a deaf RCD who is not proficient with oral communication would not choose Option 1 and 4 which involve oral discourse.

It will be shown that for every logistic decision that the therapist or RCD makes about communication, there are, on the one hand, advantages, yet on the other hand, compromises. Thus, the therapist or RCD can continually vary the use of options during a given session and between sessions, in accordance with the particular goal. One is not restricted to following one option, but should vary them flexibly as the need arises.

Option 1: Therapist or RCD Communicating Orally with Voice to Sign Interpretation

The oral method is the natural way of communicating for hearing persons, including hearing parents and hearing siblings. The hearing therapist, or RCD, or oral deaf therapist, or RCD using this first option, voices to hearing family members, while an interpreter signs in whatever form of manual communication is preferred by the deaf person: transliteration (spoken English to manually coded English system), American Sign Language, fingerspelling, or some other means. Although the RCD communicates in the presence of both hearing and deaf members, the communication is *direct* for all hearing persons while it is *indirect* (mediated through an interpreter) for the deaf member. Although this places the deaf member at a greater disadvantage than if the RCD communicated directly to him or her via manual communication (such as with Option 2), the deaf person is significantly more able to understand what is transpiring in the session than if there were no interpreter present to interpret oral dialogue.

The decision of the therapist or RCD to use this first option of oral communication is based on his or her ability to communicate orally, and predicated on the fact that he or she primarily wishes to *join with a hearing family member at a given time* by using a direct mode of communication via a common language, spoken English. In regard to the latter consideration, if an RCD uses a signed language without voice (Options 3 and 6) while communicating with hearing family members, in some cases, it precipitates some discomfort on their part. Their discomfort may be due to their resistance to accepting sign language or awkwardness about having the interpreter voice for the RCD. In any case, the parents' discomfort would be countertherapeutic until joining has properly occurred.

Options 2 and 3: Therapist or RCD Communicating via Manually Coded English or via American Sign Language—with Sign to Voice Interpretation

In these options, the therapist or RCD uses a Manually Coded English system, such as Signing Exact English, without the use of voice (Option 2), or American Sign Language without the use of voice (Option 3). The interpreter interprets sign to voice for the benefit of the hearing family members. These options represent the reverse linguistic situation of the previous option of oral communication; here, the therapist or RCD communication is *direct* for the deaf person via sign language and *indirect* (mediated through an interpreter) for the hearing persons. Thus, communication is accessible to the deaf member even when the RCD is communicating with the hearing family members. There is no information "lost" through interpretation.

It is important that the therapist or RCD utilizes the mode of manual communication which is the deaf member's primary mode. In order to join the deaf member, it is appropriate to use Option 2 if he or she uses Pidgin Sign English or Manually Coded English, as opposed to American Sign Language. However, if ASL is the deaf member's primary and preferred language, this method will prove to be linguistically inaccessible to him or her. In that case, the RCD should use Option 3 in order to increase linguistic accessibility to the deaf member.

Since there is maximal visual contact between the therapist or RCD and the deaf member, the deaf member becomes privy to all of the subtle verbal and nonverbal nuances of the RCD even when he or she is communicating with other family members. This option greatly increases the probability that the RCD or therapist can join the deaf member, because it conveys an attitude of respect for linguistic accessibility and provides a common language base. The message is, "I am altering my usual mode of communicating with hearing members out of respect for you [deaf member]."

Although this option is used primarily to converse with and join the deaf family member, it also may be used as a therapeutic intervention for conversing directly to hearing members, when proper joining has occurred and when it is therapeutically helpful to risk introducing some discomfort. Communicating to hearing parents in sign language, with sign to voice interpretation, models for them that communication need not be vocal in order to be verbal; that signed language is a sophisticated language. Once the initial awkwardness subsides, this intervention is effective in conveying a sense of "awe" that their deaf son/daughter, who may be nonvocal, is nevertheless quite linguistically competent in manual communication. *Verbal* communication is not limited to *vocal* communication.

Option 4: Therapist or RCD Communicating Orally without Interpretation

In this option, the therapist or RCD communicates orally without interpretation to the hearing and deaf members of the family. Assuming that sign language is the deaf member's primary and preferred mode of communication, it is immediately apparent that, from the perspective of maximizing conversational accessibility, this option is at best inappropriate and at worst unethical. However, I have found this option occasionally necessary particularly for the hearing RCD or therapist. As will be explained below, a deaf or hard-of-hearing RCD or therapist often need not resort to this option.

Although this option is linguistically *inappropriate* for the deaf family member, *it may be temporarily necessary to ensure that the family will return for treatment after the first session.* The RCD who suggests the use of sign language or a sign language interpreter to a family who ardently denies linguistic and other implications of deafness, is immediately confronting a rigid family rule prohibiting or disparaging the use of manual communication. In this case, premature advocacy by the RCD or therapist on behalf of the deaf member, no matter how well founded and "politically correct," may precipitate premature termination by the family.

If the RCD or therapist must use this option for the above stated reasons, it is vital to keep in mind privately that the deaf member is probably conversationally lost and may be pretending to understand much of the conversation. In addition, it is important to understand one's countertransference reactions, for example, of guilt for oppressing a deaf person in a manner similar to the stories which have been recounted by our deaf teachers and role models. However, if the RCD or therapist is empathic of the deaf family member's plight, then that empathy will be nonverbally communicated. In this case, the deaf client is often implicitly aware and approving of the RCD's intent and strategy, provided that initial joining has occurred between RCD and deaf client. Moreover, it is sometimes possible for the deaf member and RCD/therapist to meet privately and to agree on the treatment plan and strategy.

It is vital for the therapist or RCD to carefully time when and how he or she points out the deaf family member's lack of comprehension of the content of the discussion. The RCD must first join the family members who "hold the power" to influence other family members to communicate using a given methodology. Assuming that the RCD has established rapport with the "protagonist of the family" and has earned the family's respect as an expert, he or she can engage the family in figuring out ways of communicating more effectively. The RCD or therapist's first pointing out inadequate verbal communication with families at the proper time, and then "working through their feelings about it," often precipitates their expressing pent-up anger at professionals who in the past "steered us wrong . . . told us not to sign."

After appropriate linguistic communication in the session has begun, it is therapeutically *vital* for the RCD or therapist to acknowledge the deaf client's plight explicitly by eliciting and clearly explaining the reasons for not having signed and for the family (and deaf client) having participated in a game of "make believe everyone understands each other." *This, of course, is the essential therapeutic work.* This work serves as an effective catalyst towards helping the family to examine their conflicting thoughts, feelings, and behaviors about having a deaf family member.

The preceding discussion has concerned a hearing therapist or RCD who presumably would be able to understand either vocal or signed communication conversationally. This, however, is frequently not the case for a deaf or hard-of-hearing therapist or RCD whose primary receptive or expressive mode of communication is a signed language. The deaf or hard-of-hearing RCD, however, can use his or her communicative needs to decrease the resistance and defensiveness of families, and in ways that a hearing therapist/RCD cannot. Instead of the hearing therapist's blatantly asserting that the family needs manual interpretation in order to communicate effectively and, by implication, that the family has been negligent, the deaf/hard-of-hearing RCD can simply include an interpreter or insist on signing so "I will be able to understand what you are saying." In this manner, joining with the deaf member is greatly facilitated without jeopardizing the relationship with the hearing family members.

Option 5: Therapist or RCD Communicating via Simultaneous Communication without Interpretation

In this option, the therapist/RCD voices for the benefit of the hearing members, and simultaneously signs in a Pidgin or Manually Coded English system for the deaf member. Thus, no assistance from an interpreter is required, whether the RCD is directly communicating with the deaf family member or with the other hearing members; in both cases, the RCD uses simultaneous communication, often abbreviated as "sim-comm." In contrast to Option 2, when the RCD's or therapist's communication is via Manually Coded English without voice with sign to voice interpretation, this option is initially a bit less awkward for hearing family members. The RCD simultaneously communicates to all family members and has adequate control of both signed and vocal factors. For example, when the RCD communicates with parents using "sim-comm," the parents will hear the RCD's voice, not that of an interpreter as in Option 2. Furthermore, assuming that Manually Coded English is linguistically accessible to the deaf member, another advantage of this option is that the RCD can more easily convey a message to the deaf member while talking to a hearing member.

One possible disadvantage of this option has to do with clarity of communication. First, Manually Coded English is often not the deaf member's primary mode of communication. American Sign Language may prove to be more accessible. Secondly, not only is it is clearer to sign without voicing, but both modes of communication suffer when speakers attempt to use simultaneous communication (Strong & Stone-Charlson, 1987; Marmor & Petitto, 1979). In addition, Nash and Nash (1981), Woodward (1982) and many deaf people suggest that it is a cultural norm to sign without the use of voice.

A final disadvantage of this option is that it has less impact than the RCD's signing without voice. It is often helpful to demonstrate *dramatically and with impact* the sophistication of sign language, and this can best be accomplished by signing without voicing. However, as emphasized earlier, the effectiveness of this "demonstration" with a particular family member assumes that the RCD has properly joined that person. As with all of the communication options, it becomes apparent that timing considerations should dictate whether to use this option.

Option 6: Therapist or RCD Communicating via Manual Communication without Voice and without Interpretation

In this option, the therapist or RCD communicates directly with the deaf family member by using the client's primary and preferred mode of communication, such as Manually Coded English, ASL, or various pidgin modes. There is no sign to voice interpretation for the benefit of the hearing family members. This option represents the reverse situation of Option 4, which uses oral communication without voice to sign interpretation so the deaf member is conversationally isolated. Here the hearing members are conversationally isolated. As with Option 4, this option, if not used judiciously, may needlessly exclude session participants and may be at best inappropriate and at worst unethical.

However, this option has potential benefits. The impact of this option on the deaf member varies. It is likely to promote effective joining, as this option solely takes the deaf member into account, even excluding other members; it is like a "private club." One deaf child, eager to pursue a private conversation with me, exclaimed, "it is like hidden gossiping but in front of my father!" In contrast, some deaf members, in an act of loyalty (or manners) to their parents, resist this intervention, and do not wish to participate in "whispering in front of other people."

Reactions of hearing family members to the RCD using this option also vary greatly. *If, and only if,* this intervention is timed carefully in accordance with a mutual respectful relationship between RCD and hearing members, the latter will not be offended but will often report amazement and newfound respect. However, if this intervention is not done carefully, it may needlessly insult and exclude other family members. Implemented carefully, this communication option is very effective for dramatically illustrating for hearing parents that which linguists have known for over two decades, namely, that American Sign Language is a bona fide language.

It should be apparent that whatever communication mode the RCD or therapist decides to use, it has profound and complex effects on the deaf-member family. It is not a simple matter. But what about intrafamilial communication? How does an RCD or therapist enact communication among deaf and hearing family members in a family in which the hearing parents and siblings do not sign, and the deaf member's primary mode of communication is sign language? Does the RCD neglect to comment on the words and sentences that the deaf member misses, in favor of focusing on other interactions of the family session? Does the RCD modify the conversational pace of the meeting (e.g., by instructing people to speak slowly, in sequence, etc.) in order to increase the deaf member's verbal participation in the session? Does the RCD attempt to sign some or all of the discussion for the deaf member? If the deaf member has unintelligible speech, does the RCD attempt to voice for him or her for the benefit of the hearing members? Should an interpreter be present? And so on.

As with an RCD deciding on what communication to use with a family, there are no absolute answers for what mode of intrafamilial verbal communication should be utilized. As will be discussed below, the appropriateness of how or if a therapist or RCD should influence the mode of intrafamilial verbal communication is dependent on the specific rehabilitation and therapeutic objectives which have been assessed as maintaining the presenting problem. However, as a general guideline, it is usually neither feasible nor prudent for an RCD or therapist to attempt to add the task of interpreting to his or her role in the session. An RCD or clinician, even if certified as an interpreter, cannot provide effective interventions and be concerned at the same time with accurate interpretation or transliteration of manual communication and spoken English. Both are discrepant, complex, and energy-consuming tasks.

As was described in earlier publications (Harvey, 1982, 1984a,b, 1989), including an interpreter in family treatment not only has obvious linguistic effects but also has systemic ramifications which can be understood with reference to the concept from Gestalt psychology of figure-ground relationships. There is always a question concerning how "figural"—or prominent—to make deafness per se when working with a deaf-member family. Clinicians must continually vary their emphasis on generic family factors and on deafness factors, depending on the therapeutic goals at a particular time. The presence of an interpreter often serves as a catalyst to make issues of deafness more figural.

For example, during one family treatment session in which an interpreter was included, all family members spontaneously began sharing their appreciation of "how having an interpreter in the room makes communication so much easier!" During this phase of treatment, I augmented their references to the interpreter, communication, and deafness by inquiring about interactional patterns of different family members with respect to the deaf sibling at home. The father stated that he talks loudly to his deaf son; mother reported that she worries about him getting into an accident on his bicycle; and so on. Here, the presence of an interpreter served as a reminder of the deaf member's communicative needs and culture.

There are other important ways that an interpreter can make issues related to deafness more figural, or ways that an RCD or therapist can augment a family member's reaction to an interpreter. The following section summarizes two possibilities.

The RCD or therapist can track and overtly point out when the deaf family member looks at and does not look at the interpreter when conversing with another member. For example, a deaf daughter had consistently been using interpretation when discussing a mundane topic with her hearing, nonsigning father. However, she abruptly discontinued looking at the interpreter when her father brought up a "hot topic." And nobody in the family appeared to notice. It became clear that the family, including the deaf member, had participated in erecting a dysfunctional boundary or "wall" around the deaf member which excluded her from important conversations. This dynamic became clear to the family only when the therapist pointed out when the deaf daughter decided not to use interpretation. Making this frequently observed concomitant of deafness figural via the interpreter sets the stage for productive change.

An additional technique is for the RCD or therapist to ask the interpreter to *intermittently* interpret; to stop and start interpreting during a session to make the resulting difference in ease of communicative accessibility more figural. Consider a therapy segment in which there was consistent fluid exchange between a hearing, nonsigning father and a signing deaf son—fluid only because an interpreter was interpreting. When the interpreter, however, discontinued interpreting, the communicative ease and fluidity dramatically lessened and both father and son quickly became much more noticeably frustrated. Consequently, both participants more easily recognized their own long-standing frustrations with each other which had become transformed into hostility. In this case, "stressing the system" (Minuchin, 1974) facilitated therapeutic insight and the beginnings of change.

I then asked the interpreter to resume interpreting, and asked both the father and son to comment on how it felt both when the interpreter did and did not interpret. Both were able to elaborate on the marked differences. The deaf son exclaimed that "it was about time [that effective communication happened]" and began to discuss their history of disengagement and of their linguistic awkwardness with each other. The father commented that "I wish I could take her [the interpreter] home with us." Taking his wish at face value, I got my pocket calculator out, and figured the weekly cost of such an arrangement—the interpreter's hourly fee times 7 days a week times 24 hours a day—and jokingly prompted the father to begin financial negotiations. He, however, offered to learn sign language instead, joking to me that "it's cheaper." Although much more treatment was necessary to help the father follow through on his somewhat impulsive resolution, nevertheless, this intervention via the interpreter helped make conversational inaccessibility more figural and served as a transition to the next stage of treatment.

Although a detailed analysis of the evolving relationship between interpreter and therapist/RCD is beyond the scope of this chapter, it is important to mention that none of interpreter-related techniques can be successfully implemented unless the interpreter and RCD or therapist are in synch with each other, that is, unless each one is clear about what the other is doing. A detailed analysis of this important relationship is presented by Harvey (1989).

Case Example of Systemic Rehabilitation

Bruce, an 18-year-old deaf male, had requested rehabilitation services to begin vocational planning for when he would graduate from high school. Vocational counseling was initially productive, as the RCD helped him decide whether to pursue specialized post-secondary training or employment. He chose employment. However, following his graduation, Bruce failed to show up for several vocational counseling appointments and failed to follow through on various negotiated homework tasks, such as scanning job announcements or prioritizing his vocational objectives. Intermittently, during periods lasting a few weeks, Bruce would arduously follow through on tasks and would beg the RCD to find him any kind of employment. Gratified by his apparent motivation, the RCD placed him at various job sites and offered him continued vocational guidance and support. Bruce, however, easily became disenchanted with each job, and then became erratic in his work habits and attendance. Inevitably, he was fired. Although earlier psychological and vocational evaluations of Bruce, arranged by the RCD, had recommended specialized residential training and psychotherapy, he did not comply.

This pattern continued for approximately four years, until Bruce worked for an employer who was willing to tolerate, or enable, his erratic work performance and attendance for 1½ years. However, this, too, eventually ended as he was fired because of an increased number of days of work missed due to substance abuse. At this time, the RCD requested another psychological evaluation for Bruce, now age 22.

Of note, Bruce had a long history of marijuana and alcohol dependence for at least five years, and had exhibited psychotic symptomatology, such as delusions and hallucinations. During these times, he had often been violent at home. Demographic data indicated that Bruce was the third of five siblings, ranging from 13 to 26 years old, of parents who were divorced when he was 10 years old. He has sustained a profound, sensorineural, bilateral hearing loss at the age of six months as a result of meningitis. His mother, Joy, subsequently remarried Sam, himself a recovering alcoholic, and had a boy, now 13 years old. All family members, except Bruce, were hearing and did not sign fluently. Bruce's primary and preferred mode of communication was American Sign Language.

This evaluation of Bruce, conducted by the author, indicated "a psychotic picture with tenuous reality testing, impulsivity, and tendencies to withdraw . . . and risk for further decompensation." However, it further noted that it was impossible to separate the effects of psychosis per se from long-term marijuana dependence, and strongly recommended residential substance abuse treatment. It was also recommended that the RCD obtain permission from Bruce to discuss the psychometric report in a meeting which would include the RCD, myself, Bruce, Sam and Joy, his stepfather and mother, and all five siblings. A neurologic and psychiatric evaluation was also recommended to rule out medical pathology.

The following recurrent cycle contains Bruce's chemical dependency that had persistently thwarted vocational rehabilitation efforts. As with any recurrent cycle, we can arbitrarily begin at any point. Bruce requests VR counseling and funds for training and employment. The RCD provides such counseling and funds. Bruce is irresponsible on the job and either quits or is fired. The RCD confronts Bruce on his behavior and chemical dependence. Bruce, however, denies any responsibility and his addiction. His parents, hearing Bruce's complaints against the RCD, band together to criticize the RCD for her "lack of support," and they, too, request VR funds for training and employment. An so on. This cycle illustrates a common escalating pattern of Vocational Rehabilitation's providing more services only to encounter more client resistance and minimal hope for positive outcome.

The following verbatim transcripts are from the first of several meetings which occurred as described above. Present were Bruce; his parents, Sam and Joy; siblings George (age 13) and Sue (age 17); the RCD, an interpreter, and myself. The other siblings, in Bruce's words, "did not want to come." An interpreter was included at the request of the family members. The interpreter interpreted voice to sign when the hearing family members vocalized, interpreted sign to voice when Bruce signed, and interpreted sign to voice when the RCD or I signed to Bruce. The RCD and I voiced to the hearing family members, while the interpreter interpreted voice to sign.

During the first minutes of the meeting, the family communication around the RCD's and therapist's recommendations immediately became clear, namely that Joy, Sam, and Bruce were all colluding against the RCD and therapist by accusing them of being insensitive to Bruce's needs. Thus, the process which heretofore had been *un*observed because it had occurred in the privacy of the family's home was now readily observable in the RCD-therapist-family treatment session.

Sam: [to RCD] Ya know, you're not gonna stop him from drinking or from pot. He has to do that on his own time.

RCD: I know that.

Sam: Withholding a job from him is like breaking his arm. It's not gonna help any.

RCD: Uh huh.

Sam: If he gets a job and he can have responsibility. He'll probably start dropping [substances] on his own . . . But where he keeps getting no job. He worked at a year and a half at that other job washing dishes. I wouldn't have worked at it six weeks. But you keep promising you're gonna look at it for a job . . .

       He won't stop [drinking and smoking pot] cuz you're forcing him. I know I wouldn't stop. I didn't. People were telling me for years you gotta stop. You only stop when you want to and nobody else can stop you.

Joy: He has to have something. He has to have some responsibilities in life to . . .

Sam: have self-worth.

Joy: [He needs] something affirmative to plan his future on so he'll be more interested in giving himself a better life. What does he have? He has nothing.

RCD: Well, the last time we [Bruce and I] met, that was my game plan. I knew he was drinking . . . and smoking pot but not to this extent. Bruce and I set out to meet every week to look for a job.

Sam: Did you go out with Bruce?

RCD: Well, we attempted to, let me tell you what we did. You seem angry.

Sam: I am mad!

Joy: I think both of us are. I think cuz we've talked about this at home a lot and we've had a lot of frustration over this.

Sam: You're imposing rules on him to get a job. He didn't get no job, you didn't help him find a job, right? You set up rules in order for him to look for a job, right? That's the difference.

RCD: What I was doing was saying 'you take some responsibility and I'll take some responsibility and let's share in the process of seeking employment' . . . He didn't follow through with his half. I was giving him the chance. I was saying to him, I will find you a job . . .

Sam: But you didn't find him one.

RCD: Because . . .

Sam: Because why? You don't make that decision! You are there to find him a job, not to say that you can't because of his drinking or pot smoking. That will never work. I'll tell you right now that will never work. It didn't work for me. It don't work for anybody.

I then attempted, perhaps in error, to clarify my position about what Bruce needed, having had evaluated him earlier. This is a good illustration of the role conflicts inherent in serving as evaluator and therapist, because it put me in advocacy position as opposed to serving as a more neutral facilitator of change. Consequently, both Sam and Joy initially had colluded against not only the RCD but me as well, thus squelching any marital/parental disagreements or conflict. Their discord was mitigated by their mutual adversarial positions against the RCD and therapist. However, there is a hint of a conflict between Sam and Joy in terms of their different perspectives with respect to Bruce's substance abuse. As will be shown later, the RCD's refusal to continue enabling Bruce to abuse substances by providing him with job after job had the inadvertent function of stabilizing the parent's marriage.

Therapist: If I can jump in here. As you know, I tested Bruce a while ago. His thinking was very disorganized. Almost as if he were psychotic. And the problem with that is that you can't really know unless he becomes substance-free. Long term use of pot would make one as confused as someone who is psychotic.

Sam: He didn't start using it until maybe four years ago at the most, that I know of. He's been psychotic since he was born!

Joy: Well, [he began abusing substances] five years ago.

Sam: Come on, Joy, be reasonable! . . . [to therapist] I'm saying that doesn't necessarily mean he hasn't been that way before now, maybe just more . . . But you never tested him before he started smoking.

It is usually important to include siblings in family meetings, even when one person, the identified patient, is the exclusive focus. In this case, Sue and George unanimously labelled Bruce as having a drug problem and endorsed the proposed rehabilitation plan of providing residential treatment first, and then a job. Note that

Sue directly volunteered her opinion to her parents, mostly her father, after her mother interrupted the therapist by reaffirming her own position. This intervention of formally inviting sibling participation was the first step toward destabilizing the parental denial system around Bruce's substance dependence.

Therapist: [to Sue] Let me open this up a bit. Sue, what do you think about this discussion here? Do you see Bruce as having a drug or alcohol problem?

Sue: Yes, he does.

Therapist: And you [George] agree?

George: Yeah.

Sue: But he don't wanna stop.

Therapist: Ok, so if you were in [the RCD's] shoes, what would you do?

Sue: I don't know. I think I'd send him somewhere for some help . . . And then if he came back and he was fine, I'd help him get a job.

Therapist: Okay. There's two different opinions in this room. The first opinion seems to be to help him get a job which would then help him want to stop doing drugs and alcohol and the . . .

Joy: And help him boost his self-esteem.

Sue: Yeah, but I don't understand. How many times did he call work cuz he didn't want to go?

Sam: After a year and a half, you get tired of it.

Sue: But he kept doing it—he used to ask me "call my work, call my work, talk to my boss." I used to tell him, "no". He'd get mad . . . You see, you're saying "get him a job and he'll change." You don't know that he's gonna change.

Joy: I don't know that.

Sam: Give him a chance, that's what we're saying (motions to interrupt her).

Therapist: Let her talk.

Sue: But we did that before and he didn't, nothing happened, right?

Sam: He worked for a year and a half . . . After a year and a half, wouldn't you get sick of washing dishes? . . . Don't you think he has the right to try one more time?

This juncture illustrates a common situation of a VR client pitting an RCD against his parents in order to impede rehabilitation. Bruce essentially had been the go-between between the RCD and his parents, even though, in this case, the RCD had been in intermittent phone contact with them. Thus, in the following transcript, it was important for the RCD to take an active role in the conversation with Sam and Joy. Having expanded the context—or "relevant system"—beyond Bruce by including his parents and two siblings, it would now be productive for him to participate more actively in the conversation. The RCD cued Bruce to advocate his position. Note that his position, however, is unclear and, in fact, contradictory—"I wanted one day a week. Then I wanted more money. I didn't want only two days. I wanted to work for a full week so I could get more money." Bruce's apparent confusion did not appear an artifact of linguistic misunderstanding or interpreting error, as the interpreter made several verifications of communication (not included in the transcript).

RCD: We actually at that time didn't even focus on any specifics of his pot smoking or his alcohol consumption. It was only until he didn't follow through that I did these things.

Therapist: What did he not follow through on?

RCD: He would ask Sue to call and didn't come to my appointments at times. He forgot his newspapers. He'd show up a half an hour late or one time he showed up in the morning and he was supposed to meet with me in the afternoon . . . Do you [Sam] remember that he began working full-time and then decided to work part-time?

Sam: Yes, that was after about a year. His conception of time is way off . . . He doesn't know the difference between yesterday and today.

Bruce: That day, I didn't want to [work]. I wanted one day a week. Then I wanted more money. I didn't want only two days. I wanted to work for a full week so I could get more money.

Sam: And a vacation . . . He [also] wanted a raise.

RCD: And do you remember, when you started working full time, you wanted part time?

Bruce: After work was over I'd go out . . .

Sam: He'd come home, he'd park the car.

Bruce: Then I'd go out and drink. It's silly to go in, you know, to drink and then go to work. The cops might grab me. You know, I didn't want that so when work was finished I'd go out and have one, two, three beers or something and then I'd go home . . . Around eleven or twelve when work was finished, I'd go out. Go to the bar, talk, shoot the breeze with my friends.

RCD: Do you feel that alcohol or pot interfered with you at work?

Bruce: They didn't know that I was doing it. They all know that I'm deaf . . . Sometimes I'd drink and smoke pot together, not much.

Therapist: So when you arrived at work was your head confused or fuzzy?

Bruce: After work I'd go to the bar and my head would feel a little fuzzy. I would get a buzz on.

Therapist: Ok, let me ask Sam. Do you think that pot and alcohol interfered with his thinking and his responsibility on the job?

Sam: Most definitely, if he does go in that way. And I knew it because he used our car and I won't let him drive the car . . . [during] the last six months, but not the first year.

Joy: I'd say the first six months he was fine. As far as the drinking and the pot, it didn't affect him at the job or anywhere else. It was when he started saying "I don't wanna do this job any more." . . . He had to stay there to show [the RCD] that he was responsible and he didn't want to do that. Not one of my other kids, Mike, would have kept that job.

Note that Sam had dramatically begun to change his position following his conversation with the RCD by stating that "his conception of time is way off . . . He doesn't know the difference between yesterday and today." Time distortion is, of course, one symptom of long-term dependence on alcohol and marijuana. As Sam continued to shift his position, Joy immediately stepped in to counter Sam. Note also the time confusion; Sam said Bruce was fine the first year, while Joy said the first six months.

As illustrated in the next transcript, the RCD and I had a dialogue about rehabilitation/treatment goals in front of the family. We mutually decided to abandon our previous positions, "go back to square one" and acknowledged the expertise of the family. Note that Sam dramatically reversed his previous position in regards to Bruce after the RCD and I emphasized the need for accountability. Again, to emphasize an important systems theory principle, *behavior is context-based*. In an earlier context of Bruce and his parents colluding against the RCD, while excluding feedback from the siblings, Sam's position was firmly against residential treatment. Now that the context had expanded to include the siblings and therapist, Sam's position changes.

Therapist: Linda [RCD], we have not yet talked . . . There are two models here. There's what you and I were coming in with, which is that Bruce is so disorganized with drugs and alcohol that he really can't get a job until he settles that . . . It sounds to me like Sue and George are leaning in that direction as well. However, his parents, Sam and Joy, and Bruce are saying in effect, 'that's stupid . . . he needs a job that he likes and his self-esteem increases, and then he will be more able to decide whether to stop alcohol and drugs.' Where would you like to go with that in terms of us working together here?

RCD: I'm frustrated, too, and at a loss for what to do. So perhaps we can all work together to come up with a game plan. I have no objections . . . I agree that we have to share in the responsibility of [this plan]. Bruce has to consistently take some responsibility for helping himself—whether it's meeting with you [for individual therapy], meeting with me, or taking some initiative to seek employment. All of my clients do, so it's not only Bruce. . . . It's a two-way process.

Therapist: So we're back at square one. One tactic we might do now is not get so bent on selling our way of viewing 'it,' which is to say get rid of alcohol/drugs first, then job. We might want to go back to the drawing board and have an agreement amongst everybody here on what you need to do, what Bruce needs to do, and go from there. . . . Sam and Joy know Bruce better than we do. Bruce knows Bruce better than we do. And they have a model which they feel might work . . . But I think we need some accountability.

RCD: That's what I would like everyone to discuss—that accountability.

Sam: Okay, you got reasonable points. I understand that. But Bruce is not one to take that [accountability] right now. My estimation right now is that he's so far gone that a job isn't gonna help him.

Therapist: Sam, design a program! What do you think would have a chance of working? What do you think he needs?

Sam: Right now, at this stage? He's tired like hell for the last two weeks, but to try to go out and get a job now, no! The rehab place, I'll go along with Sue and George there. Maybe a rehab place to learn about what he's doing with himself. When he gets out, find him a decent job, not one washing dishes.

Therapist: Okay, I wanna get something clear. What you are saying is that you would recommend the residential treatment program. Then he gets out and Linda rolls up her sleeves with Bruce and finds a better job.

Sam: At least if he could understand what it is. He doesn't understand what drugs and alcohol are right now.

Therapist: Joy, you're the mother of this operation here. Do you agree with Sam?

Joy: Not really . . . Well I just can't. I just can't. I'm not ready to accept that route yet, that's all . . . I think getting a job is something he might enjoy. Would help to build up his self-esteem . . . I'm saying job with a drug counselor—for him to see a counselor on drugs and alcohol.

The enmeshment between Joy and Bruce became particularly clear at this point, as indicated by Joy's difficulty letting him go: "I just can't. I just can't. I'm not ready to accept that route yet, that's all." As illustrated by the next transcript, the marital discord also became clear.

Therapist: [asks Joy and Sam to sit next to each other] Could Linda and I, and the rest of us, watch you and Sam? I think that both of you have very complementary perspectives.

Joy: We disagree constantly about everything.

Therapist: Well, if you constantly agreed with each other, I'd worry about you (laughs).

Sue: Now, don't fight and scream and yell. Just talk!

Sam: You don't think it's a good idea for him [Bruce] to find out what drugs and alcohol are doing to him? He can't do that and work too, Joy.

Joy: He's gonna come home clean and be back in with the same people again and they're not gonna wanna be bothered with him . . . And who's gonna go with Bruce? He's gonna leave his whole family . . . Part of me knows [he is addicted to substances], the other part of me doesn't want to admit it.

Sam: Denial here, denial.

Joy: I know . . . He's gotten the short end of the stick all his life and you know that. Every time they say we're gonna do this, we're gonna so that, it takes months, it's not next week . . . In the meantime, this kid sits home twiddling his thumbs, having delusions, and they think he's out of his mind . . .

Joy accurately summarized the sentiment of many deaf persons of receiving disorganized, inadequate services. Sam could have supported Joy in her pain at separating from Bruce and her sympathy and/or empathy for his plight. Instead, he sarcastically said "denial here, denial." However, the apparent marital problem and/or parental conflict should not be understood as solely Sam's fault, or Joy's fault. Moreover, Bruce's difficulties should not be understood as solely *his* fault. From a systemic perspective, it is incorrect to affix blame to any one person; each person's behavior is a function of the surrounding context.

The preceding therapy excerpts illustrate the dramatic advantages of an RCD working directly with the family system around the rehabilitation client, in a sense, to provide "systemic rehabilitation." What had been an escalating conflict between Bruce and his parents against the RCD which resulted in unnecessary expenditure of VR funds and no change became dramatically transformed into a system in which father and mother openly disagreed about their definitions of the problem and joined the RCD in problem-solving. Expanding the relevant system to include the RCD, family therapist, Bruce, his parents, and two siblings set the stage for future changes to occur.

However, change does not come easy nor quickly. As stated earlier in this chapter, whether or not an intervention is effective depends on the interrelationships of systems levels at any given time. In this case, the family, RCD, and I had met two more times and, at the insistence of Bruce and Joy, the RCD agreed that VR would fund outpatient drug treatment for Bruce. During these meetings, everyone agreed that the RCD would not pursue job placement until Bruce began the process of recovery for his substance abuse.

Bruce, as he had done many times before, missed most of his drug treatment appointments, was still highly dependent on substances, and continued intermittently to become violent at home. He dropped out of treatment. The RCD and I did not hear from Bruce or his family for approximately one year. At that time, Joy called in desperation, stating that it was now time to "kick Bruce out of the house and for him to get residential treatment for pot." Why now? It became clear during a subsequent family meeting that his mother's change of attitude was precipitated by Bruce becoming intoxicated and punching his sister, Sue. Although he had done this many times before, it was different now; Sue was pregnant!

The relevant context, or recurrent cycle, in which Bruce's difficulties were embedded had shifted. Bruce's parents would no longer tolerate his out-of-control behavior, for fear of its consequences for their future grandchild. Should the RCD and I have recommended that Sue get pregnant as part of the Individualized Written Rehabilitation Plan for Bruce? Probably not. However, this case poignantly illustrates the importance of context in determining behavior.

As this chapter has illustrated, it behooves an RCD to learn how the context is interrelated with a given deaf client's vocational progress, and how to creatively intervene in the relevant system, as needed. The "client" is not necessarily an individual person, but is often a group of persons who affect the individual's vocational progress and who are, in turn, affected by it. Rather than rehabilitating an individual deaf client, the RCD provides systemic rehabilitation.

REFERENCES

Baker, C., & Cokely, D. (1980). *American Sign Language: A teacher's resource test on grammar and culture.* Silver Spring, MD: T.J. Publishers.

Bateson, G. (1971). A systems approach. *International Journal of Psychiatry, 9,* 242–244.

Bodner-Johnson, B. (1986). The family in perspective. In D.M. Luterman, *Deafness in perspective.* San Diego, CA: College-Hill Press.

Bronfenbrenner, U. (1979). *The ecology of human development.* Cambridge, MA: Harvard University Press.

Campbell, D., Draper, R., & Huffington, C. (1989). *Second thoughts on the theory and practice of the Milan approach to family therapy.* London, England: DC Associates.

Dym, B. (1987). The cybernetics of physical illness. *Family Process, 26*(1), 35–45.

Engel, G.L. (1955). Studies of ulcerative colitis. *American Journal of Medicine, 19,* 232–256.

Freeman, R.D., Malkin, S.F., & Hastings, J.O. (1975). Psychosocial problems of deaf children and their families: A comparative study. *American Annals of the Deaf, 120,* 391–405.

Greenberg, M.T. (1983). Family stress and child competence: The effects of early intervention for families with deaf infants. *American Annals of the Deaf, 128,* 407–417.

Harvey, M.A. (1982). The influence and utilization of an interpreter for deaf persons in family therapy. *American Annals of the Deaf, 127,* 821–827.

Harvey, M.A. (1984a). Family therapy with deaf persons: The systemic utilization of an interpreter. *Family Process, 23,* 205–213.

Harvey, M.A. (1984b). Rejoinder to Scott. *Family Process, 23,* 216–221.

Harvey, M.A. (1989). *Psychotherapy with deaf and hard-of-hearing persons: A systemic model.* Hillsdale, NJ: Lawrence Erlbaum Press.

Harvey, M.A., & Dym, B. (1987). An ecological view of deafness. *Family Systems Medicine, 5*(1), 52–64.

Harvey, M.A., & Dym, B. (1988). An ecological perspective on deafness. *Journal of Rehabilitation of the Deaf, 21*(3), 12–20.

Higgins, P.C. (1980). *Outsiders in a hearing world: A sociology of deafness.* Beverly Hills, CA: Sage Publications.

Hoffman, L. (1981). *Foundations of family therapy.* New York: Basic Books.

Hoffmeister, R.J. (1985). Families with deaf parents: A functional perspective. In K. Thurman (Ed.), *Handicapped families: Functional perspectives.* New York: Academic Press.

Keeny, B.P. (1983). *Aesthetics of change.* New York: The Guilford Press.

Lane, H. (1987, July 13). Is there a "psychology of the deaf?" Presented at the O.S.E.P. Conference of Research Project Directors, Boston, MA.

Levine, E.S. (1981). *The ecology of early deafness: Guides to fashioning environments and psychological assessments.* New York: Columbia University Press.

Long, G., & Harvey, M. (Eds.). (1990). *Facilitating the transition of deaf adolescents to adulthood: Focus on families.* Little Rock, AR: Univ. of Arkansas Rehabilitation Research and Training Center of Deafness/Hearing Impairment.

Luterman, D. (1979). *Counseling parents of hearing-impaired children.* Boston, MA: Little Brown & Co.

Marmor, G., & Petitto, L. (1979). Simultaneous communication in the classroom: How well is English grammar represented? *Sign Language Studies, 23,* 99–136.

McGoldrick, M., Pearce, J.K., & Giordano, G. (1982). *Ethnicity and family therapy.* New York: Guilford Press.

Mendelsohn, M., & Rozak, F. (1983). Denying disability: The case of deafness. *Family Systems Medicine, 1,* 37–47.

Mindel, E.D., & Vernon, M. (1971). *They grow in silence.* Silver Spring, MD: National Association of the Deaf.

Mindel, E.D., & Vernon, M. (1987). *They grow in silence* (2nd edition). Boston, MA: Little Brown & Co.

Minuchin, S. (1974). *Structural family therapy: Families and family therapy.* Cambridge, MA: Harvard University Press.

Moores, D.F. (1982). *Educating the deaf: Psychology, principles and practices* (2nd edition). Boston, MA: Houghton Mifflin Co.

Moses, K. (1986). Counseling: A critical point of our practice. Presented at an American Speech-Language-Hearing Association teleconference, Rockville, MD.

Nash, J.E., & Nash, A. (1981). *Deafness in society.* Lexington, MA: Lexington Books.

Padden, C. (1980). The deaf community and the culture of deaf people. *Sign language and the deaf community.* Silver Spring, MD: National Association of the Deaf.

Palmer, J.O. (1970). *The psychological assessment of children.* New York: John Wiley & Sons, Inc.

Rainer, J.D., Altshuler, K.A., & Kallman, F.Z. (1963). Psychotherapy for the deaf. In J.D. Rainer, K.Z. Altshuler, & F.Z. Kallman (Eds.), *Family and mental health problems in a deaf population.* New York: New York State Psychiatric Institute.

Rawlings, B. (1971). Characteristics of hearing-impaired students by hearing status, United States: 1970–1971. Series D., No. 10, Office of Demographic Studies, Gallaudet College.

Robinson, L.D., & Weathers, O.D. (1974). Family therapy of deaf parents and hearing children. A new dimension in psychotherapeutic intervention. *American Annals of the Deaf, 119,* 325–330.

Rogers, C.P. (1951). *Client-centered therapy: Its current practice, implications, and theory.* Boston: Houghton-Mifflin.

Schlesinger, H., & Meadow, K. (1972). *Sound and sign: Childhood deafness and mental health.* Berkeley, CA: University of California Press.

Scott, S., & Dooley, D. (1985). A structural family therapy approach for treatment of deaf children. In G.B. Anderson & D. Watson (Eds.), *Counseling deaf people: Research & practice.* Little Rock, AR: Arkansas Rehabilitation Research and Training Center on Deafness and Hearing Impairment.

Shapiro, R.J., & Harris, R. (1976). Family therapy in treatment of the deaf: A case report. *Family process, 15,* 83–97.

Shaver, K.A. (1987). Medical and psychological implications of maternal rubella and other syndromes. Presented at the 11/87 Controversies in Mental Health and Deafness Conference, Falmouth, MA.

Simon, F.B., Stierlin, H., & Wynne, C.C. (1985). *The language of family therapy: A systemic vocabulary and sourcebook.* New York: Family Process Inc.

Strong, M., & Stone-Charlson, E. (1987). Simultaneous communication: Are teachers attempting an impossible task? *American Annals of the Deaf, 132,* 376–382.

Sussman, A.E. (1976). Attitudes towards deafness: Psychology's role—past, present, and potential. In F.B. Crammette & A.B. Crammette (Eds.), *VII world congress of the World Federation of the Deaf.* Washington, DC: National Association of the Deaf.

Woodward, J. (1982). *How you gonna get to heaven if you can't talk with Jesus: On depathologizing deafness.* Silver Spring, MD: T.J. Publishers.

▶ 10

Accessibility: Legal Issues

FRANK G. BOWE
Hofstra University

*Deaf people enjoy Federal and State protection when they
seek access to "the hearing world" (i.e., the general
community). The Americans with Disabilities Act of 1990
[PL 101-336] greatly expands such protection, but it is far
from the only source of such rights. Section 504 of the
Rehabilitation Act of 1973 remains important in access to
programs receiving Federal financial assistance. In 1988,
PL 100-430, the Fair Housing Amendments Act, extended
protection to much private housing stock. The Television
Decoder Circuitry Act of 1990 [PL 101-431] promises to
expand access to television. The extent to which current
and future statutory rights of access become reality for deaf
people in America will depend principally upon how
thoroughly deaf people understand these rights and how
vigorously they seek to enforce them.*

The major federal laws according deaf people access to the general community date
from 1973. In order of enactment, the key laws are:

- **Rehabilitation Act of 1973** [PL 93-112], most recently amended in 1992 [PL
  102-569];
- **Individuals with Disabilities Education Act [IDEA]** [PL 94-142], most recently amended in 1991 [PL 102-119].

- **Technology Related Assistance for Individuals with Disabilities Act of 1988** [PL 100-407];
- **Fair Housing Amendments Act of 1988** [PL 100-430];
- **Telecommunications Accessibility Enhancement Act of 1988** [PL 100-542];
- **Americans with Disabilities Act of 1990** [PL 101-336]; and
- **Television Decoder Circuitry Act of 1990** [PL 101-431].

All except PL 100-542 and PL 101-431 extend protection to "individuals with disabilities," to use the term adopted in PL 100-407 and most subsequent legislation. That is, these are not laws specifically for deaf or hard-of-hearing persons. PL 100-542 and PL 101-431 refer to deaf and hard-of-hearing persons who use Telecommunications Devices for the Deaf [TTYs] or television decoders and make no reference to "disabilities" as such.

This immediately raises an issue stirring lively debate in the deaf community: Are deaf people "disabled"? The major federal laws include deaf people in the category of those persons who have permanent activity limitations which interfere substantially in such major life activities as working. Deaf persons are considered to be included among the persons protected by federal access laws because deaf people have a permanent medical condition (loss of hearing) which does produce an activity limitation (inability to understand conversational speech through the ear alone, as on the telephone or in meetings) in education, employment, and independent living. This does not mean that deaf individuals must consider themselves to be disabled. The issue is not one of self-perception. It is not a matter of identity. Rather, the concern at hand is that deaf people meet the statutory definition of "individuals with disabilities" and may, therefore, take advantage of the protections offered in those laws.

The fact that access laws protecting deaf people date only from 1973 also raises questions. The 197-year delay, from the founding of the Republic to 1973, was not caused by anything connected with "deaf culture." Rather, it had more to do with two things. First, the American people (including many people with disabilities themselves) traditionally have thought of handicapping conditions as "my (our) problem(s)" rather than as civil-rights issues. Thus, people sought medical and professional assistance in "coping" with the disability, rather than civil-rights legislation. Second, people with disabilities historically have been removed from the community and placed into remote "special" facilities, e.g., schools for deaf children. Thus, the issue of what rights they had in the general community seldom surfaced.

This forced removal from the community meant that people remaining in the community did not recognize access as an issue, as just about everyone who had to get around was in full possession of all "normal" facilities. It was not until the late 1960s that the concept of "normalization," which was first developed in Sweden, came to raise consciousness in America about the need to make the local community accessible (Bowe, 1978, 1990a).

At any event, between 1973 and 1990 a number of important pieces of federal legislation established rights to access for deaf as well as other persons. Each is reviewed in detail below.

FEDERAL LAWS AND DEAF PEOPLE

The Rehabilitation Act of 1973 [PL 93-112]

Title V of this Act included four major equal-protection sections. They are numbered "501," "502," "503," and "504". Each was very brief and to the point. (For an excellent short history of title V, see Scotch, 1984). Nowhere was there any effort made to separate out the needs of deaf, hard-of-hearing, or speech-impaired persons from the needs of others with "handicaps". Rather, the intent was to bring the kinds of protection afforded to members of ethnic and racial minority groups in title VI of the 1964 Civil Rights Act and to women in title IX of the Education Amendments of 1972 to the broad group of "handicapped individuals" [the term used in the 1973 Act]. Section 508 was added in 1986 and offers additional protection.

Section 501

In section 501, the Congress wanted to protect the equal-employment rights of persons with disabilities who sought jobs at, or worked in, federal agencies. Section 501 called for "affirmative action," but what it meant was "nondiscrimination" (equal employment opportunity). The section required federal agencies to provide "reasonable accommodations" for applicants and employees with handicaps. It also asked agencies to report annually on the number of employees and new hires.

According to one observer, the National Association of the Deaf (NAD) Legal Defense Fund's Marc Charmatz (1987), the record of federal agencies to date in employment of deaf people has been "deplorable". Recent figures—those for Federal Fiscal Year (FFY) 1987—indicate that the federal government employs some 5,984 deaf persons (EEOC, 1989). The agencies with the largest number of deaf employees are the U.S. Postal Service (2,417) and the Department of Defense (1,767). The two together comprise fully 70% of the total reported by 88 agencies. Advocates such as Charmatz argue that if the federal government expects the rest of the country to do better in employment of deaf people, it will have to set a better example.

Administrative regulations set by the Office of Personnel Management (OPM) and the Equal Employment Opportunity Commission (EEOC) allow agencies, but do not require them, to ignore personnel ceilings when hiring sign-language interpreters to support deaf workers. While those policies help, the budgetary constraints under which most federal agencies operate limit the practical meaning of these procedures. The reality is that many deaf "Feds" have little interpreter support except for formal meetings that are scheduled well in advance. Granted all of this, it still must be acknowledged that the level of interpreter and other support (e.g., TTYs) is better in federal agencies than it is in many state agencies or in many private-sector companies (See Chapter 11).

Section 502

The second part of title V states that federal and certain federally constructed buildings and facilities are to be accessible to persons with "physical disablities." While that category generally is defined to include deaf people, the fact that TTYs usually are regarded as "personal property" rather than as "fixed" parts of a building or facility sharply limits the application of section 502 to the access rights of deaf people. Section 502 authorizes the U.S. Architectural and Transportation Barriers Compliance Board (ATBCB), an independent Federal agency, to enforce the 1968 "Architectural Barriers Act" and the PL 90-480-based Uniform Federal Accessibility Standards (UFAS). The Act excludes "personal property" from coverage.

Nonetheless, some progress has been made. In 1985-1987, ATBCB demonstrated the feasibility of a federal TTY-Voice Relay System. That pilot project directly led to the enactment of PL 100-542 (below), which made permanent such a relay. Additionally, the UFAS specifies a minimum number of augmentative listening systems (ALSs) in auditoriums and the use of visual (flashing light) alarms and alarm systems where audible alarms are used (Bowe, 1984). The "minimum number" of ALSs depends upon the size and seating arrangement of the auditorium. The UFAS standards apply to many federal buildings and to some structures erected with federal assistance, such as housing projects.

Section 503

In the third section of title V, the Congress imposed an "affirmative action" obligation on private companies holding contracts with federal agencies worth more than $2,500 per year. Section 503 is administered by the U.S. Department of Labor. The regulations DoL has issued for section 503 differ greatly from those it released for *Executive Order 11246* [30 F.R. 12319 (Sept. 24, 1965); 41 CFR 60-1] *and for title VII* of the 1964 Civil Rights Act [42 U.S.C. section 2000e et seq.]. Let us explore some of these differences.

The Executive Order offers group protections for members of racial and ethnic minority groups and for women. It imposes affirmative action obligations on covered employers to correct the effects of past discriminatory practices. Goals and timetables are required. An individual alleging discrimination may cite numerical evidence (e.g., a paucity of class members in certain jobs) in support of a claim of discrimination. Title VII extends affirmative action obligations to small businesses having 15 or more employees and being engaged in interstate commerce.

By contrast, there are in section 503 *no numerical goals and timetables.* Section 503 focuses, *not on groups, but on individuals.* The point is that each individual is to receive fair treatment at each stage in corporate personnel processes. It is not relevant how many such persons there are. Rather, the interest is in protecting each person individually. A company may have just one disabled employee and still meet all federal requirements. Conversely, it is possible for a company to employ only disabled persons and still be in violation of section 503. Section 503 applies, not to all private employers, but only to federal contractors and subcontractors. Thus, coverage is extended to deaf persons only with 30,000 "prime contractors" and some 85,000 subcontractors employing 31 million people and doing $81 billion in contract work for the federal government (Labor, 1984).

The nation's approximately 7 million other employers, accounting for some 80 million workers, are not covered. Accordingly, *persons with disabilities, including deaf people, often turned to major corporations for employment*, believing, probably rightly, that only there or in government would they receive fair treatment.

Labor regulations add that "a handicapped individual is 'substantially limited' if he or she is likely to experience difficulty in securing, retaining, or advancing in employment because of a handicap." The word *"qualified"* is interpreted to mean "capable of performing a particular job, with reasonable accommodation to his or her handicap."

Section 503 has been the subject of numerous court cases. Of this body of case law, Labor singles out *E. E. Black, Ltd. v. Marshall*, 497 F Supp 1088, 1104 (D. C. Hawaii, 1980) for attention (Nov. 27, 1984 letter to F. Bowe from S. R. Meisinger, Deputy Under Secretary). In *Black*, the issue at hand was the definition of "handicapped individual." The case history is instructive. At the time, Labor's administrative order said that section 503 covered "every individual with an impairment which is a current bar to employment which the individual is currently capable of performing" [*E. E. Black, Ltd. v. Marshall*, No 79-0132 Civil (D. C. Hawaii)]. The Black company, however, contended that to be substantial, an impairment had to cause an individual difficulty in finding work across the entire spectrum of job opportunities, not just those jobs the individual was interested in or qualified to perform.

The Federal district court in Hawaii decided that both were wrong, but to different degrees, siding more with DoL than with Black. In denying Black's motion for summary judgment, the court said that DoL's standard was too broad because it ignored the statutory term, "substantially," and would therefore cover any person who because of an impairment is limited in employment in any way.

But the court rejected Black's interpretation as well, because it would severely limit section 503's reach and would defeat the Congressional intent to protect a broad category of persons with handicaps.

The court offered the following standard for use in case-by-case instances in which the term "qualified handicapped individual" is in question:

If an individual were disqualified from the same or similar jobs offered by employers throughout the area to which he had reasonable access, then his impairment . . .would have to be considered as resulting in a substantial handicap to employment. . . . A person who is disqualified from employment in his chosen field has a substantial handicap to employment, and is substantially limited in one of his major life activities.

[*In the Matter of Office of Federal Contract Compliance Programs v. E. E. Black, Ltd., et al.* (Case No. 77-OFCCP-7-R; Decision and Order dated Feb. 26, 1979, note 10)].

Private Right of Action

Most interpretations of section 503 state that deaf persons or others with disabilities have grievance rights in the company, and enjoy the right to file complaints with DoL. Most hold that covered persons do not, however, have the right to take their complaints to federal or state courts. That is, there is no private right of action under section 503.

Reasonable Accommodation

Every qualified handicapped individual is entitled by section 503 to reasonable accommodation to his or her known limitations. Notice that if the limitation is not known to the company, no accommodation need be considered. However, once the restriction is known to the company, the requirement is triggered. Deaf and other disabled persons may "self-identify" to the employer, thus triggering the obligation, or they may be "company identified" on the basis of visual observation or personal knowledge. Accommodations are a contractual obligation, i.e., they must be offered to qualified persons. The two exceptions recognized by the rules are those instances in which provision of an accommodation would impose an *"undue hardship"* upon the contractor (e.g., would be very costly) or would *interfere with business necessity and safety* (e.g., would jeopardize performance of work by the individual or by others in the workforce).

Accessibility

The section 503 rules refer to the American National Standards Institute (ANSI) *American National Standard for Buildings and Facilities Providing Accessibility and Useability for Physically Handicapped People.* The 1986 version of this voluntary accessibility standard is similar to the U.S. ATBCB's UFAS. The major difference for deaf people is that ANSI-1986 does not specify the number of augmentative listening systems or visual alarms. The reference to ANSI means that federal contractors must make such common-use areas as auditoriums accessible to deaf people and provide visual alarm systems where auditory systems are provided.

Section 504

Section 504 is the language that immediately follows section 503 in the 1973 Rehabilitation Act, as amended. It applies, not to contractors, but to grant recipients: i.e., to virtually all of the nation's 3,000 colleges and universities, its 15,000 school districts, and its many thousands of hospitals, social service agencies and facilities, and public libraries. In 1978, the Congress made section 504 applicable as well to federal agencies. Section 504 calls for "program accessibility" such that all programs and activities conducted by a recipient (or by an agency) must be "accessible to and usable by" disabled persons, including deaf people.

Section 504, then, is nondiscrimination rather than affirmative action in orientation. The purpose is broader than just employment. Generally, however, section 504 is similar to section 503 because neither imposes goals, timetables, or other requirements popularly associated with the words "affirmative action."

As is true with section 503 as well, the section 504 regulations issued by some 30 federal agencies refer to ANSI or UFAS for accessibility.

In 1984, the U.S. Supreme Court ruled, in the *Grove City* case, that section 504's reach extended only to specific programs or activities directly benefiting from federal financial assistance, not to the entire institution as had been understood until that time. In the case of Grove City Community College in Pennsylvania, this decision meant that only the financial aid office need comply with section 504—not the whole college. Four years later, on March 22, 1988, the Congress reversed this interpretation. The Civil Rights Restoration Act overturned the *Grove City* decision. This was an important recovery for deaf people desiring protection under section 504, because it meant that institutions receiving federal financial assistance, as do almost all of the nation's colleges and universities, must protect the rights of deaf students and faculty in all collegiate programs, not only in those that actually receive grant monies.

The "program accessibility" requirement in section 504 includes use of sign-language interpreters where needed to understand instructors, tutors, etc. However, because the supply of interpreters remains short of the demand, and because some colleges balk at paying interpreter fees, compliance has been spotty. The U.S. Congress Commission on Education of the Deaf (COED) found that just 150 American colleges and universities, or 5 percent, regularly provided interpreting and related services to undergraduate and graduate students. Again, this is a good example of how advocacy by the deaf community often is the deciding factor in whether federal laws are obeyed.

One volatile issue in many states is whether state vocational rehabilitation agencies are legally liable for interpreter costs when they send their clients to college. Some agencies have argued that they are required by title I of the Rehabilitation Act to be "last dollar" providers, that is, to exhaust all "similar services" available from other sources; and that, because colleges are required by section 504 to supply interpreter services, the colleges become "similar services" providers, thus relieving the VR agency from the obligation to pay for interpreters. No clear resolution applicable nationally has emerged as of this writing.

Private Right of Action

There is a clear private right of action under section 504. Moreover, a deaf person seeking relief need not first "exhaust administrative remedies," that is, wait for the completion of the complaint process. Other provisions of section 504, such as the "reasonable accommodation" requirement, are quite similar to those under section 503.

Section 508

PL 99-506, the 1986 Amendments to to the Rehabilitation Act, added a new section which required federal agencies to purchase, lease, or rent only "accessible" electronic office equipment. This addition recognized the reality that employment in the late 1980s and in the 1990s, in what is widely called "The Information Age", depends as much on access to equipment as it does on access to buildings. PCs and workstations purchased by federal agencies, for example, need to accept and work with speech synthesizers so that deaf persons with limited speech might use this technology. As speech recognition systems mature—the best today can understand only a few hundred words spoken by a range of people—this requirement will become more critical for deaf people.

The impact of section 508 goes beyond federal agencies, because few, if any, equipment vendors will maintain two versions of their product lines—one, accessible, for sale to federal agencies, and a second, inaccessible, for sale to other customers. Because the federal government is the world's largest buyer of electronic office equipment, section 508 virtually compels electronics companies to make and sell accessible products in all markets—meaning that deaf as well as other-disabled persons will benefit whether or not they work for federal agencies (Brill, 1989).

Individuals with Disabilities Education Act

This law started, as did the Declaration of Independence, with an indictment: A new law is needed, it said in 1975, because millions of American children with handicaps were being denied a free appropriate public education. Although the states had primary responsibility for education, they had shown that they were unwilling to assume that responsibility. Therefore, this new law had to spell out, in excruciating detail, exactly what they were now supposed to do. And to be sure no one misunderstood the intent of the legislation, the 1975 act called itself "The Education for *All* Handicapped Children Act."

IDEA, as the federal law is now called, is divided into several parts. Part A contains the indictment of existing practices, defines terms, and establishes eligibility requirements for receiving federal funds. Federal spending has been quite modest: some 8 percent of the "excess costs", or the costs above and beyond those incurred in educating other children. Part B, the heart of the Act, sets forth what state and local education agencies are expected to do. It includes a "zero reject" requirement: No child with a disability, no matter how severe, may be rejected from public schooling altogether. It establishes a whole new set of parent rights: to be fully informed, to give consent to what the school plans for their children, to contest any decision with which they disagree, to have their children tested by independent experts free of charge, and to have all educational and related services provided free of charge. Part B gives the local education agencies the job of educating children with handicaps. If local schools cannot do it, the school district has to pay all expenses for the child to receive an education somewhere else, including transportation costs.

Part C continues some special centers, including programs for deaf-blind children and postsecondary programs for deaf youth and adults, which had been created in 1970. Part D continues funds for preservice and inservice training of educators and related-services personnel. Part E continues the federal role in research, as Part F does in instructional media. Part G is a small grant program on the use of technology in special education.

Part H is an extension of Part B; it requires free family counseling and other services to infants and toddlers, from birth through age 2. States were to have a statewide system in place by 1991–1992. Parts G and H were added in 1986. IDEA now entitles children with disabilities to free public services from birth to age 18, and where state law allows, to age 21. Federal spending on Parts B and H totals some $2 billion annually. State and local governments add about ten times that much, bringing the national investment to about $30 billion.

The most controversial elements of Part B surely are the "least restrictive environment" [LRE] requirements, the "related services" provisions, and the "due process" procedures affording parents great latitude in challenging school officials' decisions. The key terms "appropriate", "unique needs", and "potential harmful effects" never have been defined, either in the law or in the implementing regulations. Accordingly, controversy rages about what these terms really mean. A review of the controversy is offered in the COED report, *Toward Equality* (Bowe, 1988). Madeline C. Will, the former Assistant Secretary for Special Education and Rehabilitative Services, regarded LRE as the core of Part B. Her successors, Dr. Robert Davila and Ms. Judith E. Heumann, have shown more understanding about the deaf community's views on this issue.

That change, if it occurs, will be welcomed by most of the deaf community. Over the past decade, most state schools for deaf children have shrunk as ever-larger numbers of deaf children attend regular public schools. The issue of quality has now surfaced in the education of deaf children. If we can establish minimum standards of what we mean by quality in teaching deaf children, we may end what many see as excessive "dumping" of such children into public school systems that are unprepared to meet their special needs. This issue is discussed in greater detail in the *Proceedings of the National Conference on Deaf and Hard-of-Hearing People*, notably Baker-Hawkins (1989) and Bowe (1989).

These issues, however emotional, are complex. The COED offered a set of proposals for resolving the difficulties now confronting the education of deaf children. The Commission's recommendations may be summarized as follows: Deaf children deserve the right to be educated in local public schools if that is the appropriate placement to meet their unique needs. However, if local schools cannot meet those needs, referral of the child to a more comprehensive facility is justified.

Approaching Equality (Bowe, 1991) offers a comprehensive review of implementation of all 52 COED recommendations. Although 50 percent were implemented within three years after COED finished its work, the record in elementary and secondary education is much weaker. Just one of the 14 COED recommendations about public schools has been implemented. As *Approaching Equality* suggests, much work remains before deaf children and youth will be assured of a quality education nationwide.

Technology-Related Assistance for Individuals with Disabilities Act of 1988 [PL 100-407]

This Act was the first ever enacted by the Congress to focus exclusively upon technology for people with disabilities. For deaf people, the most important aspects of PL 100-407 are: (1) its authorization of up to $1.5 million annually for any state to purchase, disseminate, maintain, and repair devices needed by persons of any age—TTYs, PCs, speech synthesizers, and (when commercially available at reasonable prices) voice recognition systems; and (2) its extension of the requirements of section 508 of the Rehabilitation Act to state agencies in those states receiving funds under PL 100-407.

Taken together, these two provisions of the Act offer monies for acquisition and use of modern technologies in education, employment, and independent living for deaf and other disabled persons and an assurance that equipment purchased by states, or entities of a state, will be accessible to and usable by deaf and other disabled individuals.

Fair Housing Amendments Act of 1988 [PL 100-430]

While few deaf persons have been denied the opportunity to rent, lease, or purchase housing stock, apartments, or condominums, many have had difficulty securing landlord permission for installation of flashing lights and other wiring changes. PL 100-430 makes it unlawful discrimination for a landlord to refuse a tenant permission to make such alterations in the property. However, the tenant, and not the landlord, is responsible for financing the changes. In the unusual event that a deaf person is denied equal opportunity in housing, the Act sets forth explicit, and tough, legal remedies deaf persons may pursue.

The importance of PL 100-430 extends yet further. It marks the first time deaf people and others with disabilities were granted federally protected civil rights in private-sector endeavors that do not have, in legal terminology, "a federal nexus." That is, private entities that receive no federal grants or contracts must protect the civil rights of persons with disabilities.

Telecommunications Accessibility Enhancement Act of 1988 [PL 100-542]

This Act establishes, on a permanent basis, the TTY-voice Federal Relay System demonstrated by the U.S. Architectural and Transportation Barriers Compliance

Board (see section 502, above). The new relay is staffed with seven (7) operators; the pilot project at ATBCB had only one. A new, toll-free 800 number is used. Under the pilot project, users paid all long-distance charges applicable. This relay system is available to any deaf person in the United States who wishes to reach a federal telephone that is not TTY-equipped. Thus, it makes accessible some 3 million federal phones, including those on Capitol Hill.

The Act also required the Federal Communications Commission (FCC) to complete a study of interstate relay systems prior to July 28, 1989. The FCC study concluded that the Commission has sufficient authority to require telephone companies which provide interstate telephone service to provide relay services.

RECENT DEVELOPMENTS

New and proposed measures promise expanded access for deaf people in the years to come. While not all of the changes discussed below will become law—or will be fully enforced so as to become reality for all deaf Americans—many will.

Captioning

The federal government is making itself more accessible. The U.S. House of Representatives and the U.S. Senate both passed resolutions requiring that C-Span broadcast of their floor and hearings proceedings be close-captioned; such captioning was in place in 1991. These resolutions make access to the day-to-day workings of the Congress as accessible to deaf as to other persons in the U.S.

In addition, PL 101-431, the Television Decoder Circuitry Act of 1990, requires that all new 13-inch or larger TV sets built or sold in the US after July, 1993, have a built-in capacity to receive and display closed captions. This means that the 20 million TV sets sold in the U.S. each year will be caption-ready. That compares to just 200,000 stand-alone decoders sold during the past ten years. The law establishes captioning as a permanent feature of American television. In 1991, Zenith, the sole remaining American television manufacturer, introduced several models with built-in captioning.

Americans with Disabilities Act

Even more far-reaching are the changes required by the "Americans with Disabilities Act," PL 101-336. This legislation is arguably the most important single measure ever enacted by the U.S. Congress on behalf of people with disabilities, including deaf people. The President signed the measure July 26, 1990.

The Act defines the word "disability" as "a physical or mental impairment that substantially limits one or more of the major life activities of such individuals, a record of such an impairment, or being regarded as having such an impairment." This is the definition we find in section 504. We have more than a decade of case history behind this term, although the word itself is different; it used to be "handicap."

The Act explains what is meant by "discrimination" and sets forth the "effect" standard that will apply. Covered entities—employers, hotels/motels/restaurants, public transit facilities, and telecommunications carriers—must provide opportunities that have the effect of assuring people with disabilities an equal chance to participate in or benefit from programs and activities. The Act also explains that it is not considered discrimination if opportunities were denied to people with disabilities for reasons entirely unrelated to disability.

Title I of the Act emulates title VII of the Civil Rights Act of 1964. It covers some 90 percent of employers in America—those doing commerce and employing 25 or more workers (effective July 26, 1994, the floor falls to 15 workers). These are the employers that have created most of the new jobs in the past decade, and who by all accounts will do the most hiring in the next decade. They are required to make reasonable accommodations unless doing so would impose an undue hardship on the business.

The enforcement procedures of the 1964 Act's title VII are incorporated into the ADA. Specifically, there is a private right of action, i.e., people with disabilities may go to court to enforce their rights. That option does not exist now under most interpretations of section 503. For this reason, people with disabilities likely will use the ADA rather than section 503 to gain equal opportunity in private employment. And the burden of proof on such issues as "undue burden" and "reasonable accommodation" is placed by ADA's title I squarely on the employer. Disabled people, including deaf persons, need only allege discrimination; the employer must prove that it did not occur.

In title II, the ADA explicitly requires state and local governments to comply with standards of nondiscrimination like those in section 504. For deaf people, a major implication is that "911" emergency-response centers must become accessible to TTY users. Title III of the Act requires privately operated establishments that are used by the general public—restaurants, theaters, hotels, office buildings, and recreation facilities, as well as stores, doctors' and dentists' offices and others—to be accessible to and provide equal opportunity for people with disabilities who are customers, visitors, employees, or clients. The language is parallel to that in title II of the Civil Rights Act of 1964. It is strong, sweeping language.

Title IV requires telecommunications carriers—companies like New York Telephone and its parent NYNEX, AT&T, MCI, and others—to provide services that are as equal to deaf people as they are to people who hear. This remedies a 100-year-old irony. Alexander Graham Bell's mother and wife both were deaf. He invented the telephone in an effort to help them. Instead, the telephone erected the single greatest barrier to equal opportunity for deaf people ever created. Under title IV, intrastate TTY-voice relays like that begun in January, 1989, in New York state, and interstate TTY-voice relays as well, will be required. On the other hand, title IV specifically allows telecommunications carriers to use some "improved or future technology." For example, when computer speech recognition is improved to the point that it can comprehend most of what people say, telephone companies may provide that equipment to deaf people instead of sponsoring a TTY-voice relay.

Regulations implementing ADA were issued in summer 1991. Among the many questions these rules help answer are ways stores, doctors' offices, and other places of public accommodation may become accessible to deaf people. To take one obvious example: A store may use pen and pad to communicate with a deaf customer, but a doctor probably must employ an interpreter for a deaf patient.

SUMMARY AND CONCLUSIONS

Federal laws and regulations establish a foundation from which deaf people may gain access into "the hearing world." They may attend local public schools—learning to compete against the people they will face later in the job market. If they so wish, they may compete against hearing persons in virtually any of the nation's colleges and universities, as well. Deaf people now enjoy, thanks to the Americans with Disabilities Act, equal employment opportunity with virtually all of the country's seven million employers and access rights in some five million stores, hotels, restaurants, and parks. Meanwhile, they enjoy equal access to the nation's lawmakers and to federal agencies, so as to secure services and protect rights to which they are entitled.

The major barriers facing deaf people seeking access to the general community no longer are legal in nature. Rather, they are of two kinds. First, the deaf community has not been as vocal as it needs to be in implementing and enforcing existing rights. Witness, for example, that merely one college or university in every twenty provides legally required support services such as interpreters. And second, the practical realities of money erect sizable barriers.

Access for persons using wheelchairs generally requires capital expenditures, that is, one-time design or building changes. Once accessibility features have been installed, no further costs are incurred. That, however, is not true for deaf people. Whether we are talking about TTY-voice relays or sign-language interpreters, we are dealing with "continuing" rather than capital outlays. The New York state relay, for example, costs some $12 million annually; that in California costs more than $20 million each year. Interpreters not only are expensive on an hourly basis, but we literally do not have enough of them to carry out the vision found in the Americans with Disabilities Act. That Act will require millions of companies that to date have had no obligation to hire interpreters to provide interpreting services on demand.

One solution for these problems is to make the major costs capital rather than continuing in nature. Were computer speech recognition possible now, as it may be in five to ten years (Moskowitz, 1989), telephone companies could install voice recognition systems translating speech to text, enabling deaf PC or TTY users to read what others say on the phone. Of course, existing technology already allows the obverse, i.e., translation of what a non-speaking deaf person types into voice. Such speech synthesis and recognition systems, if miniaturized, could obviate much of the need for sign-language interpreters. We would then have a situation roughly comparable to that we see now with wheelchair users. A one-time capital investment would suffice to meet the communication needs of a deaf person for a considerable period of time.

That solution does not resolve the first problem, however. For access to occur, deaf people need to advocate to protect and enforce their rights. We need to do it ourselves.

That immediately raises the question of enforcement of our rights. The right to file complaints is provided by most of the laws reviewed in this chapter. Under the Rehabilitation Act's section 501, complaints may be filed with the federal Equal Employment Opportunity Commission [EEOC]. With respect to that Act's section 502, complaints may be filed with the ATBCB. Under section 503, complaints may be filed with the U.S. Department of Labor. Section 504 provides that deaf people may file complaints with the federal agency which provides the funds to the organization or institution that discriminated; that is, were the discrimination to occur in a school or college, the complaint would be filed with the U.S. Department of Education's Office for Civil Rights. Under section 504 and under PL 94-142, complaints may also be taken to federal court.

The Americans with Disabilities Act allows deaf people who believe they have been discriminated against to file complaints with the federal Equal Employment Opportunity Commission or with the U.S. Department of Justice. The Act also affords deaf people a clear right to go to federal courts for relief. As signed by President Bush in 1990, the Act does not provide compensatory or punitive damages. These may be added later, if some version of the Civil Rights Act of 1991 is passed by the Congress. That is because the Americans with Disabilities Act states that whatever rights and privileges are offered by the Civil Rights Act of 1964, as amended, will apply to individuals with disabilities under ADA.

With respect to title IV relays, complaints may be filed with the Federal Communications Commission [FCC]. The FCC will also receive complaints about captioning under PL 101-431.

In all, deaf people enjoy vastly more protection in 1994 than they did just one generation ago. Every law reviewed in this chapter has been enacted during the past twenty years. These rights, as extensive and impressive as they are, exist only on paper until individuals who are deaf recognize that they enjoy these rights and seek to enforce them. The National Center for Law and the Deaf, at Gallaudet University, is an excellent resource for deaf people concerned about possible discrimination.

REFERENCES

Baker-Hawkins, S. (1989). Education and rehabilitation issues.In R. Brill (Ed.), *Proceedings of the National Conference on Deaf and Hard of Hearing People.* Silver Spring, MD: T. J. Publishers.

Bowe, F. (1978). *Handicapping America.* New York: Harper & Row.

Bowe, F. (1984). *Alarms.* Washington, DC: U.S. Architectural and Transportation Barriers Compliance Board.

Bowe, F. (Ed.) (1988). *Toward equality: Education of the deaf.* Washington, DC: U.S. Government Printing Office.

Bowe, F. (1989). Education and rehabilitation issues. In R. Brill (Ed.), *Proceedings of the National Conference on Deaf and Hard of Hearing People.* Silver Spring, MD: T. J. Publishers

Bowe, F. (1990a). Disabled and elderly people in the first, second, and third worlds. *International Journal of Rehabilitation Research, 13,* 1–14.

Bowe, F. (1990b). Into the private sector: Rights and people with disabilities. *Journal of Disability Policy Studies, 1,* Spring 1990, 89–101.

Bowe, F. (1991). *Approaching equality.* Silver Spring, MD: T. J. Publishers.

Brill, J. (1989). Access and opportunity: Academic computing under section 508. *Higher education and national affairs* [a newsletter of the American Council on Education, Washington, DC], May 22, 1989, unpaged insert.

Burgdorf, R. (1980). *The legal rights of handicapped persons: Cases, materials, text.* Baltimore, MD: Brookes.

Charmatz, M. (1987). A long way to go. *Gallaudet Today: 1987 legal review,* 27–29.

Equal Employment Opportunity Commission. (1989). *Annual report: 1987.* Washington, DC: U.S. Government Printing Office.

Labor. (1984). *Annual report to the Congress, U.S. Department of Labor.* Washington, DC: U.S. Department of Labor.

Moskowitz, J. (1989). The state of voice recognition. *Telocator, April,* 58–65.

Scotch, R. (1984). *From good will to civil rights.* Philadelphia: Temple University Press.

▶ 11

Accessibility to the Hearing World: Assistive Devices and Specialized Support

HOWARD E. STONE, SR.
Self Help for Hard of Hearing People, Inc. (SHHH)

T. ALAN HURWITZ
National Technical Institute for the Deaf

Many competent deaf and hard-of-hearing people are unemployed or underemployed. Others struggle to maintain their positions in the work force. Few are able to realize their potential and move up the ladder beyond stereotyped positions and the limiting conditions caused by deafness. The major problem in employment is the inherent difficulty in communication between persons with hearing loss and those with normal hearing.

This chapter will discuss the various means of alleviating communication problems. Deaf and hard-of-hearing people communicate with each other and with hearing people in ways which involve different methodologies and which often require special technology or services. A whole range of assistive devices and interpreter services is used to bridge communication gaps successfully between people with hearing loss and hearing persons.

A person seeking to alleviate these communication problems needs to know that such devices and services exist, where to find them, and how to utilize them. Above all, one must be willing to use them. In the final analysis, only the individual user can maximize the benefits of support described in this chapter.

TELECOMMUNICATIONS DEVICES AND SERVICES

In spite of the complications posed in the communications process, many persons who are deaf or hard-of-hearing have full-time jobs in business and industry. However, most of them could be more productive on the job if they had proper assistance with their special communications needs. By far the largest area of limitation for these individuals in the hearing world's workplace is that of telecommunications. There are several ways deaf and hard-of-hearing persons can be assisted in this area.

The TTY

The TTY is an acoustic modem (coupler) that makes it possible to transmit and receive typed information from one location to another through standard telephone lines. Originally called a teletypewriter, it was large, bulky, heavy, and noisy. In the 1970s, newly designed, smaller, and more portable TTYs became available.

Recently, some TTYs have been designed to be compatible with computers. A switch allows a person to choose the correct code for calling another TTY (Baudot code) or a computer (ASCII code). Many TTYs have built-in automatic answering devices that provide typed, not spoken, messages. A few models provide large print for people with vision problems. Other helpful features include a printer, memory bank, keyboard or memory dialing, full screen, rolling text, and portability.

When using a TTY, conversation is not spoken and heard; it is typed and read. Calls made from one TTY to another are private and are made without involvement of a third person. There are some restrictions, however, to using a TTY. In specific, the user needs to type, and typing is relatively more time-consuming than speaking. In addition, one cannot interrupt when the other person is typing.

Since 1980, California has distributed free TTYs to people who are unable to speak or hear over the telephone as certified by their physician or audiologist. Most states either have TTY distribution programs or will be implementing them in the near future; different procedures are used and not all provide free TTYs. Some programs are state-funded and others are funded by telephone companies. Local telephone companies will know if their state is involved in any kind of TTY distribution program.

TTY Relay Systems

Until recently, both people needed compatible equipment (a TTY) in order to call each other. There is an expanding network of TTY relay systems, some federal-, state-, or city-funded, others privately financed. With the passage of the 1990 Americans with Disabilities Act, such systems will be required. These systems connect users of TTYs with normal-hearing people using their voices on the telephone.

The relay operator serves as an intermediary for calls placed between a TTY user and a non-TTY user. Either person, the TTY user or the non-TTY user, may initiate the call. For example, the hearing-impaired person calls the relay service number via TTY. The caller gives the operator his or her name, the party to whom the call is being placed, and the phone number (and billing information if long distance).

The caller must then wait until the other party is on the line. When the operator notifies the caller that the other party is ready, the caller then types a message in the first person. The operator relays the information orally to the party contacted and subsequently relays the response to the hearing-impaired called via TTY. At the end of the conversation, it is important for the caller to say goodbye to the party. This is often overlooked and makes it awkward for the operator to formally end the conversation. Upon completion of the call, it is proper etiquette to thank the relay operator for his or her assistance. For a hearing person to contact a person with hearing loss via relay, the reverse of the above is followed.

Other Services

A number of other services are available to TTY users. These include a toll-free telephone number to connect TTY users with an AT&T operator, reduced rates on TTY toll calls, and voice/TTY relay services at no extra charge. In addition, some cities and states have TTY numbers for emergency calls.

Telephone Amplifiers

The typical telephone amplifier increases the loudness of conversation approximately 15–20 decibels, depending on how the volume is adjusted. Amplifiers may be used with or without a hearing aid, and they maybe built-in, portable, or modular. They also are described as acoustic, magnetic, or both acoustic and magnetic. This designation pertains to their ability to work with telephones having strong or weak magnetic fields. Although amplified telephones are primarily for use by hard-of-hearing people, others also use them to make sound louder in noisy work places such as computer centers, manufacturing plants, newspaper editorial rooms, and some laboratories.

Built into the handset, amplifiers come in a variety of models, some of which include rotary dial, rotary dial with pushbutton for additional loudness, pushbutton, and a touch dial that allows a range of adjustment. With rotary dial, the volume remains at the level set by the user. The pushbutton amplifier (without rotary dial) has several preset levels of loudness. The touch dial increases the volume and maintains that level until released. With touch dial amplifiers, the volume automatically returns to normal when the user hangs up. Both the touch dial and pushbutton amplifiers ensure that normal-hearing users will not be subjected to a high-volume sound when picking up the phone. Handsets with built-in amplifiers may have a hardwire or modular connection to the phone. When the amplifier is not in use, the handsets function at standard volume.

PERSONAL COMMUNICATIONS ASSISTANCE

Hearing Aids

Getting the right hearing aid is the first step in the direction of personal communications assistance. Hearing aids are produced in a variety of types and models, and each hearing aid must be selected for and adapted to the person's specified need. A hearing aid requires proper fitting to accommodate an individual's particular hearing loss level. Audiologists certified by the American Speech-Language-Hearing Association (ASHA) are trained to perform this type of fitting, as are noncertified audiologists and hearing aid dispensers licensed by states.

Many factors must be weighed and evaluated before selecting and fitting a hearing aid, if that aid is to be of optimal help to the wearer. In addition to the different types and degrees of hearing loss described in Chapter 1, physical factors need to be considered. These include the outer ear and ear canal's configuration (which affects proper fitting), the presence or absence of manual dexterity problems such as arthritic fingers (which affect the handling of hearing aid components), and special situational needs, such as the degree of physical activity in one's lifestyle.

What Can a Hearing Aid Do?

Because a hearing aid is a miniature amplification system, it can make sound louder, but it does not automatically make speech clearer. For this reason, it is not always useful as a means to remediate the difficulties of a person with poor word discrimination (difficulty interpreting the sounds of speech). The benefit an individual receives from the use of a hearing aid depends upon the nature of the hearing deficit. Nevertheless, the current generation of hearing aids can do much more than just amplify sounds. They can be constructed with the ability to filter background noise, change tonal quality, and modify the amount of power being delivered so as to control the loudness of environmental sound. With realistic expectations on the part of the user, these technical advances make hearing aids more effective.

Different Types of Hearing Aids.

Currently, there are five general types of hearing aids (and many different models of each type).

1. Canal Aid. The canal aid is the newest and smallest hearing aid. All of the components of this aid are condensed into a tiny unit, which is fitted into the ear canal. A principal attraction is the cosmetic value because it is relatively inconspicuous. Of help for mild and moderate hearing losses, these aids are typically without a "T" switch (for a telecoil that directly receives electromagnetic waves from a telephone receiver and thus assists in understanding telephone conversation). The tiny batteries may pose a handling problem for someone without good manual dexterity. The ear canal must be of suitable shape and size to accommodate the unit.

2. In-the-Ear Aid (ITE).   In this type of aid, all components are encased in a unit which fits into the outer ear bowl and the ear canal. This aid is for persons with mild to moderate hearing losses. Although they are appealing for their cosmetic value, in-the-ear aids are not totally invisible. The controls are small and for some people hard to manipulate. A telecoil is optional for some models.

3. Behind-the-Ear Aid (BTE).   In the behind-the-ear aid, all components (microphone, amplifier, and receiver) are contained in a small, curved case which fits neatly behind the ear and is connected to the ear mold by a short plastic tube. BTE aids can help hearing losses ranging from mild to profound. Some models have a tone control plus volume control and may include a "T" switch. BTE aids often can accommodate special methods of direct audio input as described below.

4. Eyeglasses Frame Aid.   This aid is similar to the behind-the-ear hearing aid except that the device is built into the temple frame piece of the glasses, with a tube from the earpiece of the glasses to the earmold. Because the eyeglasses and hearing aid are integrally connected, a need for service or repair will affect both eyes and ears, unless the person has a back-up or temporary replacement available.

5. Body Aid.   A body aid may be used by persons with a profound hearing loss needing great power in hearing aid output. Aid units are encased in a container about half the size of a cigarette pack, and are worn on the body with a cord connecting to a button-receiver snapped onto the ear mold. All body-type aids include "T" switches, but cannot connect to Direct Audio Input as described below.

6. Vibrotactile Aids.   Recently vibrotactile aids have been developed which provide for the wearer a tactile stimulation correlated with auditory input. These aids may offer profoundly deaf people new opportunities for the development of communication skills as well as an increased awareness of their environment. Since the concept is unusual, professionals as well as clients need extensive education and training in the use of such devices.

Other Aspects of Amplification

Bone-Conduction Aids
Sometimes hearing loss is caused by damage to the middle ear or conductive system which carries vibrations to the inner ear. People with conductive hearing loss may use bone-conduction hearing aids which contain vibrators anchored against the mastoid bone just behind the ear. The sound vibrations bypass the conductive system and are carried to the inner ear through the bones of the skull.

Single Hearing Aids
A person may experience major hearing impairment in one ear while the other ear is relatively unimpaired. Such a person often uses a hearing aid on the impaired ear to

improve ability to perceive the direction of sound, to help separate desired sounds from unwanted background noise, and generally to enhance listening pleasure. Often people with impairment in both ears wear only one hearing aid because of the cost or just because of personal preference. There is, however, a steady trend toward binaural fitting of hearing aids, that is, on both ears.

CROS Aids

Another adaptation sometimes used for a person with a good ear and a very impaired ear is a hearing aid which sends the sound that arrives at the poor ear to the good ear, which hears the sound normally. This type of hearing aid is called a CROS aid, an acronym for Contralateral Routing of Signal. A BICROS aid is used when both ears are impaired but one is much better than the other. Signals arriving at both ears are amplified and routed to the better ear.

The overall quality of amplification continues to improve. Such innovations as digital hearing aids and cochlear implants may greatly enhance the ability of even those with severe to profound hearing loss to use auditory information well.

"T" Switch or Telecoil

As mentioned previously, a "T"-switch operates the telecoil, also called the induction coil or induction-pickup coil. This term is used to describe that special feature on a hearing aid which uses the principle of inductive coupling. When the hearing aid is set to "T", the microphone is turned off and the induction coil or telecoil is activated to pick up electromagnetic energy, which the hearing aid then converts back to amplified sound. When the "T"-switch is used on a hearing aid, the user receives only the speech signal from the telephone. The background sounds in the room (acoustic signals not coming from the phone) are no longer amplified. Only telephones that are hearing-aid-compatible are electromagnetic sources and allow the hard-of-hearing person to communicate on the phone. ADA requires all telephones in the United States to be hearing-aid-compatible.

The "T" switch has a number of uses in addition to telephone communication, since it can link the hearing aid to other sources of electromagnetic energy, such as the induction loop system (see description below) and other types of assistive listening devices. When a hearing aid on the "T" setting is used with an induction loop system, only the signals coming from the microphone of the loop will be amplified. The purpose of the "T" switch then is to permit direct communication via the electromagnetic source without interference from other sources.

Direct Audio Input (DAI)

DAI is another recent technology aimed at minimizing the problems of sound distortion and unintelligibility due to distance from the speaker, interfering noises, and/or sound reverberation. A cord attaches to a behind-the-ear hearing aid either by fitting into a specially designed outlet right in the hearing aid or by using a slip-on connector called a "shoe." On the other end of the cord is a "jack," or plug, to connect to any type of electromechanical sound source, such as television, FM and AM radios, tape recorders, hand-held or table microphones, and FM Assistive Listening Devices. Because the hearing aid is now directly connected to any of those sound sources, the background noises which so often plague hearing-impaired people are greatly reduced. Small group conversations offer an ideal situation for using a small microphone for DAI. Its usefulness increases as the environment becomes noisier, such as in a car, or at a restaurant or party. Hand-held microphones are best for events requiring mobility; table microphones are good for meetings or conferences.

ASSISTIVE LISTENING SYSTEMS (ALSs)

Increasingly, houses of worship, theaters, meeting rooms, and other public areas throughout the country are being equipped with ALSs to help hearing-impaired persons. Passage of the *Americans With Disabilities Act of 1990* should accelerate this process.

Of more than 23 million hearing-impaired persons in the United States, close to seven million are severely hearing-impaired. They have difficulty understanding speech even with powerful hearing aids. Another two million are deaf and unable to understand speech through the auditory mode. In large room settings, hearing aid users have great difficulty hearing speakers since the aid not only amplifies the desired sound but also magnifies other sounds in the room. People with hearing impairments who do not use hearing aids often can understand the speech of people near them in a quiet room, but cannot follow spoken information in larger, noisier environments. Help can be provided through assistive listening systems which pick up speech at or close to its source, amplify it, and deliver it to the listener's ear without extraneous sound, reverberation and distortion.

Four Types of Systems

There are four types of assistive listening systems that designers and managers of meeting rooms, auditoriums, and other large environments might consider. These four ALSs accept input from existing public address systems, thereby reducing cost. However, the type of microphone and its placement at the sound source is crucial for the ALS to be effective. For example, one might use a condenser microphone 3 to 6 inches below the speaker's chin, permitting speech-reading. A variety of listening attachments (inductive telecoil couplers called neckloops, and the typical earbud or headphone type accessories) permit users of telecoil-equipped hearing aids to join others in understanding speech better with the use of an ALS.

Induction Loops (Sometimes Called "Audio" Loops)
The induction loop is simply a loop of wire which encircles the area to be served (i.e., a room, a portion of a room, or even a single chair). It can be on the floor, in the

ceiling, or embedded in the walls. The two ends of the wire are connected to an amplifier into which the sound signal is fed. The current in the loop creates an electro-magnetic field that varies in strength and frequency with the sound signal. Users sit insider the loop (and the electromagnetic field), turn their hearing aids to the "T" setting (telecoil), and set the sound to a comfortable level. This results in the sound signal moving from its source to the listener's ear without traveling through space, thus eliminating most background noise.

Radio Frequency Systems

Radio frequently systems are of two basic types, AM (Amplitude Modulated) and FM (Frequency Modulated). The difference in performance of the two radio systems is identical to the difference between AM and FM broadcasting. The AM systems typi-cally operate at low frequencies, those of the AM radio broadcast band (550 to 1600 kHz) or below. FM systems operate at higher frequencies, either the 72 to 76 MHz band or in the FM broadcast band between 88 and 108 MHz.

AM Systems

A transmitter is attached to the public address system and the sound signal is broad-cast on a preselected frequency. The listener may receive the signal via an AM radio and headset tuned to the proper frequency or via special receivers with earphones. AM systems have relatively poor sound quality. They are subject to the same sources of interference that often disrupt AM stations, and they do not perform well in build-ings with a substantial amount of structural metal. They are inexpensive and useful under certain circumstances.

FM Systems

A 1982 rule change by the Federal Communications Commission (FCC) authorized the use of FM technology in the 72 to 76 MHz band for helping hearing-impaired people. Before 1982, that band was open only for use in educational institutions for deaf people. FM technology permits the use of circuitry which eliminates the interfer-ence effects of thunderstorms and electrical apparati. The 1982 FCC regulations al-low the use of higher field strength for FM systems than for AM systems.

FM is the most versatile of all ALSs and has excellent sound quality. Transmit-ters can be either hooked up to the public address system or used alone. Personal FM transmitters can be taken anywhere easily. The portable transmitter and the receivers are about the size of a pack of cigarettes. Hearing aid users with "T" switches can use a neck loop with the portable receivers while people without "T" switches have to use ear phones.

Infrared Systems

An infrared listening system takes an auditory signal directly from a source, converts it into a modulated infrared light signal, and transmits it throughout a room. This signal is then picked up by an infrared receiver, which converts the signal back into an auditory signal. The sound is of extremely good quality. Users can choose their own settings. The system is easy to operate and is not subject to electrical interference, although bright sunlight sometimes affects the signal.

Hardwire Systems

This simply means that each listener's location is directly wired to the source of amplified sound (e.g., a wired telephone jack in pre-selected locations in a place of worship). The user plugs a headphone or earphone into the jack and receives the signal. The term hardwire has been applied retroactively after wireless technologies were developed.

ALSs have already saved many persons their jobs and enhanced the productivity of others. They are an established contribution to increased quality of life for deaf and hard-of-hearing persons.

TIPS FOR HEARING PEOPLE ON COMMUNICATING WITH DEAF AND HARD-OF-HEARING PEOPLE

Although technological devices such as those discussed above can greatly aid the communication process, appropriate techniques used by those attempting to communicate with deaf and hard-of-hearing people are also critical. Many professionals, as well as the citizen on the street, are unaware of the right techniques to maximize the opportunity for deaf and hard-of-hearing individuals to understand. The following suggestions come from the authors' own experiences as hearing-impaired individuals and from many years of experience working to facilitate communication between those with normal hearing and deaf and hard-of-hearing individuals.

Setting the Stage

Face Your Audience Directly

Always look at the deaf or hard-of-hearing person. Never talk from behind the person's back or from another room, or turn your face away while speaking. If talking with several people, face the deaf or hard-of-hearing persons. They have to see you to understand you, while hearing people do not need this visual input.

Spotlight Your Face (No Backlighting)

Face a window or a lamp so the light falls on your face to help the deaf or hard-of-hearing see your mouth as you speak. Move around to find the best lighting. If the location is very dark (for example, a car at night), postpone substantive conversation for a better place, or use a small penlight to light your face.

Rephrase if You Are Not Understood
If the deaf or hard-of-hearing person is still stuck after you have repeated, try saying the same thing in different words. If that doesn't work, write key words on a notepad.

Use Facial Expressions and Gestures
Smiles, frowns, head shakes, and hand signals are great helps in following the gist of the conversation.

Give Clues when Changing Subjects
Deaf and hard-of-hearing people get lost if you change the subject without warning. Help out by saying something like "Now I want to talk about a new subject" so they can get ready for a new situational vocabulary.

Avoid Noisy Backgrounds
Noise is a great hazard for deaf or hard-of-hearing persons, as it may block out all conversational sounds. What may be merely bothersome to you can bring physical pain when the noise is amplified by a hearing aid. So check the immediate surroundings before you start to talk. Turn off the TV, radio, garbage disposal, or vacuum, move away from a rattling air conditioner or humming equipment, and don't try to talk above the traffic noises on a busy street.

Establishing Empathy

Be Patient if Responses Seem Slow
Sounds come in blurts and blops for deaf or hard-of-hearing people with many gaps. The response of a deaf or hard-of-hearing person is slowed as a result of desperately trying to fill in those gaps and make sense of what you said. Understand this process and allow the necessary time. Also realize that the intense concentration needed to follow a conversation is extremely fatiguing. If the person seems tired, consider postponing your talk until a later time.

Stay Positive and Relaxed
If you become irritated and annoyed, your speech will deteriorate, making communication even worse.

Talk **TO** Deaf and Hard-of-Hearing Persons, not **ABOUT** Them
As one person put it, "only my ears are broken; everything else works." Be courteous in addressing individuals with hearing impairments as **PERSONS**, not as inanimate objects to talk about.

Offer Respect to Help Build Confidence
Encouragement and positive reinforcement can be of enormous benefit to deaf and hard-of-hearing persons facing the confidence-shaking strain of trying to function in the hearing world.

Get the Deaf or Hard-of-Hearing Person's Attention First
Be sure the deaf or hard-of-hearing person is aware of you before you start talking. Move around in front of the person; gently touch him or her; flick a light switch or a window shade. Note that the person is doing, so you won't cause an accident by startling him or her.

Ask how You Can Facilitate Communication
Often the deaf or hard-of-hearing person will suggest ways to improve communication, such as speaking to a better ear or moving to better light. Urge the individual to guide you.

Projecting Your Communication

Don't Shout
Shouting only makes things worse. It distorts your face and mouth so that speech-reading is impossible. Shouting causes a hearing aid to distort sound.

Speak Clearly and at a Moderate Pace
Speak more slowly and pause occasionally to let the listen keep up with you. Don't mumble. Instead, try to enunciate carefully, and clearly, using your lips. It is important not to "mouth" or speak with exaggerated expressions, as this just makes your speech harder to follow.

Don't Hide Your Mouth, Chew Food,
Chew Gum, or Smoke while Talking
All of these garble your speech and make it harder for the deaf or hard-of-hearing person to understand. Mustaches and beards are added hazards; a shorter trim might be worth considering if your conversations with a deaf or hard-of-hearing person are frequent.

OTHER TECHNOLOGICAL DEVICES

Computers

Few groups of people can benefit more from recent advances in personal computer technology than those who are deaf or hard-of-hearing. Problems that arise from "miscommunication" are basically due to a lack of information available to the deaf or hard-of-hearing person, and the personal computer provides information visually. Even a relatively inexpensive microcomputer package with a modem can do everything a TTY can, but faster and with more precision. By linking a personal computer to national telecommunication services, such as CompuServe or GEnie, a deaf or hard-of-hearing person can communicate with people literally all over the world—and on equal terms. Thus a PC can provide what is likely the only set of circumstances in which hearing loss is inconsequential. By using one of the several national electronic mail networks, a deaf or hard-of-hearing person can type a message and get an immediate reply from someone who has a PC, or can have the message delivered within hours to those who do not have computers. The vast array of informational sources (from stock reports or analysis to airline schedules) accessible with a microcomputer makes the potential for improving communication capabilities of deaf or hard-of-hearing people almost limitless. The recent emergence of "work at home" businesses, usually computer-dependent, provides a breadth of vocational opportunities for deaf or hard-of-hearing people that would have seemed impossible a few years ago.

Closed Captioning

In 1976, the FCC set aside line 21 of the television signal to be used for services to people who are deaf or hard-of-hearing. Closed captioning is the chief service. In its first five years, "closed captioning" was limited to previously taped programs. Scripts of those, including some movies, were encoded at the caption centers in advance for airing when the program was scheduled for telecast. That technique worked fine for prerecorded programs, but in 1984, computer technology, teamed with personal input of highly trained court stenographers, produced a major breakthrough. "Real-time" captioning began to bring deaf or hard-of-hearing viewers instant captions for live broadcasts.

Closed captioning is a process by which the audio portion of a television program is translated into captions (subtitles) which appear on the screen. The size of the captions vary proportionately with the size of the TV screen. On a 19-inch television screen, for instance, they are ½ inch high. The captions are easily visible—white letters against a black background, usually located at the bottom of the screen, but sometimes appearing in other locations to identify the speaker or to avoid blocking any on-screen action—they do not obstruct relevant parts of the picture. Dialogue, narration, and even the sound effects of today's best TV shows are printed so that deaf or hard-of-hearing viewers can read what they cannot hear. Because some viewers who are not deaf or hard-of-hearing find ordinary subtitles, called "open captions," distracting, special equipment, i.e., TeleCaption Adapters (decoders), are required to receive captioning. Legislation passed in 1990 by Congress required, by July 1, 1993, that all manufacturers place the necessary microchip circuitry in all television sets with larger than 13-inch screens, circuitry activated by simply turning a switch for captioning.

Alarms and Alerting Devices

For protection of the deaf or hard-of-hearing person, there are smoke, fire, and gas alarms. Vibrator or flashing devices help awaken those who cannot hear auditory alarms. A whole range of devices is available to assist in knowing when a doorbell rings (or a knock on the door occurs), the timer on the oven goes off, a car turn signal remains on, a baby cries, etc. At home or on the job, deaf people who cannot hear the phone ring can be assisted with a flashing light to attract their attention.

Devices in development include radio frequency systems in which a small receiver, the size of a pack of cigarettes, is worn in the shirt pocket and vibrates with the sound of the telephone, the doorbell, the fire alarm, the alarm clock, etc. The receiver responds instantaneously, and thus the sounds are identified by the length of the vibration. For instance, when the phone rings, the receiver will produce vibration, pause, vibration, pause, vibration, etc., easily identifying the telephone ringing. The device has no wires, no buttons, and no indicators to read, but a secure on-off switch. The receiver works throughout the house and at a short distance away from the house. It is a micropower device which will operate continuously for over a month from a single cell AA battery.

Examples of Usage

The following two examples illustrate how people can benefit from assistive devices and assistive listening systems:

Bob

Bob is a middle level employee in a large manufacturing company. His hearing continued to decline to the point where he had great difficulty on the phone, at staff meetings, and even in conversation with his co-workers. He spent considerable time with his audiologist to make sure he had the right type of hearing aid and one with a good "T" switch. He was determined to keep his job as well as to continue a well-established pattern of upward mobility. He was regarded as an excellent employee with a good future.

Bob knew that a hearing aid does not necessarily solve a person's communication problems, so he explained his problem to senior management and to his co-workers. He gave them tips on how best to communicate with him. His employers agreed to equip Bob's telephone with a flashing light to attract his attention when it rings and with an amplifier to boost the sound volume to augment Bob's hearing aids (another employee uses a TTY). Sometimes Bob uses his computer's electronic mail capability as a substitute for the telephone. He can use this for intraoffice communication as well as for contact with other company personnel in offices across the country.

Bob is sometimes required to attend meetings in locations outside his company's office. Some of these companies have installed assistive listening systems in their meeting rooms. If the system is an induction loop, Bob just flips on the "T" switch in his hearing aid and he is in business. If there is no system installed, Bob carries with him a personal FM system which permits him to function in large group meetings. He places his microphone near the speaker, turns on his FM receiver, and functions very well in those circumstances.

During informal conversations at the coffee stand, Bob uses a small directional microphone attached to his hearing aid by a long cord. He holds the microphone close to the speaker's mouth and the voice overrides the background noise. This enables Bob to stay active in the social life of his office.

Use of all the devices needed in his particular circumstances has permitted Bob to continue his work with the company of his choice and to retain a realistic expectation of advancement in that company. He illustrates how one can cope with a limiting condition in a very positive way.

Alice

Alice is an older person who lives alone. When she didn't answer her phone, her daughter sometimes left work to visit Alice personally to make sure she was all right. This situation was frustrating for both of them. They discussed the problem, visited an audiologist, purchase two hearing aids for Alice and began to search for other assistive devices to help maintain Alice's independent lifestyle.

Today, Alice has a flashing light to alert her to the doorbell or knock, the telephone ring, the smoke alarm, and the timer on her oven. She watches closed captioned television when she wants to reduce the fatigue caused by straining to hear, and she uses an infrared device on her television when she feels good and is interested in hearing the voices of characters in her favorite soaps.

She can still function on the phone with a good "T" switch on her hearing aid and use of an amplifier. Her home environment is quiet and conducive to good communication with her occasional visitor. She feels confident and secure with her capabilities restored through use of assistive devices and her hearing aid. Her daughter no longer needs to leave work to see if Alice is all right, because now she answers her phone.

There are many success stories regarding the use of assistive devices to bridge gaps between deaf and hard-of-hearing and hearing persons. Technology is very helpful but does not represent "the answer" for everyone. There are a number of reasons why some persons cannot benefit from amplification. These include poor speech discrimination, physical inability to place something in the ear, and low tolerance for amplified sound. Sign language can simplify communication for deaf and severely hard-of-hearing people. The following section will focus on all aspects of specialized language support.

USE OF INTERPRETING SERVICES

Interpreters have traditionally worked in a variety of settings, including post-secondary educational programs, rehabilitation services, and community-based activities. Just recently, we are seeing an emerging need for interpreting support for deaf or hard-of-hearing people in their workplaces in a broad range of settings in business, industry, government, education, and social services. The remainder of this chapter will focus upon different interpreting processes and how they can be most effectively utilized.

Terminology

The following is a brief discussion of three basic processes in interpreting which should clarify the role of an interpreter and introduce suggested guidelines for effective interpreting processes (Hurwitz & Witter, 1979).

Transliterating

In transliterating, an interpreter presents the spoken and signed/fingerspelled, word-for-word representations of a speaker's actual message. The exact wording may be changed so that it can be conceptually comprehended by the deaf or hard-of-hearing person. For example, if a teacher or a counselor says "I am <u>running</u> this meeting and I will ask my aide to <u>run</u> to the canteen and buy me a cup of coffee," a transliteration may be "I am controlling this meeting and I will ask my aide to go quickly to the canteen and buy me a cup of coffee."

Interpreting

From Spoken Text to Communication Mode Used by a Deaf Person.   In interpreting, an interpreter presents the spoken text in the communication mode used by the deaf or hard-of-hearing individual. This often includes American Sign Language (ASL) or a form of Pidgin Signed English (see Chapter 2). This process requires a familiarity with the content material, a diversity of language skills, and a knowledge of the attributes of mouthing words to enhance lipreading in a combined or oral interpreting situation.

From a Deaf Person's Message to Spoken English.   The interpreter repeats in spoken English the signed and/or spoken message of a deaf person. This is done when some other hearing person cannot understand the signs or speech of the deaf or hard-of-hearing person.

The Interpreting Process

An interpreter is a facilitator of communication between a deaf or hard-of-hearing person and a hearing person. An interpreter conveys the spoken message of a hearing person through the use of sign language and/or lip movements and conveys in voice the message of the hearing-impaired person. The interpreter conveys the message between the individuals but does not enter the dialogue as a contributing member of the communication.

Three individuals are involved in a successful communication event: the hearing person, the deaf or hard-of-hearing person, and the interpreter. A clear delineation and understanding of each of their respective roles, responsibilities, and rights will facilitate successful communication. Interpreting services are appropriate in a setting when a person is unable to participate fully due to communication barriers (the inability to receive spoken communication and/or express oneself intelligibly through speech).

Sign Language Interpreting

A sign language interpreter facilitates communication through the use of sign language and non-vocalized lip movements when interpreting a spoken message from other hearing individuals. There are several sign language systems which may be utilized by the sign language interpreter depending on the communication needs of the deaf or hard-of-hearing person. These sign language systems include American

Sign Language (ASL), Signed English, and Manually Coded English (Caccamise & Newell, 1987). Some deaf or hard-of-hearing persons who use sign language may prefer the use of Signed English or Manually Coded English with non-vocalized lip movements since these systems represent the spoken language in English. However, American Sign Language may be the preferred mode of communication for other individuals. Approximately 2,000 sign language interpreters are certified by the National Registry of Interpreters for the Deaf; other interpreters may have received provisional certification through other screening processes, e.g., staff-level quality assurance screening tests which are used by hiring agencies.

Oral Interpreting

An oral interpreter facilitates communication through the use of non-vocalized lip movements. The oral interpreter will rephrase or add a word or phrase to give better visibility of the spoken words on the lips. Skilled use of body language and gestures is an important part of effective oral interpreting. For the deaf or hard-of-hearing person who depends on speechreading in a setting, the oral interpreter serves an effective role. At times when a hearing person does not speak directly to a deaf or hard-of-hearing person (e.g., turns to the blackboard, gets distracted, or talks to other people during a group discussion), the speaker may not be in a position for the deaf or hard-of-hearing person to speechread effectively (Northcott, 1984).

The Role of the Interpreter

The interpreter's primary role is to be a facilitator of communication in the rehabilitation setting or in a workplace. The interpreter should interpret all communication from a deaf or hard-of-hearing person to a hearing person(s) and vice versa. Depending on the deaf or hard-of-hearing person's needs, the interpreter may also interpret comments, reports, and verbal responses of the deaf or hard-of-hearing person to other members of the workplace or rehabilitation team.

The interpreter should not encourage the deaf or hard-of-hearing person to depend too much on interpreters beyond their role in the facilitation of communication. As part of the general function of encouraging increased independence on the part of the deaf or hard-of-hearing person, the interpreter can be indirectly training the deaf or hard-of-hearing person to use an interpreter appropriately and effectively. Additionally, the deaf or hard-of-hearing person could be provided formal training to learn his or her role and responsibility in the use of an interpreter. This training may be achieved in various ways, including individualized packaged tapes and manuals, role-plays, and discussion.

The interpreter as a member of the rehabilitation team can serve an important role in the development and implementation of communication aspects of the deaf or hard-of-hearing person's Individualized Written Rehabilitation Plan (IWRP). The interpreter very often possesses a working knowledge of the client's ability to communicate in a regular rehabilitation setting or in a workplace. This information which the interpreter has acquired can assist the client's counselors and other key persons as they design and implement an appropriate rehabilitation program. The IWRP should include an indication of the desire mode of the communication for rehabilitation interpreting, that is, whether the interpreter should use American Sign Language, Manually Coded English, or Signed English, or even oral interpreting.

Dual Role Assignments and Job Descriptions

There are times when a rehabilitation agency cannot employ an interpreter on a full-time basis solely as an interpreter and may wish to assign additional responsibilities to the interpreter. This creates a dual role situation, i.e., Interpreter/Counselor, Interpreter/Social Worker, Interpreter/Tutor, Interpreter/Aide, Interpreter/Sign Language Instructor, etc. Although this type of dual role employment is generally discouraged by the interpreting profession, the reality of the situation often dictates the necessity.

If a dual role position is created it must be clearly understood by the interpreter and others involved on the team what the responsibilities of the interpreter include. The additional responsibilities should be clearly defined in the job description. It is also advisable to delineate percentages of time the interpreter will spend in each responsibility. Naturally, the interpreter must also possess the necessary qualifications for the additional responsibilities.

Each rehabilitation agency will need to develop the job description in relation to their format and requirements. However, the following sample job description is listed here to provide guidance.

Recommended Job Description for an Interpreter in a Rehabilitation Setting

General Responsibility
The interpreter serves as a member of the rehabilitation team for deaf or hard-of-hearing clients. The interpreter's main responsibility is to serve as a facilitator of communication between the deaf or hard-of-hearing client(s) and hearing individuals (i.e., counseling staff, other members of the team).

Specific Responsibilities
The interpreter functions as a member of the rehabilitation team by:

1. transliterating and/or interpreting in rehabilitation or workplace setting, as assigned;
2. transliterating and/or interpreting for other related activities, conferences, telephone calls, workshops, as assigned;
3. completing paperwork as it relates to the interpreting tasks;
4. preparing for interpreting assignments by reviewing content area, lesson plans, outlines, etc. (may need to get books related to the content area);

5. establishing physical setting in conjunction with the counselor or rehabilitation educator to optimize communication interaction;
6. meeting with counselor or a group leader on a regular basis in regard to communication needs of the clients;
7. providing information to the counselor or a group leader, clients (particularly deaf or hard-of-hearing clients), and other staff, on how to maximize benefit from interpreting services;
8. serving as a member of the IWRP team as it relates to the communication needs of the deaf or hard-of-hearing client;
9. acting as a resource person for others about interpreting;
10. participating in professional improvement activities;
11. interpreting for additional activities related to the rehabilitation process when possible.

Locating and Paying Interpreters

Generally, a vocational rehabilitation office which does not have a staff of interpreters may contact a nearby interpreter referral service agency to contract interpreting services. Deaf or hard-of-hearing persons may also obtain interpreting services by contacting the interpreter referral service agency through a TTY.

Since interpreting in the rehabilitation field is an emerging field, fee schedules for freelance interpreters have not been standardized across the nation. Normally, there is a fee for a minimum of two hours and a fee for each additional hour of service. There are variations in cost of living across the nation which impact the fee structure for freelance interpreters.

In situations where a rehabilitation agency is able to create a staff position for an interpreter, a salary guide for staff interpreters must be established within a specific district in an effort to remain in the competitive market for interpreters. The package for a staff interpreter should include a full compensation package, i.e., attractive salary and fringe benefits. The rehabilitation agency must also take into consideration the requirements for supervision and support for professional growth and development of staff interpreters.

The rehabilitation agency should hire interpreters certified by the Registry of Interpreters for the Deaf (RID), or by a quality assurance screening test procedure. The RID organization has a National Evaluation system for sign language interpreters. The evaluation is knowledge and performance-based and evaluates various modes of communication. Interpreters meeting minimal national standards are awarded a certificate based on their knowledge, skills, and attitude. Interpreters possessing different levels of certificates may be qualified to work in the rehabilitation setting, depending on clientele needs.

In recent years, programs have been established in colleges and universities to train interpreters. These programs may offer associate degrees or baccalaureate degrees in interpreting. The interpreter graduating from one of these programs has received specialized training and should offer more to a rehabilitation system as to background and knowledge as compared to a generic interpreter without any formal training. Such training often leads to a success in obtaining certification by RID or other quality assurance screening test procedures.

Guidelines in the Use of Interpreters in a Counseling Situation

The Role of the Interpreter
During a counseling session, the interpreter should stand or sit a few feet from the counselor and as close to the main object of discussion (e.g., chalkboard) as possible. The deaf or hard-of-hearing person should sit where he or she has access to the line of view of the speaker, the interpreter, and the object of discussion. Should the deaf or hard-of-hearing audience in a counseling session or a group discussion be too large for everyone to view from their areas comfortably, it is suggested that the group be broken into smaller groups, if possible.

In practice, the interpreter transliterates or interprets everything the counselor says, as well as questions and discussion from others in the audience. This is done through the use of a combination of sign language, fingerspelling, clear mouth movement (without voice), good facial and eye expressions, and body language. Should a deaf or hard-of-hearing client wish to ask a question or participate in the discussion and require assistance, the interpreter will voice-interpret the deaf or hard-of-hearing person's signed and/or spoken message into spoken English.

Regardless of the method of facilitation that the interpreter uses, it is not the role of the interpreter to replace the counselor or assume responsibility for a deaf or hard-of-hearing person's actions in the counseling session. The counselor is responsible for coordinating his or her presentation and should view the interpreter as a support for their communication, rather than as a substitute for it.

The Role of the Counselor
Counselors can assist the interpreter in delivering the best possible message to the deaf or hard-of-hearing person by providing time for the interpreter to assess the deaf or hard-of-hearing person's communication needs. Allowing time for some interaction between the interpreter and deaf or hard-of-hearing client will make the interpreter more effective in facilitating the communication process and thus enhancing the deaf or hard-of-hearing person's full participation in the meeting. Counselors can enhance their effectiveness in presenting to a deaf or hard-of-hearing person and the effectiveness of the interpreter by the following:

1. taking the time in the beginning to discuss with the interpreter and deaf or hard-of-hearing individual the role of the interpreter in the counseling session;
2. informing the interpreter of the format of the presentation, including any media to be used;

3. minimizing movement while presenting information to the deaf or hard-of-hearing person;
4. being sensitive to the "lag time" that occurs between the utterance by a presenter and the delivery of the message to the deaf or hard-of-hearing person through the interpreter;
5. providing periodic checks to make certain the deaf or hard-of-hearing person understands the presentation.

It is critically important for the counselor to understand how the interpreting process works and to cooperate with the interpreter in making sure that all deaf or hard-of-hearing persons receive and understand the essence of all communication occurring during the presentation. The following guidelines may help the counselor to interact effectively through an interpreter:

1. Do not speak too rapidly.
2. Avoid the use of colloquial expressions or idioms. Many deaf or hard-of-hearing people are unfamiliar with English idioms, and even if they understand their meaning, idioms are often difficult to lipread or translate into sign language.
3. Be careful when using jargon of technical terminology which may be unfamiliar to the interpreter or deaf or hard-of-hearing person. It would be helpful to provide a listing of these terms to the interpreter before the counseling session begins, so that the interpreter can be prepared with appropriate signs.
4. In groups, control the discussion so that only one person is talking at a time, and request those who want to speak to raise their hands and wait to be recognized by the counselor. This will enable the interpreter to finish the interpretation process and allow a deaf or hard-of-hearing person to have the same opportunity as hearing counterparts to participate in a group discussion.

Effective Use of Interpreters in Meetings

The guidelines for the effective use of interpreters in meetings in Table 11–1 were developed by the faculty and staff at the National Technical Institute for the Deaf (Lang, Basile, Cassell, Maruggi, Nace, & Holcomb, 1984). Careful consideration of these guidelines should maximize the effective use of interpreters in this type of situation.

Lighting

An interpreter should be consulted about the need to provide adequate lighting during the interpreting process. Interpreting situations which normally require additional lighting include:

1. interpreting for movies and other media presentations;
2. film and television interpreting in studios;
3. stage interpreting.

TABLE 11-1 **Guidelines for Effective Use of Interpreters in Meetings**

A. Requesting Interpreters

DO'S	DONT'S
1. Clarify the kind of interpreter needed (oral, manual, voice).	1. Assume that it won't make any difference.
2. Provide accurate and complete information about your interpreter needs.	2. Assume that detailed explanation is not needed until prior to the event.
3. Share outline of meeting with interpreter and scheduler of the interpreter referral agency.	3. Assume the content and meeting procedures won't make any difference.
4. Request an interpreter one or more weeks in advance (minimum—3 days).	4. Wait until the last minute.

B. Using Interpreters

DO'S	DONT'S
1. Arrange seating with maximum visibility between interpreter and consumers.	1. Assume participants needing interpreting services will avoid visual barriers.
2. Arrange meeting with interpreters and consumers to clarify needs.	2. Assume interpreters will automatically know what to do.
3. Maintain control as moderator.	3. Consider interpreter as a meeting moderator.
4. Encourage signers to wait for interpreters to finish before signing themselves.	4. Assume this will happen automatically.
5. Introduce interpreter and where he or she will be located.	5. Assume the participants already know them and where they are seated.
6. Enunciate formal names and places and technical terms slowly and clearly.	6. Assume interpreter is familiar with new names.
7. Read slowly.	7. Assume interpreter can keep up with fast reading.
8. Give time for deaf people to receive and process questions.	8. Assume deaf people will not participate.
9. Stop punctually.	9. Assume interpreter can stay overtime.
10. Ask for repetition when message seems unclear.	10. Assume the signer is one who is unclear.
11. Provide informal and/or formal feedback to the interpreter.	11. Assume the interpreter or the interpreter service is not interested.

Adapted from Lang, 1984

In such settings, interpreters will advise ways to ensure that sufficient lighting is available. There may be too much or too little light, distracting shadows, or too much light behind the interpreter. There are three basic lighting factors which are important for an "ideal" interpreting situation: directionality, intensity, and portability/adjustability (Siple, Cole, Steve, Litchy, Shepard, Voekl, & Hollenbeck, 1981).

A directional light source uses a reflector to focus light in a single direction.

Many lights recessed into walls and ceilings are directional lights; most household lamps are not. Lights used by interpreters should be capable of being directed in a way to optimize the deaf or hard-of-hearing person's view of the interpreter.

A light is of little help if it is not strong enough, and too strong light can cause unwanted shadows. Intensity of lighting can be adjusted by varying the distance between the light source and the illuminated object. Some lights also have variable intensity settings. An optimal lighting source for interpreting should allow adjustment of intensity for the particular situation.

Lights that are portable and adjustable allow flexibility. Because interpreting setups are usually temporary, a lightweight unit which can be easily moved is preferable. One should inform an interpreter in advance if a dark room will be used to show a movie. The interpreter can then advise one how to obtain an appropriate lighting unit for the setting.

The Interpreter and Inservice Training

Most supervisors or co-workers and many rehabilitation counselors and other key persons in the rehabilitation setting may have had no experience working with an interpreter. They are generally unfamiliar with how the interpreter can assist them as they work with deaf or hard-of-hearing clients. Sometimes, these individuals may feel threatened by the presence of another adult in the room. Often they may expect too much or too little from the interpreter. There may be a tendency to add inappropriate functions to the interpreter's role. A formal inservice training for supervisors and employees would provide information about interpreting and assist the interpreter and supervisor or group leader in establishing an effective and productive relationship.

During inservice training, individuals in the setting who have had no previous experience or contact with an interpreter will be curious about why the interpreter is in the room. The group leader and the interpreter will need to make preparations to explain about deaf culture or deaf issues and the role of the interpreter. Some workplaces may invite a deaf or hard-of-hearing adult skilled in the use of an interpreter to speak to the supervisor(s) and co-worker(s) about sign language and interpreting. This activity should be followed up and reinforced when a formal meeting takes place, and other individuals in the meeting should be encouraged to ask any questions they have about this arrangement.

At the workplace or in a rehabilitation setting, the supervisor of the counselor may include time for the interpreter or the deaf or hard-of-hearing person to provide informal sign language instruction. The interpreter's, or the deaf or hard-of-hearing person's, responsibilities for sign language instruction, if any, should be clearly outlined in his or her job descriptions.

Personnel's Use of Interpreters

Since the interpreter has not been hired as a supervisor or a counselor, it is not the responsibility of the interpreter to assume any of the responsibilities to execute a diagnosis and evaluation, assist in doing IWRP paperwork, determine and/or modify a rehabilitation plan, or counsel or advise a client. The interpreter may not make any rehabilitation decisions in lieu of the counselor, respond for the client, or respond for the counselor. If the interpreter is doing things other than interpreting, that person should not be labeled as an interpreter and the job description should clearly outline the job responsibilities of the individual.

As with any other professional, the interpreter requires ongoing training and continual upgrading. By participating in professional organizations such as the RID, the interpreter will have the opportunity to meet regularly with other interpreters to share information and stay current on professional events. Those interpreters certified by the RID are guided by a Code of Ethics (RID, 1979; see Appendix 11.1). Interpreters working in a rehabilitation setting or in a workplace setting will find this Code of Ethics helpful in determining appropriate courses of action.

In a rehabilitation setting which operates a special unit for deaf or hard-of-hearing clients, the interpreter will generally report to the coordinator of services for deaf or hard-of-hearing clients or that person's designee. The coordinator usually is responsible for hiring, evaluations, and any other administrative or supervisory responsibilities, as dictated by the rehabilitation agency. The coordinator should make sure the procedures are in place to provide both counselors and interpreters the opportunity to resolve role conflicts or other problems which might arise. In this setting, it is the responsibility of the coordinator to develop and clarify the communication philosophy of the program and to help the interpreter develop the skills necessary to function consistently with program goals.

In rehabilitation agencies with no on-site services for deaf or hard-of-hearing clients, the agency administrator becomes the interpreter's immediate supervisor. As such, the supervisor must develop procedures to guarantee that the interpreter is hired and evaluated by a qualified person. The supervisor will also need to develop procedures to cover interpreters' illnesses and resolution of counselor/interpreter role conflict. It will probably be necessary to seek assistance form outside the agency. Regional or state programs serving deaf or hard-of-hearing students and the local chapter of the RID will provide assistance to rehabilitation agencies. In some states, a Commission for the Deaf or an Office of Deafness may be able to assist rehabilitation agencies in this area.

When developing an interpreter's schedule, it is important to remember that interpreting is physically exhausting. It is wise to arrange the interpreter's schedule so that lecture and non-lecture settings are mixed whenever possible. The interpreter should not be completely scheduled from early morning to late afternoon. Periodic breaks need to be arranged throughout the day to maintain maximum efficiency.

Issues which need to be addressed by a rehabilitation agency which is involved in a decision to provide an interpreting service to a deaf or hard-of-hearing person are multi-faceted. For instance, many agencies are not aware of the costs involved in hiring an interpreter and are often unprepared to cover the expenses from their budget. Careful planning is required in advance to build into their operating budget costs for interpreting services. The fee schedule utilized by agencies for payment of interpreters for clientele service should be competitive with the current market rate for interpreters in other non-rehabilitation settings (Hurwitz, 1986a).

There is a critical shortage of qualified interpreters to meet the growing demand in many area, including rural areas and other areas where interpreter training programs are lacking (Hurwitz, 1986a). There continues to be a prevailing concern about the scarcity of qualified interpreters to work with deaf and hard-of-hearing clients in vocational rehabilitation related programs and services. The fee structure for interpreters working with deaf and hard-of-hearing clients is often noncompetitive with the existing market for freelance interpreters. There is a need to develop policies, procedures, strategies, and materials for the evaluation and employment of non-certified interpreters, which should help these interpreters to identify their specific needs for interpreter skill development, and eventual certification (Hurwitz, 1991).

A study conducted by Joyce and Mathay (1986) revealed that a significant number of cases which were unsuccessful case closures were largely attributed to the lack of counselor's skills to communicate effectively in sign language with their deaf and hard-of-hearing clients, particularly those who are low achieving and do not possess adequate communication and language skills to be able to use an interpreter in the rehabilitation process. The result of the study has profound implications on the qualifications of counselors and interpreters who work with special populations of deaf and hard-of-hearing adults.

There must be a viable mechanism in which deaf and hard-of-hearing people, interpreters, and consumers (e.g., rehabilitation agencies) can work together to address a realm of issues related to recruiting, training, employing, supervising, evaluating, and certifying interpreters. As previously mentioned, job titles, job descriptions, roles, and responsibilities of interpreters must be spelled out clearly so that hiring agencies who do not understand the nature and purpose of interpreting will not unnecessarily abuse the interpreter's role. Those who supervise interpreters must be both knowledgeable about interpreting and be qualified to handle this function of supervision.

Recently the critical issue of overuse syndrome (carpal tunnel syndrome, tendonitis, bursitis, burnout, etc.) has drawn much attention. This problem seems to be increasing in the United States. For instance, the National Technical Institute for the Deaf spent approximately $60,000 in one year for Worker's Compensation related to the disabilities of interpreters, primarily as a result of the overuse syndrome. We must find a way to take care of our interpreters. Many qualified interpreters are leaving the field of interpreting because of this problem.

The Commission on Education of the Deaf (Bowe, 1988) has identified a problem with standards never having been established for training and certifying interpreters working in rehabilitation settings. Part of the problem is that Section 315 of the Rehabilitation Act of 1973, amended in 1978, has never been funded to support this need. This funding is necessary to implement Section 504 and the recently passed Americans with Disabilities Act (see Chapter 10) which require that all recipients of federal funding provide reasonable accommodation to disabled persons in post-secondary, rehabilitation, mental health, medical, and work settings.

Finally, but not least important, there is a problem with effective voice interpreting for deaf or hard-of-hearing people. Hurwitz (1986b) demonstrated that interpreters, regardless of their training and experience, have considerable difficulty voice interpreting for deaf or hard-of-hearing people in American Sign Language and, even, in some version of Manually Coded English. This has serious implications for a deaf or hard-of-hearing person who has a need to participate fully in the rehabilitation process or in a workplace and requires the services of a skilled voice interpreter. Further research work is needed in this area of study. Training deaf or hard-of-hearing people to be effective consumers of interpreting services is one way of alleviating this problem, but at the same time, interpreters will need to find some ways to improve their voice interpreting skills. It has often been said that interpreters would have to be totally immersed in a deaf world in order to be able to acquire, develop, and refine their receptive sign language skills and voice interpreting skills.

CONCLUSIONS

This chapter introduced some basic principles relevant to the use of assistive devices and interpreters in rehabilitation settings or in workplaces. The implications of assistive devices which can be used as an access to the rehabilitation process were discussed. The roles of the interpreter, the counselor, and the deaf or hard-of-hearing person were delineated. For many people, this process is a new one. Appropriate selection of assistive devices and the interpreter, and cooperation among all individuals involved in the interpreting process will ensure the smooth, productive, and effective implementation of the rehabilitation service.

APPENDIX

Registry of Interpreters for the Deaf, Inc.

The Registry of Interpreters for the Deaf (RID), Inc., refers to individuals who may perform one or more of the following services.

Interpret

Spoken English to American Sign Language
American Sign Language to Spoken English

Transliterate

Spoken English to Manually Coded English/Pidgin Sign English
Manually Coded English/Pidgin Sign English to Spoken English
Spoken English to Non-Audible Spoken English

Gesticulate/Mime, etc.

Spoken English to Gesture, Mime, etc.
Gesture, Mime, etc., to Spoken English

The Registry of Interpreters for the Deaf (RID), Inc., has set forth the following principles of ethical behavior to protect and guide the interpreter/transliterator, the consumers (hearing and deaf or hard-of-hearing), and the profession, as well as to ensure for all, the right to communicate.

This Code of Ethics applies to all members of the RID and all certified non-members.

While these are general guidelines to govern the performance of the interpreter/transliterator generally, it is recognized that there are ever-increasing numbers of highly specialized situations that demand specific explanation. It is envisioned that the RID will issue appropriate guidelines for all of these situations.

Code of Ethics

1.   INTERPRETERS/TRANSLITERATORS SHALL KEEP ALL ASSIGNMENT-RELATED INFORMATION STRICTLY CONFIDENTIAL.

Guidelines

Interpreters/transliterators shall not reveal information about any assignment.

Even seemingly unimportant information could be damaging in the wrong hands. Therefore, to avoid this possibility, interpreters/transliterators must not say anything about an assignment. In cases where meeting or information becomes a matter of public record, interpreters/transliterators shall use discretion in discussing such meetings or information.

If a problem arises between the interpreter/transliterator and any person involved in an assignment, the interpreter/transliterator should first discuss it with the person involved. If no solution can be reached, then both should agree on a third person who could advise them.

When instructing interpreter trainees by the method of sharing actual experiences, the trainers shall not reveal any of the following information: (a) name, sex, age, etc., of the consumer; (b) day of the week, time of the day, time of the year the situation took place; (c) location, including city, state, or agency; (d) other persons involved; and (e) unnecessary specifics about the situation.

It requires only a minimum amount of information to identify the parties involved.

2.   INTERPRETERS/TRANSLITERATORS SHALL RENDER THE MESSAGE FAITHFULLY, ALWAYS CONVEYING THE CONTENT AND SPIRIT OF

THE SPEAKER, USING LANGUAGE MOST READILY UNDERSTOOD
BY THE PERSON(S) WHOM THEY SERVE.

Guidelines

Interpreters/transliterators are not editors and must transmit everything that is said in exactly the way it was intended. This is especially difficult when the interpreter disagrees with what is being said or feels uncomfortable with "how" something is stated. Interpreters/transliterators must remember that they are not responsible for what is said, only for conveying it accurately. If the interpreter's/transliterator's own feelings interfere with rendering the message accurately, he or she shall withdraw from the situation.

While working from spoken English to sign or non-audible spoken English, interpreters/transliterators should communicate in the manner most easily understood or preferred by deaf and hard-of-hearing consumers, be it American Sign Language, Manually Coded English, fingerspelling, paraphrasing in Non-Audible Spoken English, gesturing, drawing, or writing, etc. It is important for interpreters/transliterators and deaf and hard-of-hearing persons to spend some time adjusting to each other's way of communicating prior to the actual assignment. When working from sign to Non-Audible Spoken English, the interpreter/transliterator shall speak the language used by the hearing person in the spoken form, be it English, Spanish, French, etc.

3. INTERPRETERS/TRANSLITERATORS SHALL NOT COUNSEL, ADVISE, OR INTERJECT PERSONAL OPINIONS.

Guidelines

Just as interpreters/transliterators may not omit anything which is said, they may not add anything to the situation, even when they are asked to do so by other parties involved.

An interpreter/transliterator is only present in a given situation because two or more people have difficulty communicating, and thus the interpreter's/transliterator's only function is to facilitate communication. He or she shall not become personally involved because in so doing, he or she accepts some responsibility for the outcome, which does not rightly belong to the interpreter/transliterator.

4. INTERPRETERS/TRANSLITERATORS SHALL ACCEPT ASSIGNMENTS USING DISCRETION WITH REGARD TO SKILL, SETTING, AND THE CONSUMERS INVOLVED.

Guidelines

Interpreters/transliterators shall only accept assignments for which they are qualified. However, when an interpreter/transliterator does not possess the necessary skills for a particular assignment, this situation should be explained to the consumer(s). If the consumer(s) agrees that the services are needed regardless of skill levels, then the available interpreter/transliterator should use his or her best judgment about accepting or rejecting the assignment.

Certain situations may prove uncomfortable for some interpreters/transliterators and consumers. Religious, political, racial, or sexual differences, etc., can adversely affect the facilitating role. Therefore, an interpreter/transliterator shall not accept assignments which he or she knows will involve such situations.

Interpreters/transliterators shall generally refrain from providing services in situations where family members, or close personal or professional relationships may affect impartiality, since it is difficult to mask inner feelings. Under these circumstances, especially in legal settings, the ability to prove oneself unbiased when challenged is lessened. In emergency situations, it is realized that the interpreter/transliterator may have to provide services for family members, friends, or close business associates. However, all parties should be informed that the interpreter/transliterator may not become personally involved in the proceedings.

5. INTERPRETERS/TRANSLITERATORS SHALL REQUEST
   COMPENSATION FOR SERVICES IN A PROFESSIONAL AND
   JUDICIOUS MANNER.

Guidelines

Interpreters/transliterators shall be knowledgeable about fees which are appropriate to the profession, and be informed about the current suggested fee schedule of the national organization. A sliding scale of hourly and daily rates has been established for interpreters/transliterators in many areas. To determine the appropriate fee, interpreters/transliterators should know their own level of skill, level of certification, length of experience, nature of the assignment, and the local cost of living index.

There are circumstances when it is appropriate for interpreters/transliterators to provide services without charge. This should be done with discretion, taking care to preserve the self-respect of the consumers. Consumers should not feel that they are recipients of charity. When providing gratis services, care should be taken so that the livelihood of other interpreters/transliterators will be protected. A freelance interpreters/transliterator may depend on this work for a living, and therefore must charge for services rendered, while persons with other full-time work may perform the service as a favor without feeling a loss of income.

6. INTERPRETERS/TRANSLITERATORS SHALL FUNCTION IN A
   MANNER APPROPRIATE TO THE SITUATION.

Guidelines

Interpreters/transliterators shall conduct themselves in such a manner that brings respect to themselves, the consumers and the national organization. The term "appropriate manner" refers to: (a) dressing in a manner that is in contrast to the skin tone and is not distracting, and (b) conducting oneself in all phases of an assignment in a manner befitting a professional.

7. INTERPRETERS/TRANSLITERATORS SHALL STRIVE TO FURTHER KNOWLEDGE AND SKILLS THROUGH PARTICIPATION IN WORKSHOPS, PROFESSIONAL MEETINGS, INTERACTION WITH PROFESSIONAL COLLEAGUES, AND READING OF CURRENT LITERATURE IN THE FIELD.
8. INTERPRETERS/TRANSLITERATORS, BY VIRTUE OF MEMBERSHIP IN OR CERTIFICATION BY THE RID, INC., SHALL STRIVE TO MAINTAIN HIGH PROFESSIONAL STANDARDS IN COMPLIANCE WITH THE CODE OF ETHICS.

Revision: October, 1979.

REFERENCES

Bowe, F. (1988). *Towards equality in education of the deaf.* Washington, DC: Commission on Education of the Deaf.

Caccamise, F., & Newell, W. (1987). Assessing sign communication skills via interview techniques. In C. Padden (Ed.), *Proceedings of the Fourth National Symposium on Sign Research and Teaching* (pp. 168–177).

Hurwitz, T.A., & Witter, A. (1979). Principles of interpreting in an education environment. In M. Bishop (Ed.), *Mainstreaming: Practical ideas for educating hearing-impaired students.* Washington, DC: Volta Bureau.

Hurwitz, T.A. (1986a). White paper on vocational rehabilitation services of deaf and hard-of-hearing clients. Albany, NY: *New York State Office of Vocational Rehabilitation.*

Hurwitz, T.A. (1986b). A study of two factors relative to effective voice interpreting. *Journal of Interpretation, 3,* 53–61.

Hurwitz, T.A. (1991). Quality of communication service for deaf and hard-of-hearing clients: Current issues and future directions. *Journal of the American Deafness and Rehabilitation Association, 25*(1), 1–7.

Joyce, E., & Mathay, G. (1986). A study of closed cases: Implications for the administration of deafness rehabilitation services. *Journal of Rehabilitation of the Deaf, 20,* 5–13.

Lang, H.G., Basile, M.L., Cassell, D., Maruggi, E.A., Nace, M., & Holcomb, B.R. (1984). Guidelines for effective communication among hearing-impaired and hearing professionals in small group meetings. *American Annals of the Deaf, 129,* 333–337.

Northcott, W. (1984). *Oral interpreting: Principles and practices.* Baltimore, MD: University Park Press.

Siple, L., Cole, J., Steve, M., Litchy, D., Shepard, J., Voekl, K., & Hollenbeck, N. (1981). *The interpreter as a stage manager: Student handbook.* Rochester, NY: National Technical Institute for the Deaf.

Registry of Interpreters for the Deaf (1979). Code of ethics (Revised). *Registry of Interpreters for the Deaf Journal,* Silver Spring, MD.

▶ 12

Considerations in the Acquisition of Employment

JAMES J. DECARO
Rochester Institute of Technology

PATRICIA A. MUDGETT-DECARO
DOUGLAS D. NOBLE
University of Rochester

When viewed from the perspective of a deaf person, or any individual for that matter, a job marks the commencement of a career in pursuit of earning a living and living a life. It is essential, therefore, that employment be considered within a career development context when working with people who are deaf.

For purposes of this discussion, a simple six-stage career development continuum is illustrative. The first four stages of the continuum are from the Comprehensive Career Education Matrix (CCEM), a model of career development developed at the Ohio State University. The fifth and sixth stages are suggested by DeCaro and Areson (1983). The six stages of the continuum are as follows: awareness, exploration, preparation, specialization, employment acquisition, and career maintenance and enhancement (Figure 12–1).

As can be seen, a job occupies one point on the temporal continuum of a career. For example, a person pursuing a career in the rehabilitation profession can move through a variety of occupations, e.g., counselor, program administrator, faculty member, and the like. The acquisition of employment may occur several different times during the career of an individual.

A person will bring the variety of interests, skills, and knowledge, developed during the prior four stages of the career development continuum, to the process of

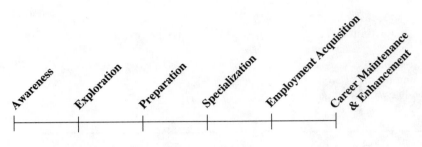

FIGURE 12-1 **Career Development Continuum**

seeking employment. These interests, knowledge, and skills will significantly influence employment acquisition, and cannot be ignored.

It would be shortsighted to view acquisition of a job as the sole goal in working with a person who is deaf, even though productive employment is a very important outcome of the rehabilitation process. As has been pointed out, a person will hold a variety of jobs in his or her lifetime. To focus upon initial employment and not to facilitate independence means that a deaf individual is being relegated to a role of continued future dependence in the lifelong process of acquiring employment. That is, each time a deaf person is seeking a new position, it means a return to the rehabilitation process. In effect, if we don't foster and develop independence, we may be propagating a perpetual client.

The reader will note that the fifth stage on the career development matrix is labeled "employment acquisition" and not "job placement." Compare and contrast the term "placement" with the term "acquisition." The former term evokes images of putting someone someplace. The term "placement" seems to imply passivity on the part of the deaf person, that is, something is being done to or for the person. Appropriately, in sign language the sign most often used for "placement" is the sign "to put."

The term "acquisition," on the other hand, summons up an impression of the active process of bringing toward, implied by the sign "to get." These authors, therefore, suggest that the term job "acquisition," or "acquisition of employment," may be more appropriate. Therefore, these terms are used in this chapter.

With this as background, the authors will address job acquisition with two foci: working with employers and working with deaf people. The reader will note that the former is given more attention, but not because working with employers is more important than working with deaf people. Rather, working with employers is an area that has traditionally received less attention in the employment acquisition process. The authors discuss a number of potential barriers to employment, offer some suggestions for overcoming these, and also suggest that the rehabilitation counselor is in an excellent position to act as an educator of employers in these areas. The authors also suggest that the rehabilitation counselor be a leader in establishing and maintaining a partnership that involves the employer, counselor, and the deaf client.

On the other hand, the rehabilitation counselor, historically, has spent considerable time with the deaf client. In this regard, the authors first discuss the possibility that deaf people have been somewhat limited in their employment opportunities and suggest that this need not be the case. The authors go on to discuss job-seeking skill training for deaf people and the actual job-search processes which may be useful for the rehabilitation counselor and the deaf client.[1]

WORKING WITH EMPLOYERS

Most employers have very little knowledge about disabilities, and about deafness in particular, since it occurs in such a low incidence in the general population. Employers, therefore, will have a variety of uncertainties regarding employment of such people. Rochlin, a former Executive Director of the President's Committee on Employment of People with Disabilities, has indicated that much of business and industry wants to provide equal opportunity to people with a disability but doesn't know how to go about doing it. He suggests that business and industry can find solutions by seeking the expertise of people with disabilities and organizations that work with and for them (Rochlin & Liebers, 1981).

Ewell and Price (1986) have suggested that a key to successful employment is providing the employer or potential employer with an understanding of deafness and its implications for the workplace. Specifically, Schein, Delk, and Hooker (1980) have recommended that orienting supervisors to deafness can be a very valuable activity.

The rehabilitation counselor is in an excellent position to act as a resource and consultant to employers in the hiring of people who are deaf. The attitudes of business leaders toward deaf people are subject to modification as a result of a disability awareness seminar (Perry & Apostal, 1986). Workshops presented to supervisors, co-workers, and hiring personnel in business can be very useful. Further, working one-on-one with employers, supervisors, and the like is a very productive strategy that has proven to be successful.

Potential Barriers to Employment

We will first turn to a framework that can be helpful in interpreting and addressing the concerns of employers regarding the hiring of people who are deaf. DeCaro (1980), and DeCaro and Egelston-Dodd (1982), identified two general classes of barriers that can impede the acquisition of a job by a deaf person: environmental and attitudinal. Environmental barriers are those physical or structural impediments to accessing employment. Included in this category would be such impediments as telephones, instruction manuals, audible fire signals, and the like. Attitudinal barriers are those perceptions regarding deafness, real or imagined, that mitigate against a deaf person's acquiring employment. There may be no impediment to acquisition of a particular job other than the attitude, of an employer, rehabilitation counselor, parent, or a deaf person, that deaf people are not suited for the job. An employer, for example, may be reluctant to start a worker who is deaf on a job because it has never been done previously. One result is that a deaf person's career could be comprised of successive stereotypical jobs.

Attitudinal and environmental barriers are confronted by deaf people early in their career development. The attitudes of parents, teachers, counselors, and significant others have a strong influence on how deaf people define themselves and their capabilities. In an effort to identify the attitudes of parents and teachers toward deaf people training for entry into selected careers, an attitude measure was developed and applied at a school for the deaf in England (DeCaro, Evans, & Dowaliby, 1982), Italy (DeCaro, Dowaliby, & Maruggi, 1983), and South Africa (Naidoo, 1985). In all three countries, the parents' and teachers' expressed advice to deaf people was consistently more negative for those occupations for which safety and communication are significant considerations. In those occupations in which a person could function in relative isolation and safety, there was no significant difference between the expressed advice to a deaf or hearing person. Clearly, safety and communication considerations had a very strong influence upon the ratings given to the occupations in all three countries.

Safety and communications appear to play an important role in the guidance that parents and teachers provide to deaf people who are considering preparing for a career. Career opportunity advisors at the National Center on Employment of the Deaf at the National Technical Institute for the Deaf have found that these same two concerns are often raised by potential employers of deaf people. Further, these observations are confirmed by a body of literature. Phillips noted that, "The employability of deaf persons is restricted, since employers are safety conscious and see deafness as an occupational hazard. They fear that the deaf worker will be hurt on the job" (Phillips, 1975, p. 7). Further, Schein et al. (1980) found that three categories of concern were expressed by supervisors of deaf employees: (1) use of sound recording devices, i.e., the telephone, dictaphone, and other information-transcribing devices; (2) use of machinery, i.e., safety considerations in areas where machinery is in use; and (3) jobs dealing with the public, i.e., jobs where an individual would need considerable public contact and thus be required to communicate with a variety of people. Finally, Hopkins et al. (1987) found that employers stated that they need assistance in learning how to communicate with a deaf person to facilitate the hiring process.

Clearly, employer concerns about safety and communication influence their willingness to offer a position to a deaf person or even to consider a deaf person for employment. Therefore, some evidence regarding these critical areas of concern follows. A counselor who is conversant in these details will be in a good position to educate employers regarding the realities with regard to safety and communication.

Safety
Despite the concerns of employers, there is a documented history of deaf people working very successfully and safely in a variety of occupations. First, over forty

years ago, the Bureau of Labor Statistics conducted a survey (Kossoris & Hammond, 1948) in which it was found that workers with impairments were as safe as their co-workers. For example, the number of minor injuries which required only first aid were identical for impaired and non-impaired workers. Further, the records for injuries that resulted in death, permanent impairment, or absence from work for at least one day was better for the impaired workers than for other workers.

Historically, Lavos and Jones (1946) report that deaf workers were rated as at least as safe as the average hearing worker. In fact, none of the deaf workers in their study were rated as involved in more accidents than the average hearing worker, and none were rated as observing safety rules less than the average hearing worker.

More recently, Staub (1974) found that, for deaf and hard-of-hearing production workers in a heavy metal fabrication industry, there was no significant difference in the frequency of injuries on the job for hearing-impaired and non-hearing-impaired long-term employees. In 1973, Hjort found that there was no significant difference in the mean days absent per year due to occupational injuries between the deaf and hearing employees in an aerospace industry.

Finally, DuPont Corporation (1981) reported that people with disabilities are "equal to the task" of employment. The safety of employees with a hearing impairment was rated as superior to that of their normally hearing peers. This was also found to be true for both job performance and attendance. These findings were essentially the same as the findings of a prior study conducted by DuPont (Sears, 1974). Thus as Menchel and Ritter (1984) conclude, "If proper precautions are taken, hearing-impaired employees are no more of a safety risk than those with normal hearing" (p. 49).

The attitudes of employers about the ability of a deaf person to function safely in the work environment can create barriers to the deaf person's being considered for a position and successfully acquiring a position. It is therefore critical that a counselor be prepared to bring the above information to the attention of an employer.

In addition to information about the safety records of deaf employees, it is important to make employers aware of those accommodations that can make the workplace more hospitable with regard to the safety of the deaf employee, and for that matter, any employee. A very useful resource manual was developed by a team of faculty and staff at the National Technical Institute for the Deaf, for use by and with employers (Fritz & Smith, 1985). In that volume, a series of safety tips are recommended and these are paraphrased below:

1. Set up a buddy system for dealing with emergency situations.
2. Determine which of the sounds in the environment need to be translated into visual or tactile signals and acquire the appropriate signaling devices.
3. When a deaf employee works at night or during weekends, holidays, and the like, security personnel should be notified.

Further, it is important to educate employers about the variety of signaling devices that are available for use in business and industry (Castle, 1980, 1982). These devices, if installed in the work environment, provide a deaf person with visual alarm signals to replace audible alarms. These devices are relatively inexpensive and easy to install.

As noted previously, safety is an issue about which many employers are concerned, however, the literature clearly indicates that deaf people are safe employees. As has been pointed out, information about safety must be a component of any education or interaction with potential employers of people who are deaf.

Communication

In the work environment, messages are sent and received every day by employees, supervisors, customers, and the like. The successful job performance of an employee can be contingent upon the ability of the employee to send and receive a message. Clearly, the communication barriers that exist in a work environment profoundly affect deaf workers' ability to resolve problems that arise in that environment on a daily basis. Thus, most employers are concerned about the ability of the potential deaf employee to communicate in the work environment.

Prior to being able to address employers' concerns, it is important that a counselor understand the general nature of the communication that occurs in the workplace as well as the specific kind of communication required in a particular employment setting. A study conducted by Stuckless, Singer, and Walter (1974) can help provide some insights in this regard. These researchers found that 50 percent of the reported communication episodes in the workplace were initiated by the employee, and 50 percent were initiated by others, e.g., colleagues, supervisors, and the like. They also found that 52 percent of an employee's communication was with fellow employees in the same department, and 13 percent with employees in another department. These researchers further found that communication occurred in the employee's own workplace 61 percent of the time, and 15 percent of the time in a fellow employee's workplace. In addition, a full 78 percent of the communication took place on a one-to-one basis, with small group and large group communication accounting for only 15 percent and 2 percent respectively. Finally, 12 percent of all the employees' communication involved telecommunication. While such "communication demographics" will vary from occupation to occupation, these data illustrate the type of communication that occurs in the workplace and the relative proportion of time that is devoted to each.

The communication that occurs in the workplace can be partitioned into four categories for the purpose of considering accommodations: telecommunications, one-to-one, small group, and large group. A counselor must be able to address each with authority with an employer in order to provide some measure of assurance that deaf people have the capability of overcoming the potential barriers to communication in each setting. A brief discussion of each category follows. (See Chapter 11 for a description of the technologies discussed here.)

Employers are often concerned about *telecommunications,* as illustrated by a question often encountered by counselors working with employers: How will this deaf person be able to use the telephone? At a time when innovative telecommunications technology is available for use in the workplace, there is no reason why a deaf person should be barred from employment because of the alleged barriers created by the telephone. New technology such as TTYs, electronic messaging systems, fax technology, and relay systems can provide deaf people with full access to communication via the telephone network. Employers must be made aware that TTYs are available and can make the telephone accessible to deaf employees. In fact, a study conducted by Polaroid Corporation (Bell, 1981) provided evidence that the installation of TTYs resulted in a decrease in the absenteeism of its deaf workers.

The advent of the electronic office has resulted in more and more workstations being equipped with computers or computer terminals. As a result, electronic message systems are becoming an integral part of day-to-day business communications. In addition, fax technology is having, and will continue to have, a profound effect upon the flow of communication in the workplace. Both of these technologies are resulting in a decreasing dependence upon voice communication in the transmission and reception of messages in the workplace.

Another innovation which is becoming increasingly available across the country is the telephone relay service (Deaf Life, 1989). Very few potential employers are aware of such services, and educating them about their availability can be very useful in addressing concerns about telephone accessibility. The Telecommunication Accessibility Act of 1988 mandates that the Federal Communication Commission explore ways of addressing interstate relay services and report back to Congress regarding their findings. Clearly, telephone relay services are a valuable accommodation to overcome telecommunication barriers.

As has been pointed out previously, the vast majority of communication that occurs in the workplace is on a *one-to-one basis*. This is an important piece of data, since in such a setting each party needs to focus only upon the message being sent by the other, and the pace of communication can be varied to facilitate the communication process. Employers need to be aware that one-to-one communication is the type that is most comfortable for a deaf employee, since he or she will be able to accommodate to the styles of co-workers and they will be able to accommodate to him or her.

For example, Foster (1987) found that deaf employees used a variety of one-to-one strategies for communicating on the job: speech reading, voice, writing, sign, fingerspelling, and gesturing. She indicates that the deaf employees she interviewed utilized a variety of special strategies either to encourage or to facilitate communication between themselves and their co-workers: humor; teaching some signs and fingerspelling; teaching co-workers to speak slowly and clearly, face them, and be willing to repeat the message; and finding a key co-worker to serve as a communication mediator or informant.

Foster also indicated that, "Hearing co-workers who demonstrated patience, a willingness to communicate needs of deaf people were the easiest to work with" (p. 3). Thus, finding a willing co-worker can be very helpful as well. In fact, the deaf employees in Hjort's (1973) study reported that the majority of their hearing co-workers were helpful regarding interpersonal communications. These examples indicate that people are ready and willing but need to be taught, and/or learn, the various strategies to facilitate communication.

A few words about interpreters in one-to-one settings are appropriate. Employers need to be made aware of the potential value of interpreters in the facilitation of communication. Unfortunately, it will not always be practical or feasible to have an interpreter available for the daily one-to-one communication that occurs in the work-place. However, when a message is critical or complex, it will be to everyone's advantage to assure that a certified interpreter is available for those deaf people who use sign language (see Chapter 11).

Small and large group communication settings will often be meetings at which there will be more than one presenter and at which a deaf person will be expected to participate along with his or her hearing peers. Training sessions and weekly work group meetings are typical of such communication settings. Employers will be con-cerned that a deaf applicant for a position is able to derive benefit from such meetings and workplace interactions. As has been pointed out previously, the rehabilitation professional is in a good position to act as a resource and trainer for those in industry regarding the facilitation of communication in meetings and training sessions.

For example, employers need to be aware that using interpreters in large and small group settings has been acknowledged to be a tremendous asset in the facilita-tion of communication (Bowe, Delk, & Schein, 1973; MacArthur, 1981; Smith, 1979). Further, since such meetings do not occur with undue frequency in most work settings, it is cost effective to make an interpreter available. Smith (1979) has identi-fied a variety of interpreting strategies that are used in industry. The services range from hiring a fully qualified professional interpreter to using an individual who has been given some sign language training by the company. Clearly, however, the qual-ity of the skills of the interpreter will have a direct impact upon the quality of the message that is sent, and ultimately received, by the person who is depending on the interpreter.

In addition to interpreting, the value of providing notetaking services for a deaf person who is involved in small or large group meetings should be pointed out. It has been found that such services are invaluable in a teaching/learning setting (Osguthorpe, Whitehead, & Bishop, 1978).

Other Considerations

In addition to safety and communications barriers, there are other considerations that should be a part of an employer education program. Two are presented below: lan-guage issues and social-cultural issues.

For many deaf individuals, the language of United States business and industry, English, may not be their primary language. Presenting such a person with a compli-cated application form could constitute a considerable obstacle (Arnold, 1977; Steffanic, 1982). Employment screening tests that are heavily dependent upon verbal content to test the competencies of persons to perform some task or to solve problems can also present an obstacle to deaf persons. On the whole, deaf people, irrespective of their native intelligence, have not historically performed well on tests that are heavily dependent upon verbalizable knowledge (Furth, 1966). As discussed in Chapter 7, the results of such testing can give a very erroneous picture of the abilities of a deaf person taking the test. The salient point here is that the use of such tests with deaf people may be inappropriate unless the items on the test actually measure essential job-related abilities. Employers must be informed that testing which is heavily dependent upon English language may be acting to systematically screen out highly qualified deaf people from employment. This could present an employer with two types of potential problems: a resource pool of qualified potential employees is being ignored, and exposure to possible discrimination litigation.

Mutual misinterpretation of the social meaning of a message or interaction can arise between deaf and hearing persons. That is, inadvertent violations of each other's norms of behavior can result in deaf and hearing people interpreting the behavior of others as inappropriate or rude.

Individuals make use of their own experiences and cultural norms in evaluating the appropriateness and quality of the words and actions of others. There has been a tendency to focus upon violations of hearing norms by deaf persons, since deaf people function within a predominantly hearing world. Historically, therefore, many of the behaviors of deaf people have been characterized as immature, egocentric, impulsive, and the like (Myklebust, 1964; Levine, 1960). These characteristics are often explained as a developmental lag caused by insufficient and inappropriate social interactions (Meadow, 1980) (see Chapter 4).

In the past 20 years, however, linguistic studies (Klima & Bellugi, 1979; Stokoe, 1980), sociological studies (Higgins, 1980; Nash & Nash, 1981), and recent anthropological studies (Padden & Humphries, 1988) have offered an alternate interpretation. That is, they suggest that what has been classified as inappropriate behavior is possibly the result of languages, cultures, or experiences coming into conflict.

For example, after observing several deaf persons engaged in a typical conversation, several hearing students in a sign language class taught by one of these authors asked, "Why are deaf people always so emotional?" The normal use of hands and arms by a deaf person who is signing could be interpreted as a lack of control or emotionalism by a hearing person in our culture, since hearing people who exhibit similar behaviors are often categorized as odd, drunk, or even crazy. Similarly, facial expressions such as those grammatically encoded in sign language are easily interpreted as emotionality by the untrained observer. In contrast, deaf people comment upon the coldness and dullness of hearing people, based upon the lack of body movement and facial expression.

Clearly, rehabilitation professionals, employers, deaf people, or hearing fellow employees will be confronted with possible misunderstandings in the social interactions that are inherent in the work environment. Sorting out the sources of such misunderstandings will be a challenging task; two approaches are recommended:

1. A professional working directly with deaf people should be familiar with the cultural norms of the deaf community, and the specific differences between them and the norms of the dominant culture.
2. There should be in-depth discussions between rehabilitation professionals, deaf clients, and employers, regarding the meanings and interpretations of specific behaviors and communications, from the viewpoint of both the deaf client and the hearing society. This can serve as an educational process for all involved.

Job Restructuring and Job Modification

Rochlin, DeCaro, and Clarcq (1985) have indicated that job restructuring and job modification are two ways of accommodating a deaf person in the workplace. They point out that, while the two terms are often used synonymously, they are quite different types of accommodation. *Job restructuring* means the actual changing of the job duties that the person is asked to perform. Such accommodations are often very difficult to realize in companies that have established job descriptions or have negotiated such job descriptions with unions. Changes in the job duties of an employee who is deaf could also result in morale problems with co-workers who may find that they consequently need to assume additional duties or responsibilities. Further, the deaf person may be subject to criticism from fellow employees doing the same job because he or she is viewed as a member of a privileged class.

In contrast, Rochlin et al. (1985) indicate that *job modification* means changing the way the work is done and not the duties that are to be performed. In job modification, the performance expectations remain the same but how the job is done is allowed to differ. Many companies have structured practices and procedures, not only regarding the tasks that are to be performed, but also how they should be performed. These procedures, while generally developed to facilitate the most efficient means of performing a job, do not consider the unique skills, abilities and needs of a deaf person. Rochlin et al. (1985) suggest that "disabled people should be allowed to do their work in any way possible, as long as it is safe and the outcome meets expectations" (p. 21). The authors indicate that,

> A critical consideration in the job modification process is the manager's willingness to accept a disabled person doing the work in a manner that is different from the norm. Managers need to assure that assigned tasks are accomplished in accordance with the established performance objectives and not be concerned about how the tasks are accomplished. Managers must work with employees to determine how their skills and abilities can be used to the fullest in the accomplishment of assigned tasks. (p. 21)

Partnerships

Prior to concluding this section, it is important to cover one more issue. Rochlin et al. (1985) have argued for a partnership between people with disabilities, employers, and educational/rehabilitation personnel in the competitive employment of people with disabling conditions. They suggest that such a partnership is of benefit to all those who participate. Business and industry benefit because the partnership can lead to a pool of reliable, productive, and qualified employees. Educational/rehabilitation personnel can benefit since the partnership can lead to successful job entry and the long-term career placement for people who are deaf. People with disabilities can benefit from this partnership since it can open careers previously not available to them. Such partnerships can result in deaf people fulfilling the need to accomplish and produce, which they share with their hearing peers.

Partnerships, then, are mutually beneficial relationships that require an equal commitment on the part of participants.

An Example Strategy

Establishing a partnership is more easily said than operationalized. For this reason, an example strategy that can be used by a rehabilitation professional in a local community follows.

First, it is recommended that the counselor establish an industrial advisory committee whose role is to provide advice and counsel, and not necessarily serve as a pool of potential employers. Selection of advisory committee members might start with identifying corporations that have a proven commitment to equal opportunity and affirmative action hiring within the community. An influential individual from one of these corporations, who is very knowledgeable regarding the activities of the business community (e.g., through the Chamber of Commerce), would be an appropriate representative. Lists of members of the boards of trustees of community service organizations, such as the United Way, can serve as starting points for identifying individuals who might be potential members for the industrial advisory committee.

Second, once selected, the advisory committee should be used to help identify corporations that are hiring and have a demonstrated record of innovation in employment and hiring practices. Further, the advisory group can recommend influential individuals within corporations that may have a personal interest in disability; these people can serve as key contacts within a corporation. In each instance where the National Center on Employment of the Deaf has established a partnership with a corporation, there has been an influential champion for people with disabilities within the corporation. The champion either had a relative or close friend with a disability, was disabled him- or herself, or had worked with a person with a disability who had positively influenced his or her life.

Third, the key contacts within corporations should be directly approached by the counselor. In those instances where a member of the advisory group knows a contact person well, the advisory group member may be able to provide an introduction. In the initial interaction, the counselor should clearly detail that the purpose is to discuss the establishment of a partnership and not the immediate identification of employment opportunities. An individual in business and industry will be justifiably skeptical and will need to be provided evidence that the counselor is worthy of trust.

Therefore, the counselor must be prepared to present appropriate evidence of his or her credibility, dependability, and expertise, as well as that of the organization he or she represents. References to employers with whom the counselor has worked often can be very helpful.

Fourth, the counselor should determine if the corporation is willing to consider the hiring of people who are deaf and at the same time present to the contact the value of hiring deaf people. The counselor should draw upon his or her knowledge of successful deaf employees in the community in order to provide concrete evidence.

Fifth, the counselor should work with the contact to determine key personnel within the corporation who should be involved in establishing an ongoing relationship or partnership aimed at the employment of people who are deaf. Once these key individuals have been identified, it is appropriate to work toward the provision of a seminar or workshop for these individuals that details: (1) the value of an ongoing partnership, (2) the value of deaf employees in the workplace, and (3) how concerns that arise in the workplace with regard to safety, communication, and the like can be handled. It is often helpful to invite to the workshop a successful deaf worker and his or her supervisor who can speak to various employment-related issues, since employers will take very seriously the testimony of a fellow employer.

Sixth, the counselor should work with selected session participants to develop an action plan which is tailored to the needs and structure of the organization. Minimally, the action plan should include the following: an identification of targets of employment opportunity within the company, the support that the counselor is able to provide initially and as follow-up should a deaf person be hired, the type of educational experiences that will be provided to potential hiring managers regarding deafness, the training experiences that will be made available to a hiring manager regarding accommodations and supervision, and a mechanism by which the employer can provide feedback regarding the utility of the relationship.

There are as many ways of establishing a partnership as there are counselors and employers. The above example is but one approach and is intended to provide a counselor with a heuristic model that can be used in establishing a partnership.[2]

Reasons for the Dearth of Partnerships
Partnerships are rare, and one could ask what has obstructed their formation. As has already been pointed out, there has been significant resistance on the part of employers with regard to hiring people with disabling conditions. However, this does not fully account for the lack of formation of such partnerships. Flannigan (1974) suggests that rehabilitation professionals have a fundamental distaste for activities that require "contact with an alien public" (p. 209), that is, employers. Further, Minton (1977) suggests that many counselors feel that going out to talk to employers about hiring people with disabilities is not professional and is akin to a salesperson's "hawking" a product. One significant obstacle to the formation of partnerships may very well be the attitudes that are held by counselors toward employers, as well as the attitudes they have about themselves, and their professional identity. Clearly, this is

an area about which a rehabilitation professional, or one preparing for the profession, should do some introspection.

Legal Issues

As described in Chapter 10, there are a variety of state and federal statutes that relate to the employment of people who have disabling conditions. Most employers are very well aware of these statutes and will seldom need to be reminded of their existence. In fact, most employers are more aware of the implications of such legislation than those of us in the business of rehabilitation or education. It is the recommendation of these authors that legislation regarding the employment of people who have disabilities be used as a source of leverage with employers only as a last resort. Doing so is not very conducive to the establishment of partnerships and these authors suggest that people with handicapping conditions should present themselves to employers on the basis of their *abilities* rather than on the basis of employers' *responsibilities* under federal or state statutes.

WORKING WITH DEAF PEOPLE

Historically, deaf people have found ample employment opportunities as printers, tailors, shoemakers, and janitors. These occupations are ones in which an individual works alone and is not required to have a lot of interaction with others. In three of these occupations, noise is a consideration, i.e., the environment in which an individual works is rather noisy. As has been pointed out previously, attitudes about the needs and abilities of deaf people can significantly limit their employment opportunities.

These authors suggest that almost any occupation can be made accessible to a deaf person who possesses the innate intelligence to do the job. For example, most people would consider it rather a foolish proposition to consider a profoundly deaf person as a telephone installer but the following case study demonstrates the opposite:

Z, in his forties, unable to hear since birth, was a long-time employee in the pressroom of a newspaper. His job was soon to become a casualty of automation so he decided to relocate. He applied for a position as a telephone installer with a telephone company.

Three major problems had to be overcome in order for Z to be able to do a satisfactory job.

First, he was faced with the challenge of how to communicate with customers. This was solved by giving Z a company business card that states, "My name is Z, station installation technician. I am totally deaf. I am here to do the work you requested. Please show me what you would like done." He then gives the customer a pad and pencil and thus messages are exchanged.

A second problem was that Z could not use the standard test set, that is, the portable handset that installers carry, since he could not hear the dial tone, ringing, or a busy signal. This challenge was overcome by the husband of Z's pole climbing instructor, who was a former telephone installer. He modified the test set to use small lights to give Z visual indications of the various sounds.

The most difficult problem to resolve was how Z would communicate with various departments inside the company from the field. This was solved by equipping him with a portable TTY.

No other special allowances were made for Z and he is expected to meet the same productivity and quality of work objectives of established for all installers. He has more than succeeded and, in merchandising, outsells his co-workers.

Is it worth the effort and expense to employ someone like Z? Two statements of co-workers answer this question definitively. His foreman said, "If there are more like Z around, I will take all I can get." The other comment was from a clerk in the control center who stated that when she learned that a deaf installer had been hired said, "I just know it will not work." When queried later, she said, ". . . it has worked and I am so glad, because Z is such a great guy." (paraphrased from Rochlin & Liebers, 1981)

The appropriateness of certain employment opportunities naturally depends upon whether the person with a disability possesses the technical and other competencies needed for a position. For example, an individual who possesses no training or education in drafting should not pursue a job as a draftsperson.

Data collected as a part of a follow-up of graduates of 24 schools and programs for the deaf (MacLeod-Gallinger, 1989) indicate, however, that factors other than education may be having an effect. For example, deaf graduates, both male and female, were under-represented by a factor of approximately four in the ranks of managerial and professional specialties as compared to their hearing peers. On the other hand, deaf graduates were over-represented by a factor of approximately two in service occupations. As mentioned previously, education and the attitudes of employers may contribute significantly to this circumstance. However, it is important to consider the possibility that rehabilitation counselors and others (DeCaro, Evans, & Dowaliby, 1982) may be channeling and limiting the employment opportunities of deaf people.

Job Seeking Skills Training

Minton (1977) suggests that clients seeking employment are often in need of training in four basic areas: how to find work, where to find work, how to apply for employment, and how to act in the employment interview. Anderson (1985) has identified a variety of what he refers to as "employability skills" that a deaf person should possess. Under the category of *job-seeking skills* he identifies five major skill areas: acquiring job leads, writing letters of inquiry, telephoning, organizing a job search, and completing applications. In the area of *job interviewing* he lists five skill areas: adequately representing one's skills and abilities, responding to employer questions, dealing with concerns about deafness, demonstration of self-confidence, and effective use of an interpreter in the interview. Veatch (1982) has developed materials, available from the National Association for the Deaf, that can be useful to both the deaf person and the counselor in addressing many of the areas identified by Minton and Anderson.

Many of the programs that address training in job-seeking skills can be traced to Azrin's work on the "job club" (Azrin, Flores, & Kaplan, 1977) and an extensive manual describing this approach is readily available (Azrin & Besalel, 1980). The job club approach provides detailed instruction to participants in obtaining job leads, establishing job contacts, documenting prior work history, and preparation for an interview. This approach has been successfully applied in a variety of rehabilitation situations (Azrin, Besalel, Wisotezek, McMorrow, & Bechtel, 1982; Azrin, Philip, Thienes-Hontos, & Besalel, 1981).

Several investigators have reported the successful application of the job club approach with people who are deaf. Long (1988; Long & Davis, 1986) details work with deaf clients in the Tulsa Speech and Hearing Association/Projects With Industry job-seeking training project. Seven topics were reported as being included in the training program: developing resumes, identifying job leads, making initial contacts, setting up the interview, completing applications, executing the interview, and doing follow-up. In addition, Torretti (1983) reports the successful application of the job club approach with a group of deaf people being served by the Southwest Center for the Hearing-Impaired in San Antonio, Texas. Further, Dwyer (1983) has also reported successfully applying the job club approach to deaf students at Waubonsee Community College.

A survey of 29 job-seeking skills development programs (Herbert, 1988) identified five broad program content areas: job selection, written documentation of work skills and abilities related to obtaining a job interview, job interview preparation, job interview behaviors, and job-keeping skills. The assessment of work values, interests, and abilities of a client was all but ignored in the 29 programs surveyed. Further, assessments regarding placement readiness were reported to have been conducted using measures that are generally experimental. Herbert (1988), therefore, made several excellent recommendations to improve job-seeking skill training:

1. Use standardized tests to assess job-seeking readiness.
2. Devote greater time to exploring with participants the feasibility of work skills and interests.
3. Devote greater time to developing skills at informational interviews, that is, a participant using interviews to gather labor market and job lead information.
4. Instruct participants to be proactive in addressing potential employer concerns regarding hiring people with disabling conditions.
5. Increase attention to issues related to personal appearance as it relates to getting a job (dressing for success), and the use of nonverbal cues.

6. Address the various strategies for coping with being the unsuccessful candidate for a position.
7. Give additional attention to the skills necessary for maintaining employment.

The rehabilitation professional has a significant role to play as a teacher-mentor in the development of job-seeking skills. Job-seeking skills development should be an integral component of the services provided to a deaf person, since such training can reduce the dependency of the client. The rehabilitation professional who has knowledge of the repertoire of strategies that are used in job-search skill training is well placed to assist deaf people.

The Search Process

Once the deaf person has acquired the job-seeking skills, he or she is ready to implement the actual job-search process. This section provides the reader with a sampling of job-search strategies.

The actual search for a job should be a shared effort, with the locus of responsibility shifted as far as possible to the deaf person. Flannigan (1974) suggests that structuring and executing the job-search should be shared, with the client ". . . shouldering as much of the burden as possible, short of collapse" (p. 117). He suggests that the more job ready the client is, the less assistance he or she will require. Client involvement in the job-search process can be thought of as a continuum ranging from the client assuming full responsibility for the job-search with minimal assistance from a rehabilitation professional, to the rehabilitation professional assuming a major role in the process (Ouellette & Dwyer, 1983). It is interesting to note that rehabilitation professionals are reported to spend relatively little time on the placement process (6 to 10 percent), in large part, because they report not having the time to do so (Zandy & James, 1977a; 1977b; 1979; Ouellette & Dwyer, 1983).

As an initial step in the job-search process, it is recommended that the rehabilitation professional and the deaf client determine, in collaboration, the role the rehabilitation professional will play in the process. This having been decided, there are some strategies described in the literature that can facilitate the job-search process, irrespective of whether the deaf person or the rehabilitation professional assumes the major responsibility for the process.

Flannigan (1974) and Ugland (1977) suggest the use of manufacturer indexes of industry lists for the area in which a job-search is being conducted. Such resources are readily available from the local Chamber of Commerce or local industry/management councils. In addition, the yellow pages of the telephone directory can provide a fairly comprehensive listing of various businesses in a locality. Further, many professional and trade organizations publish lists of their membership; for example, the membership list of the American Association of General Contractors. Mallik and Moretti (1982) have suggested that labor unions can serve as a source of information about possible employment opportunities. Labor market reviews and occupational trend and outlook publications can be acquired from state and local labor department offices. Finally, federal, state, and local civil service bulletins can serve as an excellent resource.

Approaching employers and their personnel offices, with a resume in hand, is to be recommended. The sequence of "hitting the pavement," making such contacts, and later following up indicates interest and motivation.

Attempts have been made to systematize the job-search process (Geist & Calzaretta, 1982; Vandergroot & Swirsky, 1980). On the whole, however, the literature would tend to indicate that the job-search process is more of an art than it is a science. These authors tend to agree with an observation by Flannigan (1974) that any activity that is feasible, and not criminal or a violation of ethical standards, should be used in executing a job search.

CONCLUSION

There are attitudinal and environmental barriers that can act as impediments to the acquisition of employment of people who are deaf. As has been pointed out previously, these barriers can be overcome, depending upon the willingness and the creativity of deaf people, employers, and rehabilitation professionals. Education and partnerships are very useful methods for beginning to systematically dismantle the work site barriers to employment of deaf people.

These authors take the position that deaf people should play as large a role in the acquisition of employment as their abilities will permit. However, attitudes and opinions of rehabilitation professionals, employers, and others will mediate their interpretation of what deaf people can do. The tendency to underestimate the abilities of deaf people has led many employers, parents, teachers, and rehabilitation professionals to do things "for" deaf people. To combat this, these authors suggest that a deaf person should be provided the freedom and opportunity to assume all the responsibilities that he or she can withstand, short of collapse.

Some strategies that can facilitate the acquisition of employment have been presented in this chapter, with a clear recognition that job acquisition is more of an art than it is a science. Job-seeking skills development has been shown to be an extremely useful method for cultivating independence in the employment acquisition process. The rehabilitation professional who is knowledgeable in the various methods for developing job-search skills is well placed to implement training and educational programs to facilitate the acquisition of such skills. The job-search section of this chapter is by no means comprehensive and provides an introduction to some practical approaches.

Prior to ending this chapter, a few final words of counsel are offered. First, it is important to remember that deaf people as "people" first and foremost. Second, the employment acquisition process should be approached from an "ability" rather than a "disability" perspective, i.e., on the basis of what a person can do. Finally, the professional working in the field should never lose a sense of humor. Those in the helping professions should take the job to be done seriously but should not take themselves too seriously. By maintaining an appropriate perspective regarding the job to be done, we will be better able to serve people who are deaf.[3]

ENDNOTES

1. In preparing this chapter, an annotated bibliography of over 100 articles was developed (Noble, 1988). This bibliography is available upon request from the Staff Resource Center at NTID. Further, an annotated bibliography on the employment of deaf people has been compiled by the National Center on Employment of the Deaf (1988) and is also available from the Staff Resource Center at NTID. Finally, Ritter and Hopkins (1985) have prepared a bibliography related to deafness that is available from the American Library Association.
2. The authors would like to acknowledge the advice and counsel regarding partnerships provided by Professor Paul Seidel of the National Center on Employment of the Deaf at the National Technical Institute for the Deaf.
3. The authors wish to acknowledge the perspective provided by Patricia Laird, Esq., senior legislative analyst, U.S. House of Representatives Subcommittee on Select Education.

REFERENCES

Amrin, C., & Bullis, M. (1985). The job club approach to placement: A viable tool? *Journal of Rehabilitation of the Deaf, 19*(1–2), 18–22.

Anderson, G.B. (1985). Employability enhancement skills training for deaf rehabilitation clients. In D. Watson, G. Anderson, & M. Taff-Watson (Eds.), *Integrating human resources, technology and systems in deafness* (pp. 306–312). Silver Springs, MD: American Deafness and Rehabilitation Association.

Arnold, M.V. (1977). Affirmative action and employment of deaf persons: How rehabilitation personnel can help. *Journal of Rehabilitation of the Deaf, 10*(4), 9–16.

Azrin, N., & Besalel, V. (1980). *Job club counselor's manual.* Baltimore, MD: University Park Press.

Azrin, N., Besalel, V., Wisotezek, I., McMorrow, M., & Bechtel, R. (1982). Behavioral supervision versus informational counseling of job seeking in the job club. *Rehabilitation Counseling Bulletin, 25*(4), 212–218.

Azrin, N., Flores, T., & Kaplan, S. (1977). Job finding club: A group assisted program for obtaining employment. *Behavior Research and Therapy, 13,* 17–27.

Azrin, N., & Philip, R. (1979). The job club method for the job handicapped: A comparative outcome study. *Rehabilitation Counseling Bulletin, 23*(2), 144–155.

Azrin, N., Philip, R., Thienes-Hontos, P., & Besalel, V. (1981). Follow-up of welfare benefits received by job club clients. *Journal of Vocational Behavior, 18*(3), 253–254.

Bell, R. (1981). *Polaroid: A look at its hearing-impaired members.* Unpublished manuscript, Polaroid Corporation, Cambridge, MA.

Bowe, F.G., Delk, M.T., & Schein, J.D. (1973). Barriers to the full employment of deaf people in federal government. *Journal of Rehabilitation of the Deaf, 6*(4), 1–15.

Castle, D.L. (1980). *Telecommunication training for the deaf.* Rochester, NY: Rochester Institute of Technology, National Technical Institute for the Deaf.

Castle, D.L. (1982). *Telephone training for the deaf.* Rochester, NY: Rochester Institute of Technology, National Technical Institute for the Deaf.

Deaf Life. (1989, March). *The boom in telephone relay services.* Rochester, NY: MSM Productions, Author.

DeCaro, J.J. (1980). Design for access: Implications for disabled people. *Journal of the Greater London Association of the Disabled, 5*(3), 3–5.

DeCaro, J.J., & Areson, A.A. (1983). Career assessment and advising of the technical college student. In D. Watson, G. Anderson, S. Ouellette, & N. Ford (Eds.), *Vocational evaluation of hearing-impaired persons: Research and practice* (pp. 77–92). Little Rock, AR: University of Arkansas, Arkansas Rehabilitation Research and Training Center.

DeCaro, J.J., Dowaliby, F., & Maruggi, E.A. (1983). A cross cultural examination of parents' and teachers' expectations for deaf youth regarding careers. *British Journal of Educational Psychology, 53,* 358–363.

DeCaro, J.J., & Egelston-Dodd, J. (1982). Towards a dialogue regarding careers for deaf youth. *Journal of the British Association of Teachers of the Deaf, 6*(6), 155–161.

DeCaro, J.J., Evans, L., & Dowaliby, F.J. (1982). Advising deaf youth to train for various occupations: Attitudes of significant others. *British Journal of Educational Psychology, 52,* 220–227.

DuPont Corporation (1981). *Equal to the task* (1981 DuPont survey on employment of the handicapped). Washington, DC: Author.

Dwyer, C.L. (1983). Job-seeking and job-retention skill training with hearing-impaired clients. In D. Watson, G. Anderson, N. Ford, P. Marut, & S. Ouellette (Eds.), *Job placement of hearing-impaired persons: Research and practice* (pp. 17–26). Little Rock, AR: University of Arkansas, Arkansas Rehabilitation Research and training Center.

Ewell, E.G., & Price, B.J. (1986). Preparing an employer to work with a hearing-impaired employee. In D. Watson, G. Anderson, & M. Taff-Watson (Eds.), *Integrating human resources, technology and systems in deafness* (pp. 352–364). Silver Springs, MD: American Deafness and Rehabilitation Association.

Flannigan, T.W. (1974, March). What ever happened to placement? *Vocational Guidance Quarterly,* 209–213.

Flannigan, T.W. (1977). Placement: Beyond the obvious. *Behavior Research and Therapy, 13,* 116–120.

Foster, S.B. (1987). Employment experiences of deaf college graduates: An interview study. *Journal of Rehabilitation of the Deaf, 21*(1), 1–15.

Foster, S.B. (1988, October). *Dealing with barriers in the workplace: Strategies used by deaf people in response to difficult situations at work.* Paper presented at the 18th Southeast Regional Institute of Deafness, Memphis, TN.

Fritz, G., & Smith, N. (1985). *The hearing-impaired employee: An untapped resource.* San Diego, CA: College Hill Press.

Furth, H.G. (1966). *Thinking without language: Psychological implications of deafness.* New York, NY: Free Press.

Geist, C.S., & Calzaretta, W.A. (1982). *A placement handbook for counseling disabled people.* Springfield, IL: Charles C. Thomas Publisher.

Herbert, J.T. (1988). Content analysis of placement skills training: A survey of job seeking skills programs. *Journal of Job Placement, 4*(2), 9–14.

Higgins, P.C. (1980). *Outsiders in a hearing world: A sociology of deafness.* Beverly Hills, CA: Sage Publications.

Hjort, W.L. (1973). Comparison of deaf and hearing workers in an aerospace industry in Southern California. *Dissertation Abstracts International, 33,* 3173B. (University Microfilms No. 72–33, 931)

Hopkins, K., Licata, C., Berl, R., Cox, J., Grosshans, R., Kelley, C., Menchel, R., Morley, L., Rees, M., & Staufer, E. (1987). *Educational outreach project final report of the subcommittee on employers/providers of placement services.* Unpublished manuscript, Rochester Institute of Technology, National Technical Institute for the Deaf, Rochester, NY.

Klima, E.S., & Bellugi, U. (1979). *The signs of language.* Cambridge, MA: Harvard University Press.

Kossoris, M.D., & Hammond, H.S. (1948). Work performance of physically impaired workers. *Monthly Labor Review* (Bulletin 923 of the Bureau of Labor Statistics), Reprinted by the President's Committee on Employment of the Handicapped, Washington, DC.

Lavos, G., & Jones, E.W. (1946). The deaf worker in industry: A descriptive study of fifty-six deaf workers engaged in manufacturing during the war. *American Annals of the Deaf, 91,* 154–176.

Levine, E.S. (1960). *The psychology of deafness: Techniques of appraisal for rehabilitation.* New York, NY: Columbia University Press.

Long, N.M. (1988). Job-seeking skills training with deaf rehabilitation clients. In S.T. Boone, & G.A. Long (Eds.), *Enhancing the employment of deaf persons* (pp. 57–69). Springfield, IL: Charles C. Thomas Publisher.

Long, N.M., & Davis, G. (1986). Self-directed job-seeking skills training: Utilization in a project with industry program for the deaf. In D. Watson, G. Anderson, & M. Taff-Watson (Eds.), *Integrating human resources, technology and systems in deafness* (pp. 313–324). Silver Springs, MD: American Deafness and Rehabilitation Association.

MacArthur, P.F. (1981). *Observation of deaf professionals who have achieved staff, supervisory or management positions within the business sector.* Unpublished graduate project, California State University, Northridge, CA.

MacLeod-Gallinger, J. (1989). *Secondary school graduate followup program for the deaf: Annual report for 1988.* Unpublished manuscript, Rochester Institute of Technology, Rochester, N.Y.

Mallik, K., & Moretti, V. (1982). Unions as a resource in job placement. *Journal of Rehabilitation, April-May-June,* 20–24.

Meadow, K.P. (1980). *Deafness and child development.* Berkeley, CA: University of California Press.

Menchel, R.S., & Ritter, A. (1984). Keep deaf workers safe. *Personnel Journal, 63*(8), 49–51.

Minton, E.B. (1977). Job placement: Strategies and techniques. *Rehabilitation Counseling Bulletin, 21*(2),141–149.

Myklebust, H.R. (1964). *The Psychology of deafness: Sensory deprivation, learning, and adjustment.* New York, NY: Grune & Stratton.

Naidoo, R.M. (1985). *An examination of parents' and teachers' expressed attitudes towards careers for Indian deaf youth.* Unpublished masters thesis, University of Natal, Pietermaritzburg, South Africa.

Nash, J.E., & Nash, A. (1981). *Deafness in society.* Lexington, MA: Lexington Books.

National Center on Employment of the Deaf (1988). *An annotated bibliography of literature related to the employment of deaf persons.* Rochester, NY: Rochester Institute of Technology, National Technical Institute for the Deaf, Author.

Noble, D.D. (1988). *Annotated bibliography: Job placement of deaf workers.* Unpublished manuscript: Rochester Institute of Technology, National Technical Institute for the Deaf, Rochester, NY.

Osguthorpe, R.T., Whitehead, B.D., & Bishop, M.E. (1978). Training and managing paraprofessionals as tutor notetakers for mainstreamed deaf students. *American Annals of the Deaf, 123*(5), 563–571.

Ouellette, S., & Dwyer, C. (1983). An analysis of employment search, development and placement strategies currently employed with hearing impaired persons in the United States. *Journal of Rehabilitation of the Deaf, 17*(3), 13–20.

Padden, C., & Humphries, T. (1988). *Deafness in America: Voices from a culture.* Cambridge, MA: Harvard University Press.

Perry, D.C., & Apostal, R.A. (1986). Modifying attitudes of business leaders toward disabled persons. *Journal of Rehabilitation, 52*(4), 35–38.

Phillips, G.B. (1975). An exploration of employer attitudes concerning employment opportunities for deaf people. *Journal of Rehabilitation of the Deaf, 9*(2), 1–9.

Ritter, A.L., & Hopkins, K.A. (1985). *A deafness collection: Selected and annotated.* Chicago, IL: American Library Association.

Rochlin, J.F., DeCaro, J.J., & Clarcq, J.R. (1985). Competitive employment of disabled people: The need for a partnership. *Journal of Rehabilitation, 51*(2), 19–23.

Rochlin, J.F., & Liebers, D.E. (1981). *American Telephone and Telegraph presentation to the NTID National Advisory Group.* Unpublished manuscript. (Available from the Staff Resource Center of the National Technical Institute for the Deaf at Rochester Institute of Technology)

Salomone, P.R., & Usdane, W.M. (1977). Client-centered placement revisited: A dialogue on placement philosophy. *Rehabilitation Counseling Bulletin. 21*(2), 85–91.

Schein, J.D., Delk, M.T., & Hooker, S. (1980). Overcoming barriers to the full employment of deaf people in federal government. *Journal of Rehabilitation of the Deaf, 13*(3), 15–21.

Sears, J.H. (1974). The able disabled. *Journal of Rehabilitation, March-April,* 19–22.

Smith, M.F. (1987). *Vocational rehabilitation and related programs for persons with handicaps* (Congressional Research Report Number 87–569 EPW). Washington, DC: Congressional Research Service.

Smith, T.M. (1979). Communication needs of deaf people in industry. Journal *of Rehabilitation of the Deaf, 13*(2), 6–10.

Staub, C.S. (1974, January). Hearing loss and accidents. *Sound and Vibration,* 22–23.

Steffanic, D.J. (1982). *Reasonable accommodations for deaf employees in white collar jobs* (Report Number OPRD–82–6). Washington, DC: United States Office of Personnel Management, Office of Personnel Research and Development.

Stokoe, W.C. (1980). *Sign and culture.* Silver Springs, MD: Linstok Press.

Stuckless, E.R., Singer, C.S., & Walter, G.G. (1974). *Communication and work: Implications for the deaf worker.* Unpublished manuscript, Rochester Institute of Technology, National Technical Institute for the Deaf, Rochester, NY.

Torretti, W.M. (1983). The placement process with severely disabled deaf people. In D.

Watson, G. Anderson, N. Ford, P. Marut, & S. Ouellette (Eds.), *Job placement of hearing-impaired persons: Research and practice* (pp. 55–71). Little Rock, AR: University of Arkansas, Arkansas Rehabilitation Research and Training Center.

Ugland, R.P. (1977). Job seeker's aids: a systematic approach for organizing employer contacts. *Rehabilitation Counseling Bulletin, 21*(2), 107–116.

Usdane, W.M., & Salomone, P.R. (1977). Reconceptualization of the placement process: A dialogue. *Rehabilitation Counseling Bulletin, 21*(2), 92–101.

Vandergroot, D., & Swirsky, J. (1980). Applying a systems view to placement and career services in rehabilitation: A survey. *Journal of Applied Rehabilitation Counseling, 11*(3), 149–155.

Veatch, D.J. (1982). *How to get the job you really want.* Silver Springs, MD: National Association of the Deaf.

Wolfe, M.A. (1987). *Survey of state statutes concerning employment discrimination of handicapped persons* (Congressional Research Service Report Number 87–561 A). Washington, DC: Congressional Research Service.

Zandy, J.L., & James, L.F. (1977a). A review of research on job placement. *Rehabilitation Counseling Bulletin, 21*(2), 150–157.

Zandy, J.L., & James, L.F. (1977b). Time spent on placement. *Rehabilitation Counseling Bulletin, 21*(1), 31–35.

Zandy, J.L., & James, L.F. (1979). The problem with placement. *Rehabilitation Counseling Bulletin, 22*(5), 439–442.

Index

MacArthur, P.F., 276
MacLeod-Gallinger, J., 91, 95, 143, 282
macro approach
  used in assessment, 114
  used in case study, 130–132
Maestas y Moores, J., 57
Maher, P., 177
Mahoney, G., 66
Mahoney, M., 160
mainstreaming, in education, 6, 59–60
Malkin, S.F., 190
Mallik, K., 284
manual communication, 5, 9, 208–209
Manually Coded English (MCE)
  interpreting services for, 253–254
  teacher training programs, 22
  used in education, 5, 20–21, 22
  used in systemic rehabilitation, 204, 205, 207, 208
Manuele, C.A., 123
Marlatt, G., 160, 172
Marmor, G., 16, 22, 207
Marshak, L.E., 1
Martin, D.S., 35, 46, 106, 159
Maruggi, E.A., 272
Mathay, G., 156, 262
Matthews, K., 22
maturity, social, 61
Maxwell, M., 22, 27
McAnally, P., 19
McCrone, W., 159, 177
MCE (*See* Manually Coded English)
McGill-Franzen, 26
McGoldrick, M., 200
McGowan, J., 86
McHugh, D.F., 93, 94
McKee, B., 63, 72
McMorrow, M., 283
Meadow, K.P., 16, 38, 52, 54, 55, 56, 57, 58, 60, 61, 62, 63, 66, 67, 68, 73, 75, 119, 190, 203, 277
Meadow Pictorial Scale of Self Image, 119
Meadow-Kendall Social-Emotional Assessment Inventory for Deaf Students, 119
measures, daily function vs., 63–64
Meath-Lang, B., 63, 69
mediation, as tool for cognitive development, 16
meetings, interpreters used in, 258, 259
Meichenbaum, D., 105, 106, 159, 160, 161, 164, 166, 169, 172, 174
Melton, W., 88, 89
memory, component of performance tests, 37–38

Menchel, R.S., 272, 273
Menchetti, B.M., 137
Mendelsohn, M., 190
meningitis, causing hearing loss, 3
mental health/illness
  cognitive-behavioral psychotherapy used, 159–161
  emotional disturbance in deaf population, 73
  hospitalization for, 73–74
  identifying needs for rehabilitation counseling, 158
  need for in rehabilitation counseling, 156–157
  treatment issues, 74–75
mental retardation, deafness and, 39–40
Mertens, D., 59, 60
Merwin, J.C., 106
micro approach
  used in assessment, 114
  used in case study, 127–130
Microcomputer Evaluation and Screening Assessment (MESA), 96
Miller, J.K., 60
Miller, M., 44
Millin, J.P., 4
Mindel, E.D., 177, 190, 203
Minnesota Clerical, 125
Minton, E.B., 280, 282
Minuchin, S., 191, 210
Moeller, M.P., 43
Moores, A., 26
Moores, D.F., 5, 6, 7, 23, 26, 36, 37, 52, 57, 59, 64, 68, 75, 76, 196, 197
Moretti, V., 284
Morley, L., 272
morphology, syntactic development and, 18–19
Morrison, J., 85
Moses, K., 190
Moskowitz, J., 235
Mudgett-DeCaro, P.A., 269
Mullis, I., 88, 91
Munson, H.L., 92
Munson, J.L., 60
Myers, J.R., 144
Myers, P., 157
Myklebust, H.R., 26, 37, 119, 277

Nadolsky, J.M., 114
Naidoo, R.M., 272
Nash, A., 207, 277
Nash, J.E., 207, 277
National Project on Career Education, 92
Nestle, G., 66